MIKE'S PLACE

A TRUE STORY OF LOVE, BLUES, AND TERROR IN TEL AVIV

JACK BAXTER
JOSHUA FAUDEM
KOREN SHADMI

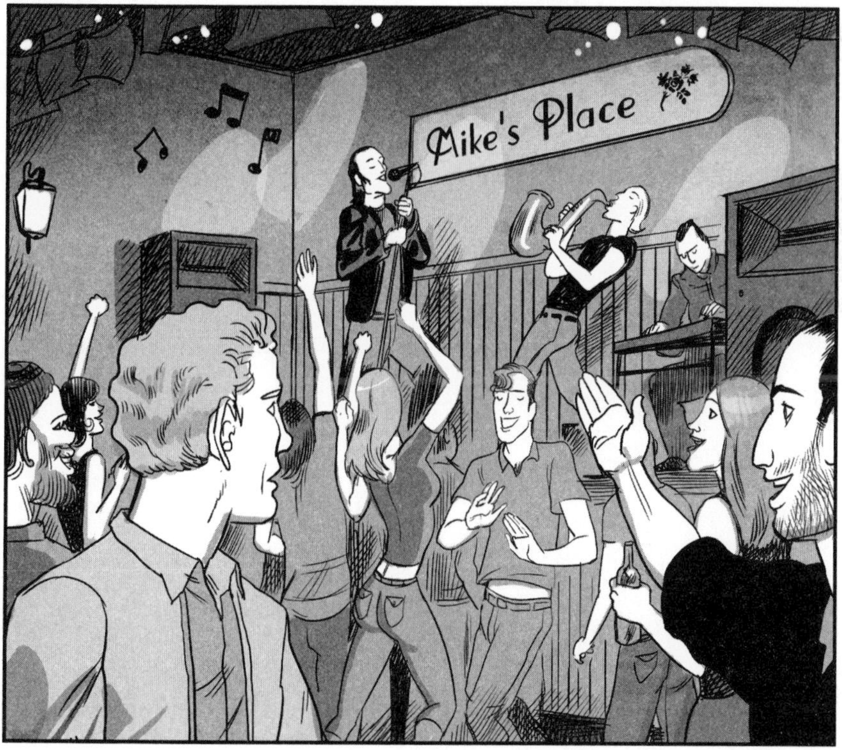
Mike's Place

First Second
New York

For my beloved wife, Fran
—Jack Baxter

For Avi "Gooch" Saragosi (1970-2012)
—Joshua Faudem

First Second

Text copyright © 2015 by Jack Baxter and Joshua Faudem
Art copyright © 2015 by Koren Shadmi

Published by First Second
First Second is an imprint of Roaring Brook Press, a division of Holtzbrinck Publishing Holdings
Limited Partnership
175 Fifth Avenue, New York, New York 10010

Cataloging-in-Publication Data is on file at the Library of Congress.

ISBN 978-1-59643-857-6

First Second books may be purchased for business or promotional use.
For information on bulk purchases please contact Macmillan Corporate and Premium Sales
Department at (800) 221-7945 x5442 or by email at specialmarkets@macmillan.com.

"Time Will Change Everything" copyright © Barry Gilbert. Reprinted by permission of Barry Gilbert

First edition 2015
Book design by Roberta Pressel and Danielle Ceccolini
Printed in the United States of America

10 9 8 7 6 5 4 3 2 1

I

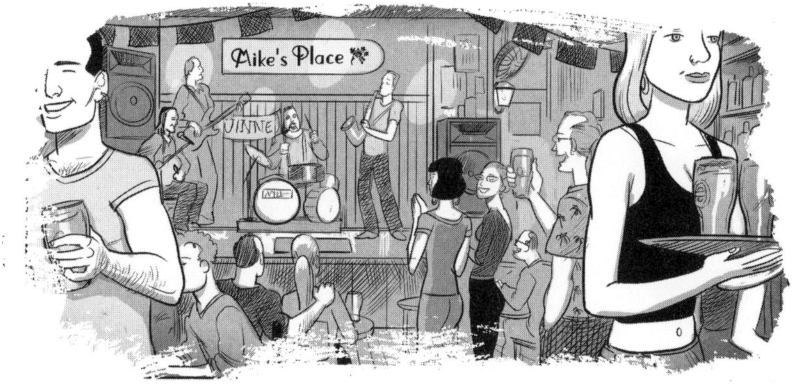
Mike's Place

"O mankind, truly We have created you male and female, and have made you nations and tribes that you may know one another . . ."

—Qur'an

ISRAEL, WEDNESDAY, FEBRUARY 19, 2003

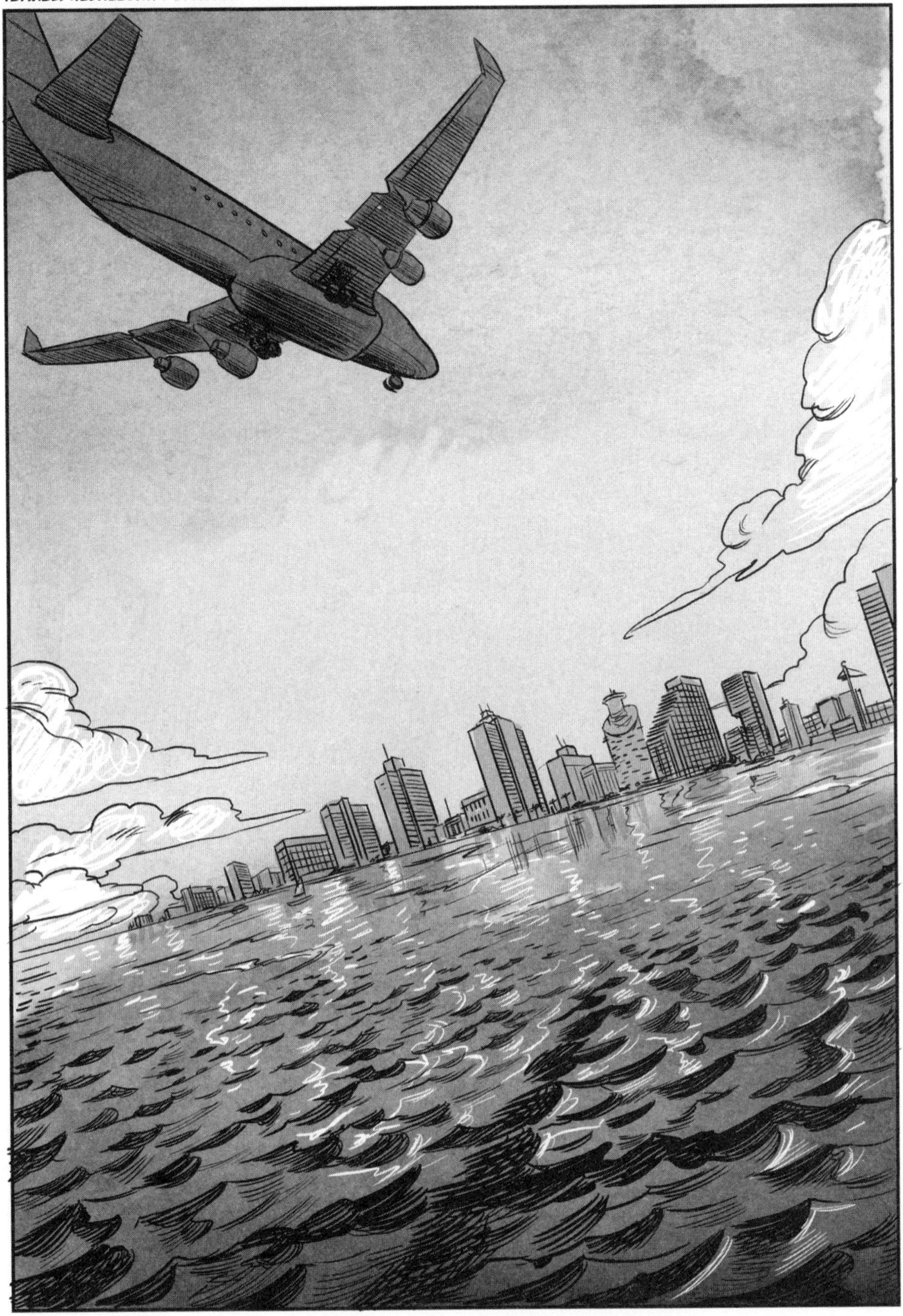

BEN GURION AIRPORT

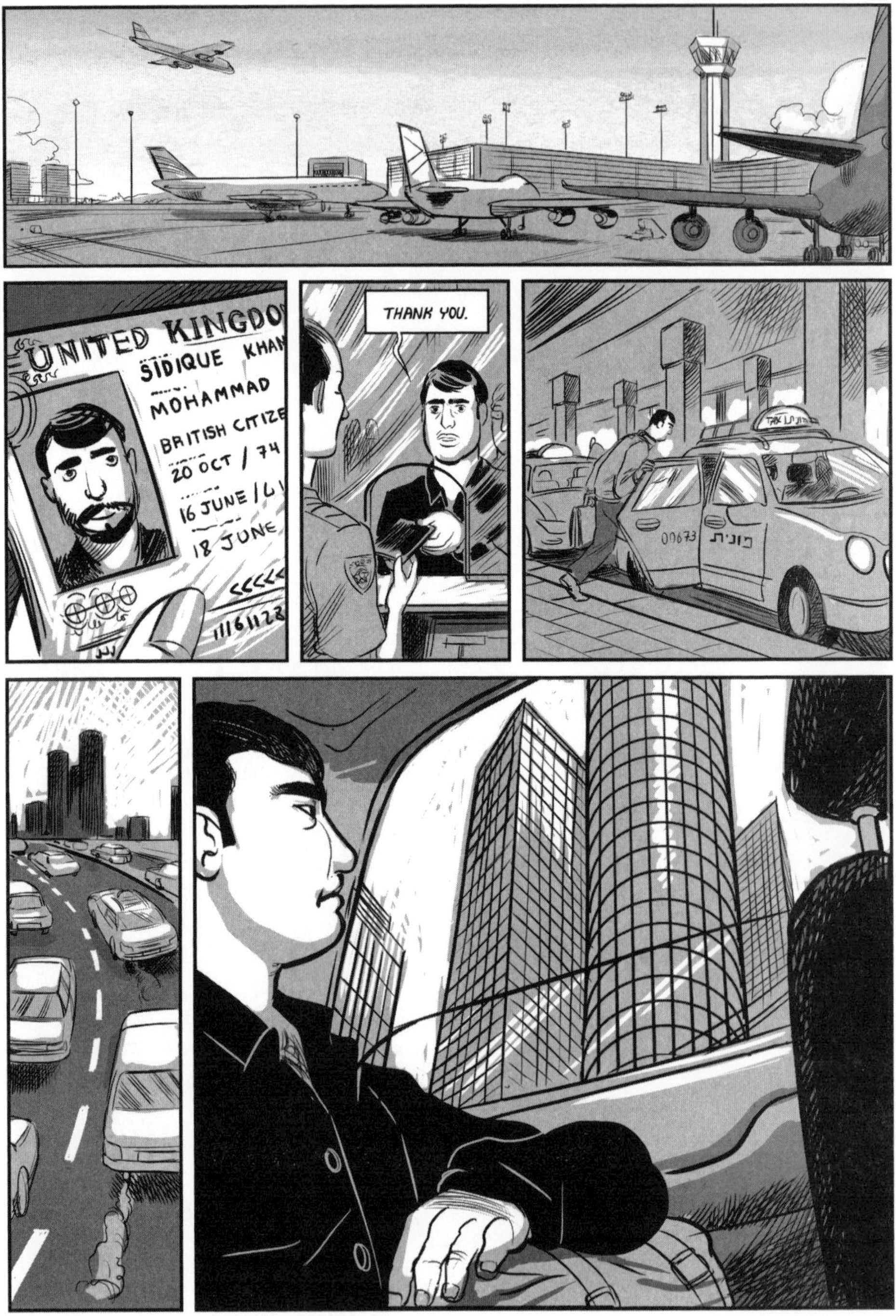
UNITED KINGDO
SIDIQUE KHAN
MOHAMMAD
BRITISH CITIZE
20 OCT / 74
16 JUNE
18 JUNE
THANK YOU.
00673
מונית

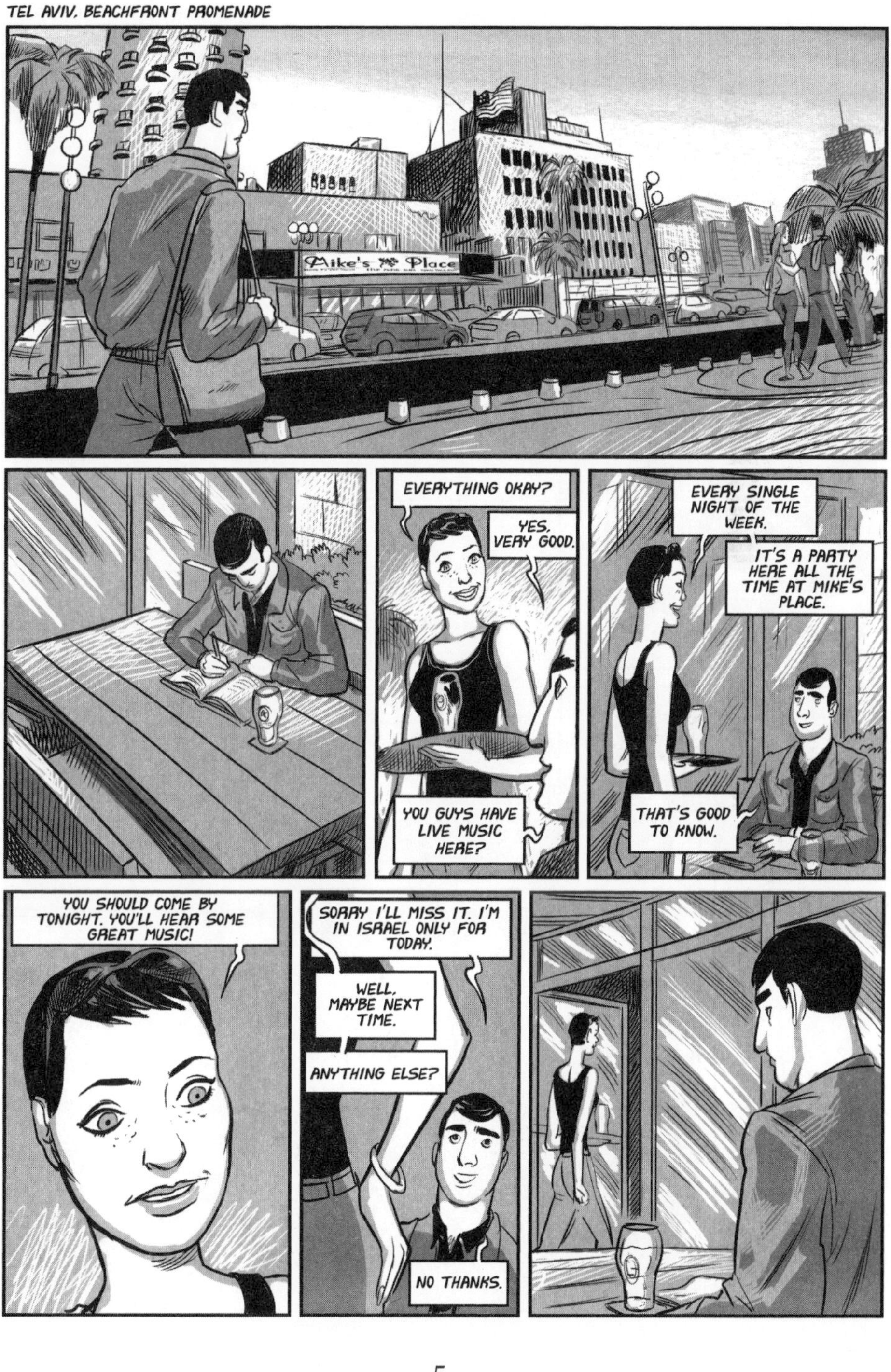
TEL AVIV, BEACHFRONT PROMENADE
Mike's Place
EVERYTHING OKAY?
YES, VERY GOOD.
YOU GUYS HAVE LIVE MUSIC HERE?
EVERY SINGLE NIGHT OF THE WEEK.
IT'S A PARTY HERE ALL THE TIME AT MIKE'S PLACE.
THAT'S GOOD TO KNOW.
YOU SHOULD COME BY TONIGHT. YOU'LL HEAR SOME GREAT MUSIC!
SORRY I'LL MISS IT. I'M IN ISRAEL ONLY FOR TODAY.
WELL, MAYBE NEXT TIME.
ANYTHING ELSE?
NO THANKS.

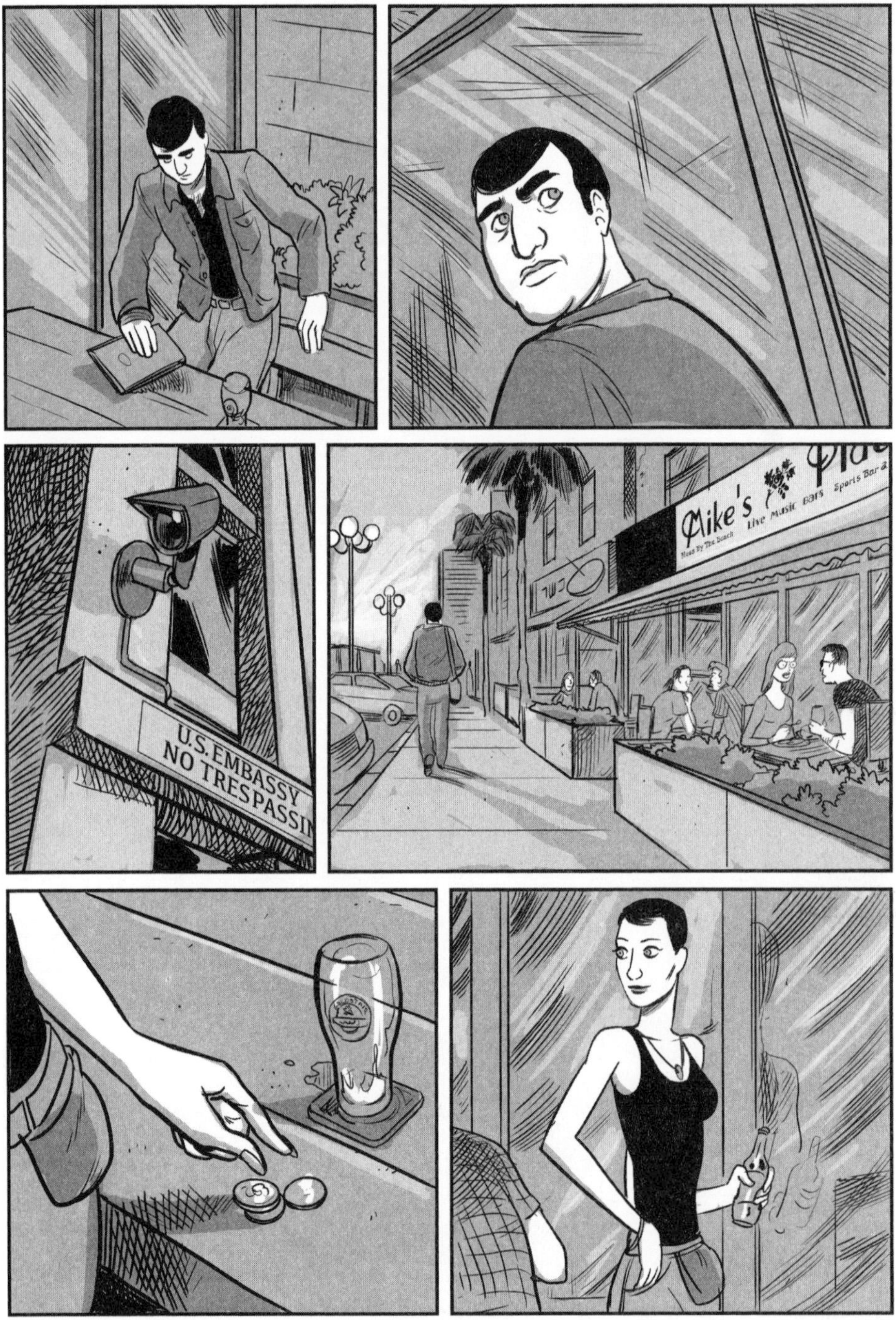
U.S. EMBASSY
NO TRESPASSIN
Mike's
Live Music Bars
Sports Bar &

HASHALOM COURT, TEL AVIV, APRIL 3, 2003

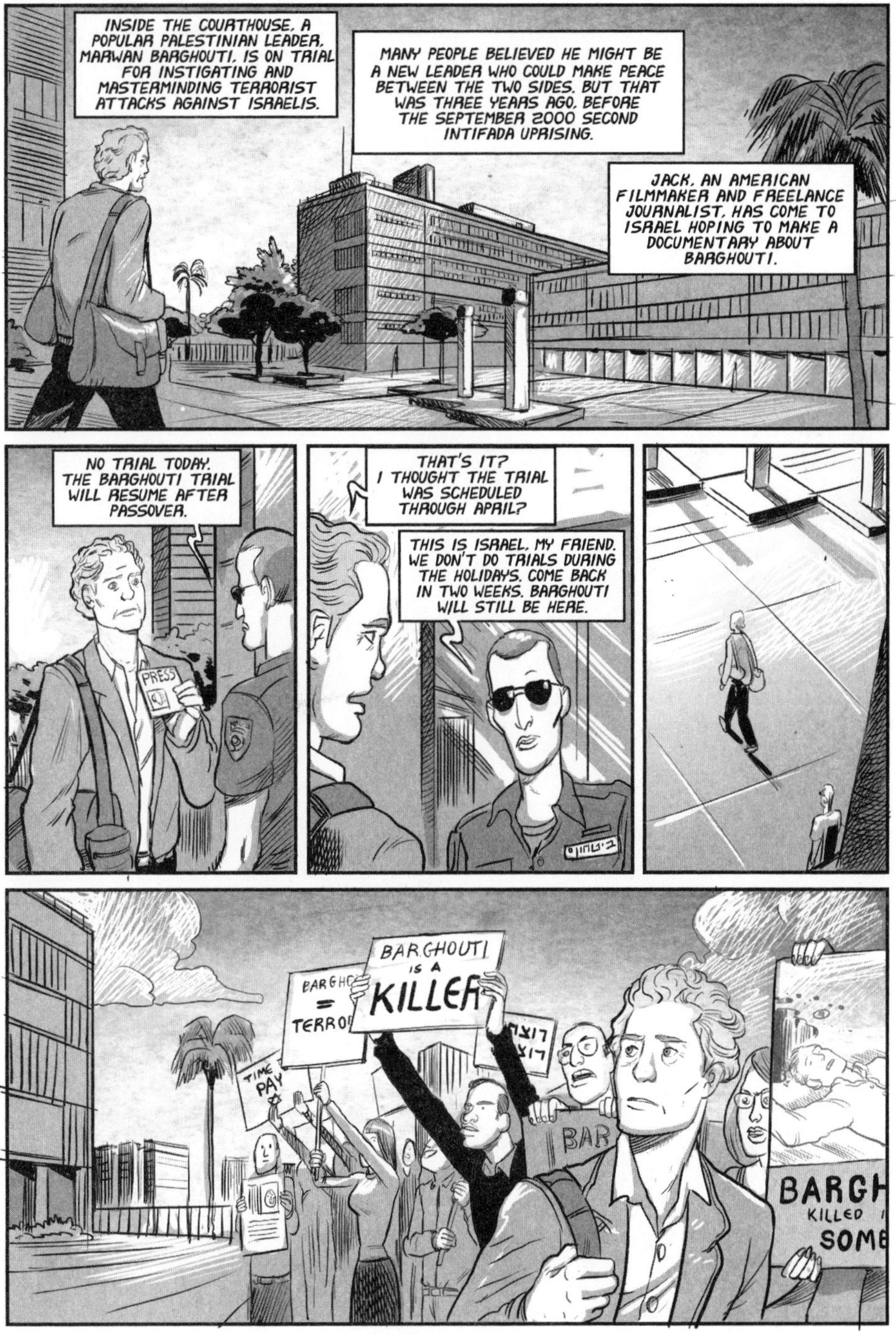

INSIDE THE COURTHOUSE, A POPULAR PALESTINIAN LEADER, MARWAN BARGHOUTI, IS ON TRIAL FOR INSTIGATING AND MASTERMINDING TERRORIST ATTACKS AGAINST ISRAELIS.
MANY PEOPLE BELIEVED HE MIGHT BE A NEW LEADER WHO COULD MAKE PEACE BETWEEN THE TWO SIDES. BUT THAT WAS THREE YEARS AGO, BEFORE THE SEPTEMBER 2000 SECOND INTIFADA UPRISING.
JACK, AN AMERICAN FILMMAKER AND FREELANCE JOURNALIST, HAS COME TO ISRAEL HOPING TO MAKE A DOCUMENTARY ABOUT BARGHOUTI.
NO TRIAL TODAY. THE BARGHOUTI TRIAL WILL RESUME AFTER PASSOVER.
PRESS
THAT'S IT? I THOUGHT THE TRIAL WAS SCHEDULED THROUGH APRIL?
THIS IS ISRAEL, MY FRIEND. WE DON'T DO TRIALS DURING THE HOLIDAYS. COME BACK IN TWO WEEKS. BARGHOUTI WILL STILL BE HERE.
BARGHO = TERRO
BARGHOUTI IS A KILLER
TIME PAY
BAR
BARGH KILLED SOME

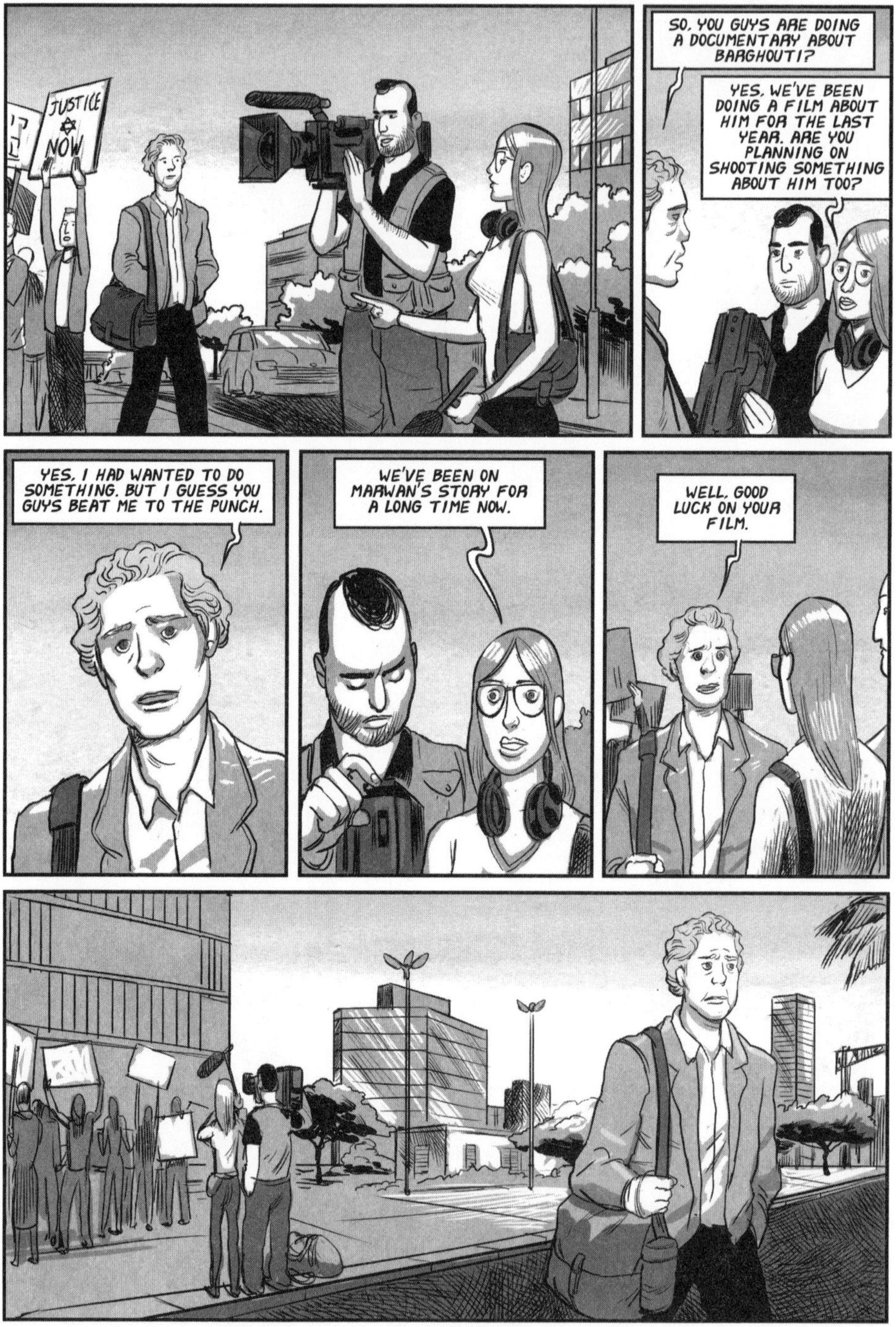
JUSTICE NOW
SO, YOU GUYS ARE DOING A DOCUMENTARY ABOUT BARGHOUTI?
YES, WE'VE BEEN DOING A FILM ABOUT HIM FOR THE LAST YEAR. ARE YOU PLANNING ON SHOOTING SOMETHING ABOUT HIM TOO?
YES, I HAD WANTED TO DO SOMETHING. BUT I GUESS YOU GUYS BEAT ME TO THE PUNCH.
WE'VE BEEN ON MARWAN'S STORY FOR A LONG TIME NOW.
WELL, GOOD LUCK ON YOUR FILM.

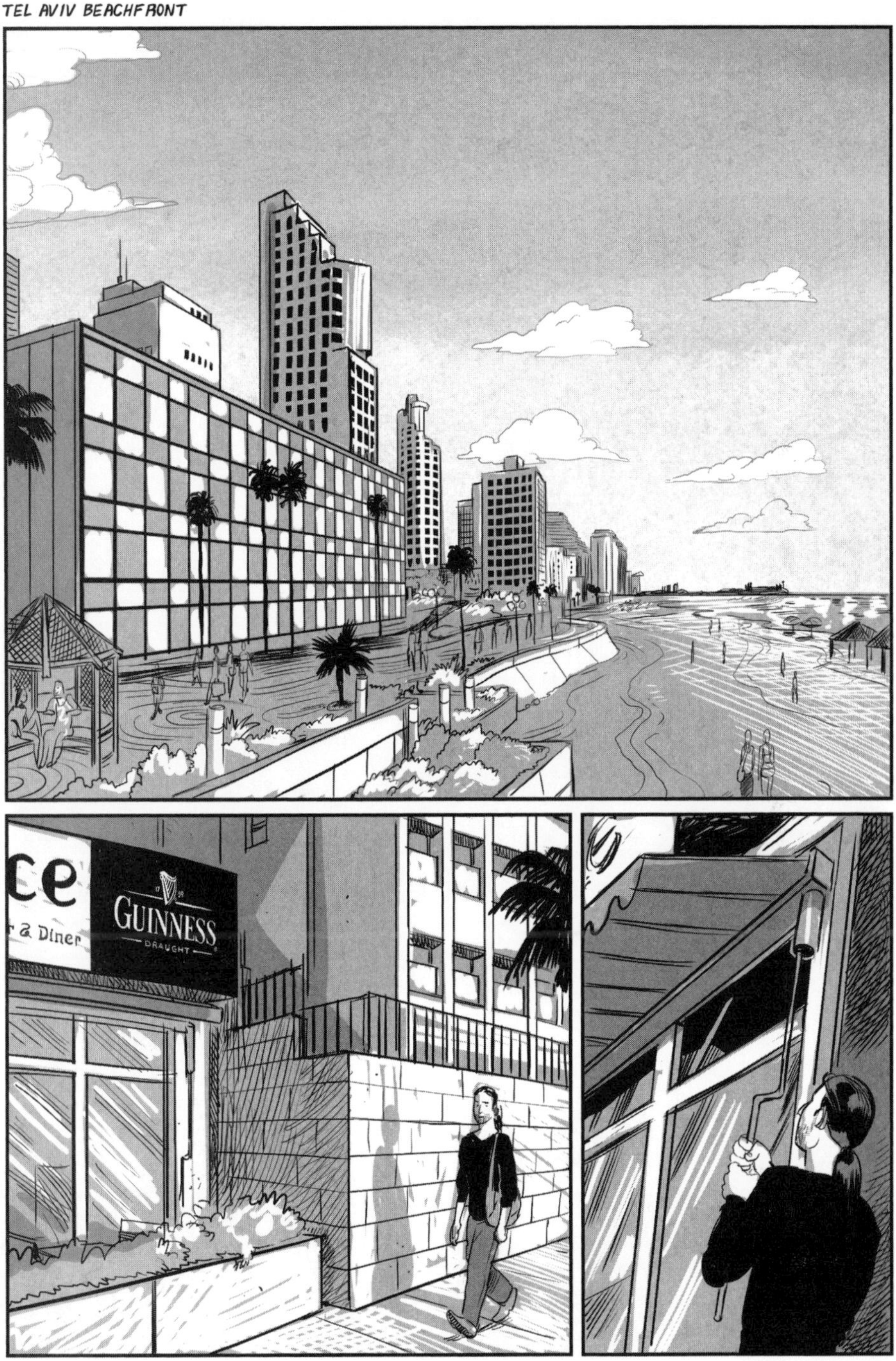
TEL AVIV BEACHFRONT
ce
r & Diner
GUINNESS
DRAUGHT

Mike's Place
Blues By The Beach
Live Music Bars
Sports Bar & Diner

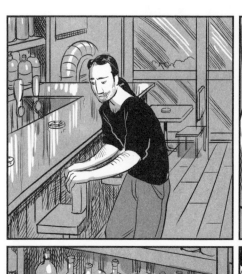

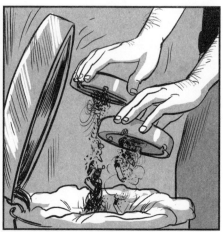

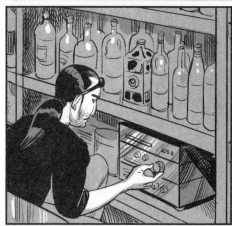

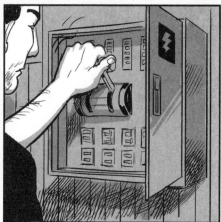

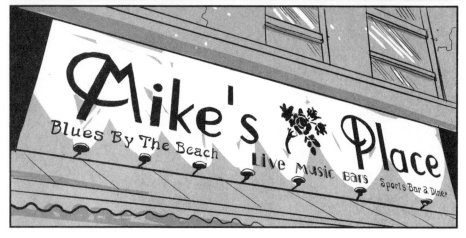

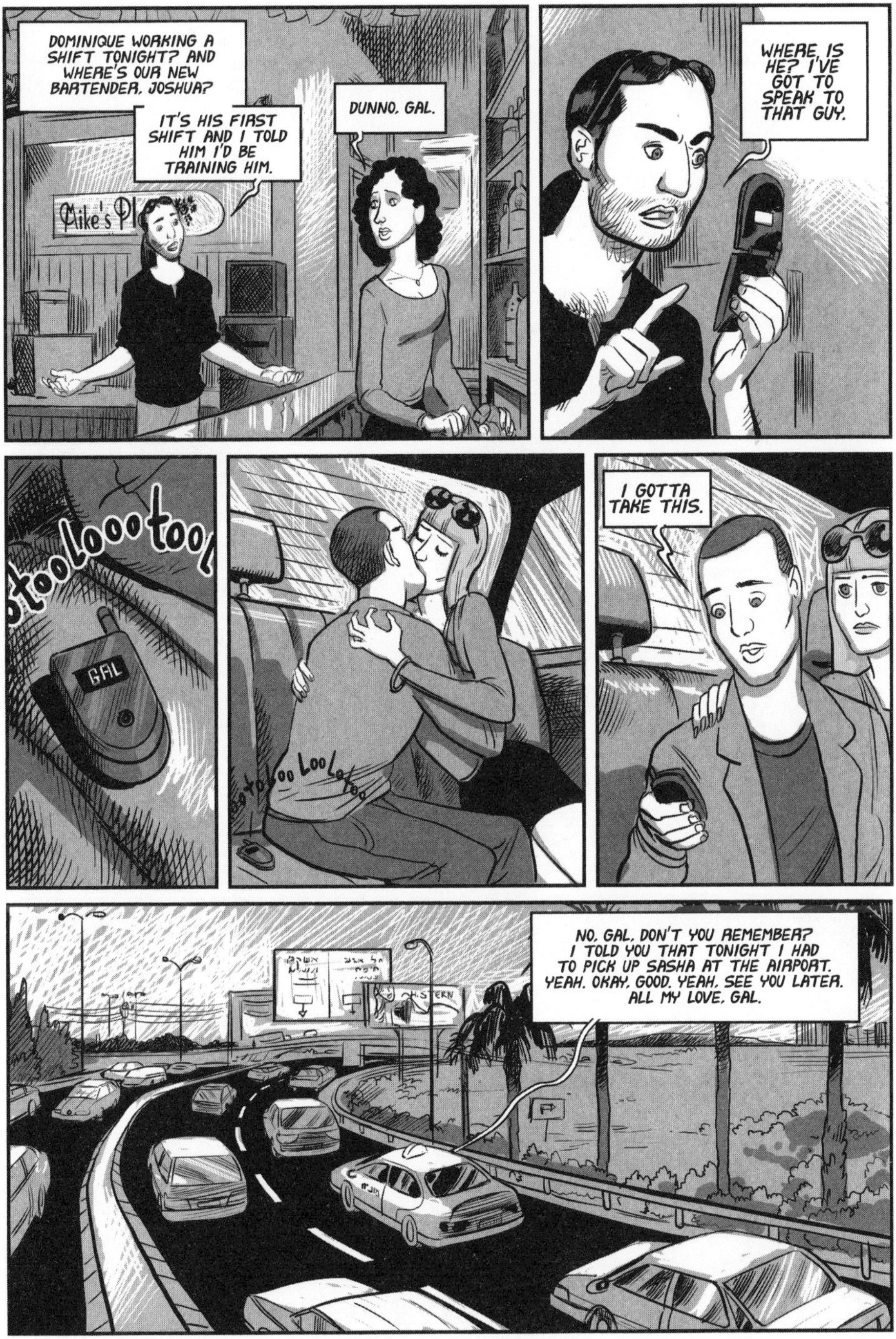
DOMINIQUE WORKING A SHIFT TONIGHT? AND WHERE'S OUR NEW BARTENDER, JOSHUA?
IT'S HIS FIRST SHIFT AND I TOLD HIM I'D BE TRAINING HIM.
DUNNO, GAL.
Mike's Pl
WHERE IS HE? I'VE GOT TO SPEAK TO THAT GUY.
tootooLooootool
GAL
tootoo LooLatoo
I GOTTA TAKE THIS.
H.STERN
NO, GAL, DON'T YOU REMEMBER? I TOLD YOU THAT TONIGHT I HAD TO PICK UP SASHA AT THE AIRPORT. YEAH. OKAY, GOOD. YEAH, SEE YOU LATER. ALL MY LOVE, GAL.

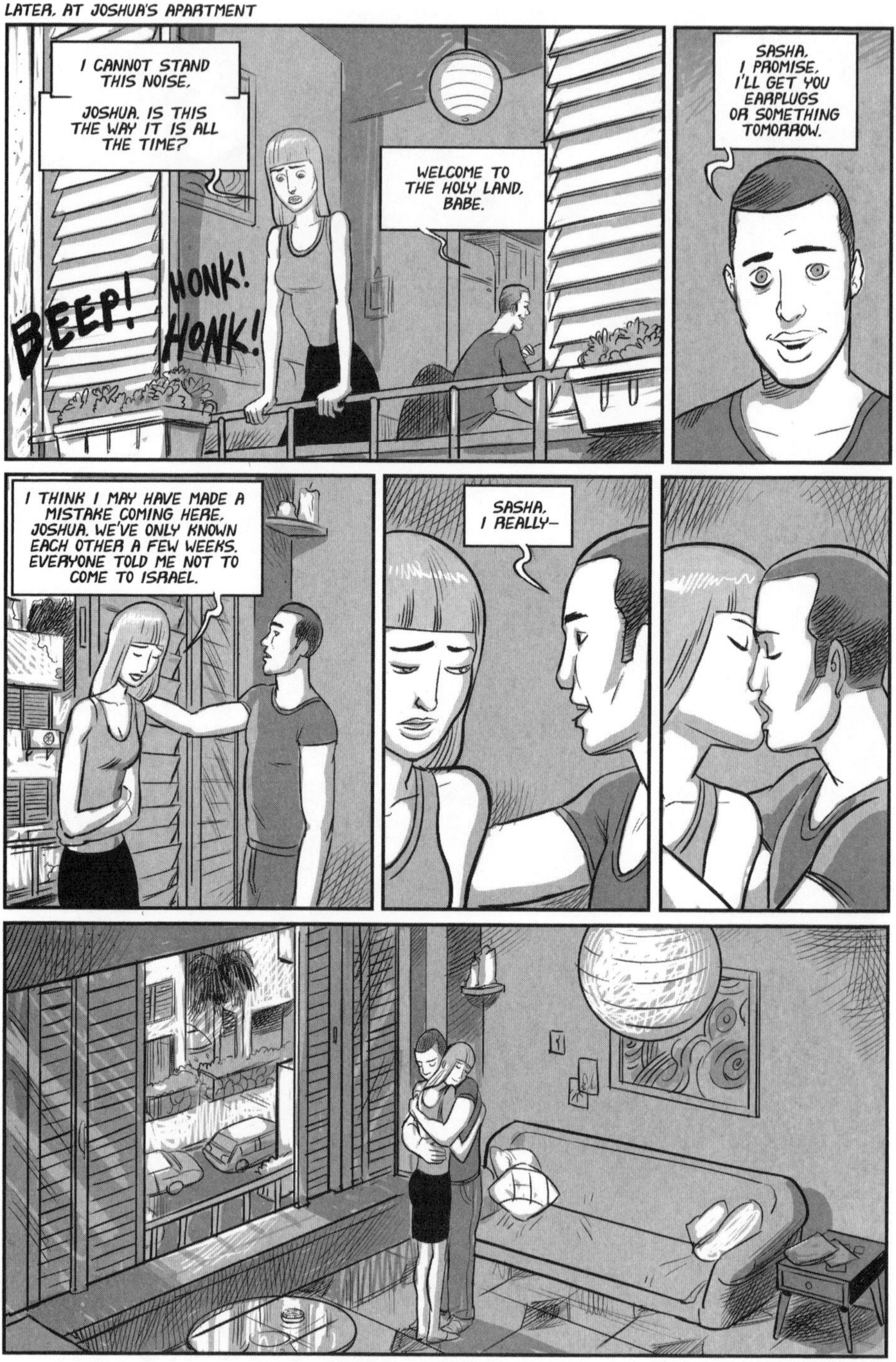
LATER, AT JOSHUA'S APARTMENT
I CANNOT STAND THIS NOISE,
JOSHUA. IS THIS THE WAY IT IS ALL THE TIME?
WELCOME TO THE HOLY LAND, BABE.
BEEP!
HONK! HONK!
SASHA, I PROMISE, I'LL GET YOU EARPLUGS OR SOMETHING TOMORROW.
I THINK I MAY HAVE MADE A MISTAKE COMING HERE, JOSHUA. WE'VE ONLY KNOWN EACH OTHER A FEW WEEKS. EVERYONE TOLD ME NOT TO COME TO ISRAEL.
SASHA, I REALLY—

ALLENBY BRIDGE CHECKPOINT CROSSING INTO ISRAEL FROM JORDAN

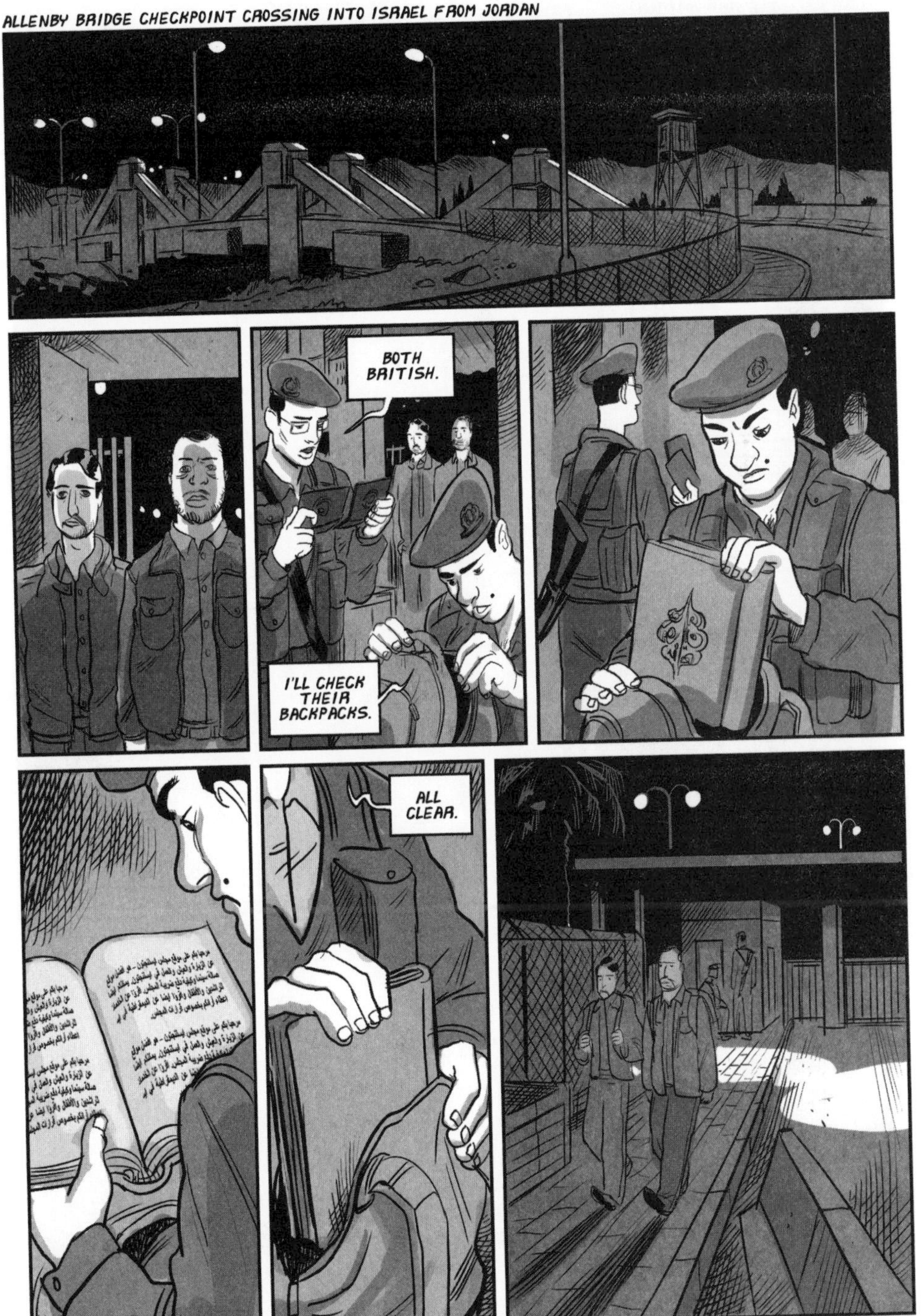
BOTH BRITISH.
I'LL CHECK THEIR BACKPACKS.
ALL CLEAR.

TEL AVIV, THE AMI HOTEL

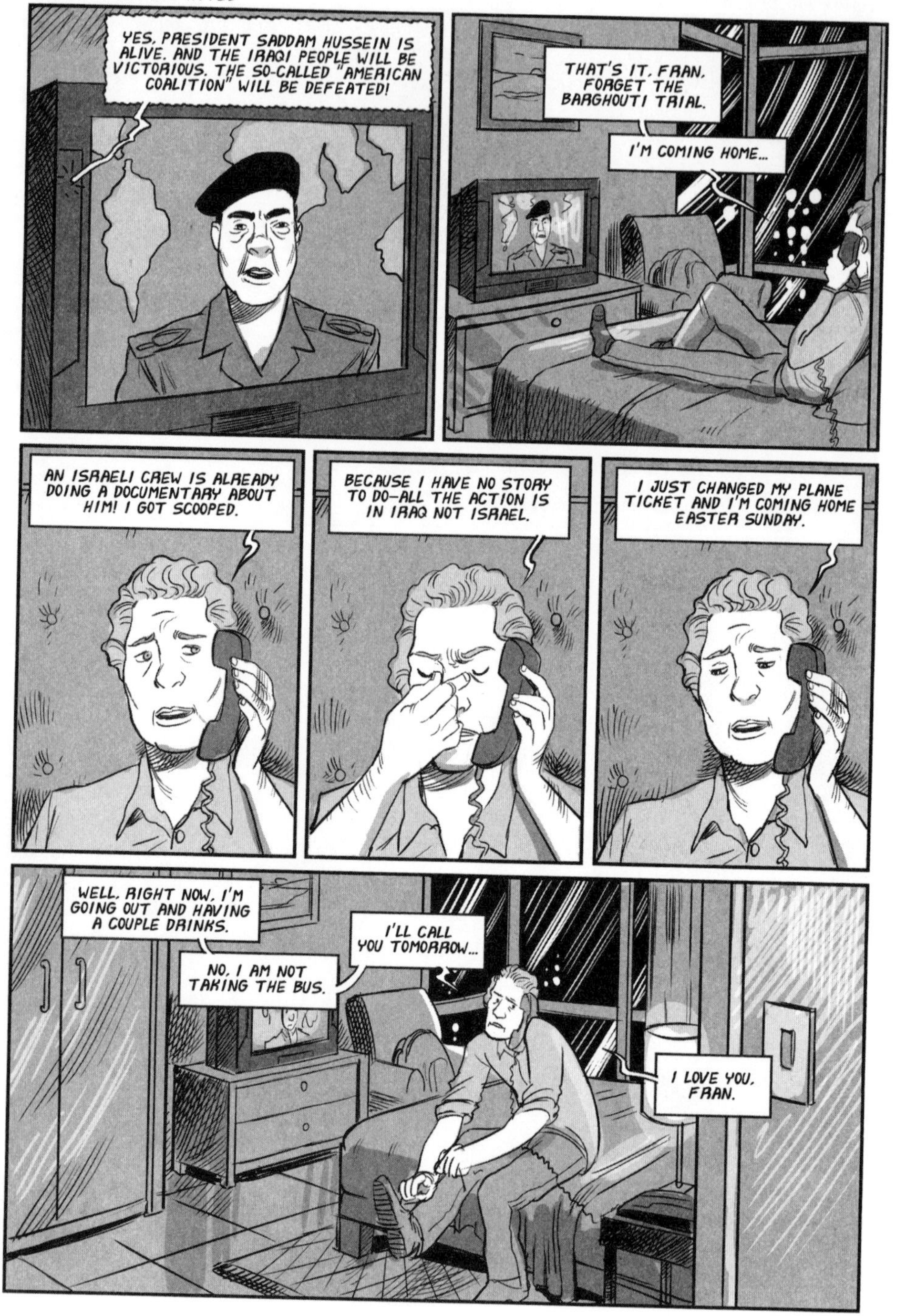
YES, PRESIDENT SADDAM HUSSEIN IS ALIVE. AND THE IRAQI PEOPLE WILL BE VICTORIOUS. THE SO-CALLED "AMERICAN COALITION" WILL BE DEFEATED!
THAT'S IT, FRAN. FORGET THE BARGHOUTI TRIAL.
I'M COMING HOME...
AN ISRAELI CREW IS ALREADY DOING A DOCUMENTARY ABOUT HIM! I GOT SCOOPED.
BECAUSE I HAVE NO STORY TO DO—ALL THE ACTION IS IN IRAQ NOT ISRAEL.
I JUST CHANGED MY PLANE TICKET AND I'M COMING HOME EASTER SUNDAY.
WELL, RIGHT NOW, I'M GOING OUT AND HAVING A COUPLE DRINKS.
NO, I AM NOT TAKING THE BUS.
I'LL CALL YOU TOMORROW...
I LOVE YOU, FRAN.

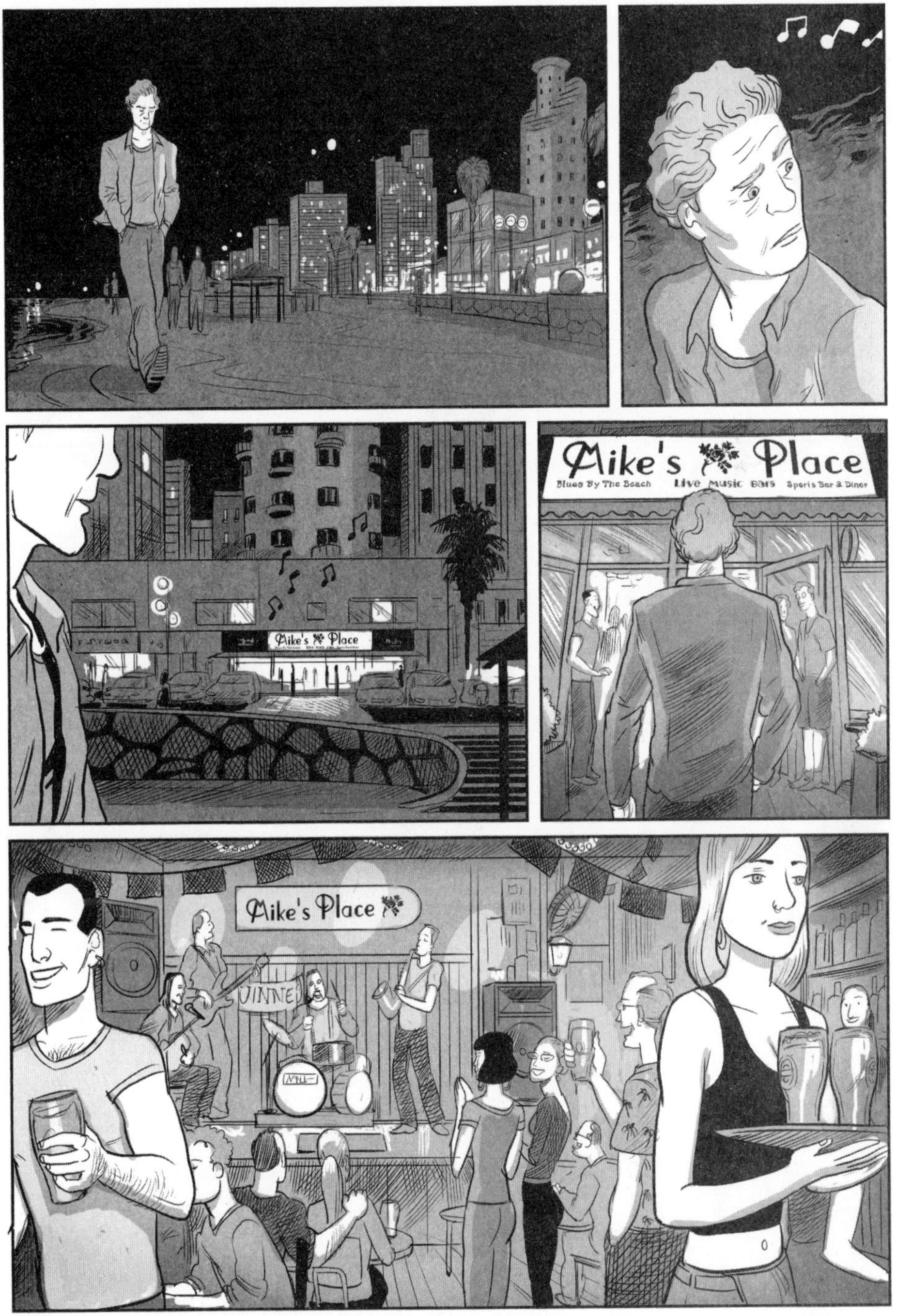
Mike's Place
Blues By The Beach
Live Music Bars
Sports Bar & Diner
Mike's Place

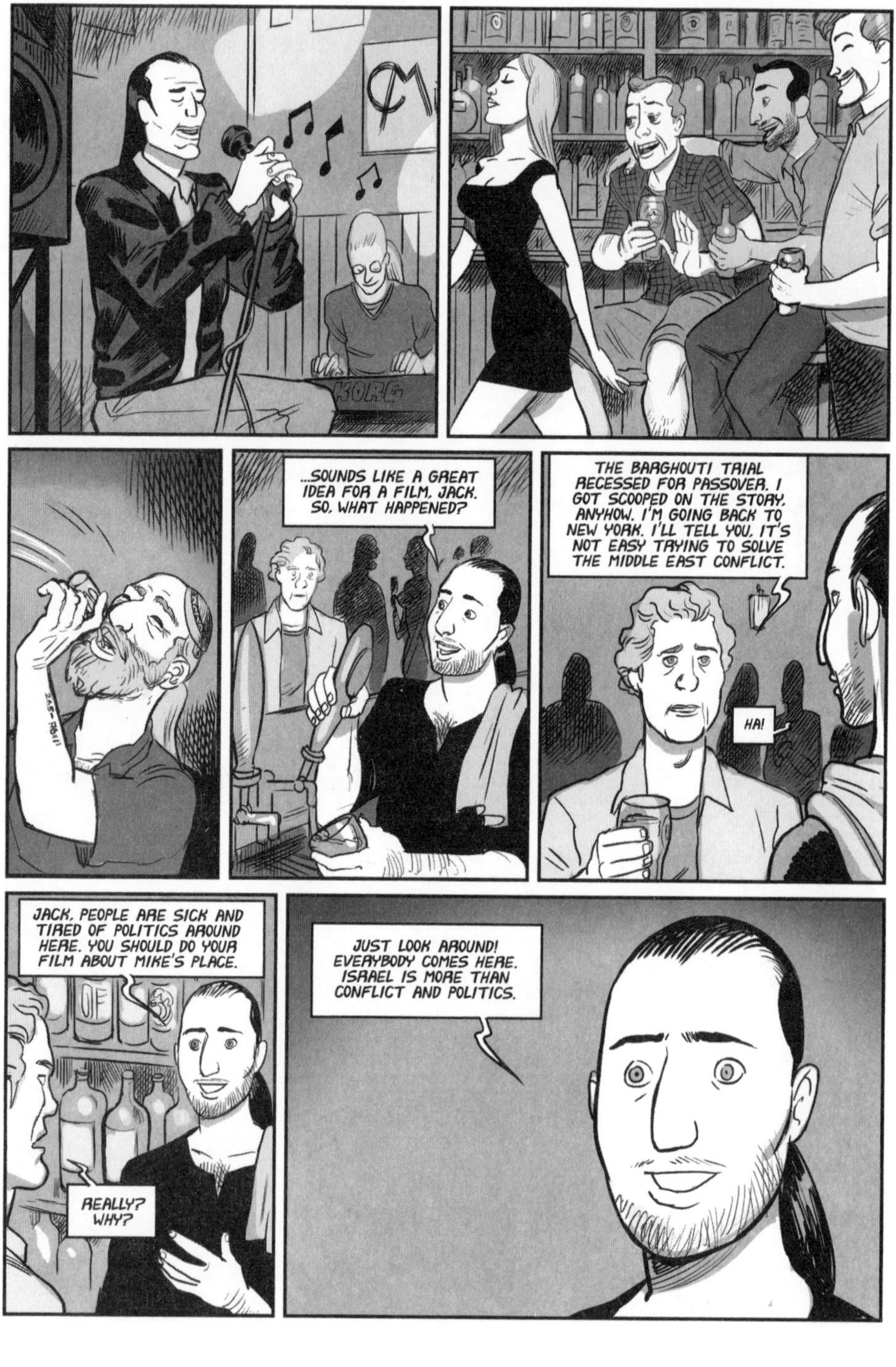
KORG
...SOUNDS LIKE A GREAT IDEA FOR A FILM, JACK. SO, WHAT HAPPENED?
THE BARGHOUTI TRIAL RECESSED FOR PASSOVER. I GOT SCOOPED ON THE STORY. ANYHOW, I'M GOING BACK TO NEW YORK. I'LL TELL YOU, IT'S NOT EASY TRYING TO SOLVE THE MIDDLE EAST CONFLICT.
HA!
JACK, PEOPLE ARE SICK AND TIRED OF POLITICS AROUND HERE. YOU SHOULD DO YOUR FILM ABOUT MIKE'S PLACE.
REALLY? WHY?
JUST LOOK AROUND! EVERYBODY COMES HERE. ISRAEL IS MORE THAN CONFLICT AND POLITICS.

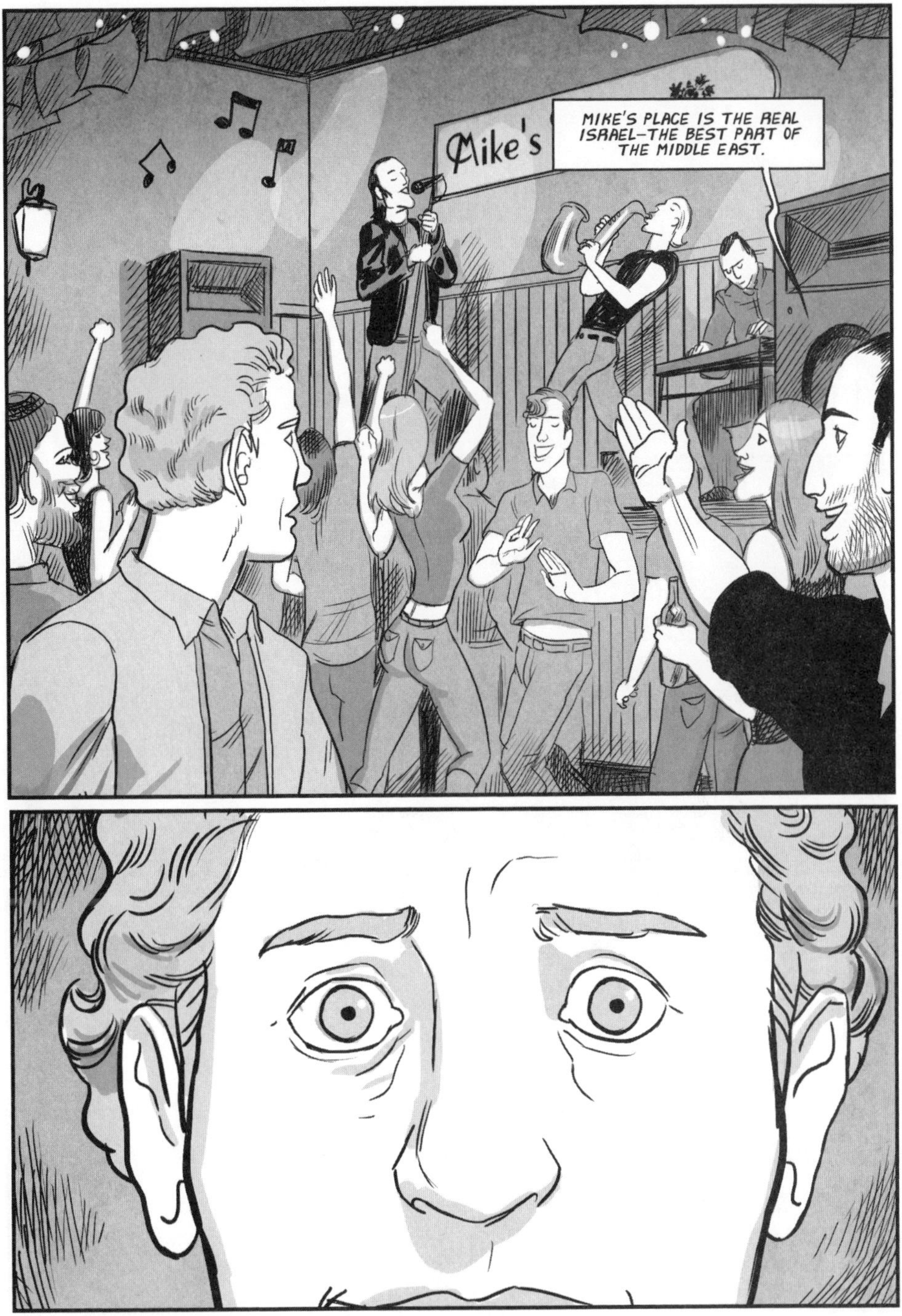
Mike's
MIKE'S PLACE IS THE REAL ISRAEL—THE BEST PART OF THE MIDDLE EAST.

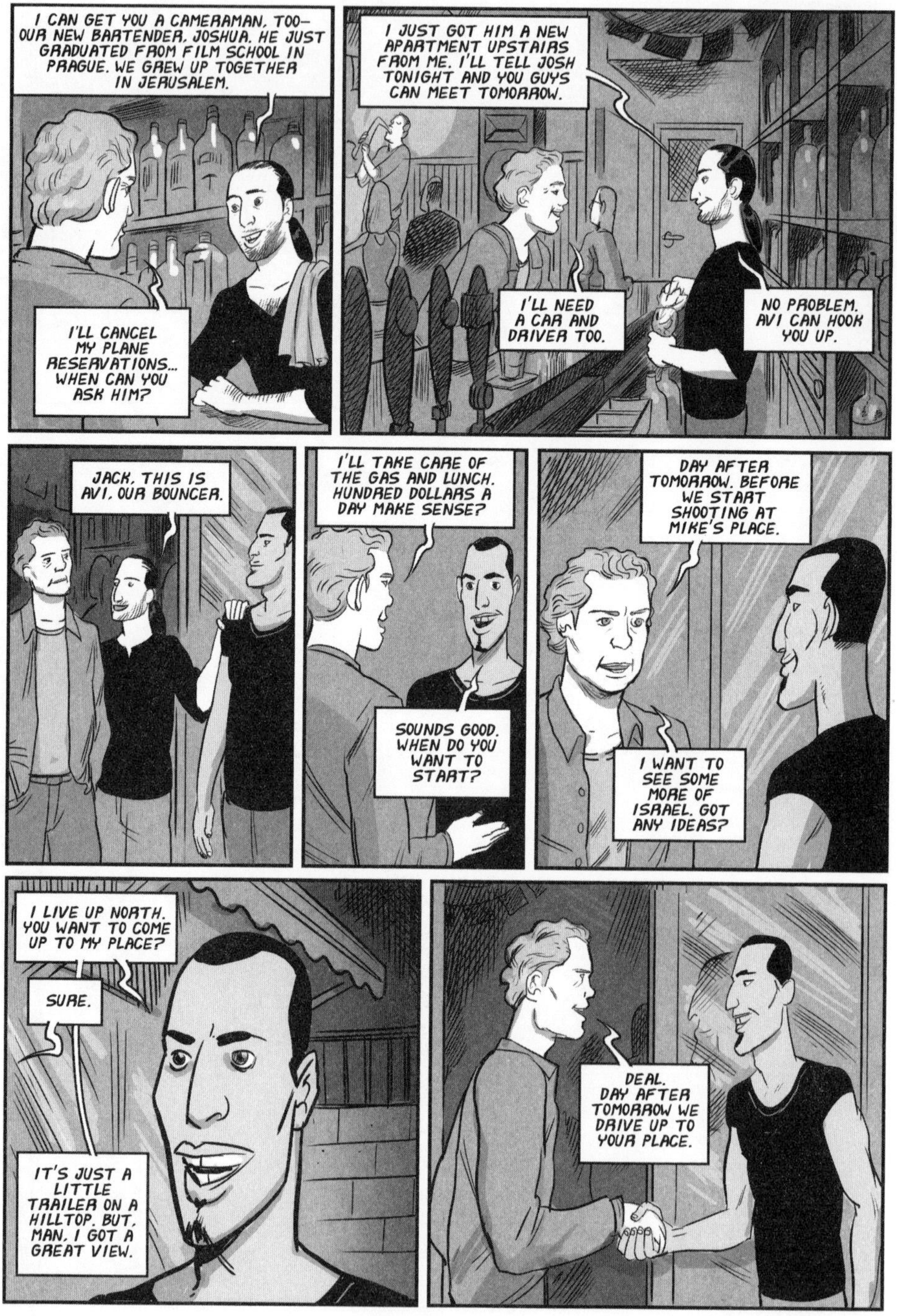
I CAN GET YOU A CAMERAMAN, TOO—OUR NEW BARTENDER, JOSHUA. HE JUST GRADUATED FROM FILM SCHOOL IN PRAGUE. WE GREW UP TOGETHER IN JERUSALEM.
I'LL CANCEL MY PLANE RESERVATIONS... WHEN CAN YOU ASK HIM?
I JUST GOT HIM A NEW APARTMENT UPSTAIRS FROM ME. I'LL TELL JOSH TONIGHT AND YOU GUYS CAN MEET TOMORROW.
I'LL NEED A CAR AND DRIVER TOO.
NO PROBLEM. AVI CAN HOOK YOU UP.
JACK, THIS IS AVI, OUR BOUNCER.
I'LL TAKE CARE OF THE GAS AND LUNCH. HUNDRED DOLLARS A DAY MAKE SENSE?
SOUNDS GOOD. WHEN DO YOU WANT TO START?
DAY AFTER TOMORROW. BEFORE WE START SHOOTING AT MIKE'S PLACE.
I WANT TO SEE SOME MORE OF ISRAEL. GOT ANY IDEAS?
I LIVE UP NORTH. YOU WANT TO COME UP TO MY PLACE?
SURE.
IT'S JUST A LITTLE TRAILER ON A HILLTOP. BUT, MAN, I GOT A GREAT VIEW.
DEAL. DAY AFTER TOMORROW WE DRIVE UP TO YOUR PLACE.

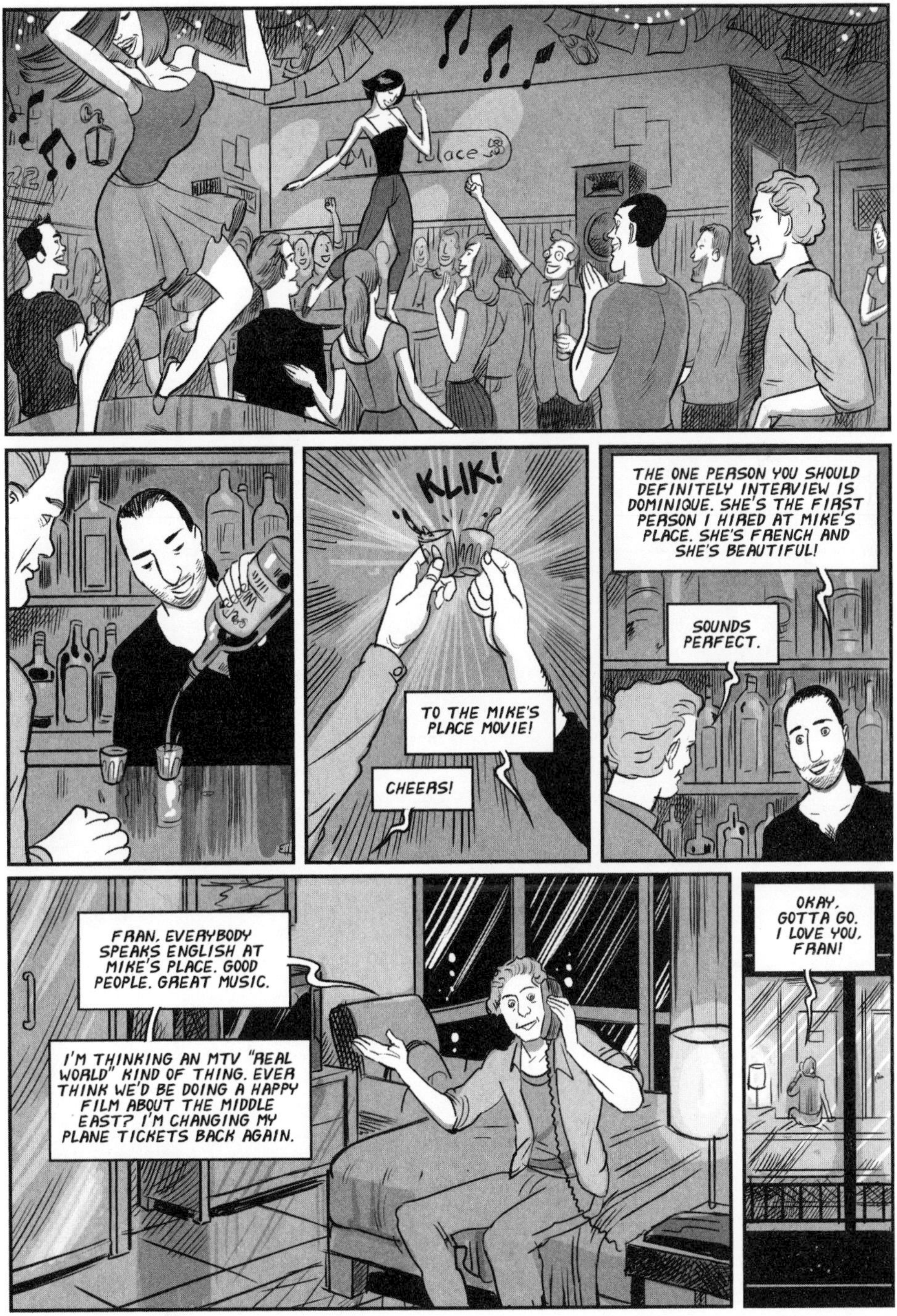
Mike's Place
KLIK!
TO THE MIKE'S PLACE MOVIE!
CHEERS!
THE ONE PERSON YOU SHOULD DEFINITELY INTERVIEW IS DOMINIQUE. SHE'S THE FIRST PERSON I HIRED AT MIKE'S PLACE. SHE'S FRENCH AND SHE'S BEAUTIFUL!
SOUNDS PERFECT.
FRAN. EVERYBODY SPEAKS ENGLISH AT MIKE'S PLACE. GOOD PEOPLE. GREAT MUSIC.
I'M THINKING AN MTV "REAL WORLD" KIND OF THING. EVER THINK WE'D BE DOING A HAPPY FILM ABOUT THE MIDDLE EAST? I'M CHANGING MY PLANE TICKETS BACK AGAIN.
OKAY, GOTTA GO. I LOVE YOU, FRAN!

THE NEXT DAY, JACK AND JOSHUA MEET AT MIKE'S PLACE

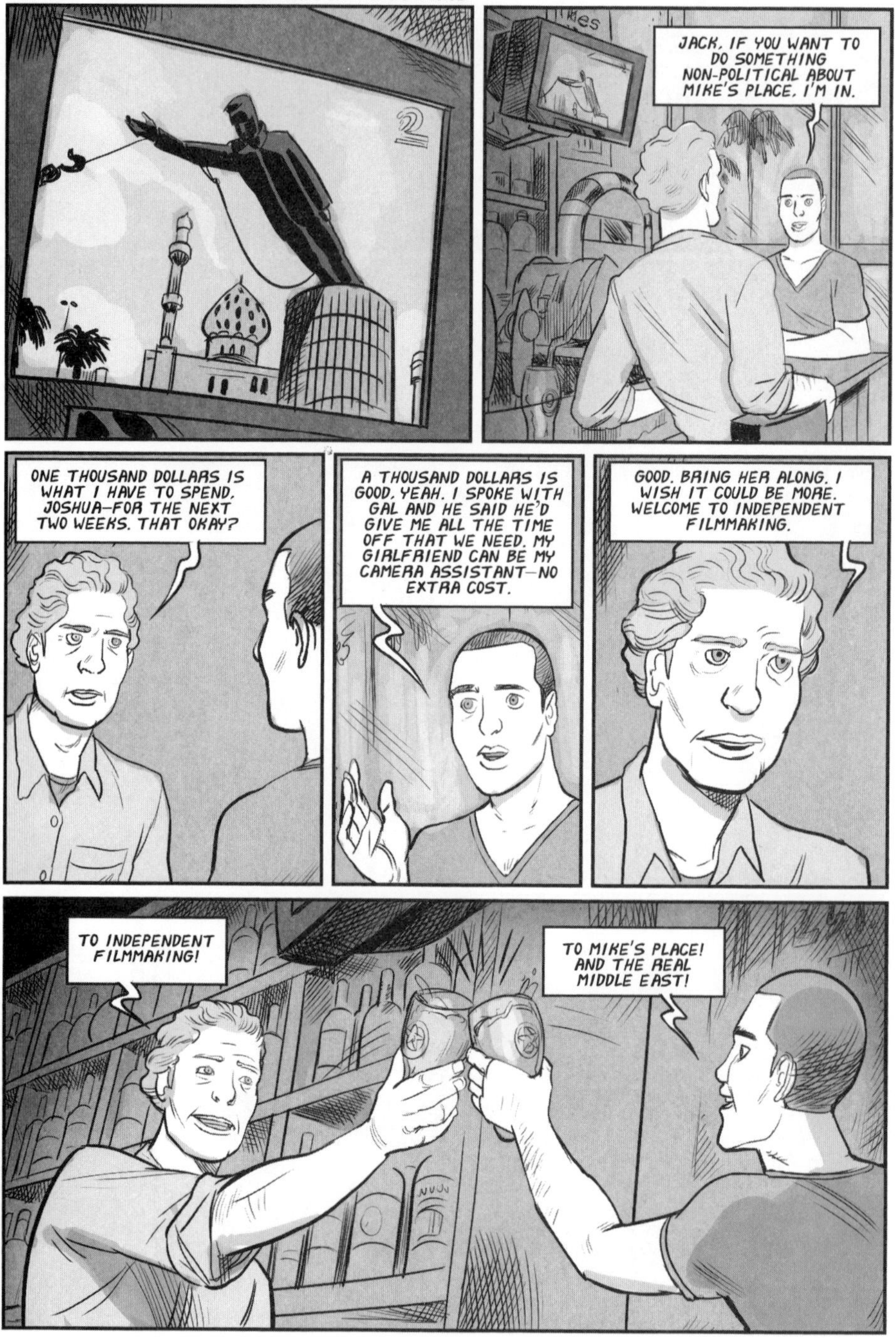
JACK, IF YOU WANT TO DO SOMETHING NON-POLITICAL ABOUT MIKE'S PLACE, I'M IN.
ONE THOUSAND DOLLARS IS WHAT I HAVE TO SPEND, JOSHUA—FOR THE NEXT TWO WEEKS. THAT OKAY?
A THOUSAND DOLLARS IS GOOD, YEAH. I SPOKE WITH GAL AND HE SAID HE'D GIVE ME ALL THE TIME OFF THAT WE NEED. MY GIRLFRIEND CAN BE MY CAMERA ASSISTANT—NO EXTRA COST.
GOOD. BRING HER ALONG. I WISH IT COULD BE MORE. WELCOME TO INDEPENDENT FILMMAKING.
TO INDEPENDENT FILMMAKING!
TO MIKE'S PLACE! AND THE REAL MIDDLE EAST!

SHUK HACARMEL OUTDOOR MARKET

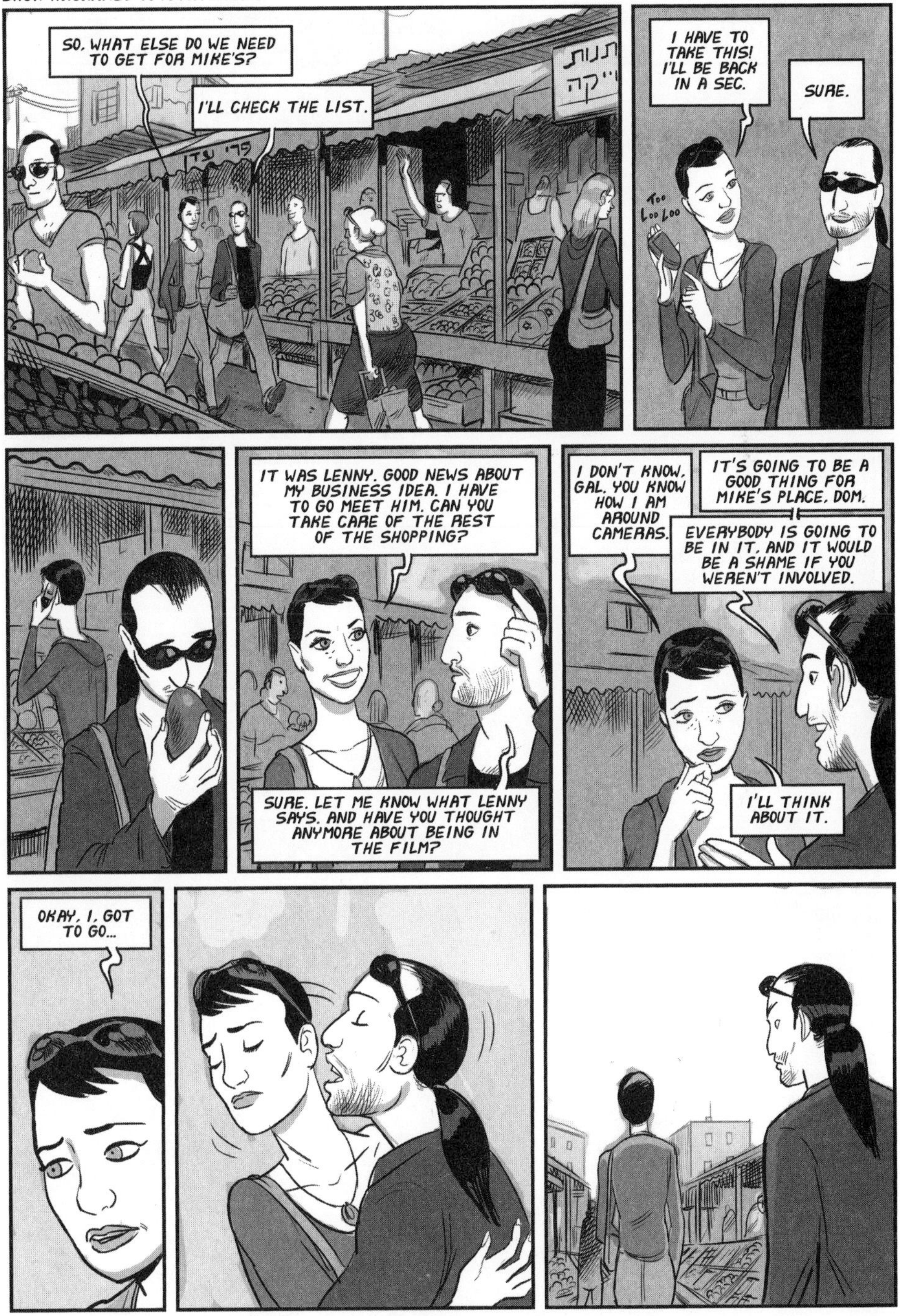

SO, WHAT ELSE DO WE NEED TO GET FOR MIKE'S?
I'LL CHECK THE LIST.
I HAVE TO TAKE THIS! I'LL BE BACK IN A SEC.
Too Loo Loo
SURE.
IT WAS LENNY. GOOD NEWS ABOUT MY BUSINESS IDEA. I HAVE TO GO MEET HIM. CAN YOU TAKE CARE OF THE REST OF THE SHOPPING?
SURE. LET ME KNOW WHAT LENNY SAYS. AND HAVE YOU THOUGHT ANYMORE ABOUT BEING IN THE FILM?
I DON'T KNOW, GAL. YOU KNOW HOW I AM AROUND CAMERAS.
IT'S GOING TO BE A GOOD THING FOR MIKE'S PLACE, DOM.
EVERYBODY IS GOING TO BE IN IT, AND IT WOULD BE A SHAME IF YOU WEREN'T INVOLVED.
I'LL THINK ABOUT IT.
OKAY, I, GOT TO GO...

OLD JAFFA HOSTEL ROOFTOP

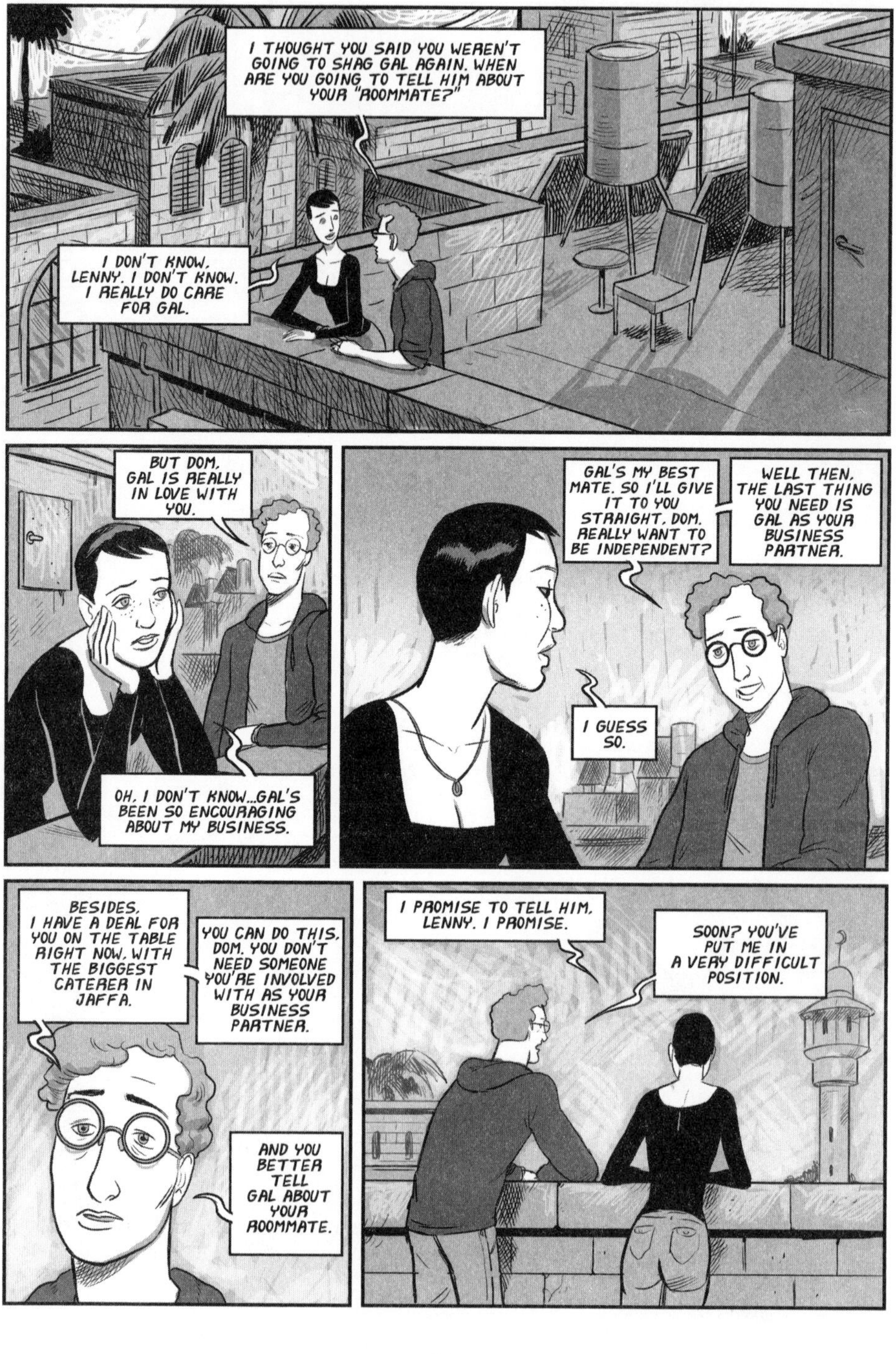
I THOUGHT YOU SAID YOU WEREN'T GOING TO SHAG GAL AGAIN. WHEN ARE YOU GOING TO TELL HIM ABOUT YOUR "ROOMMATE?"
I DON'T KNOW, LENNY. I DON'T KNOW. I REALLY DO CARE FOR GAL.
BUT DOM, GAL IS REALLY IN LOVE WITH YOU.
OH, I DON'T KNOW...GAL'S BEEN SO ENCOURAGING ABOUT MY BUSINESS.
GAL'S MY BEST MATE, SO I'LL GIVE IT TO YOU STRAIGHT, DOM. REALLY WANT TO BE INDEPENDENT?
WELL THEN, THE LAST THING YOU NEED IS GAL AS YOUR BUSINESS PARTNER.
I GUESS SO.
BESIDES, I HAVE A DEAL FOR YOU ON THE TABLE RIGHT NOW, WITH THE BIGGEST CATERER IN JAFFA.
YOU CAN DO THIS, DOM. YOU DON'T NEED SOMEONE YOU'RE INVOLVED WITH AS YOUR BUSINESS PARTNER.
AND YOU BETTER TELL GAL ABOUT YOUR ROOMMATE.
I PROMISE TO TELL HIM, LENNY. I PROMISE.
SOON? YOU'VE PUT ME IN A VERY DIFFICULT POSITION.

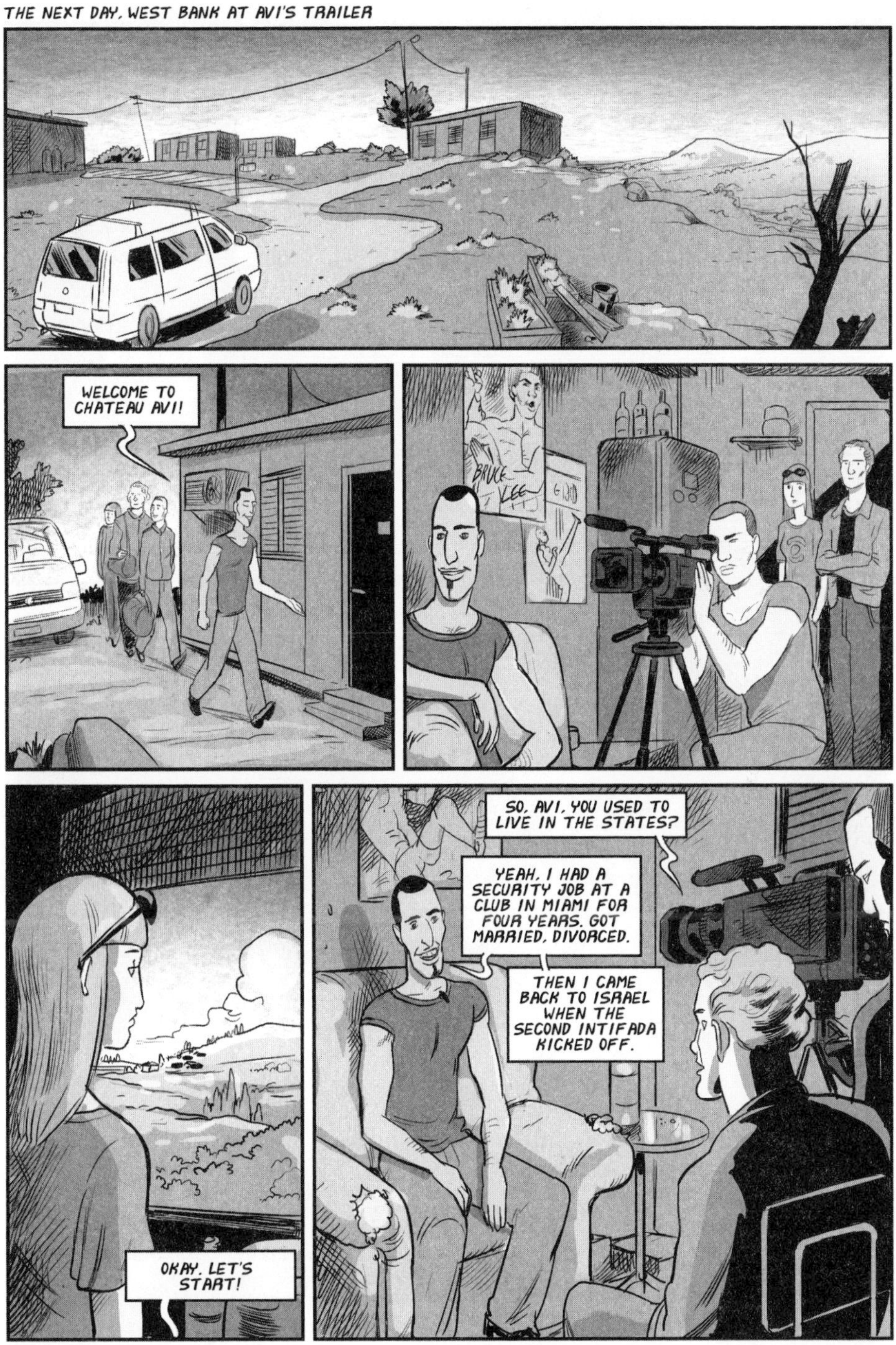
THE NEXT DAY, WEST BANK AT AVI'S TRAILER
WELCOME TO CHATEAU AVI!
OKAY. LET'S START!
SO, AVI, YOU USED TO LIVE IN THE STATES?
YEAH, I HAD A SECURITY JOB AT A CLUB IN MIAMI FOR FOUR YEARS. GOT MARRIED, DIVORCED.
THEN I CAME BACK TO ISRAEL WHEN THE SECOND INTIFADA KICKED OFF.

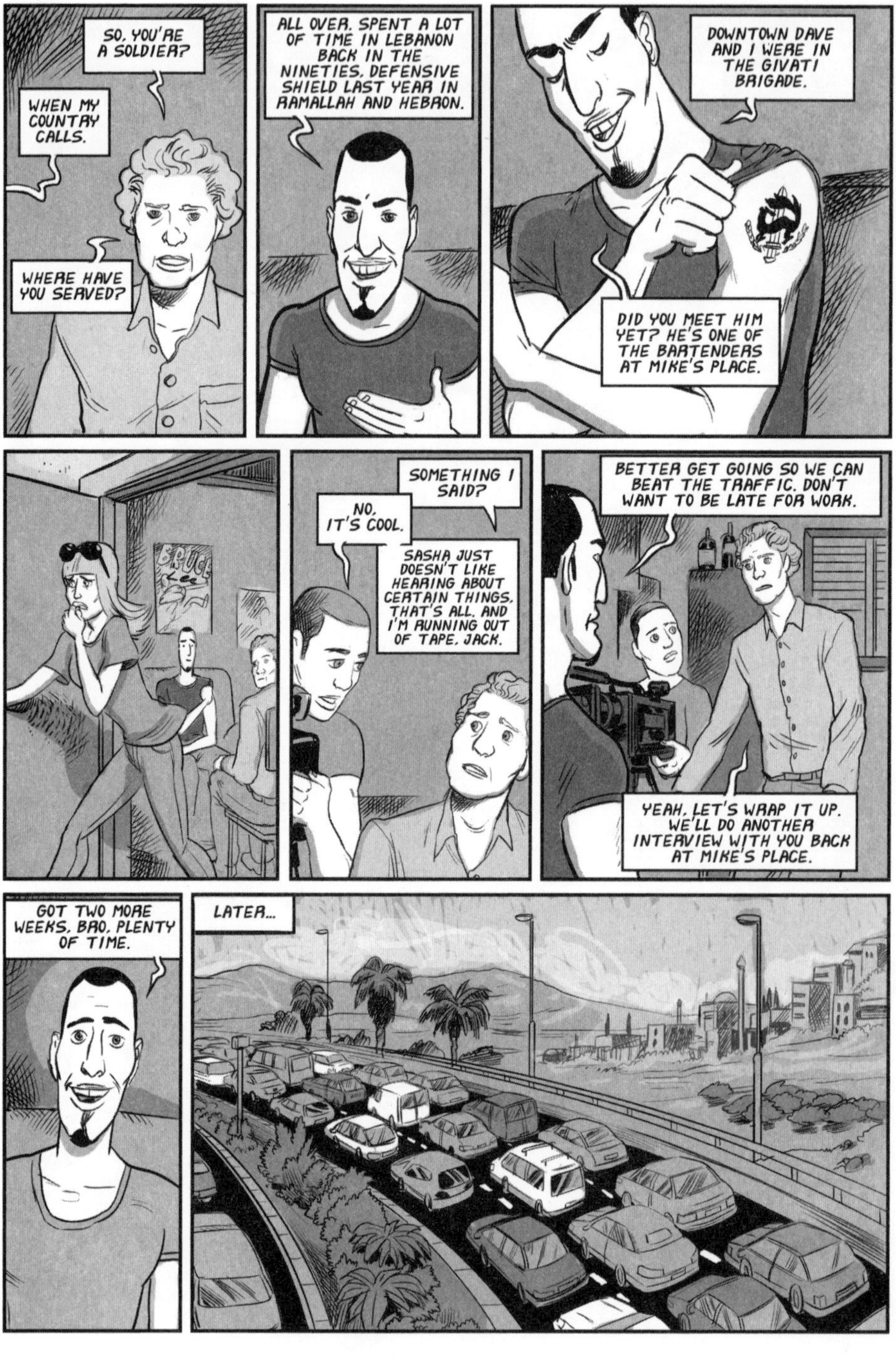
SO, YOU'RE A SOLDIER?
WHEN MY COUNTRY CALLS.
WHERE HAVE YOU SERVED?
ALL OVER. SPENT A LOT OF TIME IN LEBANON BACK IN THE NINETIES. DEFENSIVE SHIELD LAST YEAR IN RAMALLAH AND HEBRON.
DOWNTOWN DAVE AND I WERE IN THE GIVATI BRIGADE.
DID YOU MEET HIM YET? HE'S ONE OF THE BARTENDERS AT MIKE'S PLACE.
BRUCE LEE
SOMETHING I SAID?
NO, IT'S COOL.
SASHA JUST DOESN'T LIKE HEARING ABOUT CERTAIN THINGS, THAT'S ALL. AND I'M RUNNING OUT OF TAPE, JACK.
BETTER GET GOING SO WE CAN BEAT THE TRAFFIC. DON'T WANT TO BE LATE FOR WORK.
YEAH, LET'S WRAP IT UP. WE'LL DO ANOTHER INTERVIEW WITH YOU BACK AT MIKE'S PLACE.
GOT TWO MORE WEEKS, BRO, PLENTY OF TIME.
LATER...

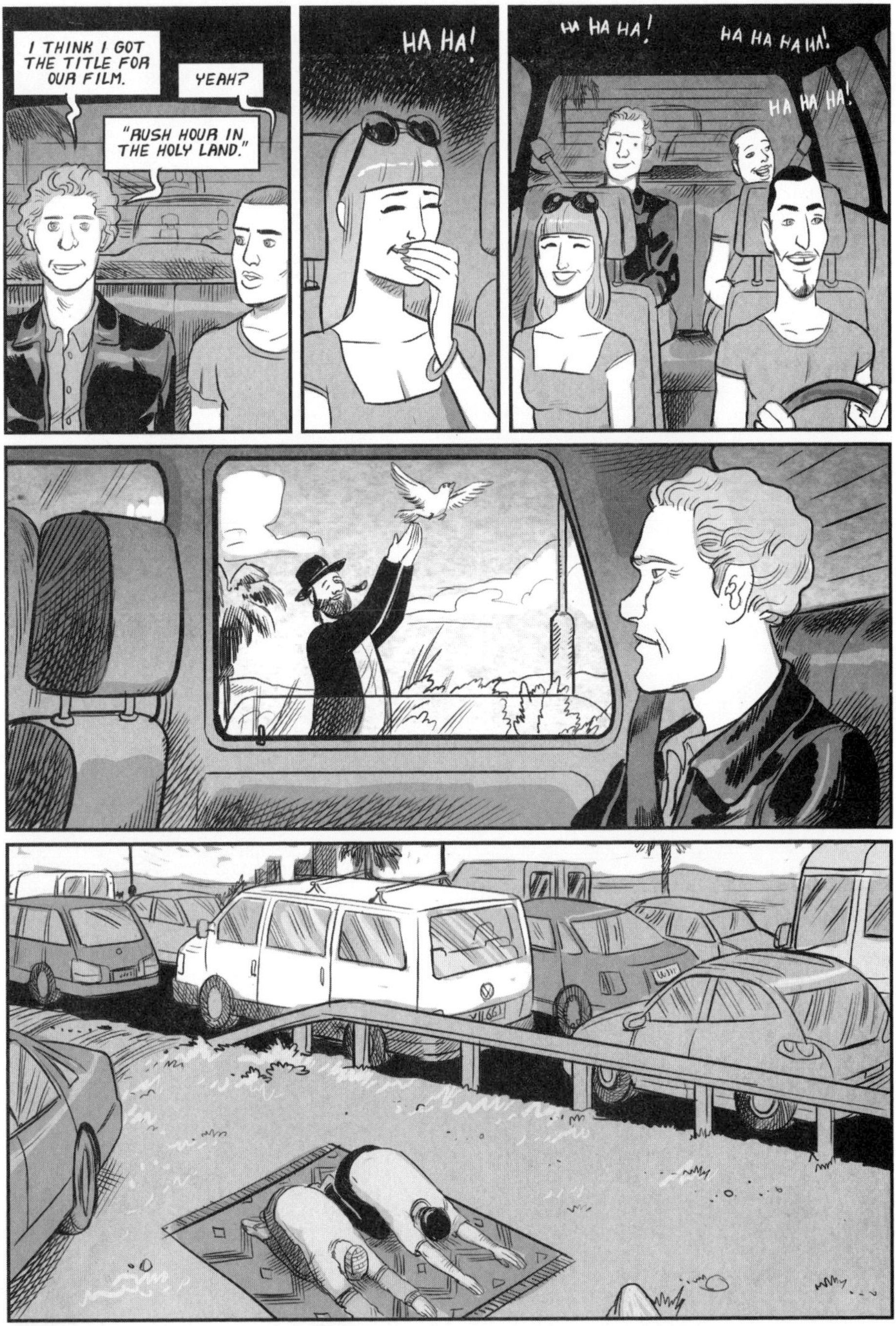
I THINK I GOT THE TITLE FOR OUR FILM.
YEAH?
"RUSH HOUR IN THE HOLY LAND."
HA HA!
HA HA HA!
HA HA HA HA!
HA HA HA!

II

"Truly those who believe, and the Jews, and the Christians, and the Sabaeans—whoever believes in God and the Last Day and performs virtuous deeds—surely their reward is with their Sustainer, and no fear shall come upon them, neither shall they grieve."

—Qur'an

EREZ CHECKPOINT CROSSING INTO GAZA STRIP

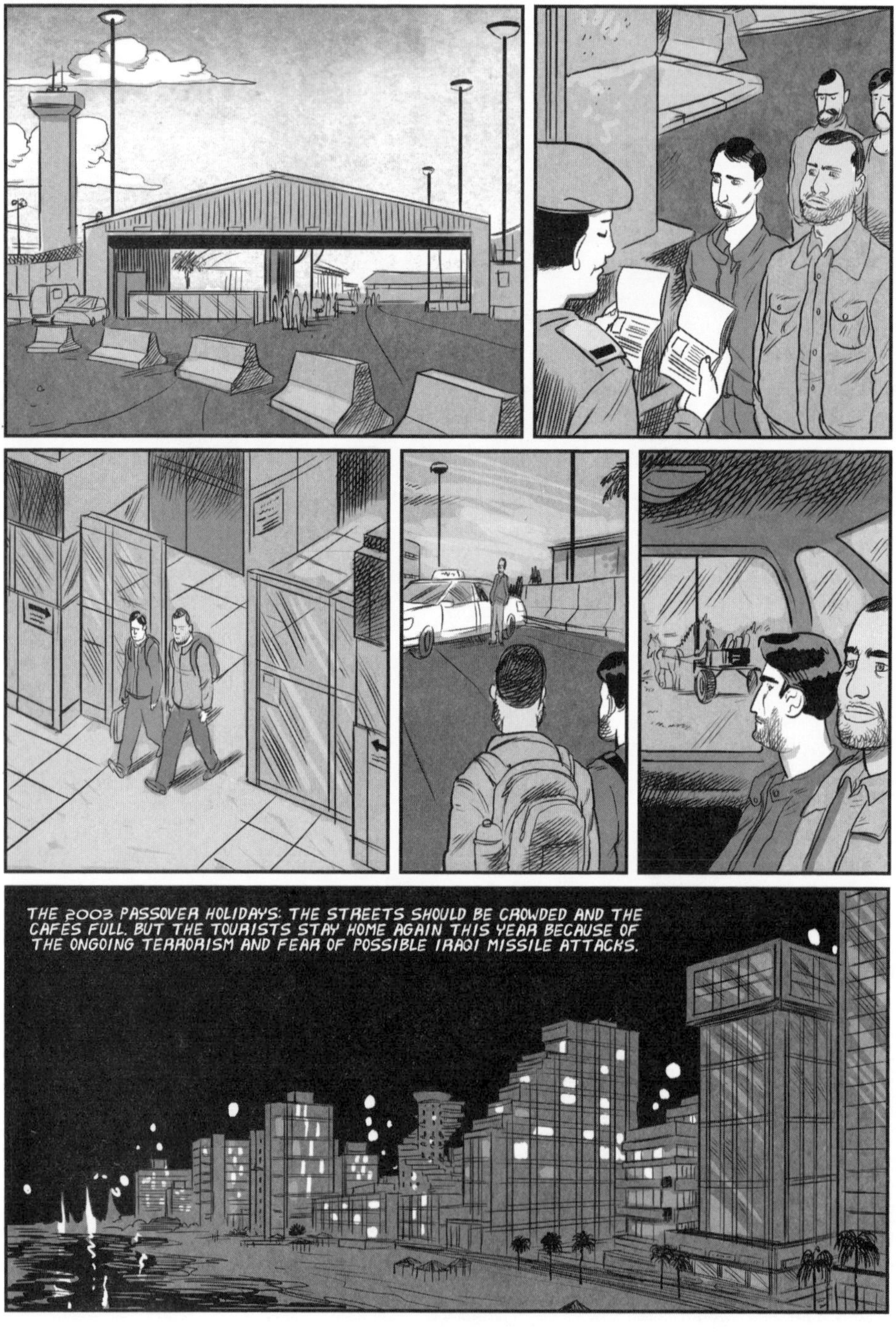
THE 2003 PASSOVER HOLIDAYS: THE STREETS SHOULD BE CROWDED AND THE CAFÉS FULL. BUT THE TOURISTS STAY HOME AGAIN THIS YEAR BECAUSE OF THE ONGOING TERRORISM AND FEAR OF POSSIBLE IRAQI MISSILE ATTACKS.

HEY, LOUIE, I GOT ONE CHEESEBURGER DELUXE AND TWO ISRAELI SALADS.

GOT IT.

WHERE'S THE AMERICAN?

JACK'S TIRED. HE SAID WE'D RESCHEDULE AND START TOMORROW. THEY GOT CAUGHT UP AT AVI'S PLACE.

OH, AVI'S IN IT TOO? MAYBE I WILL DO HIS FILM. WHAT THE HELL, RIGHT? I AM NOT DOING IT ALONE THOUGH. GAL, YOU MUST BE WITH ME FOR THE INTERVIEW.

HEY, YOU KNOW I'M THERE FOR YOU, DOM.

HAVE YOU THOUGHT ANYMORE ABOUT GOING INTO BUSINESS TOGETHER? I'M READY TO WRITE A CHECK RIGHT NOW AND MAKE YOU THE PASTRY QUEEN OF TEL AVIV.

THANK YOU, GAL. LET'S TALK AFTER THE HOLIDAYS.

COOL.

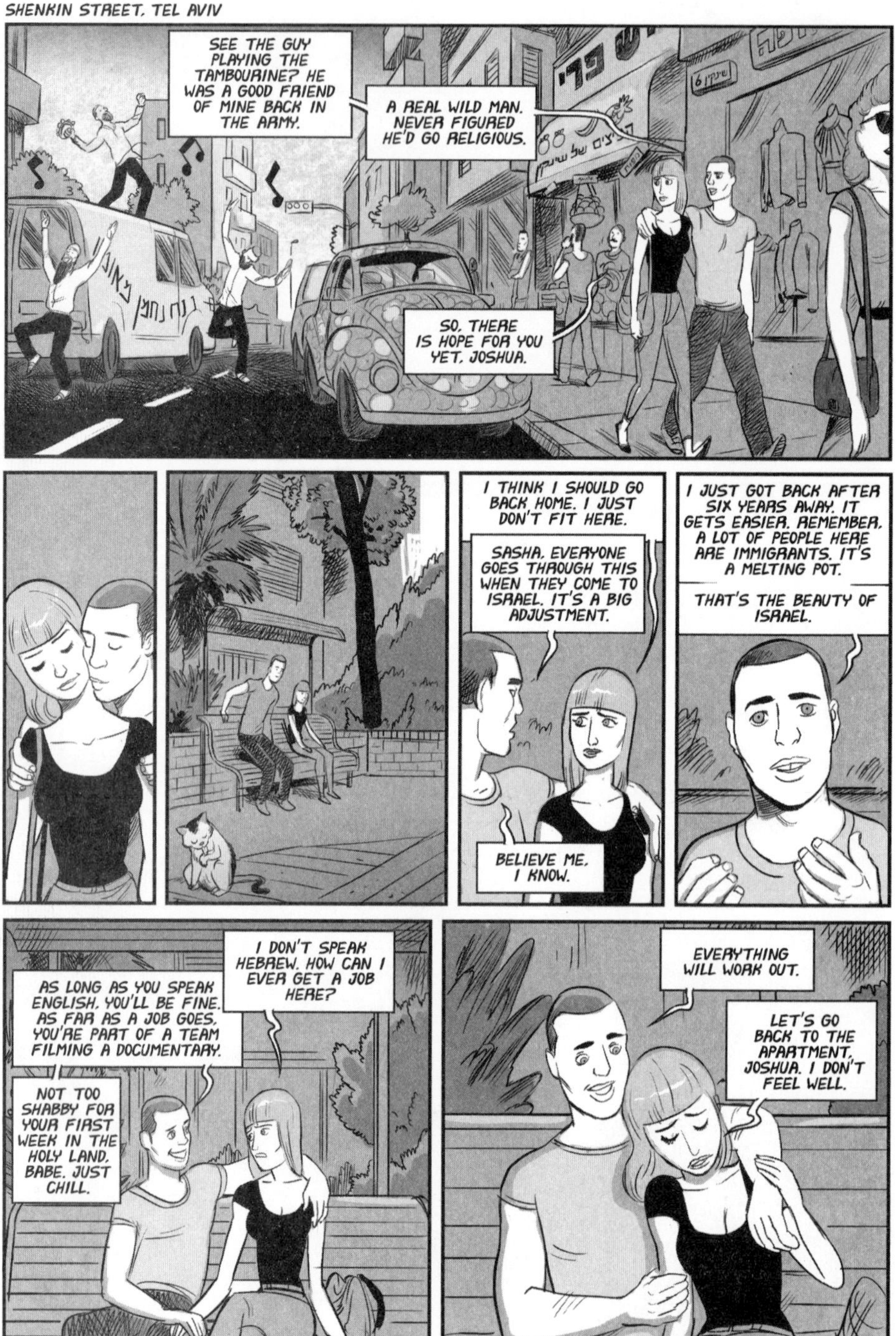
SHENKIN STREET, TEL AVIV
SEE THE GUY PLAYING THE TAMBOURINE? HE WAS A GOOD FRIEND OF MINE BACK IN THE ARMY.
A REAL WILD MAN. NEVER FIGURED HE'D GO RELIGIOUS.
SO, THERE IS HOPE FOR YOU YET, JOSHUA.
I THINK I SHOULD GO BACK HOME. I JUST DON'T FIT HERE.
SASHA, EVERYONE GOES THROUGH THIS WHEN THEY COME TO ISRAEL. IT'S A BIG ADJUSTMENT.
BELIEVE ME, I KNOW.
I JUST GOT BACK AFTER SIX YEARS AWAY. IT GETS EASIER. REMEMBER, A LOT OF PEOPLE HERE ARE IMMIGRANTS. IT'S A MELTING POT.
THAT'S THE BEAUTY OF ISRAEL.
I DON'T SPEAK HEBREW. HOW CAN I EVER GET A JOB HERE?
AS LONG AS YOU SPEAK ENGLISH, YOU'LL BE FINE. AS FAR AS A JOB GOES, YOU'RE PART OF A TEAM FILMING A DOCUMENTARY.
NOT TOO SHABBY FOR YOUR FIRST WEEK IN THE HOLY LAND, BABE. JUST CHILL.
EVERYTHING WILL WORK OUT.
LET'S GO BACK TO THE APARTMENT, JOSHUA. I DON'T FEEL WELL.

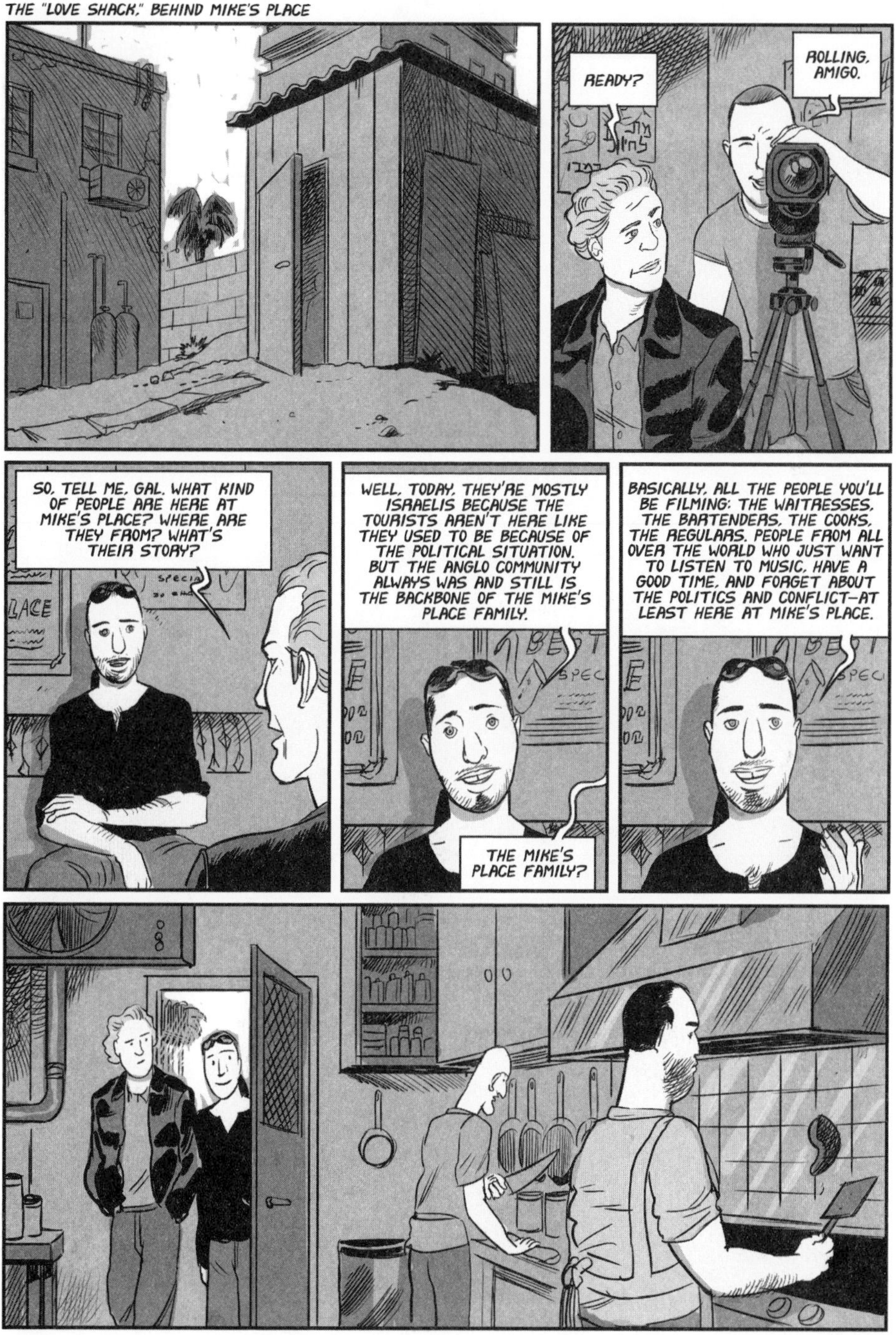
THE "LOVE SHACK," BEHIND MIKE'S PLACE
READY?
ROLLING, AMIGO.
SO, TELL ME, GAL. WHAT KIND OF PEOPLE ARE HERE AT MIKE'S PLACE? WHERE ARE THEY FROM? WHAT'S THEIR STORY?
WELL, TODAY, THEY'RE MOSTLY ISRAELIS BECAUSE THE TOURISTS AREN'T HERE LIKE THEY USED TO BE BECAUSE OF THE POLITICAL SITUATION. BUT THE ANGLO COMMUNITY ALWAYS WAS AND STILL IS THE BACKBONE OF THE MIKE'S PLACE FAMILY.
THE MIKE'S PLACE FAMILY?
BASICALLY, ALL THE PEOPLE YOU'LL BE FILMING: THE WAITRESSES, THE BARTENDERS, THE COOKS, THE REGULARS. PEOPLE FROM ALL OVER THE WORLD WHO JUST WANT TO LISTEN TO MUSIC, HAVE A GOOD TIME, AND FORGET ABOUT THE POLITICS AND CONFLICT—AT LEAST HERE AT MIKE'S PLACE.

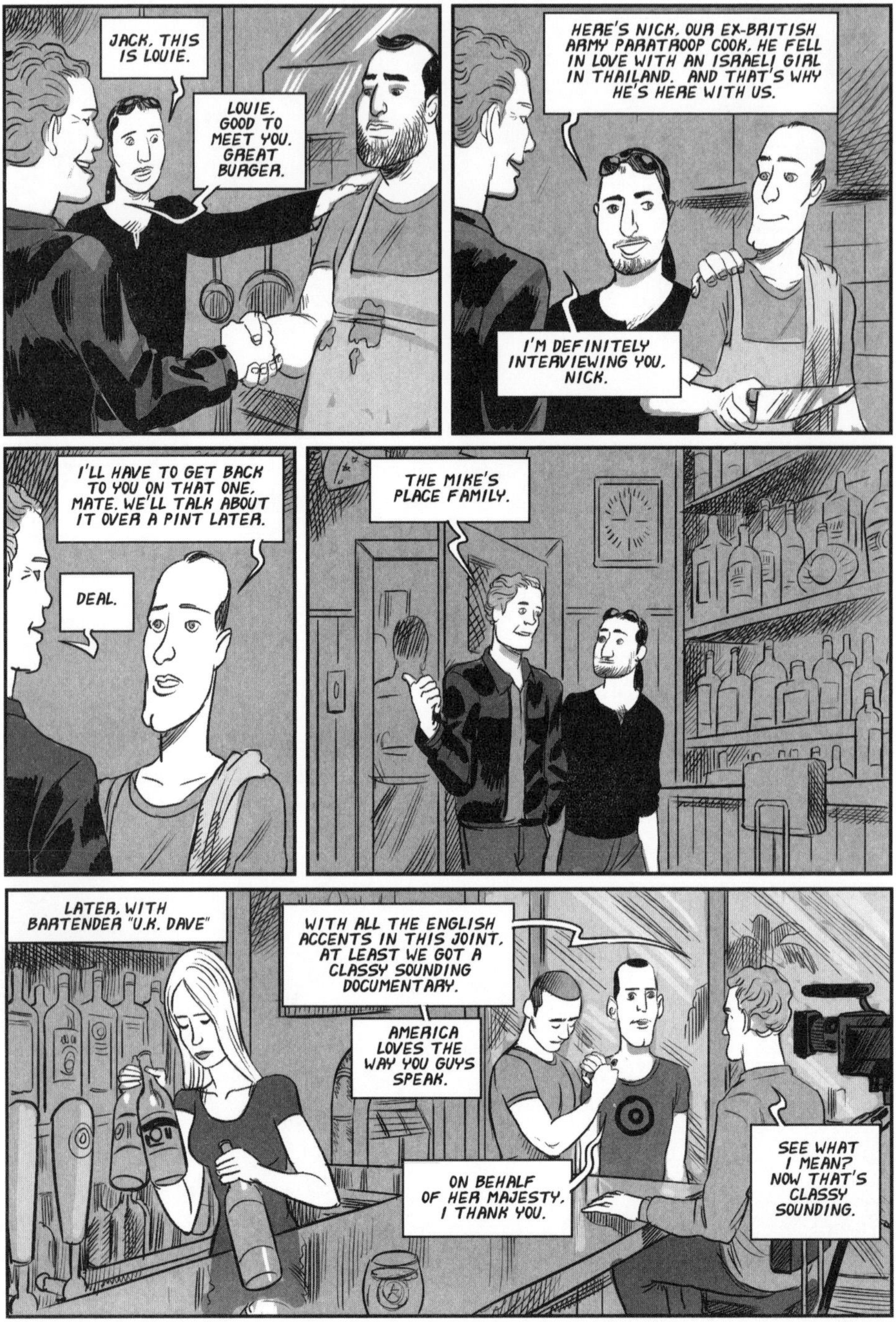
JACK, THIS IS LOUIE.
LOUIE, GOOD TO MEET YOU. GREAT BURGER.
HERE'S NICK, OUR EX-BRITISH ARMY PARATROOP COOK. HE FELL IN LOVE WITH AN ISRAELI GIRL IN THAILAND. AND THAT'S WHY HE'S HERE WITH US.
I'M DEFINITELY INTERVIEWING YOU, NICK.
I'LL HAVE TO GET BACK TO YOU ON THAT ONE, MATE. WE'LL TALK ABOUT IT OVER A PINT LATER.
DEAL.
THE MIKE'S PLACE FAMILY.
LATER, WITH BARTENDER "U.K. DAVE"
WITH ALL THE ENGLISH ACCENTS IN THIS JOINT, AT LEAST WE GOT A CLASSY SOUNDING DOCUMENTARY.
AMERICA LOVES THE WAY YOU GUYS SPEAK.
ON BEHALF OF HER MAJESTY, I THANK YOU.
SEE WHAT I MEAN? NOW THAT'S CLASSY SOUNDING.

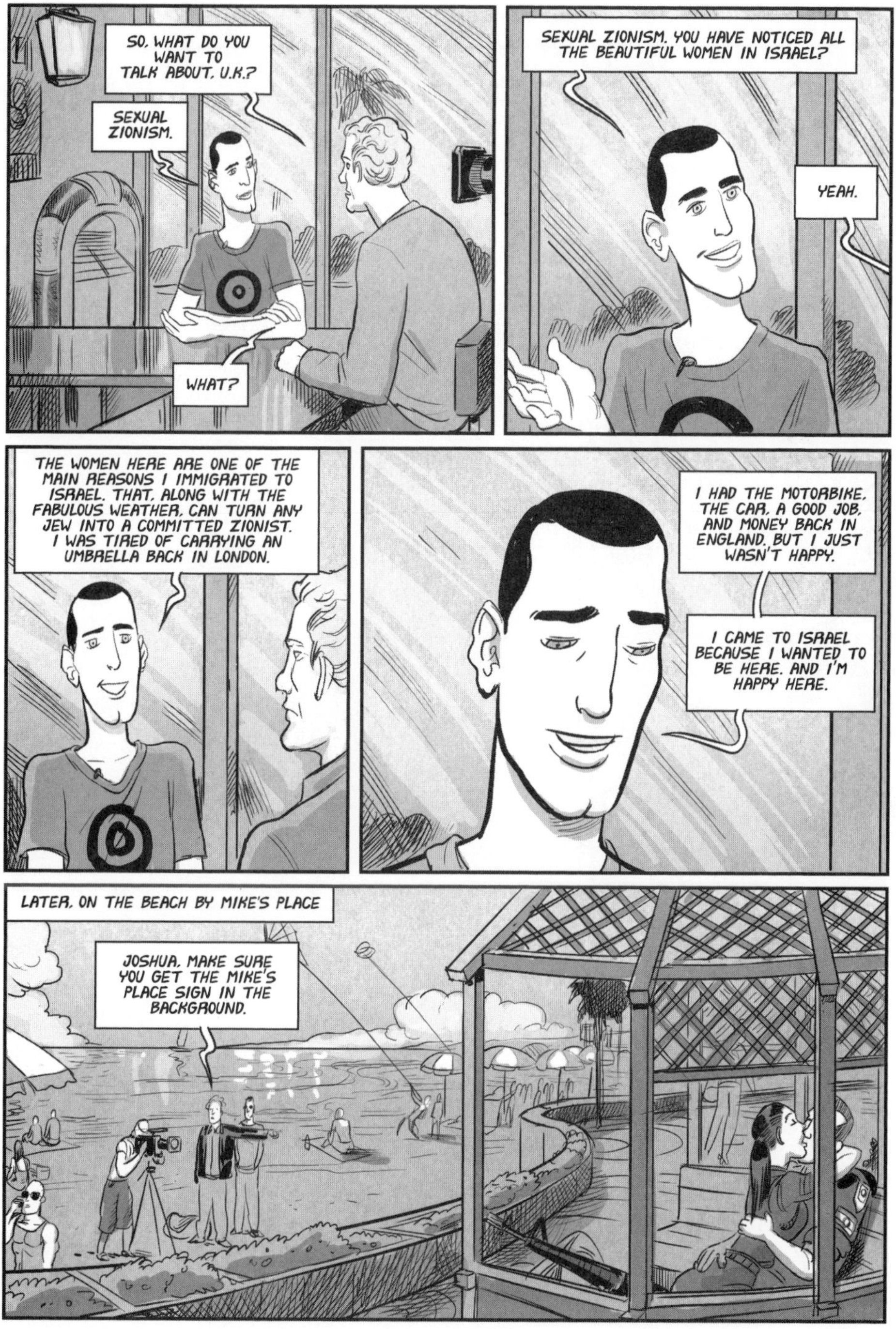
SO, WHAT DO YOU WANT TO TALK ABOUT, U.K.?
SEXUAL ZIONISM.
WHAT?
SEXUAL ZIONISM. YOU HAVE NOTICED ALL THE BEAUTIFUL WOMEN IN ISRAEL?
YEAH.
THE WOMEN HERE ARE ONE OF THE MAIN REASONS I IMMIGRATED TO ISRAEL. THAT, ALONG WITH THE FABULOUS WEATHER, CAN TURN ANY JEW INTO A COMMITTED ZIONIST. I WAS TIRED OF CARRYING AN UMBRELLA BACK IN LONDON.
I HAD THE MOTORBIKE, THE CAR, A GOOD JOB, AND MONEY BACK IN ENGLAND. BUT I JUST WASN'T HAPPY.
I CAME TO ISRAEL BECAUSE I WANTED TO BE HERE. AND I'M HAPPY HERE.
LATER, ON THE BEACH BY MIKE'S PLACE
JOSHUA, MAKE SURE YOU GET THE MIKE'S PLACE SIGN IN THE BACKGROUND.

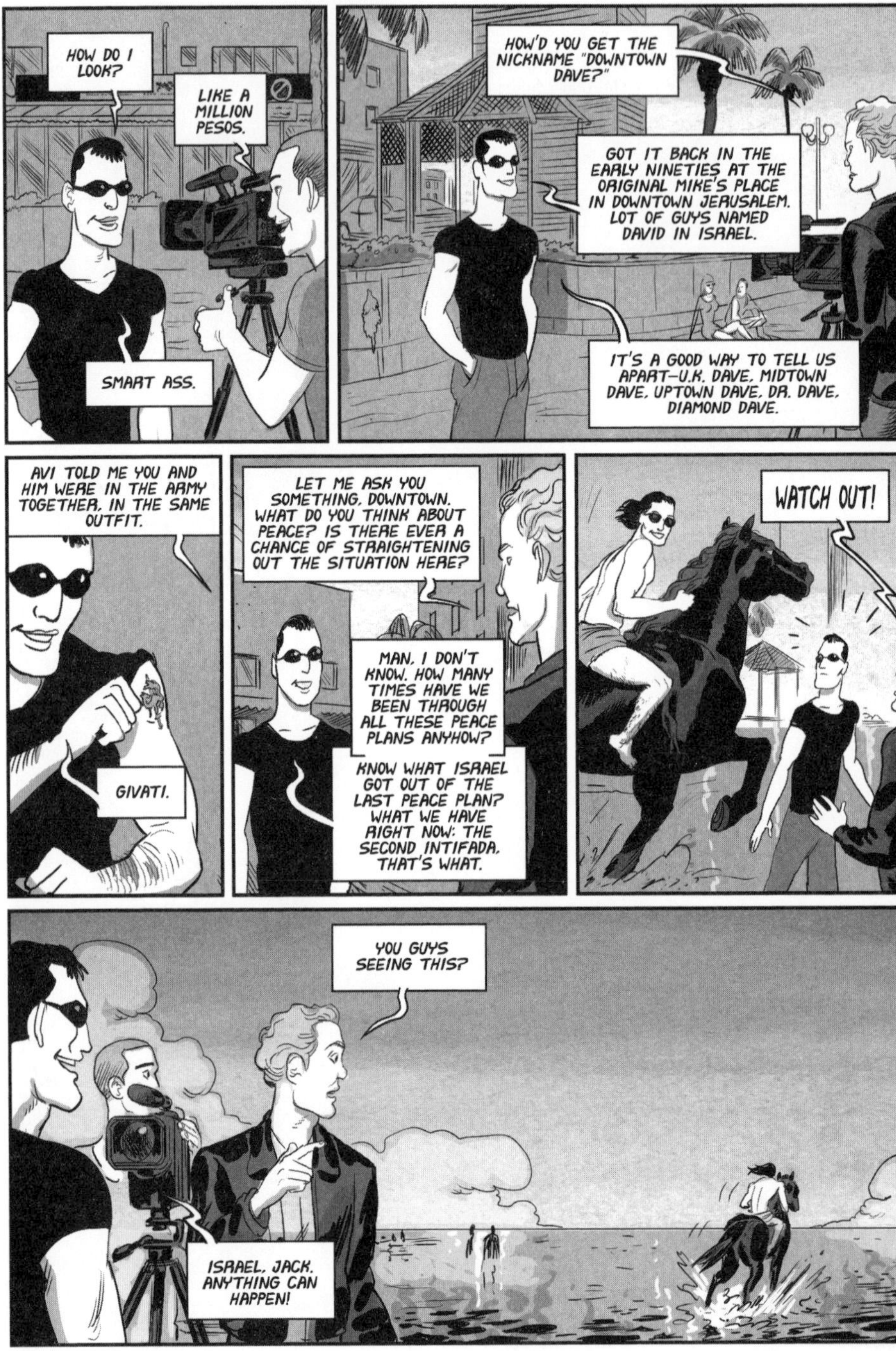
HOW DO I LOOK?
LIKE A MILLION PESOS.
SMART ASS.
HOW'D YOU GET THE NICKNAME "DOWNTOWN DAVE?"
GOT IT BACK IN THE EARLY NINETIES AT THE ORIGINAL MIKE'S PLACE IN DOWNTOWN JERUSALEM. LOT OF GUYS NAMED DAVID IN ISRAEL.
IT'S A GOOD WAY TO TELL US APART—U.K. DAVE, MIDTOWN DAVE, UPTOWN DAVE, DR. DAVE, DIAMOND DAVE.
AVI TOLD ME YOU AND HIM WERE IN THE ARMY TOGETHER, IN THE SAME OUTFIT.
GIVATI.
LET ME ASK YOU SOMETHING, DOWNTOWN. WHAT DO YOU THINK ABOUT PEACE? IS THERE EVER A CHANCE OF STRAIGHTENING OUT THE SITUATION HERE?
MAN, I DON'T KNOW. HOW MANY TIMES HAVE WE BEEN THROUGH ALL THESE PEACE PLANS ANYHOW?
KNOW WHAT ISRAEL GOT OUT OF THE LAST PEACE PLAN? WHAT WE HAVE RIGHT NOW: THE SECOND INTIFADA. THAT'S WHAT.
WATCH OUT!
YOU GUYS SEEING THIS?
ISRAEL, JACK. ANYTHING CAN HAPPEN!

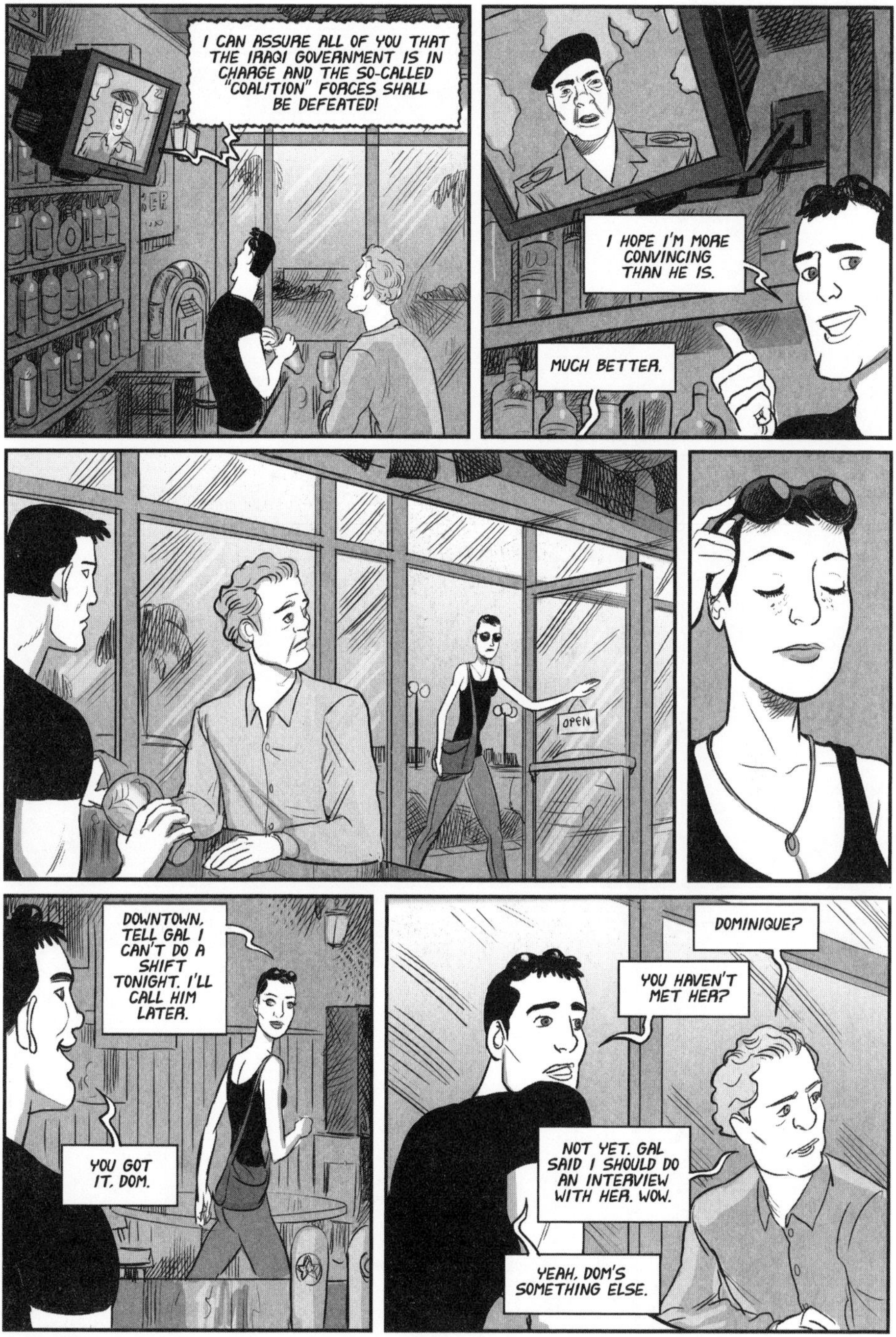
I CAN ASSURE ALL OF YOU THAT THE IRAQI GOVERNMENT IS IN CHARGE AND THE SO-CALLED "COALITION" FORCES SHALL BE DEFEATED!
I HOPE I'M MORE CONVINCING THAN HE IS.
MUCH BETTER.
OPEN
DOWNTOWN, TELL GAL I CAN'T DO A SHIFT TONIGHT. I'LL CALL HIM LATER.
YOU GOT IT, DOM.
DOMINIQUE?
YOU HAVEN'T MET HER?
NOT YET. GAL SAID I SHOULD DO AN INTERVIEW WITH HER. WOW.
YEAH, DOM'S SOMETHING ELSE.

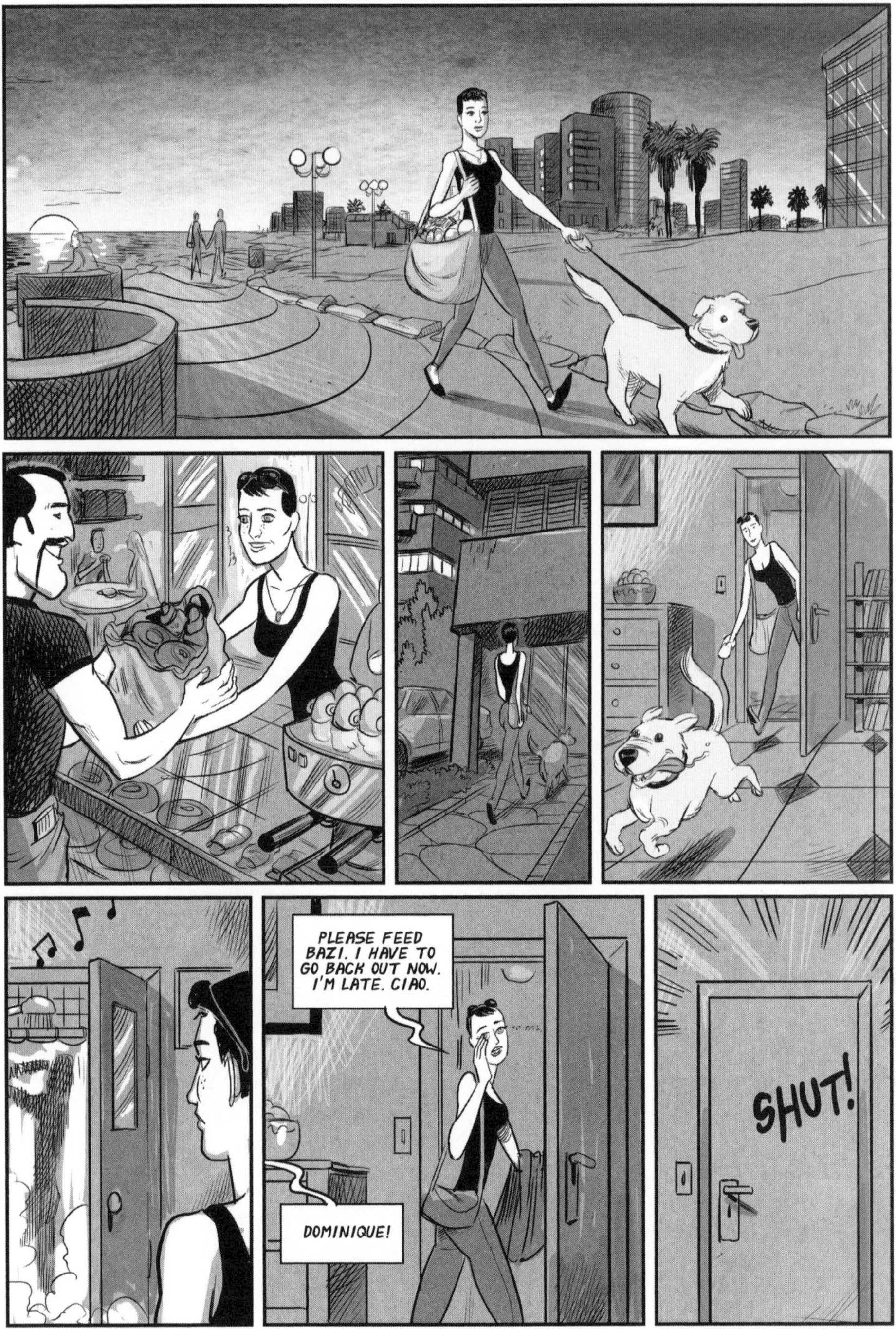
PLEASE FEED BAZI. I HAVE TO GO BACK OUT NOW. I'M LATE. CIAO.
DOMINIQUE!
SHUT!

ALLENBY STREET, FORTUNE-TELLER SHOP

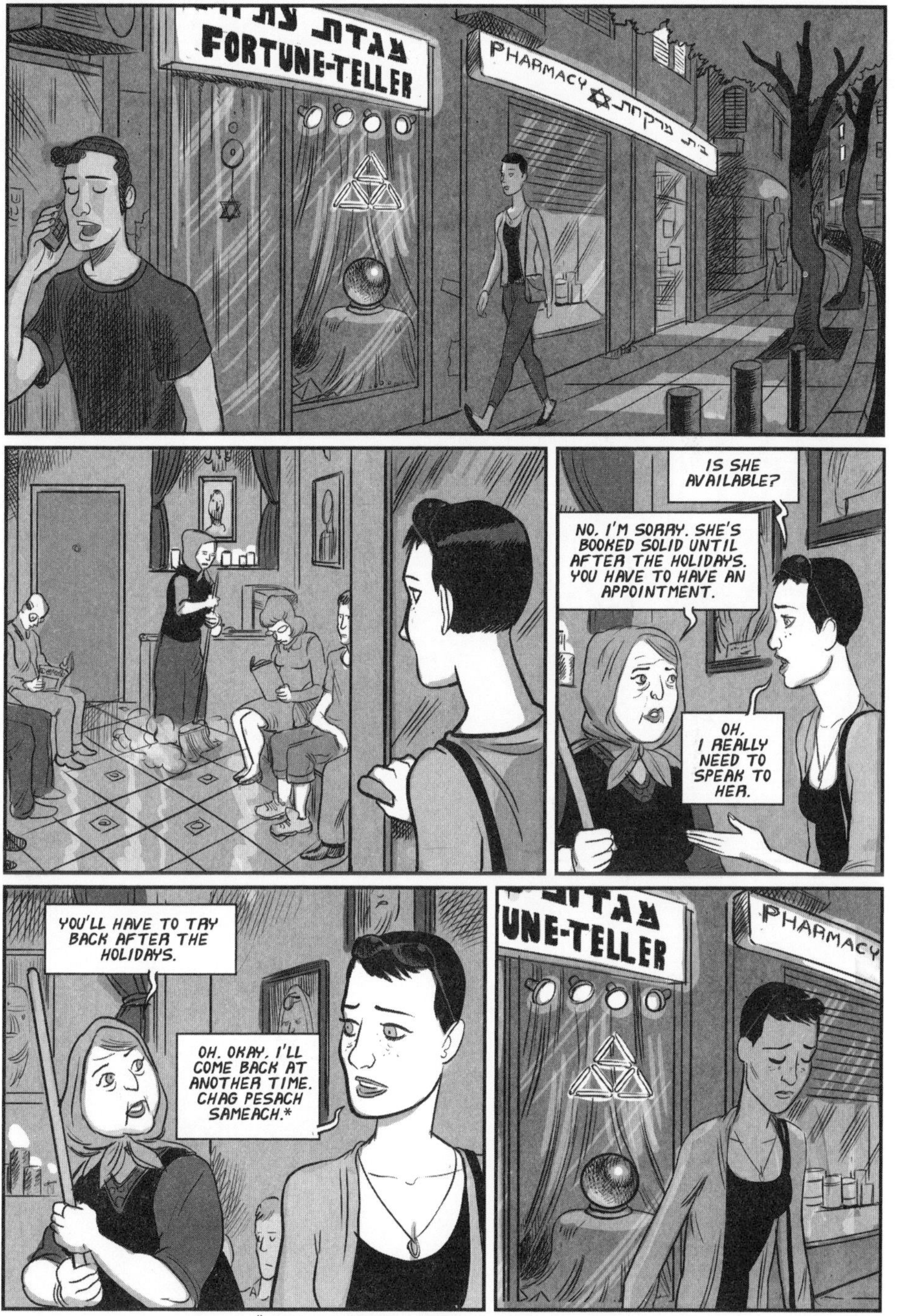
FORTUNE-TELLER
PHARMACY
בית מרקחת
IS SHE AVAILABLE?
NO, I'M SORRY. SHE'S BOOKED SOLID UNTIL AFTER THE HOLIDAYS. YOU HAVE TO HAVE AN APPOINTMENT.
OH, I REALLY NEED TO SPEAK TO HER.
YOU'LL HAVE TO TRY BACK AFTER THE HOLIDAYS.
OH. OKAY. I'LL COME BACK AT ANOTHER TIME. CHAG PESACH SAMEACH.*
UNE-TELLER
PHARMACY

*HAPPY PASSOVER HOLIDAYS.

AMI HOTEL

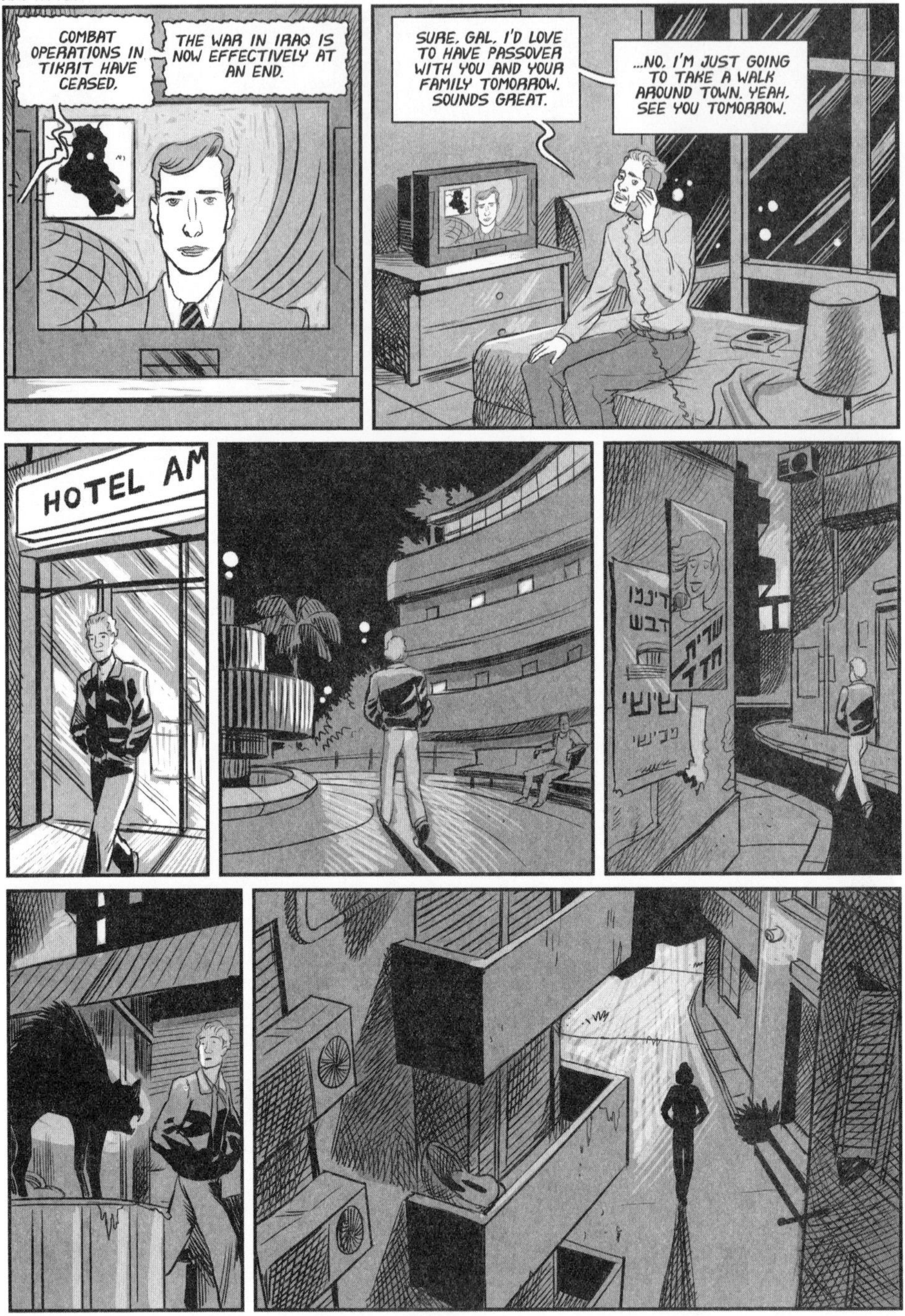
COMBAT OPERATIONS IN TIKRIT HAVE CEASED.
THE WAR IN IRAQ IS NOW EFFECTIVELY AT AN END.
SURE, GAL, I'D LOVE TO HAVE PASSOVER WITH YOU AND YOUR FAMILY TOMORROW. SOUNDS GREAT.
...NO, I'M JUST GOING TO TAKE A WALK AROUND TOWN. YEAH, SEE YOU TOMORROW.
HOTEL AM
שרית חדד
שישי

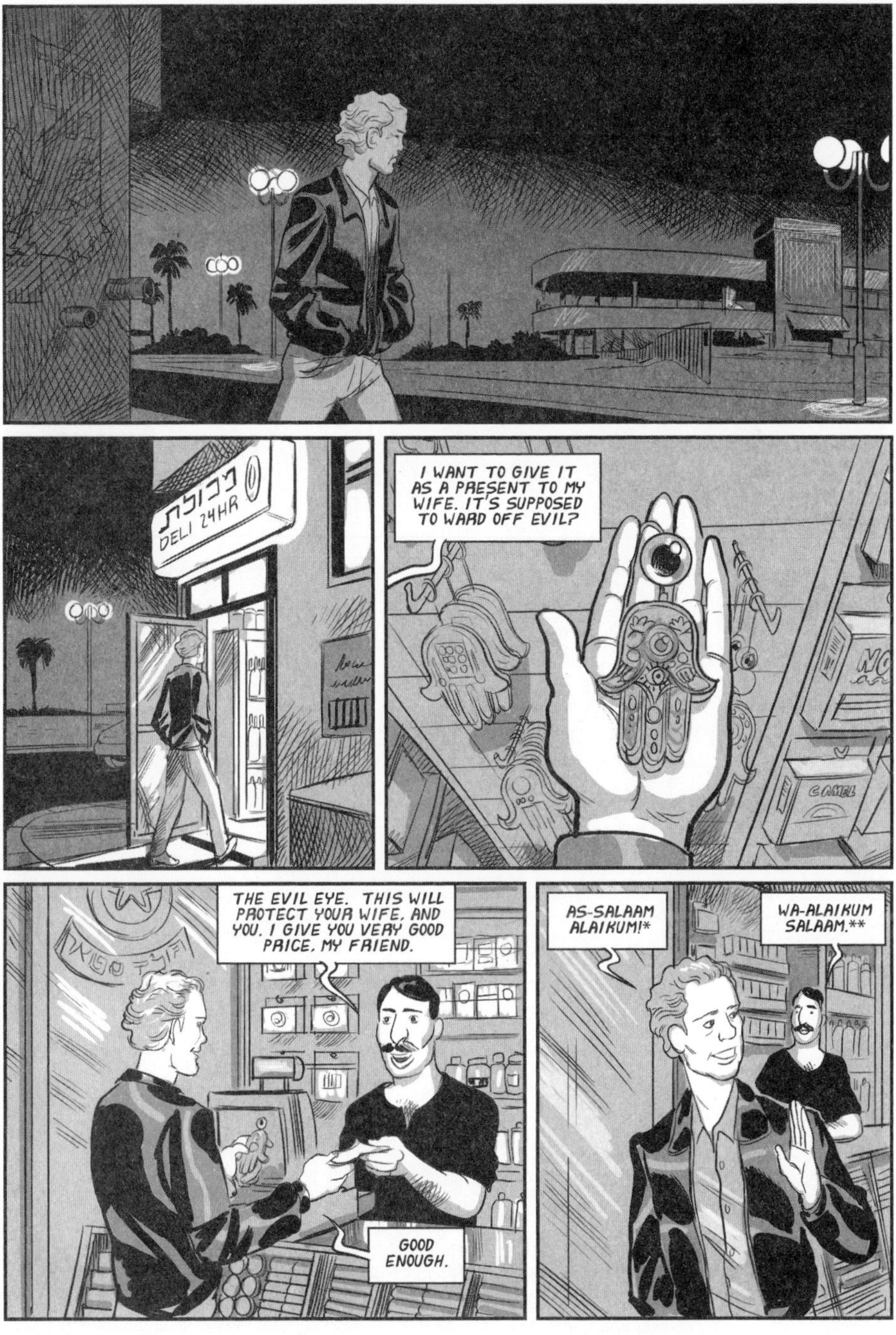
DELI 24HR
I WANT TO GIVE IT AS A PRESENT TO MY WIFE. IT'S SUPPOSED TO WARD OFF EVIL?
CAMEL
THE EVIL EYE. THIS WILL PROTECT YOUR WIFE, AND YOU. I GIVE YOU VERY GOOD PRICE, MY FRIEND.
GOOD ENOUGH.
AS-SALAAM ALAIKUM!*
WA-ALAIKUM SALAAM.**

*PEACE TO YOU!
**AND TO YOU, PEACE.

JOSHUA'S APARTMENT

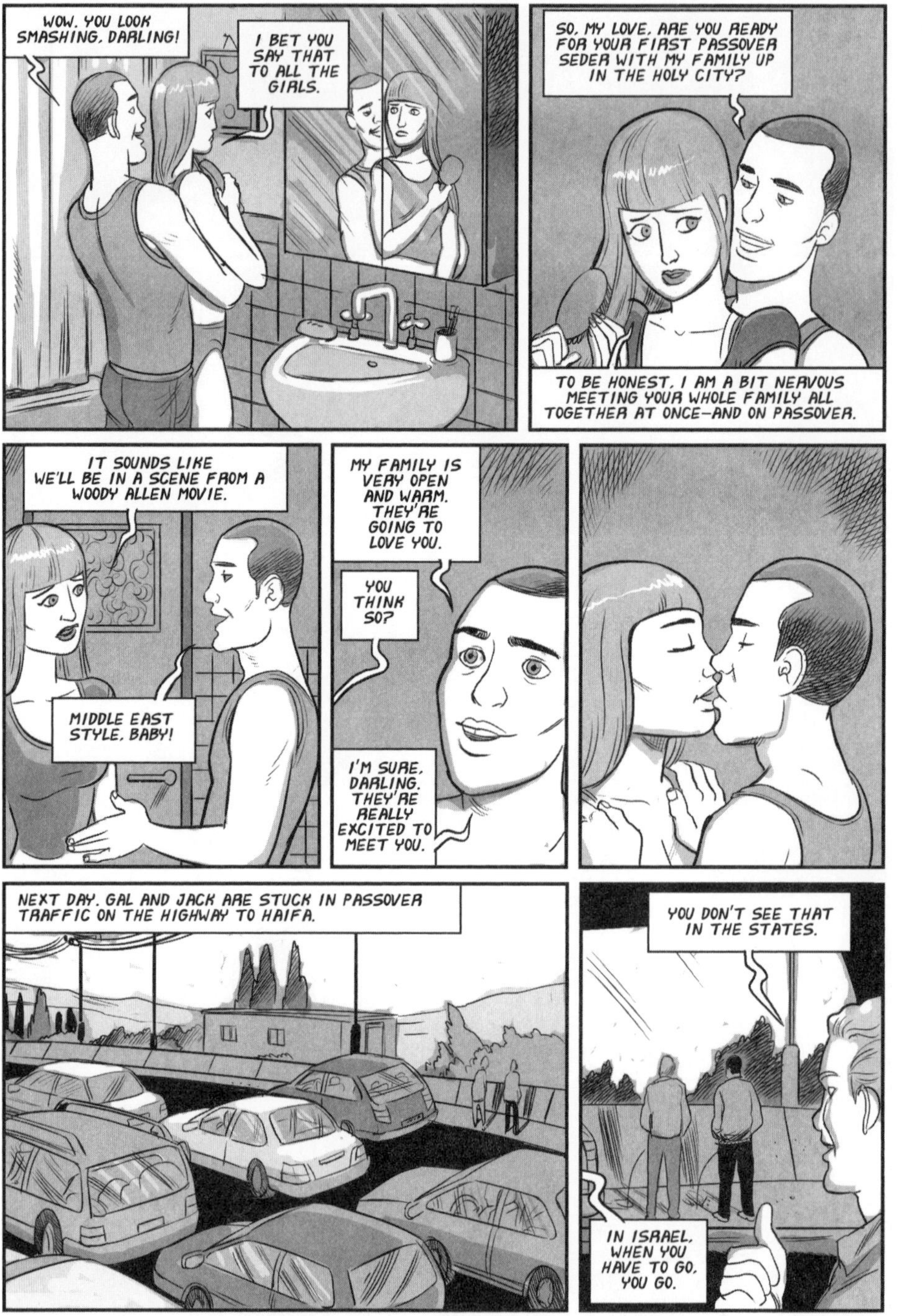
WOW. YOU LOOK SMASHING, DARLING!
I BET YOU SAY THAT TO ALL THE GIRLS.
SO, MY LOVE. ARE YOU READY FOR YOUR FIRST PASSOVER SEDER WITH MY FAMILY UP IN THE HOLY CITY?
TO BE HONEST, I AM A BIT NERVOUS MEETING YOUR WHOLE FAMILY ALL TOGETHER AT ONCE—AND ON PASSOVER.
IT SOUNDS LIKE WE'LL BE IN A SCENE FROM A WOODY ALLEN MOVIE.
MIDDLE EAST STYLE, BABY!
MY FAMILY IS VERY OPEN AND WARM. THEY'RE GOING TO LOVE YOU.
YOU THINK SO?
I'M SURE, DARLING. THEY'RE REALLY EXCITED TO MEET YOU.
NEXT DAY. GAL AND JACK ARE STUCK IN PASSOVER TRAFFIC ON THE HIGHWAY TO HAIFA.
YOU DON'T SEE THAT IN THE STATES.
IN ISRAEL, WHEN YOU HAVE TO GO, YOU GO.

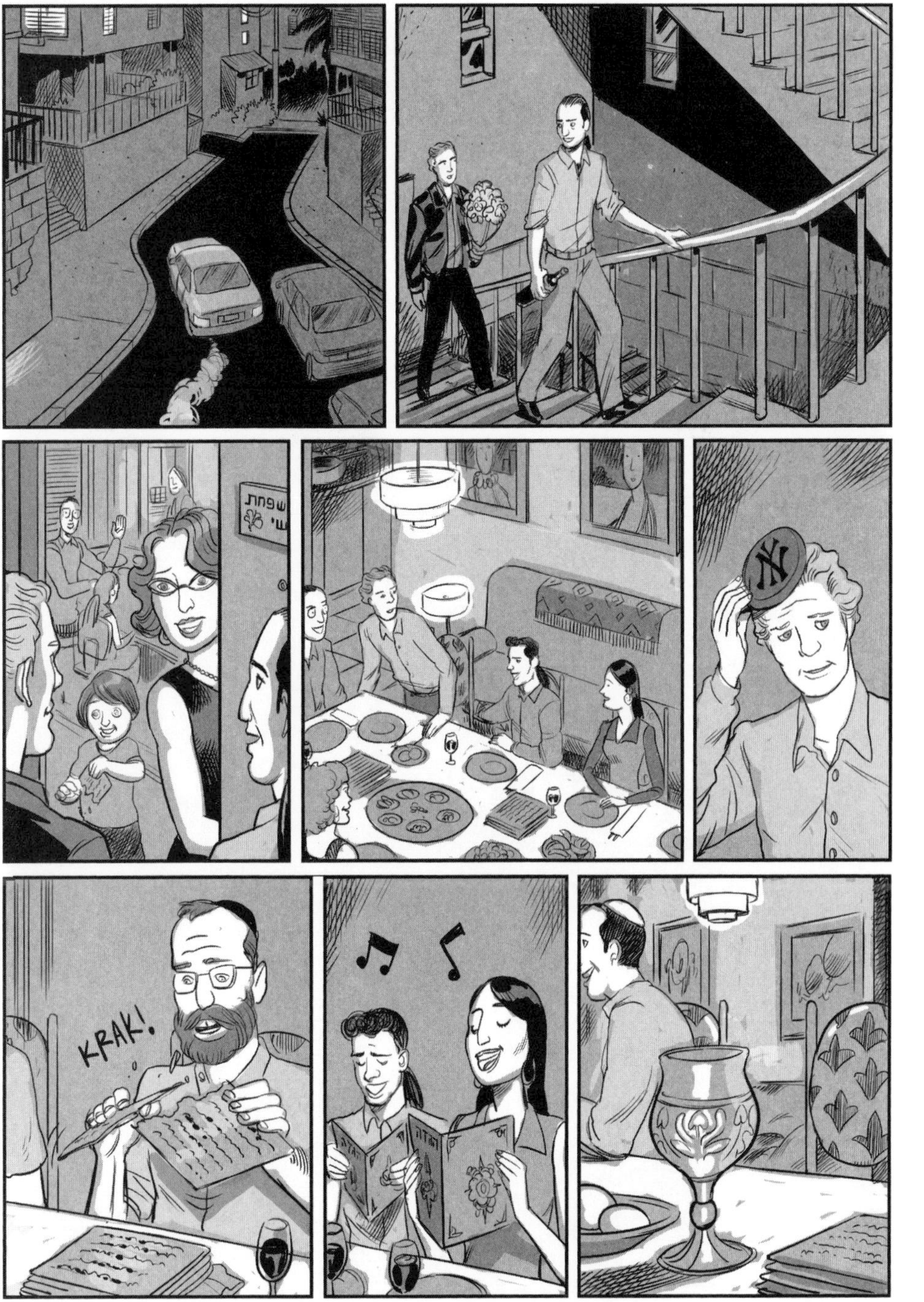
KRAK!

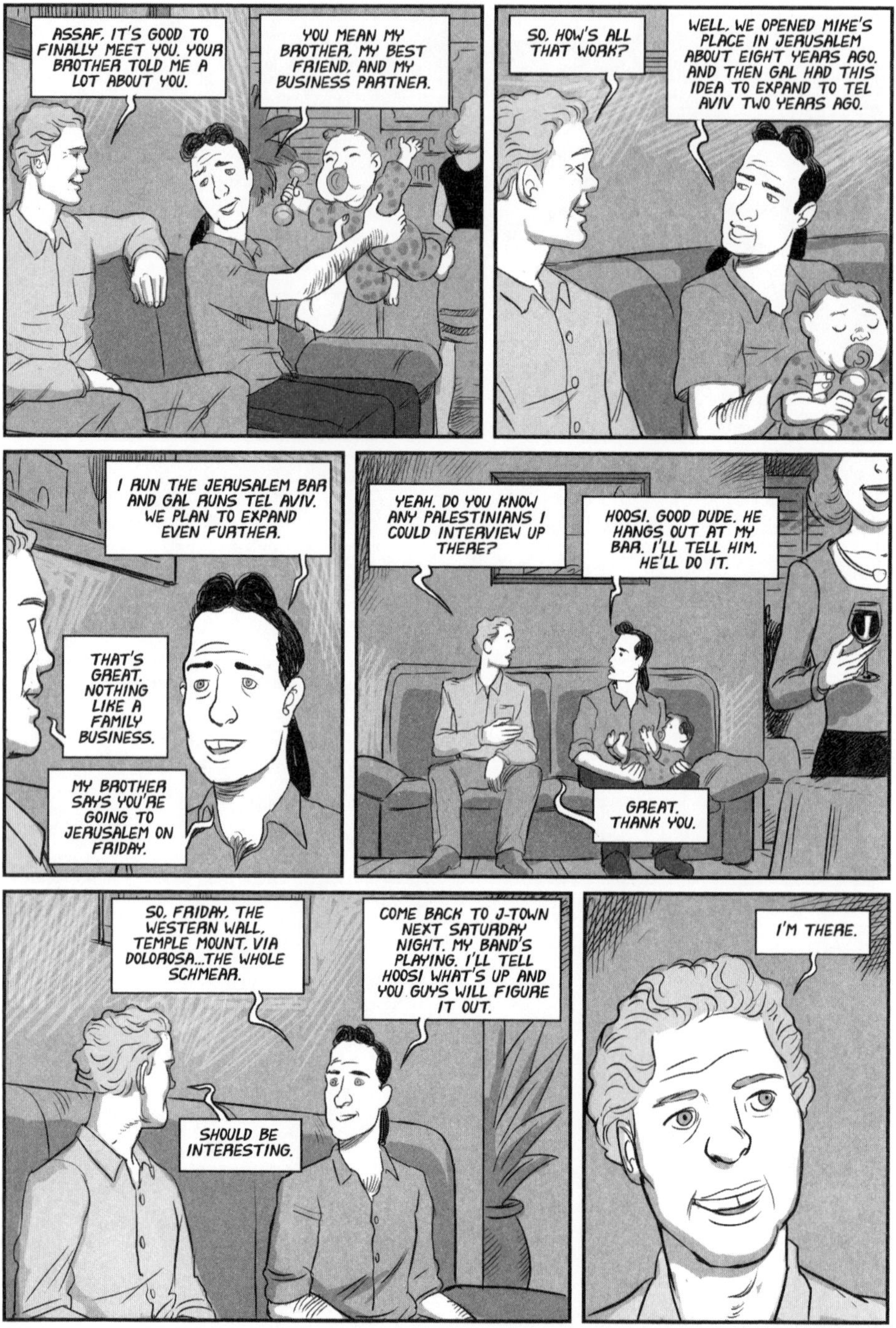
ASSAF, IT'S GOOD TO FINALLY MEET YOU. YOUR BROTHER TOLD ME A LOT ABOUT YOU.
YOU MEAN MY BROTHER, MY BEST FRIEND, AND MY BUSINESS PARTNER.
SO, HOW'S ALL THAT WORK?
WELL, WE OPENED MIKE'S PLACE IN JERUSALEM ABOUT EIGHT YEARS AGO. AND THEN GAL HAD THIS IDEA TO EXPAND TO TEL AVIV TWO YEARS AGO.
I RUN THE JERUSALEM BAR AND GAL RUNS TEL AVIV. WE PLAN TO EXPAND EVEN FURTHER.
THAT'S GREAT. NOTHING LIKE A FAMILY BUSINESS.
MY BROTHER SAYS YOU'RE GOING TO JERUSALEM ON FRIDAY.
YEAH. DO YOU KNOW ANY PALESTINIANS I COULD INTERVIEW UP THERE?
HOOSI. GOOD DUDE. HE HANGS OUT AT MY BAR. I'LL TELL HIM. HE'LL DO IT.
GREAT. THANK YOU.
SO, FRIDAY. THE WESTERN WALL, TEMPLE MOUNT, VIA DOLOROSA...THE WHOLE SCHMEAR.
SHOULD BE INTERESTING.
COME BACK TO J-TOWN NEXT SATURDAY NIGHT. MY BAND'S PLAYING. I'LL TELL HOOSI WHAT'S UP AND YOU GUYS WILL FIGURE IT OUT.
I'M THERE.

DAMASCUS GATE, THE OLD CITY OF JERUSALEM, GOOD FRIDAY

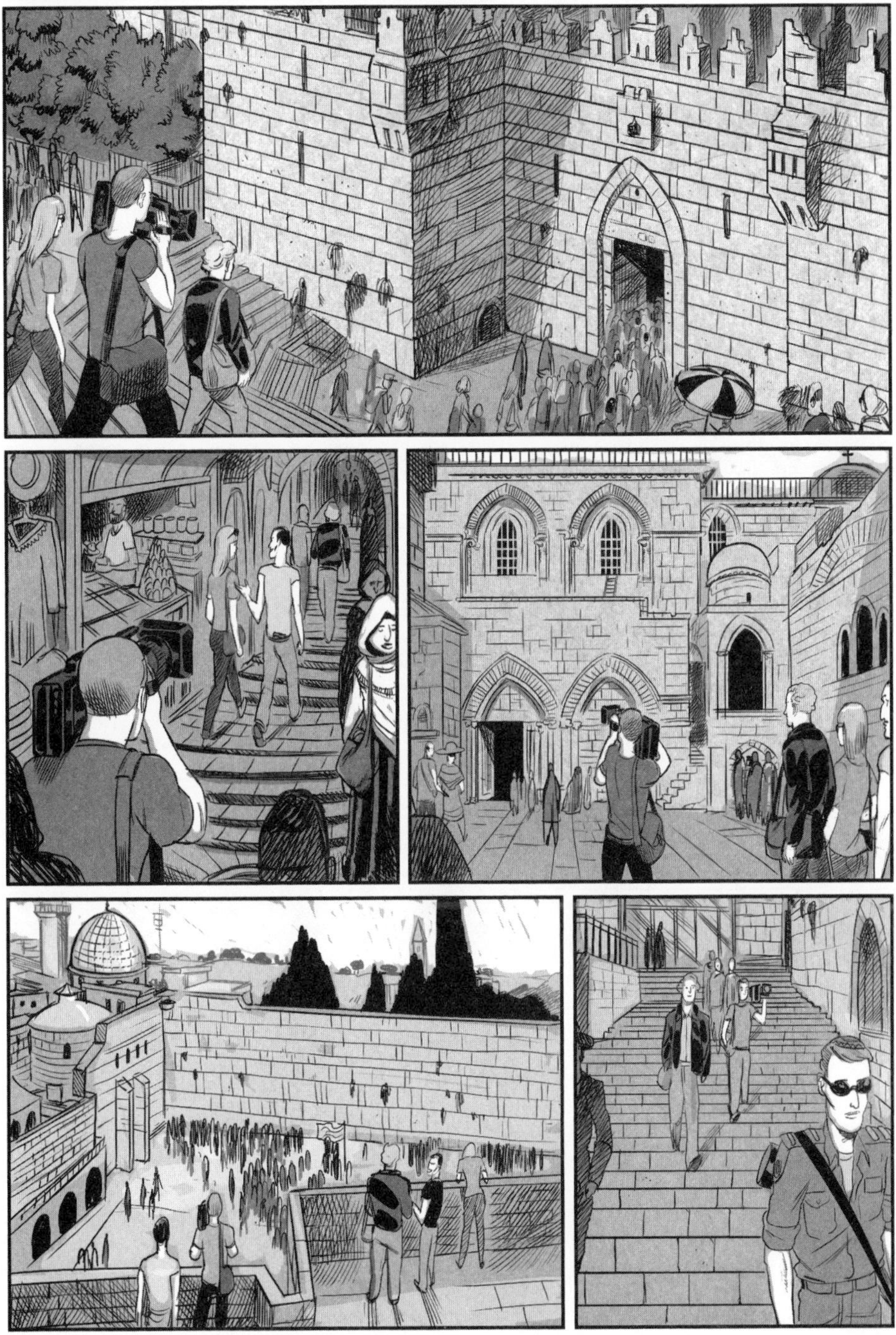

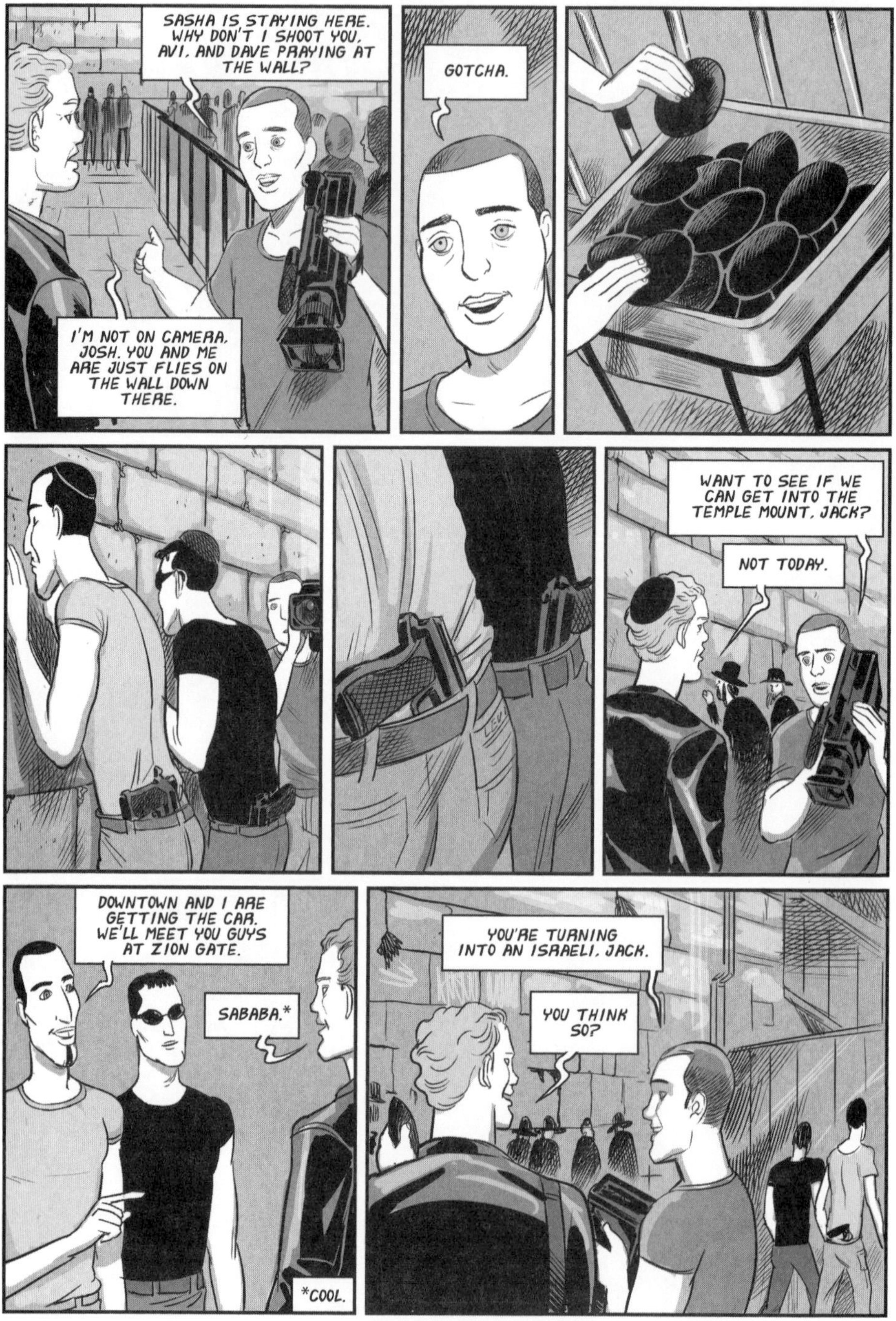
SASHA IS STAYING HERE. WHY DON'T I SHOOT YOU, AVI, AND DAVE PRAYING AT THE WALL?
I'M NOT ON CAMERA, JOSH. YOU AND ME ARE JUST FLIES ON THE WALL DOWN THERE.
GOTCHA.
WANT TO SEE IF WE CAN GET INTO THE TEMPLE MOUNT, JACK?
NOT TODAY.
DOWNTOWN AND I ARE GETTING THE CAR. WE'LL MEET YOU GUYS AT ZION GATE.
SABABA.*
*COOL.
YOU'RE TURNING INTO AN ISRAELI, JACK.
YOU THINK SO?

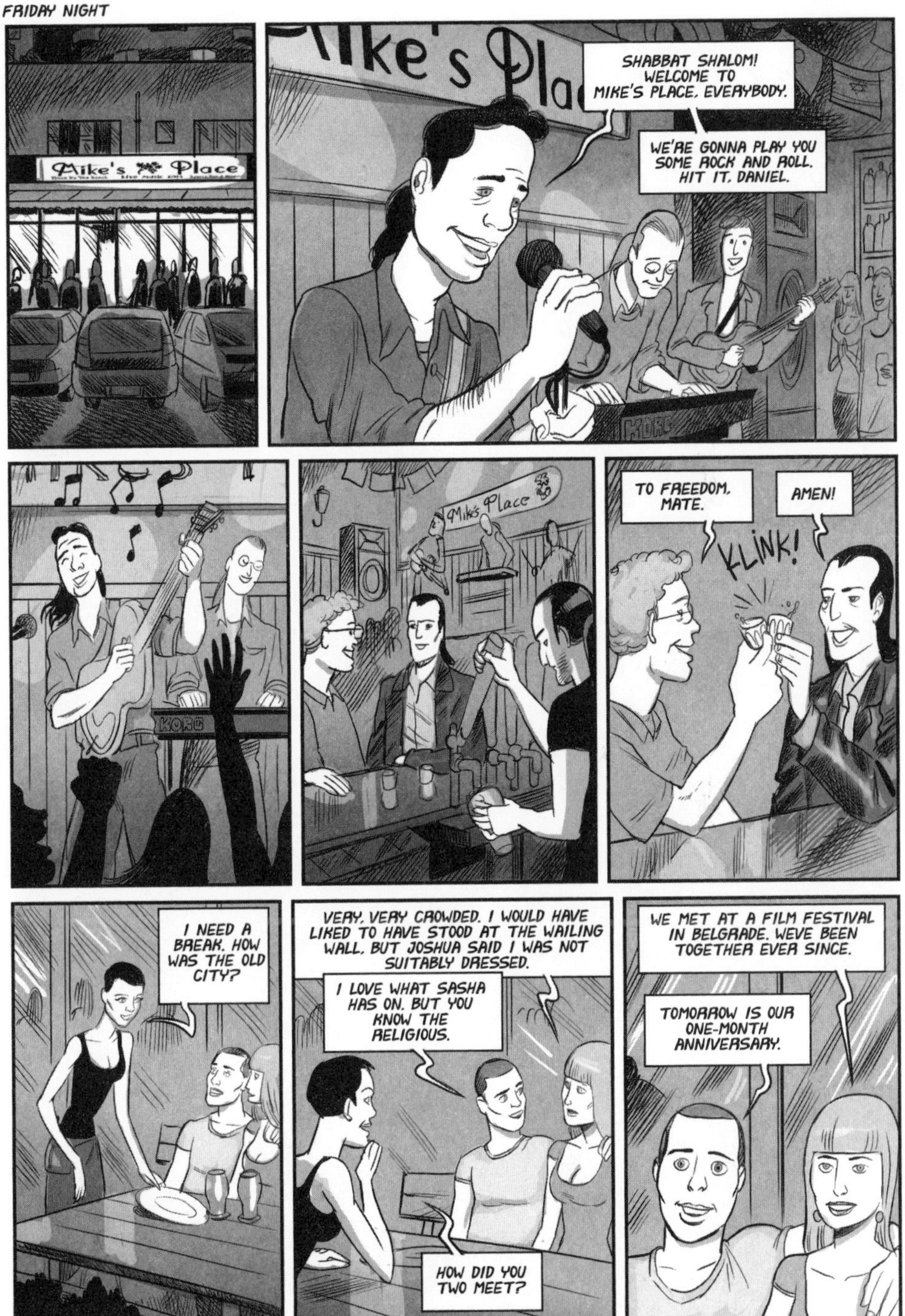
FRIDAY NIGHT
Mike's Place
SHABBAT SHALOM! WELCOME TO MIKE'S PLACE, EVERYBODY.
WE'RE GONNA PLAY YOU SOME ROCK AND ROLL. HIT IT, DANIEL.
KORG
Mike's Place
TO FREEDOM, MATE.
AMEN!
KLINK!
I NEED A BREAK. HOW WAS THE OLD CITY?
VERY, VERY CROWDED. I WOULD HAVE LIKED TO HAVE STOOD AT THE WAILING WALL, BUT JOSHUA SAID I WAS NOT SUITABLY DRESSED.
I LOVE WHAT SASHA HAS ON. BUT YOU KNOW THE RELIGIOUS.
HOW DID YOU TWO MEET?
WE MET AT A FILM FESTIVAL IN BELGRADE. WEVE BEEN TOGETHER EVER SINCE.
TOMORROW IS OUR ONE-MONTH ANNIVERSARY.

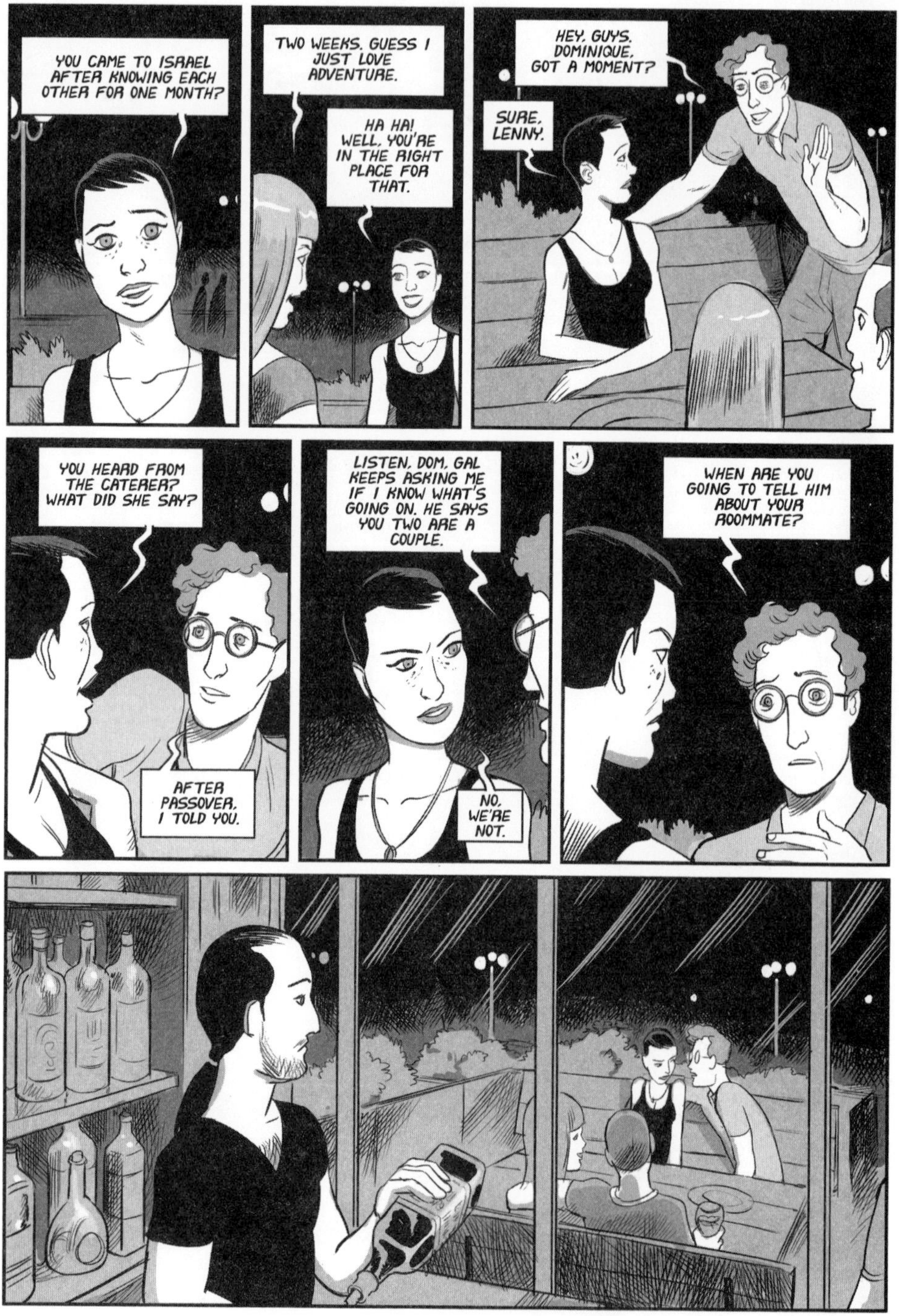
YOU CAME TO ISRAEL AFTER KNOWING EACH OTHER FOR ONE MONTH?
TWO WEEKS. GUESS I JUST LOVE ADVENTURE.
HA HA! WELL, YOU'RE IN THE RIGHT PLACE FOR THAT.
HEY, GUYS. DOMINIQUE, GOT A MOMENT?
SURE, LENNY.
YOU HEARD FROM THE CATERER? WHAT DID SHE SAY?
AFTER PASSOVER, I TOLD YOU.
LISTEN, DOM, GAL KEEPS ASKING ME IF I KNOW WHAT'S GOING ON. HE SAYS YOU TWO ARE A COUPLE.
NO, WE'RE NOT.
WHEN ARE YOU GOING TO TELL HIM ABOUT YOUR ROOMMATE?

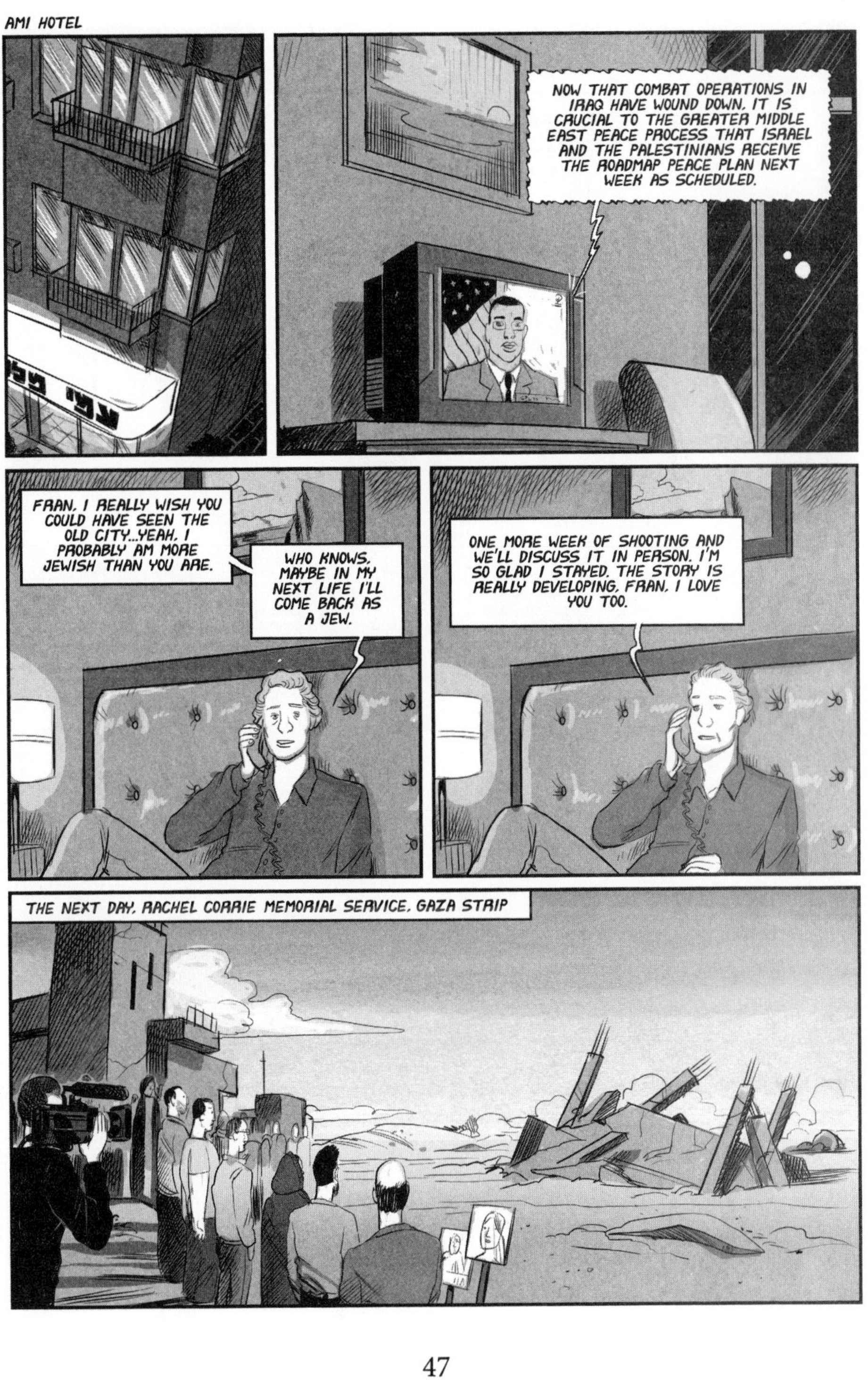
AMI HOTEL
NOW THAT COMBAT OPERATIONS IN IRAQ HAVE WOUND DOWN, IT IS CRUCIAL TO THE GREATER MIDDLE EAST PEACE PROCESS THAT ISRAEL AND THE PALESTINIANS RECEIVE THE ROADMAP PEACE PLAN NEXT WEEK AS SCHEDULED.
FRAN, I REALLY WISH YOU COULD HAVE SEEN THE OLD CITY...YEAH, I PROBABLY AM MORE JEWISH THAN YOU ARE.
WHO KNOWS, MAYBE IN MY NEXT LIFE I'LL COME BACK AS A JEW.
ONE MORE WEEK OF SHOOTING AND WE'LL DISCUSS IT IN PERSON. I'M SO GLAD I STAYED. THE STORY IS REALLY DEVELOPING, FRAN. I LOVE YOU TOO.
THE NEXT DAY, RACHEL CORRIE MEMORIAL SERVICE, GAZA STRIP

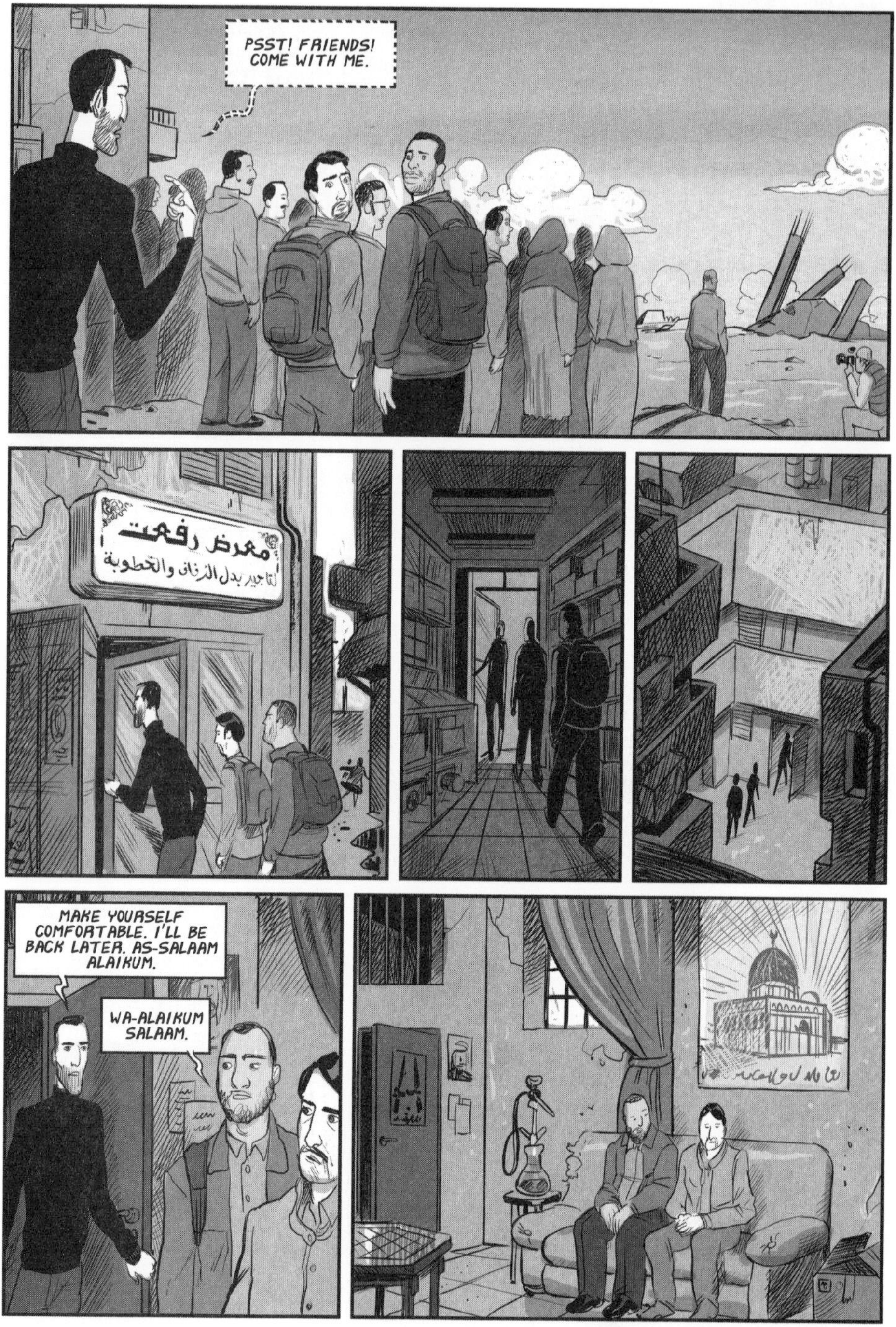
PSST! FRIENDS! COME WITH ME.
معرض رفعت
لتاجير بدل الزفاف والخطوبة
MAKE YOURSELF COMFORTABLE. I'LL BE BACK LATER. AS-SALAAM ALAIKUM.
WA-ALAIKUM SALAAM.

BACK AT MIKE'S PLACE

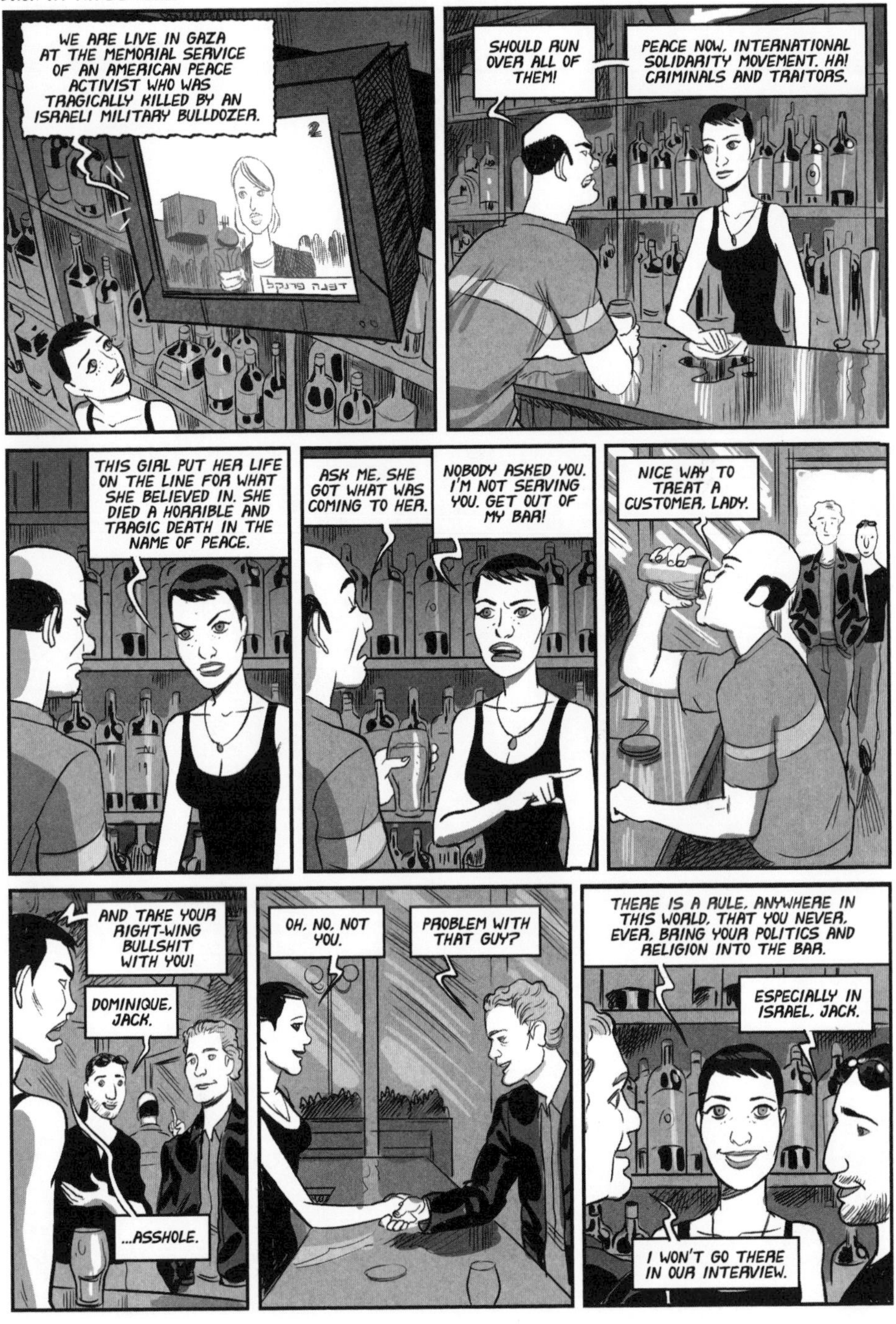
WE ARE LIVE IN GAZA AT THE MEMORIAL SERVICE OF AN AMERICAN PEACE ACTIVIST WHO WAS TRAGICALLY KILLED BY AN ISRAELI MILITARY BULLDOZER.
SHOULD RUN OVER ALL OF THEM!
PEACE NOW, INTERNATIONAL SOLIDARITY MOVEMENT. HA! CRIMINALS AND TRAITORS.
THIS GIRL PUT HER LIFE ON THE LINE FOR WHAT SHE BELIEVED IN. SHE DIED A HORRIBLE AND TRAGIC DEATH IN THE NAME OF PEACE.
ASK ME, SHE GOT WHAT WAS COMING TO HER.
NOBODY ASKED YOU. I'M NOT SERVING YOU. GET OUT OF MY BAR!
NICE WAY TO TREAT A CUSTOMER, LADY.
AND TAKE YOUR RIGHT-WING BULLSHIT WITH YOU!
DOMINIQUE, JACK.
...ASSHOLE.
OH, NO, NOT YOU.
PROBLEM WITH THAT GUY?
THERE IS A RULE, ANYWHERE IN THIS WORLD, THAT YOU NEVER, EVER, BRING YOUR POLITICS AND RELIGION INTO THE BAR.
ESPECIALLY IN ISRAEL, JACK.
I WON'T GO THERE IN OUR INTERVIEW.

LATER, THE "LOVE SHACK" IN THE BACK OF MIKE'S PLACE

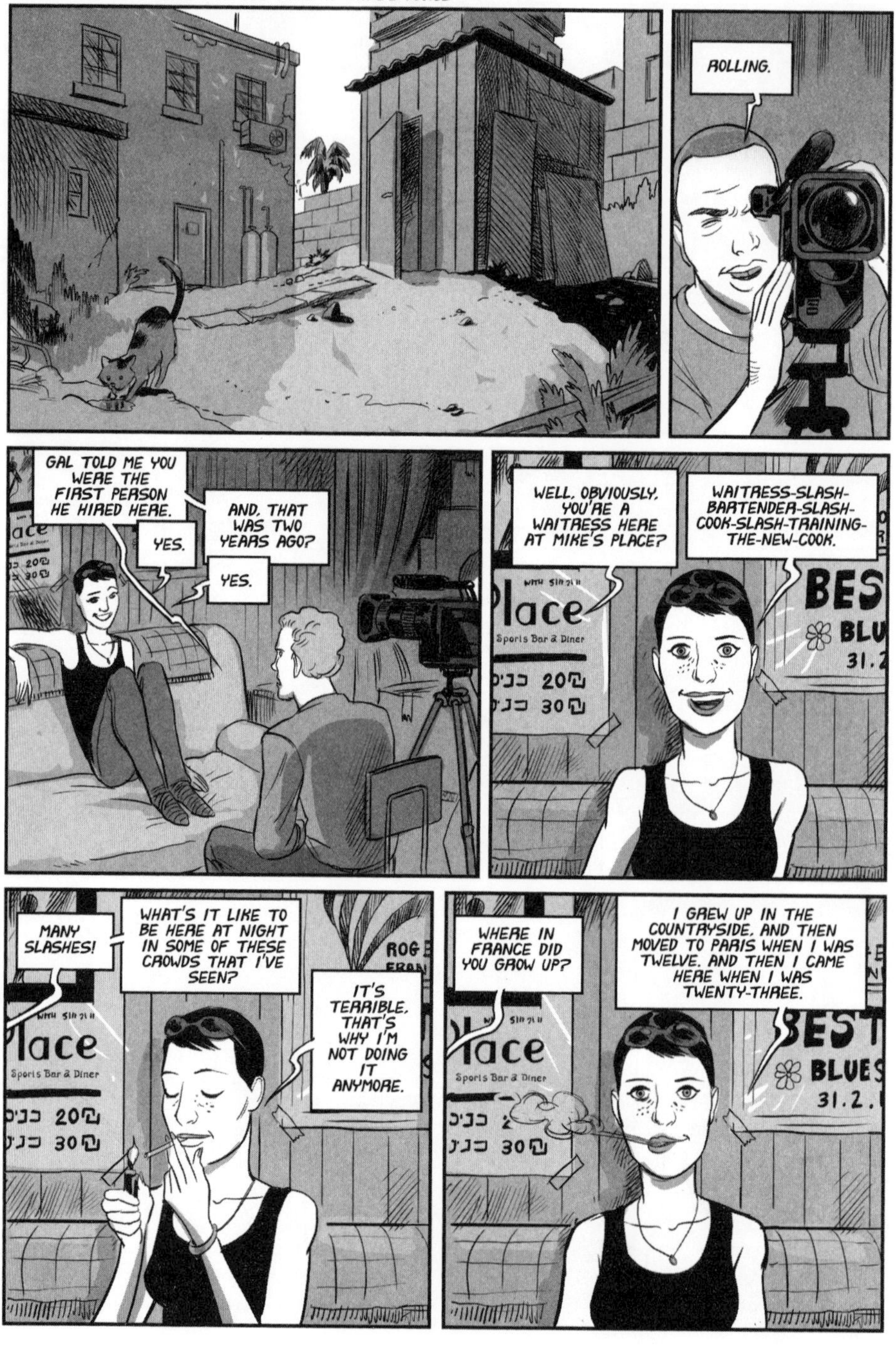
ROLLING.
GAL TOLD ME YOU WERE THE FIRST PERSON HE HIRED HERE.
YES.
AND, THAT WAS TWO YEARS AGO?
YES.
WELL, OBVIOUSLY, YOU'RE A WAITRESS HERE AT MIKE'S PLACE?
WAITRESS-SLASH-BARTENDER-SLASH-COOK-SLASH-TRAINING-THE-NEW-COOK.
MANY SLASHES!
WHAT'S IT LIKE TO BE HERE AT NIGHT IN SOME OF THESE CROWDS THAT I'VE SEEN?
IT'S TERRIBLE, THAT'S WHY I'M NOT DOING IT ANYMORE.
WHERE IN FRANCE DID YOU GROW UP?
I GREW UP IN THE COUNTRYSIDE, AND THEN MOVED TO PARIS WHEN I WAS TWELVE, AND THEN I CAME HERE WHEN I WAS TWENTY-THREE.

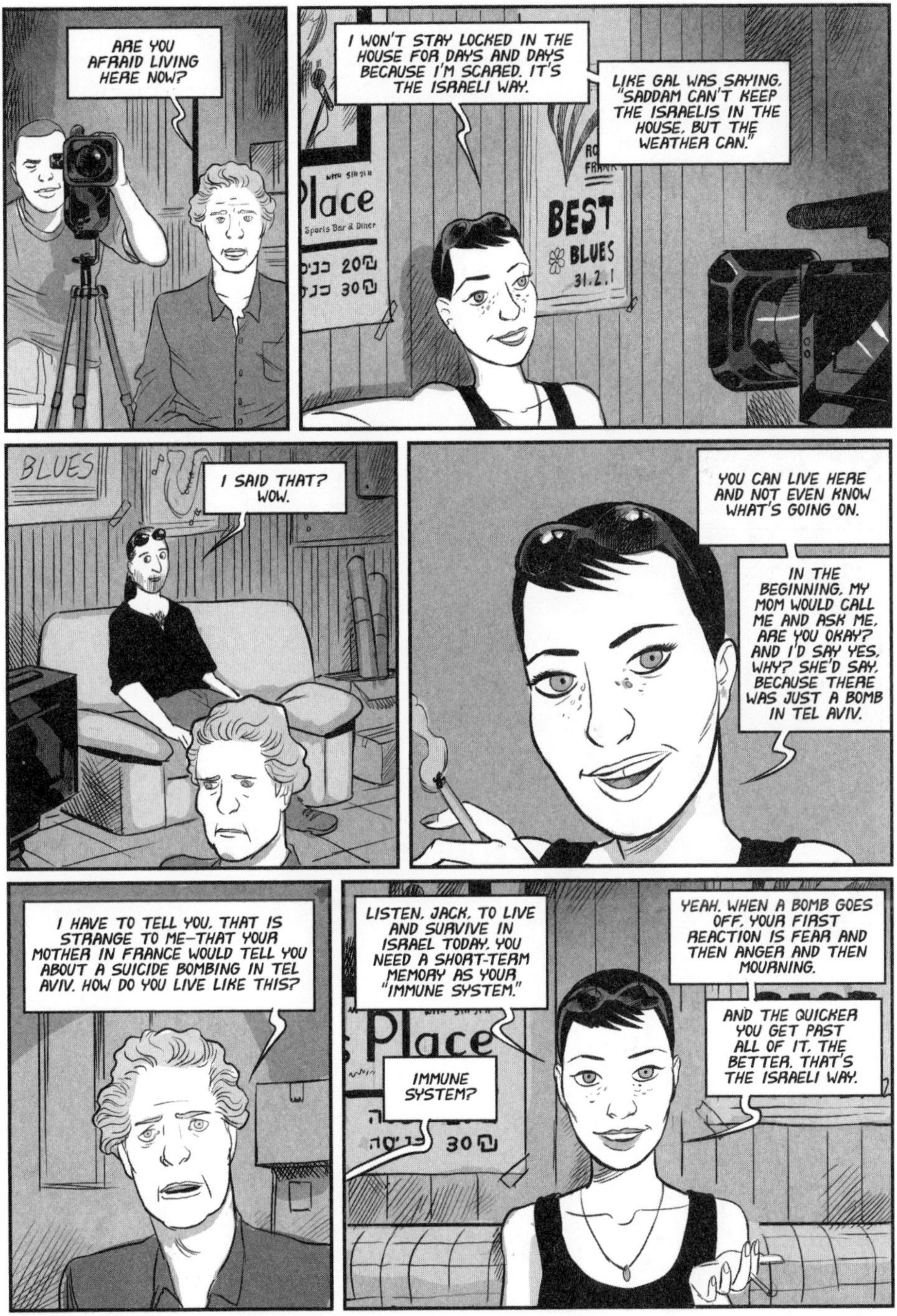
ARE YOU AFRAID LIVING HERE NOW?
I WON'T STAY LOCKED IN THE HOUSE FOR DAYS AND DAYS BECAUSE I'M SCARED. IT'S THE ISRAELI WAY.
LIKE GAL WAS SAYING, "SADDAM CAN'T KEEP THE ISRAELIS IN THE HOUSE, BUT THE WEATHER CAN."
Place
Sports Bar & Diner
BEST
BLUES
31.2.1
BLUES
I SAID THAT? WOW.
YOU CAN LIVE HERE AND NOT EVEN KNOW WHAT'S GOING ON.
IN THE BEGINNING, MY MOM WOULD CALL ME AND ASK ME, ARE YOU OKAY? AND I'D SAY YES, WHY? SHE'D SAY, BECAUSE THERE WAS JUST A BOMB IN TEL AVIV.
I HAVE TO TELL YOU, THAT IS STRANGE TO ME—THAT YOUR MOTHER IN FRANCE WOULD TELL YOU ABOUT A SUICIDE BOMBING IN TEL AVIV. HOW DO YOU LIVE LIKE THIS?
LISTEN, JACK, TO LIVE AND SURVIVE IN ISRAEL TODAY, YOU NEED A SHORT-TERM MEMORY AS YOUR "IMMUNE SYSTEM."
IMMUNE SYSTEM?
YEAH. WHEN A BOMB GOES OFF, YOUR FIRST REACTION IS FEAR AND THEN ANGER AND THEN MOURNING.
AND THE QUICKER YOU GET PAST ALL OF IT, THE BETTER. THAT'S THE ISRAELI WAY.

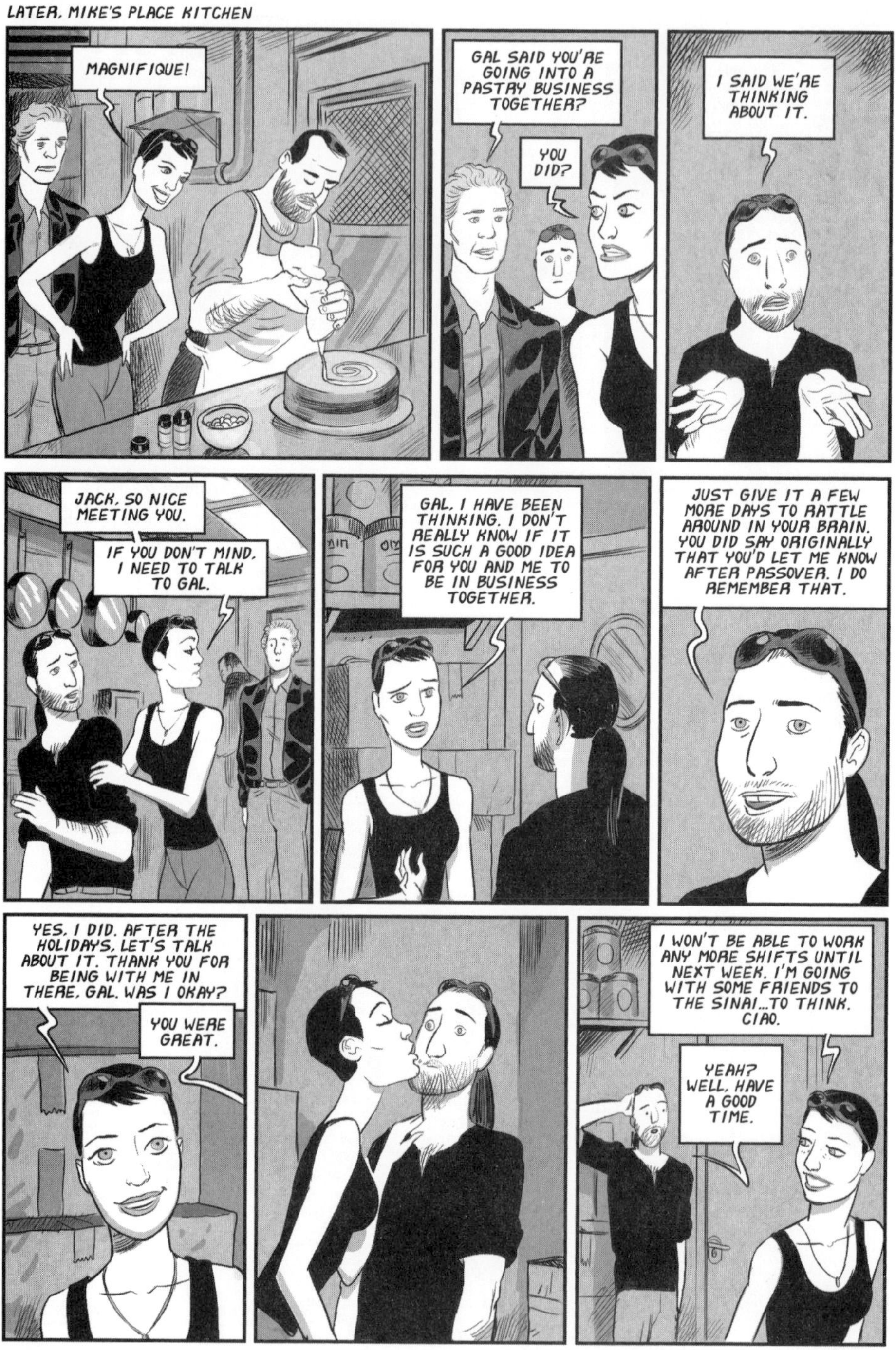
LATER, MIKE'S PLACE KITCHEN
MAGNIFIQUE!
GAL SAID YOU'RE GOING INTO A PASTRY BUSINESS TOGETHER?
YOU DID?
I SAID WE'RE THINKING ABOUT IT.
JACK, SO NICE MEETING YOU.
IF YOU DON'T MIND, I NEED TO TALK TO GAL.
GAL, I HAVE BEEN THINKING. I DON'T REALLY KNOW IF IT IS SUCH A GOOD IDEA FOR YOU AND ME TO BE IN BUSINESS TOGETHER.
JUST GIVE IT A FEW MORE DAYS TO RATTLE AROUND IN YOUR BRAIN. YOU DID SAY ORIGINALLY THAT YOU'D LET ME KNOW AFTER PASSOVER. I DO REMEMBER THAT.
YES, I DID. AFTER THE HOLIDAYS, LET'S TALK ABOUT IT. THANK YOU FOR BEING WITH ME IN THERE, GAL. WAS I OKAY?
YOU WERE GREAT.
I WON'T BE ABLE TO WORK ANY MORE SHIFTS UNTIL NEXT WEEK. I'M GOING WITH SOME FRIENDS TO THE SINAI...TO THINK. CIAO.
YEAH? WELL, HAVE A GOOD TIME.

NEXT DAY, JAFFA MEDICAL CLINIC

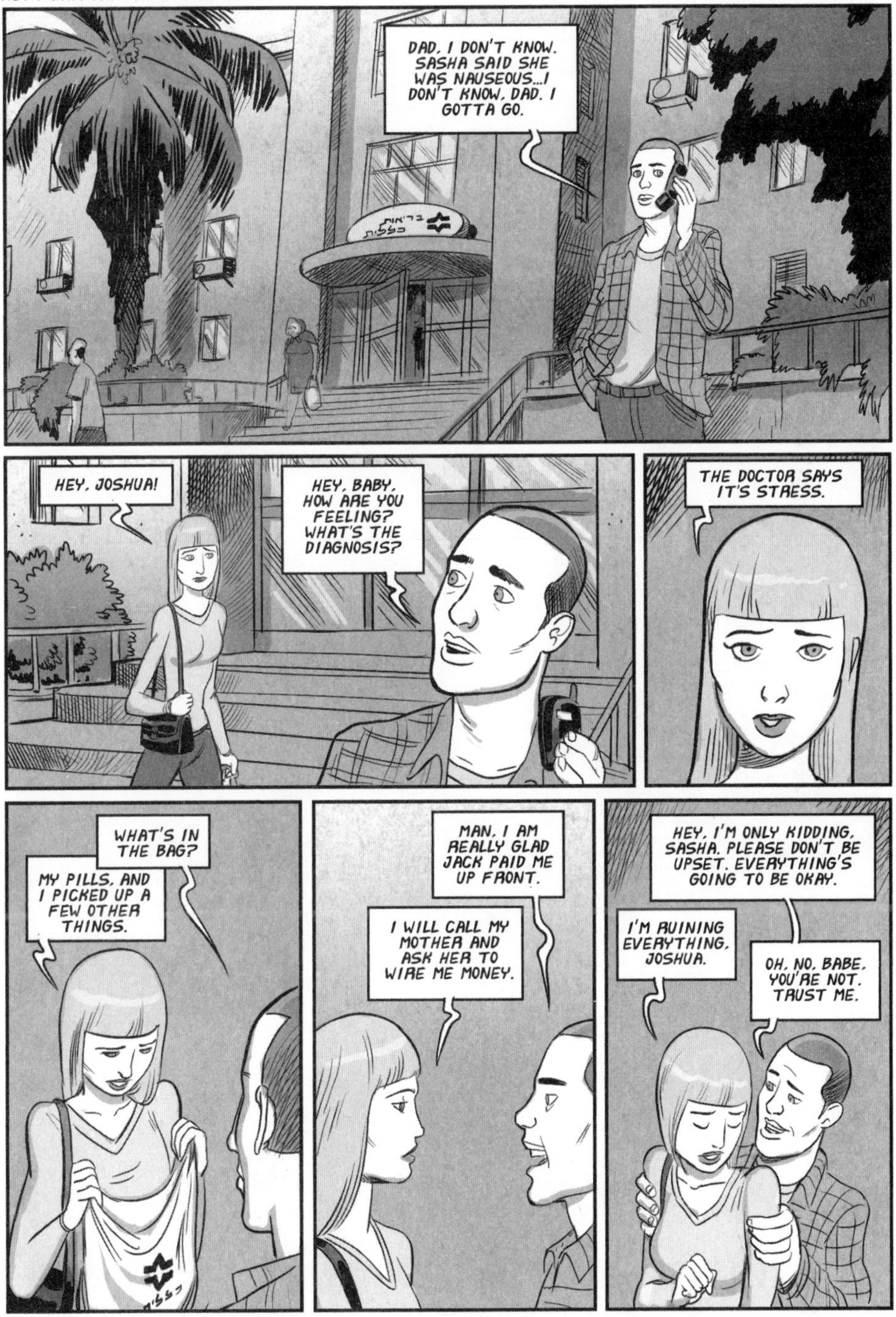

DAD, I DON'T KNOW. SASHA SAID SHE WAS NAUSEOUS...I DON'T KNOW, DAD. I GOTTA GO.
HEY, JOSHUA!
HEY, BABY, HOW ARE YOU FEELING? WHAT'S THE DIAGNOSIS?
THE DOCTOR SAYS IT'S STRESS.
WHAT'S IN THE BAG?
MY PILLS, AND I PICKED UP A FEW OTHER THINGS.
MAN, I AM REALLY GLAD JACK PAID ME UP FRONT.
I WILL CALL MY MOTHER AND ASK HER TO WIRE ME MONEY.
HEY, I'M ONLY KIDDING, SASHA. PLEASE DON'T BE UPSET. EVERYTHING'S GOING TO BE OKAY.
I'M RUINING EVERYTHING, JOSHUA.
OH, NO, BABE, YOU'RE NOT. TRUST ME.

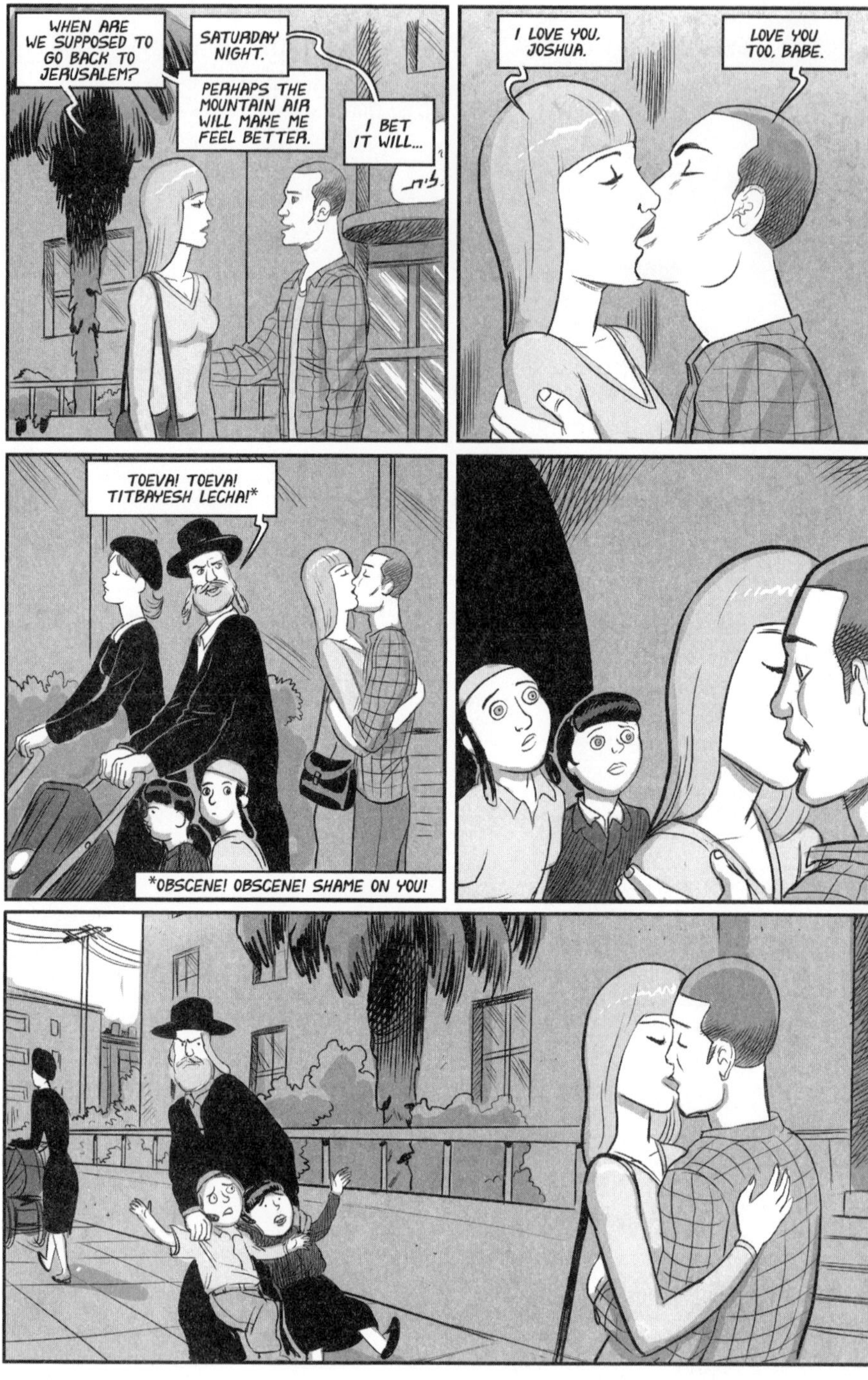
WHEN ARE WE SUPPOSED TO GO BACK TO JERUSALEM?
SATURDAY NIGHT.
PERHAPS THE MOUNTAIN AIR WILL MAKE ME FEEL BETTER.
I BET IT WILL...
I LOVE YOU, JOSHUA.
LOVE YOU TOO, BABE.
TOEVA! TOEVA! TITBAYESH LECHA!*
*OBSCENE! OBSCENE! SHAME ON YOU!

SATURDAY NIGHT, THE ROAD TO JERUSALEM

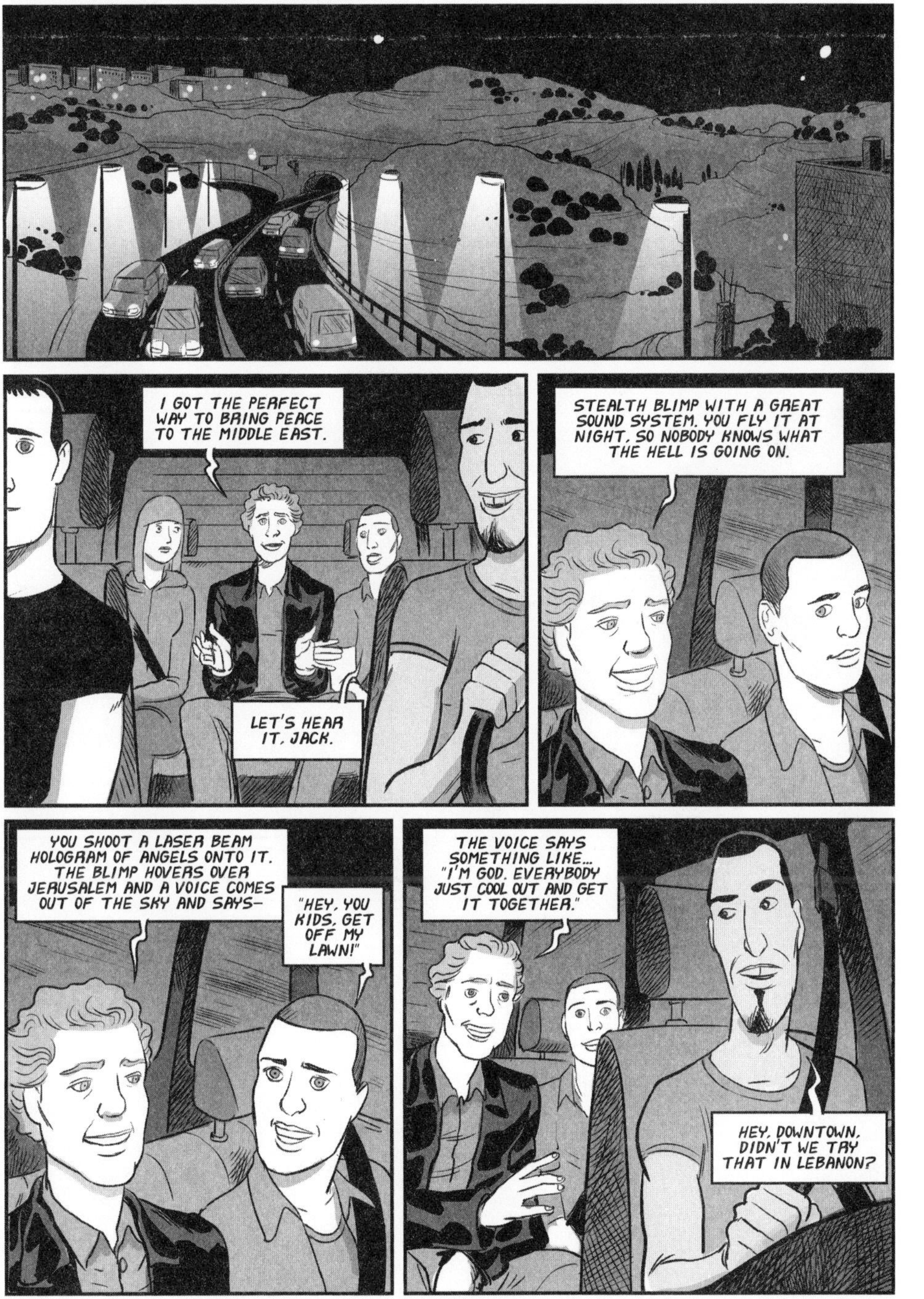

I GOT THE PERFECT WAY TO BRING PEACE TO THE MIDDLE EAST.
LET'S HEAR IT, JACK.
STEALTH BLIMP WITH A GREAT SOUND SYSTEM. YOU FLY IT AT NIGHT, SO NOBODY KNOWS WHAT THE HELL IS GOING ON.
YOU SHOOT A LASER BEAM HOLOGRAM OF ANGELS ONTO IT. THE BLIMP HOVERS OVER JERUSALEM AND A VOICE COMES OUT OF THE SKY AND SAYS–
"HEY, YOU KIDS, GET OFF MY LAWN!"
THE VOICE SAYS SOMETHING LIKE... "I'M GOD. EVERYBODY JUST COOL OUT AND GET IT TOGETHER."
HEY, DOWNTOWN, DIDN'T WE TRY THAT IN LEBANON?

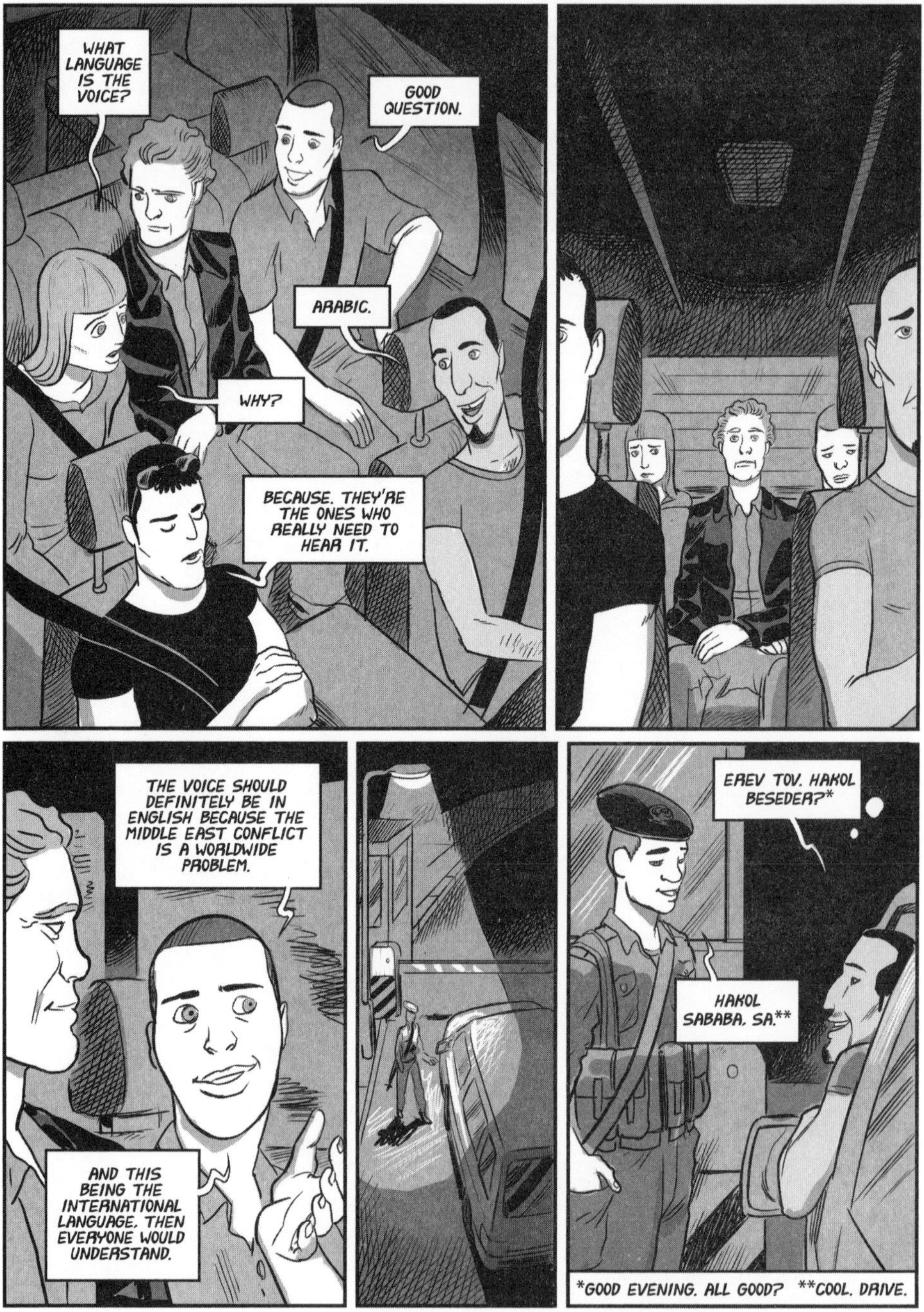
WHAT LANGUAGE IS THE VOICE?
GOOD QUESTION.
ARABIC.
WHY?
BECAUSE. THEY'RE THE ONES WHO REALLY NEED TO HEAR IT.
THE VOICE SHOULD DEFINITELY BE IN ENGLISH BECAUSE THE MIDDLE EAST CONFLICT IS A WORLDWIDE PROBLEM.
AND THIS BEING THE INTERNATIONAL LANGUAGE, THEN EVERYONE WOULD UNDERSTAND.
EREV TOV. HAKOL BESEDER?*
HAKOL SABABA, SA.**
*GOOD EVENING. ALL GOOD? **COOL. DRIVE.

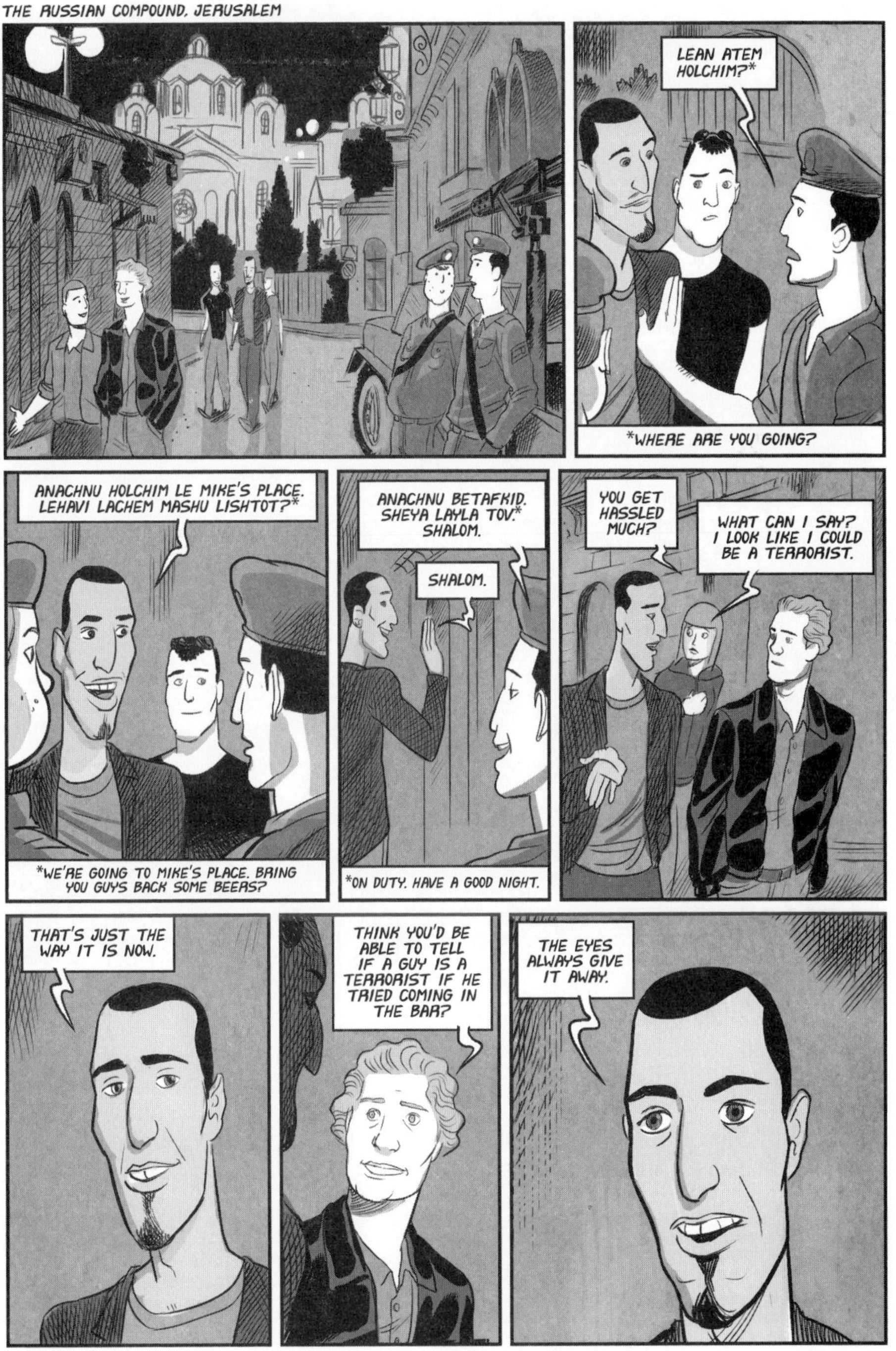
THE RUSSIAN COMPOUND, JERUSALEM
LEAN ATEM HOLCHIM?*
*WHERE ARE YOU GOING?
ANACHNU HOLCHIM LE MIKE'S PLACE. LEHAVI LACHEM MASHU LISHTOT?*
*WE'RE GOING TO MIKE'S PLACE. BRING YOU GUYS BACK SOME BEERS?
ANACHNU BETAFKID. SHEYA LAYLA TOV.* SHALOM.
SHALOM.
*ON DUTY. HAVE A GOOD NIGHT.
YOU GET HASSLED MUCH?
WHAT CAN I SAY? I LOOK LIKE I COULD BE A TERRORIST.
THAT'S JUST THE WAY IT IS NOW.
THINK YOU'D BE ABLE TO TELL IF A GUY IS A TERRORIST IF HE TRIED COMING IN THE BAR?
THE EYES ALWAYS GIVE IT AWAY.

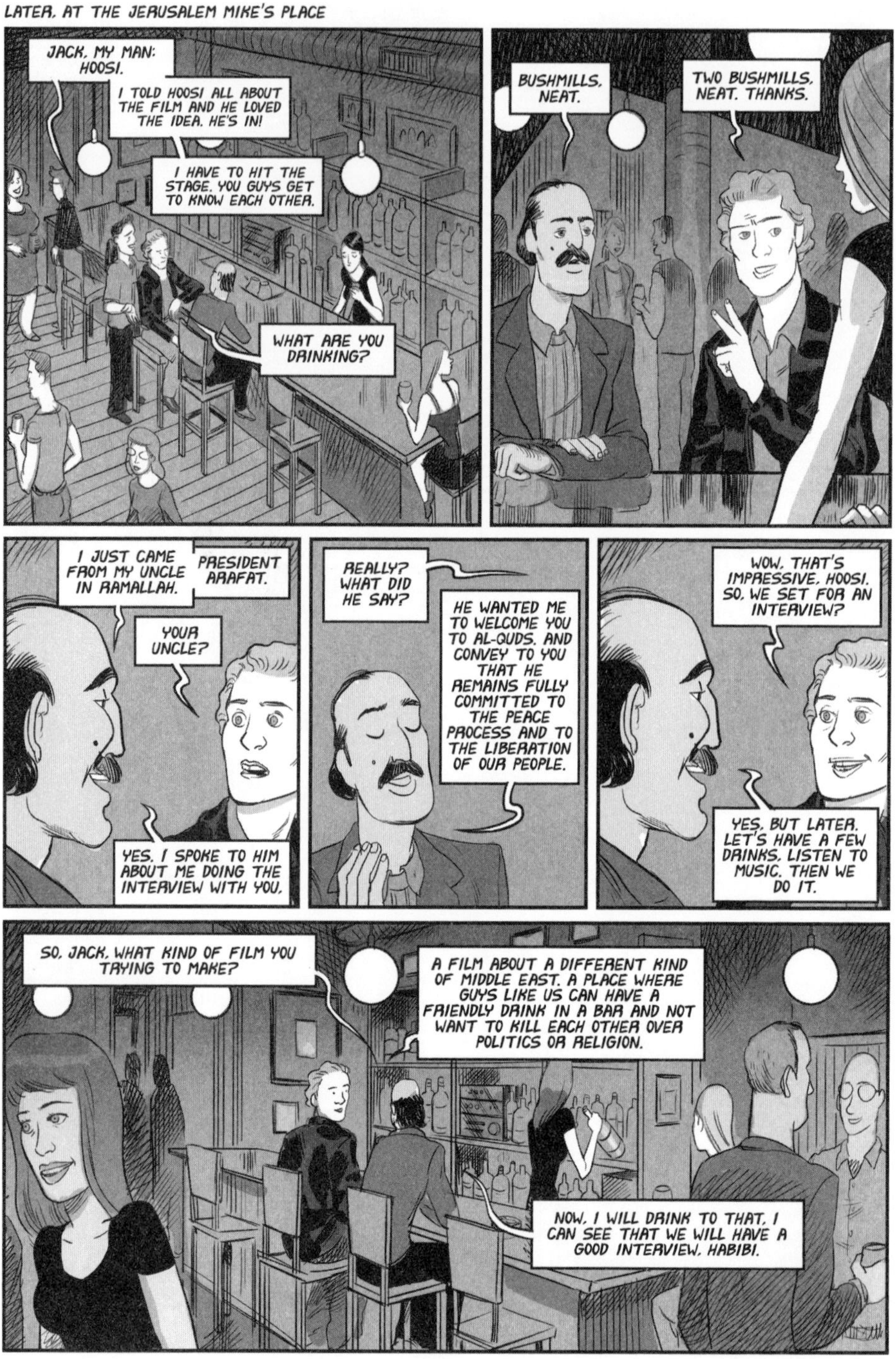
LATER, AT THE JERUSALEM MIKE'S PLACE
JACK, MY MAN: HOOSI.
I TOLD HOOSI ALL ABOUT THE FILM AND HE LOVED THE IDEA. HE'S IN!
I HAVE TO HIT THE STAGE. YOU GUYS GET TO KNOW EACH OTHER.
WHAT ARE YOU DRINKING?
BUSHMILLS, NEAT.
TWO BUSHMILLS, NEAT. THANKS.
I JUST CAME FROM MY UNCLE IN RAMALLAH.
YOUR UNCLE?
PRESIDENT ARAFAT.
YES. I SPOKE TO HIM ABOUT ME DOING THE INTERVIEW WITH YOU.
REALLY? WHAT DID HE SAY?
HE WANTED ME TO WELCOME YOU TO AL-QUDS. AND CONVEY TO YOU THAT HE REMAINS FULLY COMMITTED TO THE PEACE PROCESS AND TO THE LIBERATION OF OUR PEOPLE.
WOW, THAT'S IMPRESSIVE, HOOSI. SO, WE SET FOR AN INTERVIEW?
YES, BUT LATER. LET'S HAVE A FEW DRINKS, LISTEN TO MUSIC, THEN WE DO IT.
SO, JACK, WHAT KIND OF FILM YOU TRYING TO MAKE?
A FILM ABOUT A DIFFERENT KIND OF MIDDLE EAST. A PLACE WHERE GUYS LIKE US CAN HAVE A FRIENDLY DRINK IN A BAR AND NOT WANT TO KILL EACH OTHER OVER POLITICS OR RELIGION.
NOW, I WILL DRINK TO THAT. I CAN SEE THAT WE WILL HAVE A GOOD INTERVIEW, HABIBI.

III

"Let there be no compulsion in religion. Truth stands out clearly from error; whoever rejects evil and has faith in God has grasped the most trustworthy, unfailing handhold . . ."

— Qur'an

KLAK-KSH

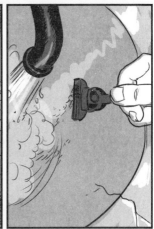

THIS WILL SERVE YOU WELL IN YOUR MISSION.

MAY GOD BE WITH YOU.

COURAGE, MY BROTHERS.

SALAAM ALAIKUM.

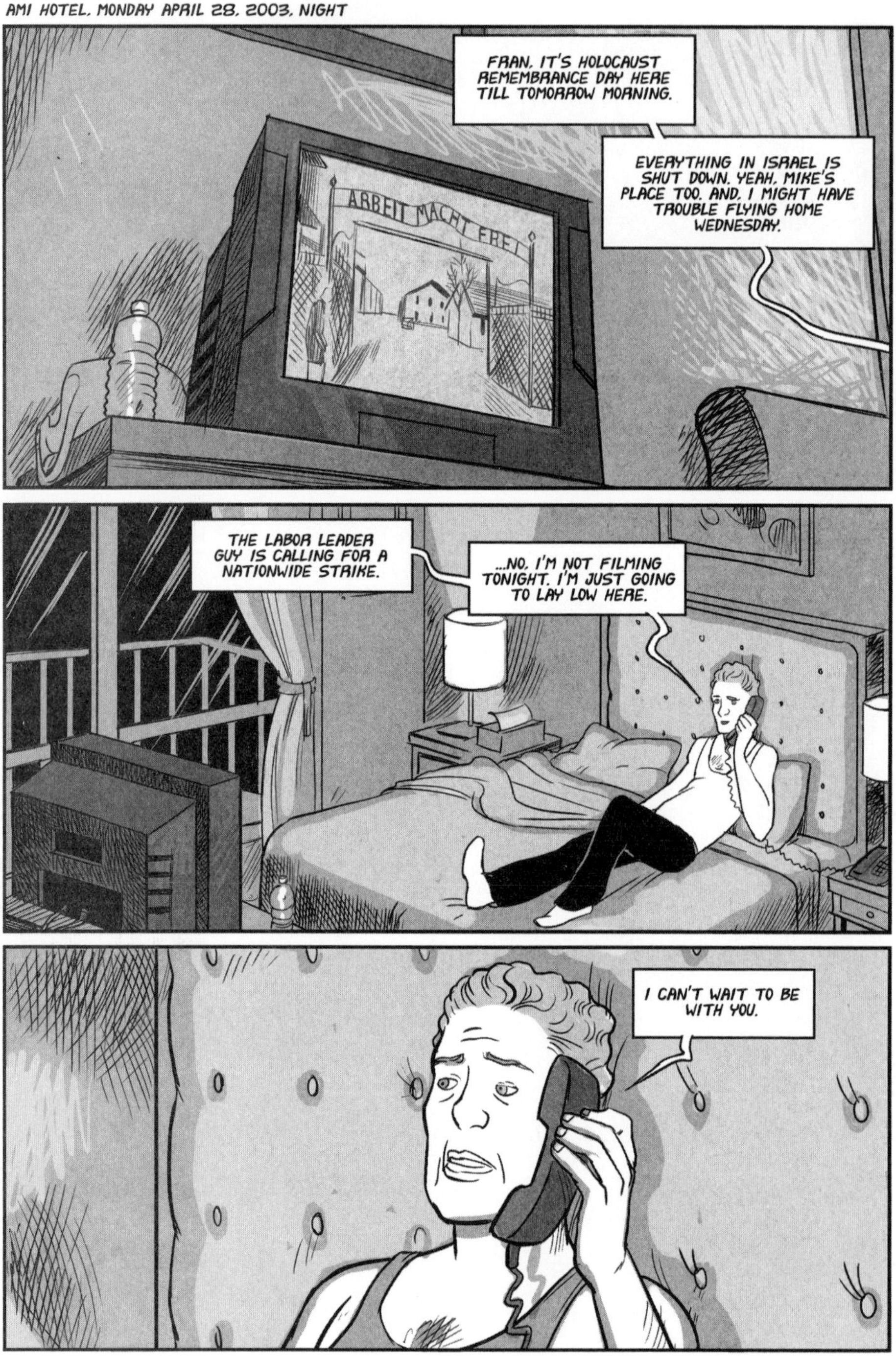
AMI HOTEL, MONDAY APRIL 28, 2003, NIGHT
FRAN, IT'S HOLOCAUST REMEMBRANCE DAY HERE TILL TOMORROW MORNING.
EVERYTHING IN ISRAEL IS SHUT DOWN. YEAH, MIKE'S PLACE TOO. AND, I MIGHT HAVE TROUBLE FLYING HOME WEDNESDAY.
ARBEIT MACHT FREI
THE LABOR LEADER GUY IS CALLING FOR A NATIONWIDE STRIKE.
...NO, I'M NOT FILMING TONIGHT. I'M JUST GOING TO LAY LOW HERE.
I CAN'T WAIT TO BE WITH YOU.

DOWNTOWN DAVE'S APARTMENT ON BEN YEHUDA STREET, SAME NIGHT

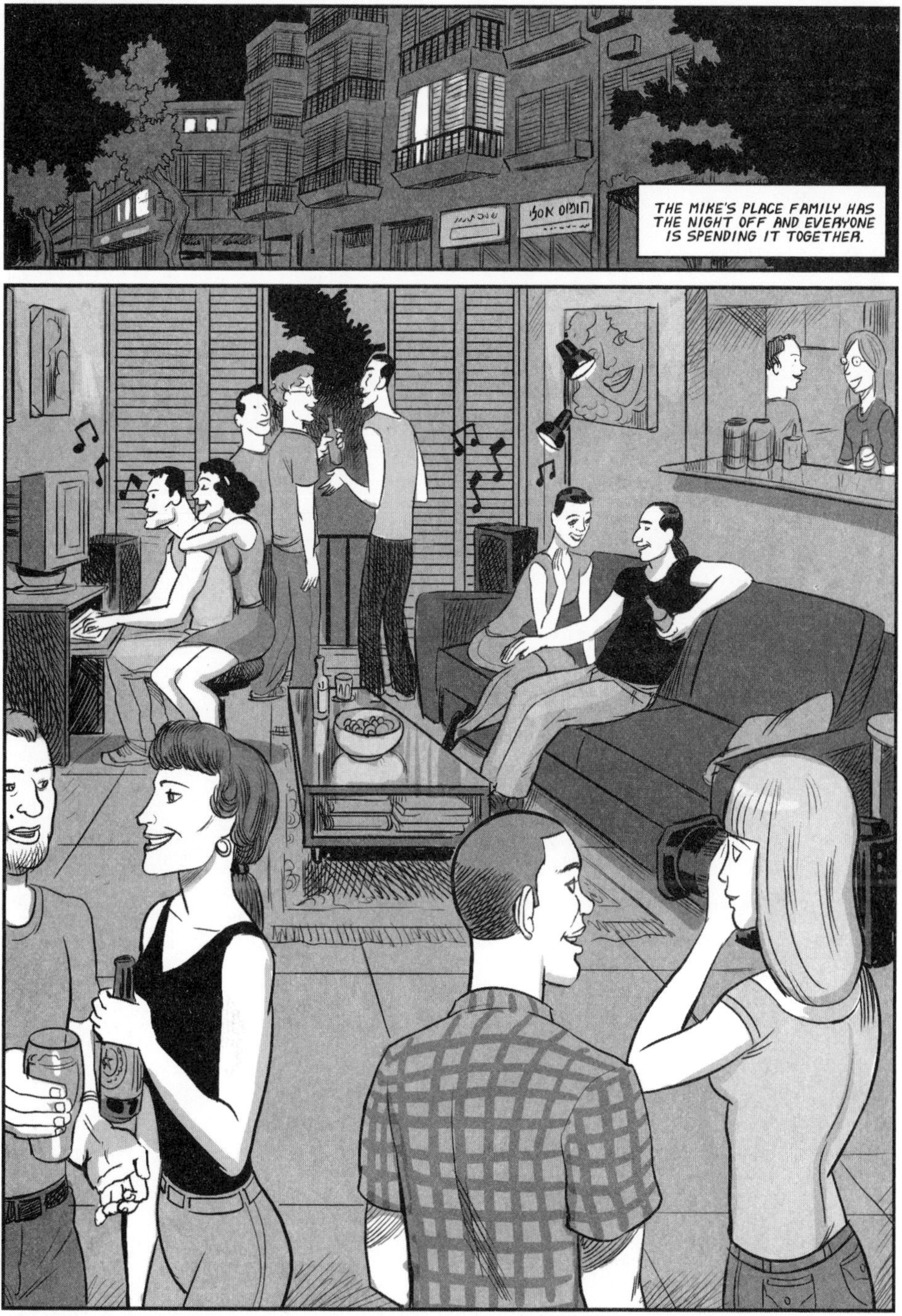
THE MIKE'S PLACE FAMILY HAS THE NIGHT OFF AND EVERYONE IS SPENDING IT TOGETHER.

WHERE'S JACK?

BACK IN HIS HOTEL ROOM, CURLED UP WITH A GOOD HOLOCAUST MOVIE.

OREC

THIS IS VERY STRANGE, JOSHUA.

WHAT?

TODAY IS HOLOCAUST DAY. AND WE ARE IN ISRAEL FILMING A PARTY. IT'S SO BIZARRE.

OREC

HEY, GAL, SASHA WANTS TO KNOW WHY YOU'RE PARTYING ON YOM HASHOAH.

SASHA, EVERYDAY IN ISRAEL IS HOLOCAUST REMEMBRANCE DAY.

WE PARTY FOR THE SIX MILLION WHO NEVER HAD THE CHANCE.

OREC

AMEN TO THAT!

KEEP SHOOTING, SASHA.

OREC

OKAY. SO WE HAVE FOUR DAYS A YEAR THAT MIKE'S PLACE IS CLOSED. AND THAT'S WHY TONIGHT WE CAN ACTUALLY GET ALL OF OUR BARTENDERS HERE. AND NOT AT MIKE'S PLACE.

HAHAHAHA!!

OREC

NEXT MORNING, SIRENS SIGNAL THE END OF HOLOCAUST REMEMBRANCE DAY

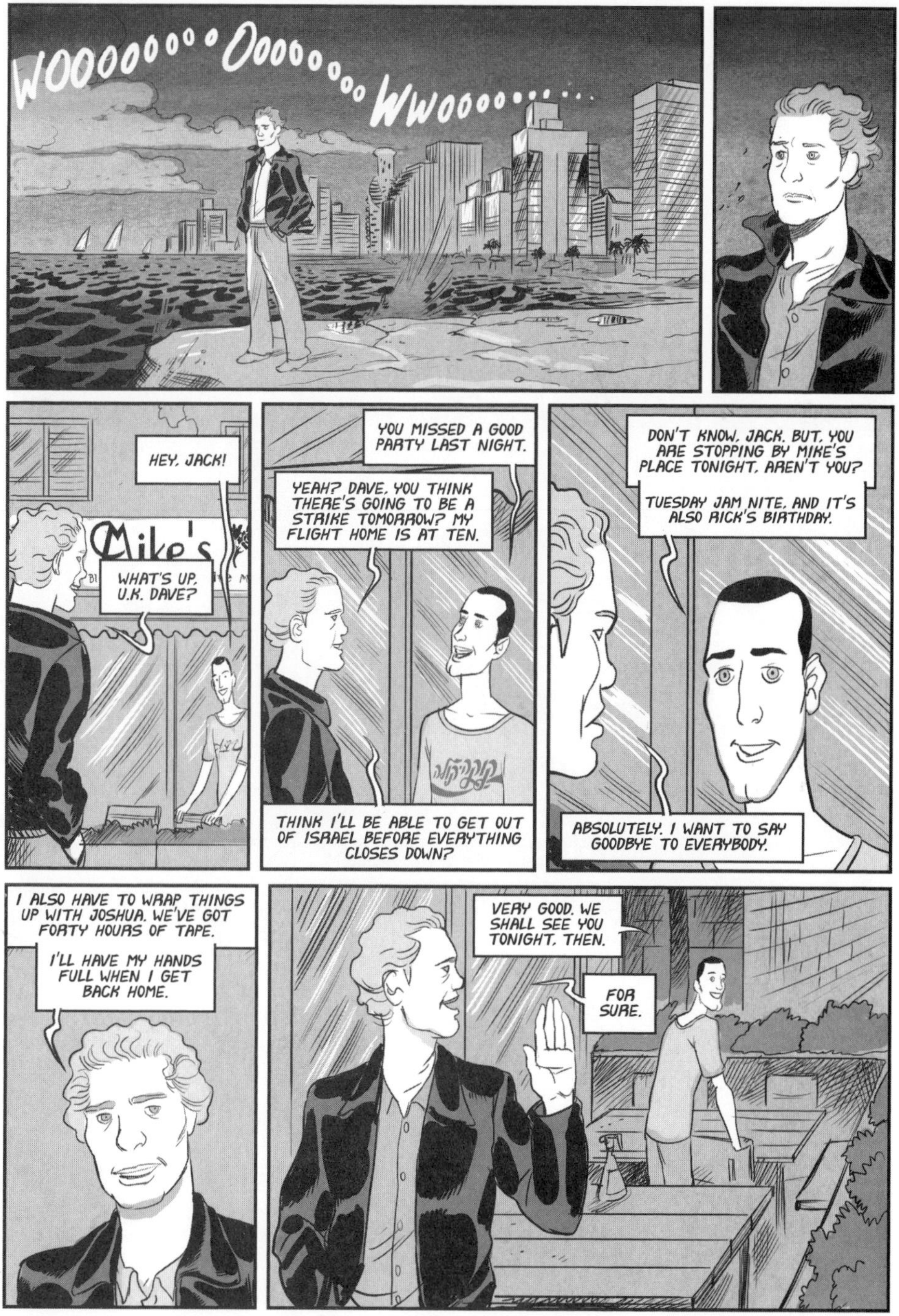
WOOOOOOOO OOOOOOOO WWOOOOO.....
HEY, JACK!
WHAT'S UP, U.K. DAVE?
YOU MISSED A GOOD PARTY LAST NIGHT.
YEAH? DAVE, YOU THINK THERE'S GOING TO BE A STRIKE TOMORROW? MY FLIGHT HOME IS AT TEN.
THINK I'LL BE ABLE TO GET OUT OF ISRAEL BEFORE EVERYTHING CLOSES DOWN?
DON'T KNOW, JACK. BUT, YOU ARE STOPPING BY MIKE'S PLACE TONIGHT, AREN'T YOU?
TUESDAY JAM NITE, AND IT'S ALSO RICK'S BIRTHDAY.
ABSOLUTELY. I WANT TO SAY GOODBYE TO EVERYBODY.
I ALSO HAVE TO WRAP THINGS UP WITH JOSHUA. WE'VE GOT FORTY HOURS OF TAPE.
I'LL HAVE MY HANDS FULL WHEN I GET BACK HOME.
VERY GOOD. WE SHALL SEE YOU TONIGHT, THEN.
FOR SURE.

OLD JAFFA HOSTEL, SAME DAY

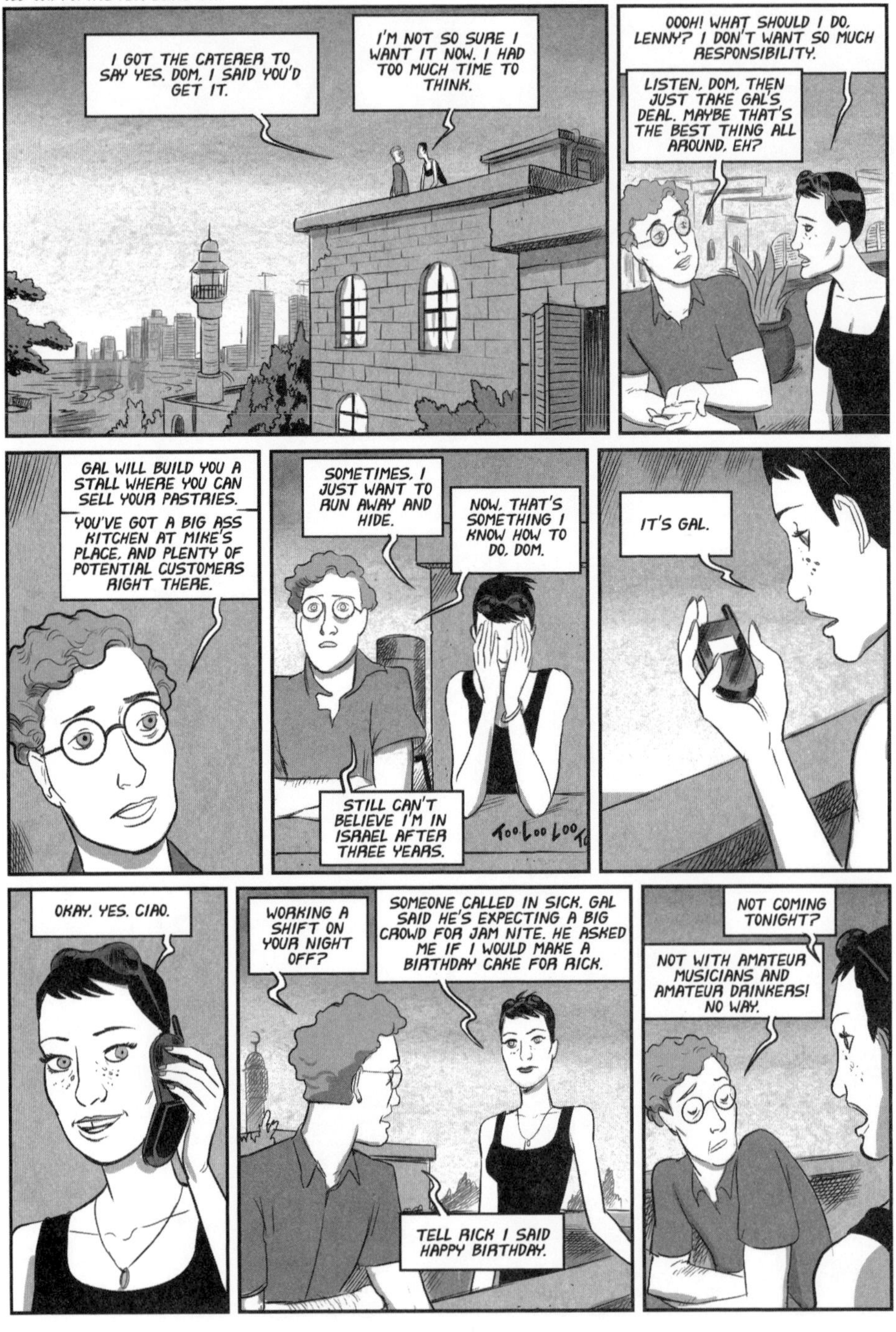
I GOT THE CATERER TO SAY YES. DOM, I SAID YOU'D GET IT.
I'M NOT SO SURE I WANT IT NOW. I HAD TOO MUCH TIME TO THINK.
OOOH! WHAT SHOULD I DO, LENNY? I DON'T WANT SO MUCH RESPONSIBILITY.
LISTEN, DOM, THEN JUST TAKE GAL'S DEAL. MAYBE THAT'S THE BEST THING ALL AROUND, EH?
GAL WILL BUILD YOU A STALL WHERE YOU CAN SELL YOUR PASTRIES.
YOU'VE GOT A BIG ASS KITCHEN AT MIKE'S PLACE, AND PLENTY OF POTENTIAL CUSTOMERS RIGHT THERE.
SOMETIMES, I JUST WANT TO RUN AWAY AND HIDE.
NOW, THAT'S SOMETHING I KNOW HOW TO DO, DOM.
STILL CAN'T BELIEVE I'M IN ISRAEL AFTER THREE YEARS.
TOO LOO LOO TO
IT'S GAL.
OKAY. YES. CIAO.
WORKING A SHIFT ON YOUR NIGHT OFF?
SOMEONE CALLED IN SICK. GAL SAID HE'S EXPECTING A BIG CROWD FOR JAM NITE. HE ASKED ME IF I WOULD MAKE A BIRTHDAY CAKE FOR RICK.
TELL RICK I SAID HAPPY BIRTHDAY.
NOT COMING TONIGHT?
NOT WITH AMATEUR MUSICIANS AND AMATEUR DRINKERS! NO WAY.

GAZA, EREZ CHECKPOINT CROSSING INTO ISRAEL

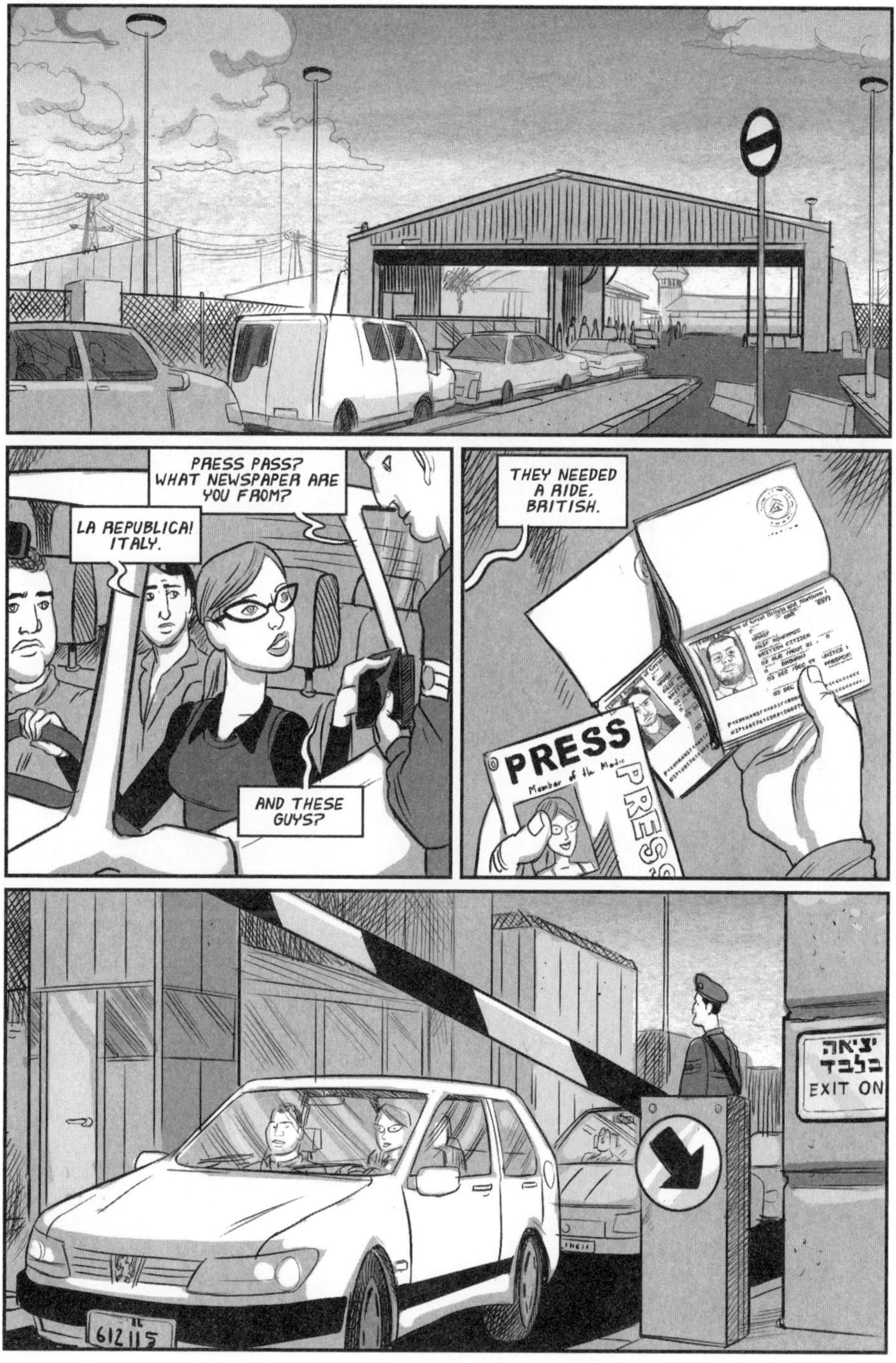
PRESS PASS? WHAT NEWSPAPER ARE YOU FROM?
LA REPUBLICA! ITALY.
AND THESE GUYS?
THEY NEEDED A RIDE. BRITISH.
PRESS
Member of the Media
EXIT ON

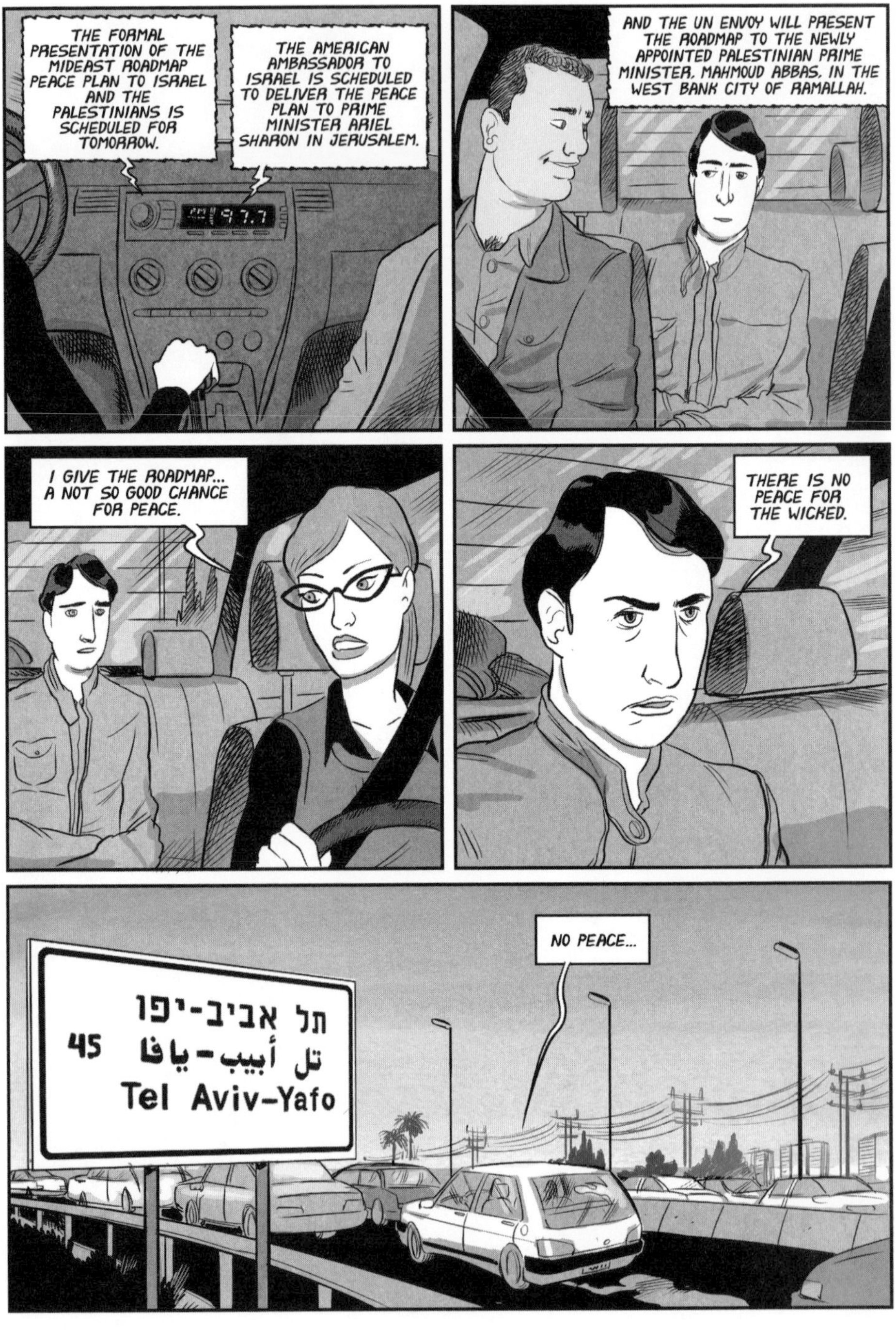
THE FORMAL PRESENTATION OF THE MIDEAST ROADMAP PEACE PLAN TO ISRAEL AND THE PALESTINIANS IS SCHEDULED FOR TOMORROW.
THE AMERICAN AMBASSADOR TO ISRAEL IS SCHEDULED TO DELIVER THE PEACE PLAN TO PRIME MINISTER ARIEL SHARON IN JERUSALEM.
97.7
AND THE UN ENVOY WILL PRESENT THE ROADMAP TO THE NEWLY APPOINTED PALESTINIAN PRIME MINISTER, MAHMOUD ABBAS, IN THE WEST BANK CITY OF RAMALLAH.
I GIVE THE ROADMAP... A NOT SO GOOD CHANCE FOR PEACE.
THERE IS NO PEACE FOR THE WICKED.
תל אביב-יפו
45
تل أبيب-يافا
Tel Aviv-Yafo
NO PEACE...

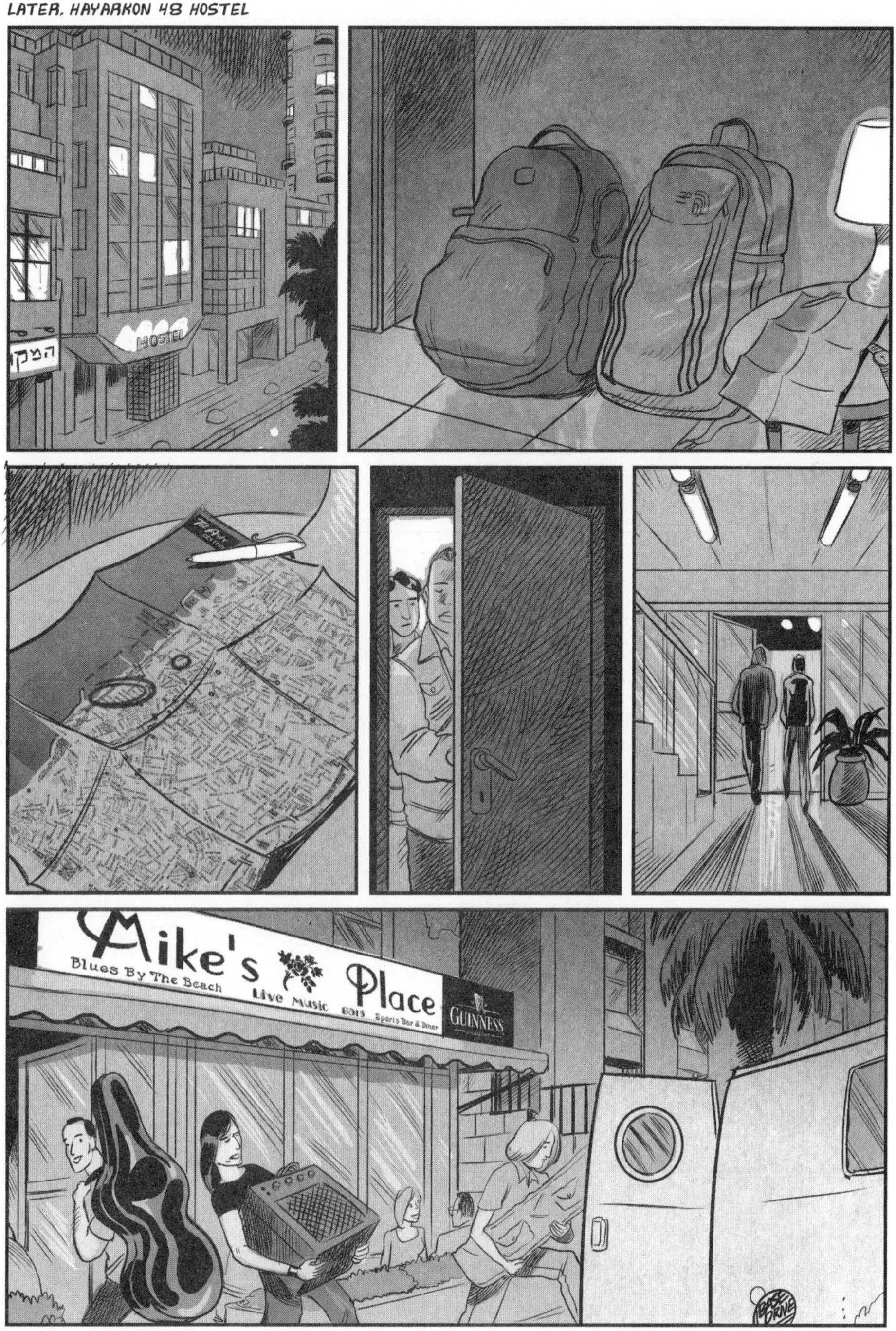
LATER, HAYARKON 48 HOSTEL
HOSTEL
Mike's Place
Blues By The Beach
Live Music
Sports Bar & Diner
GUINNESS

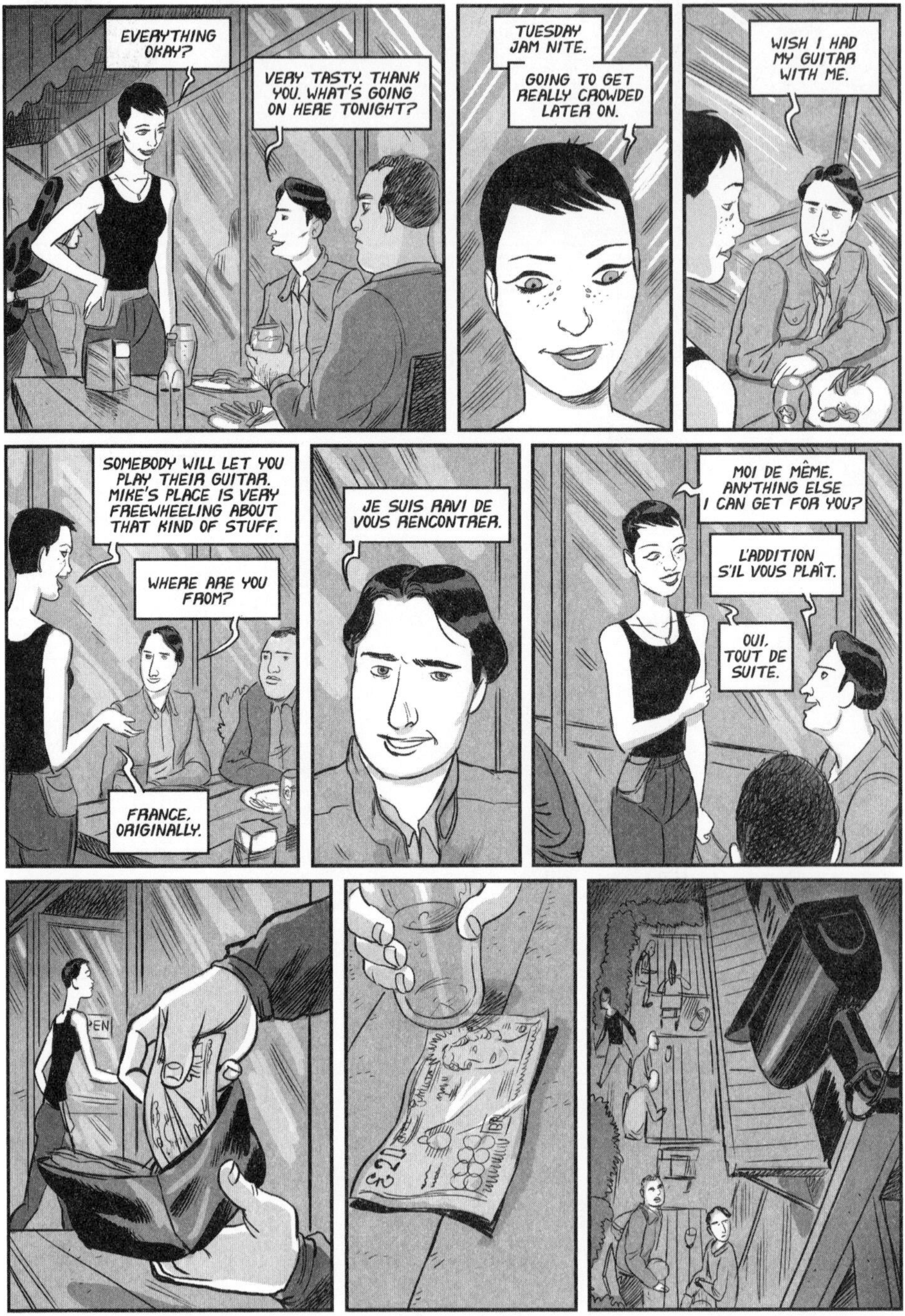
EVERYTHING OKAY?
VERY TASTY. THANK YOU. WHAT'S GOING ON HERE TONIGHT?
TUESDAY JAM NITE.
GOING TO GET REALLY CROWDED LATER ON.
WISH I HAD MY GUITAR WITH ME.
SOMEBODY WILL LET YOU PLAY THEIR GUITAR. MIKE'S PLACE IS VERY FREEWHEELING ABOUT THAT KIND OF STUFF.
WHERE ARE YOU FROM?
FRANCE, ORIGINALLY.
JE SUIS RAVI DE VOUS RENCONTRER.
MOI DE MÊME. ANYTHING ELSE I CAN GET FOR YOU?
L'ADDITION S'IL VOUS PLAÎT.
OUI, TOUT DE SUITE.
PEN

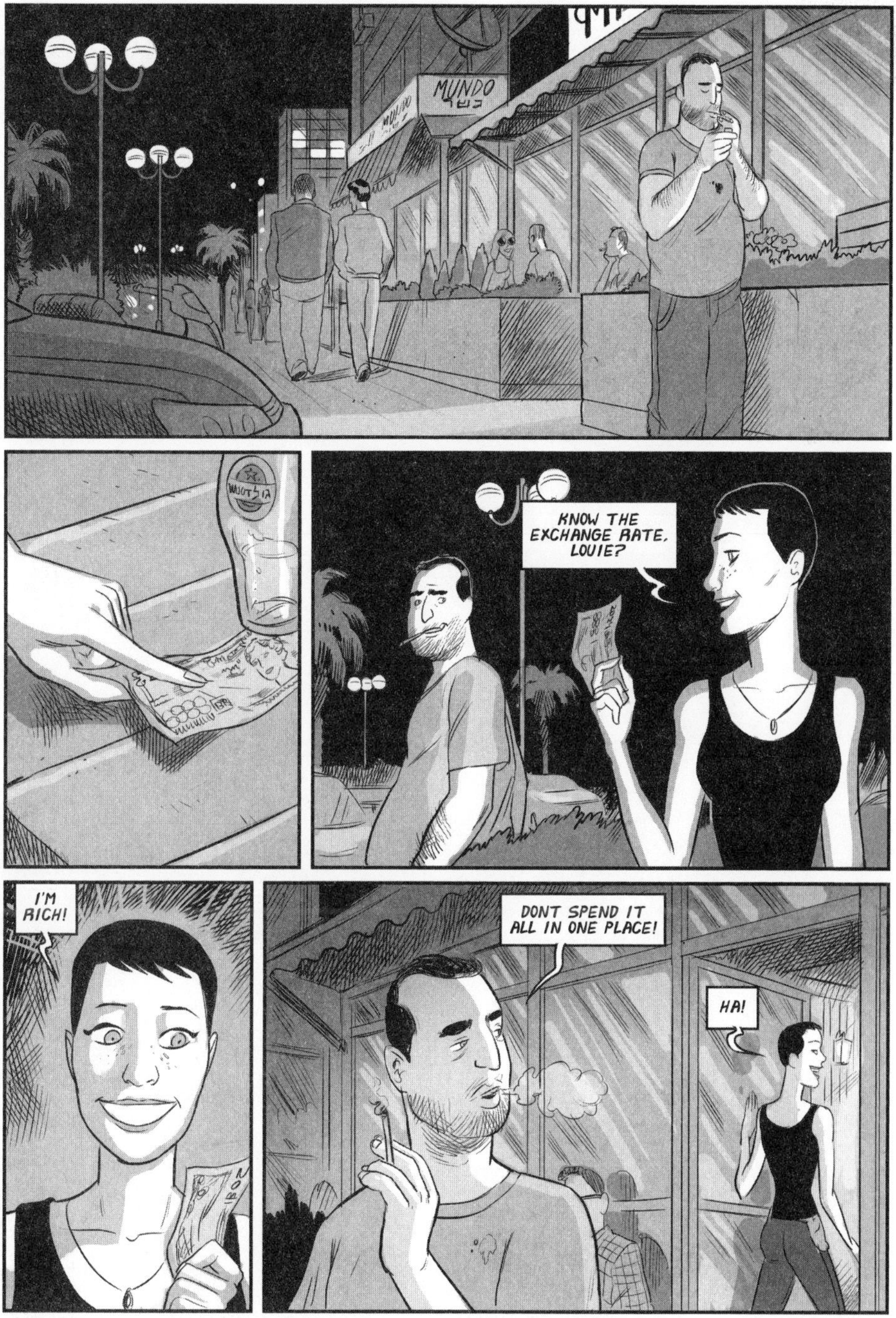
MUNDO
KNOW THE EXCHANGE RATE, LOUIE?
I'M RICH!
DONT SPEND IT ALL IN ONE PLACE!
HA!

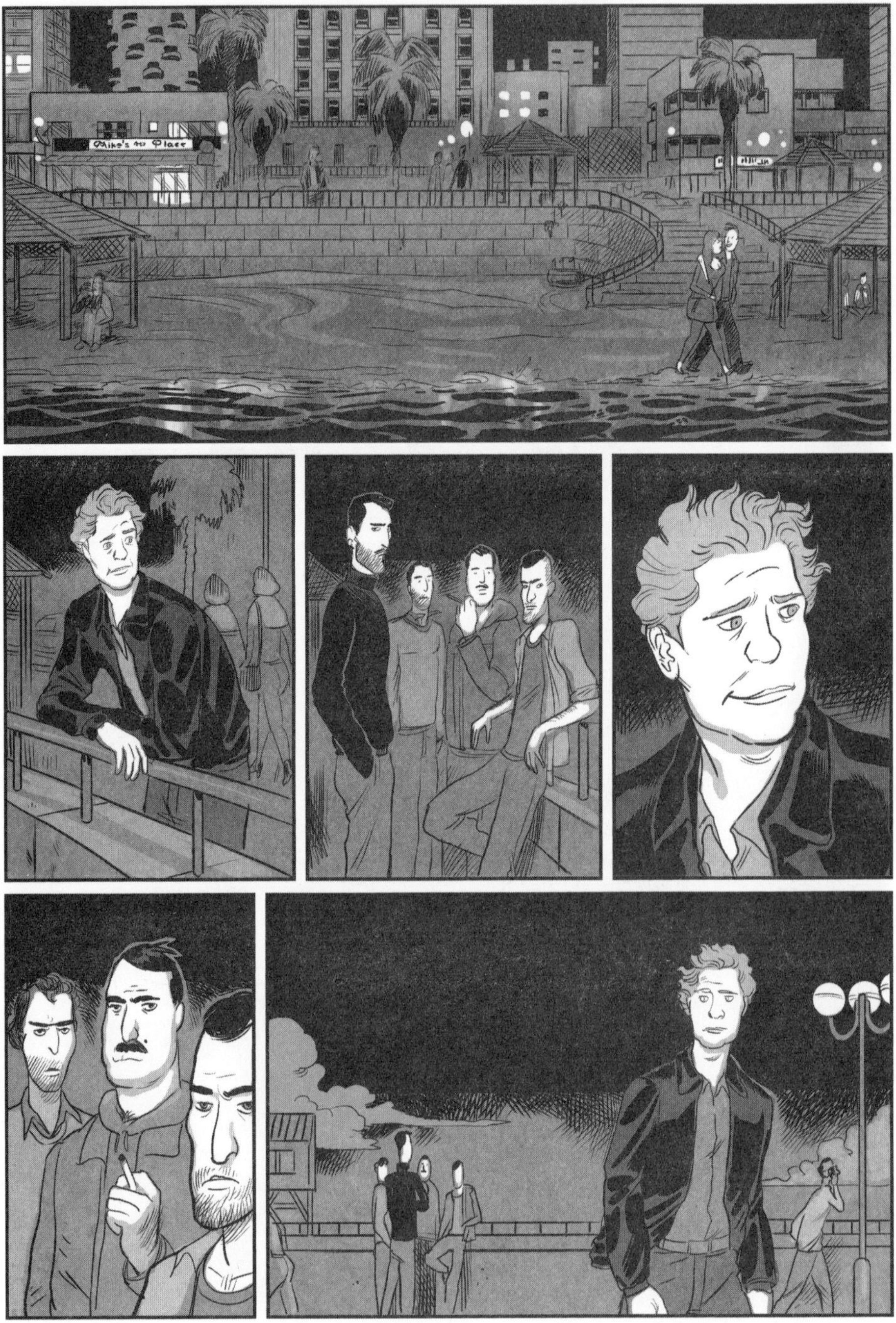
Mike's Place

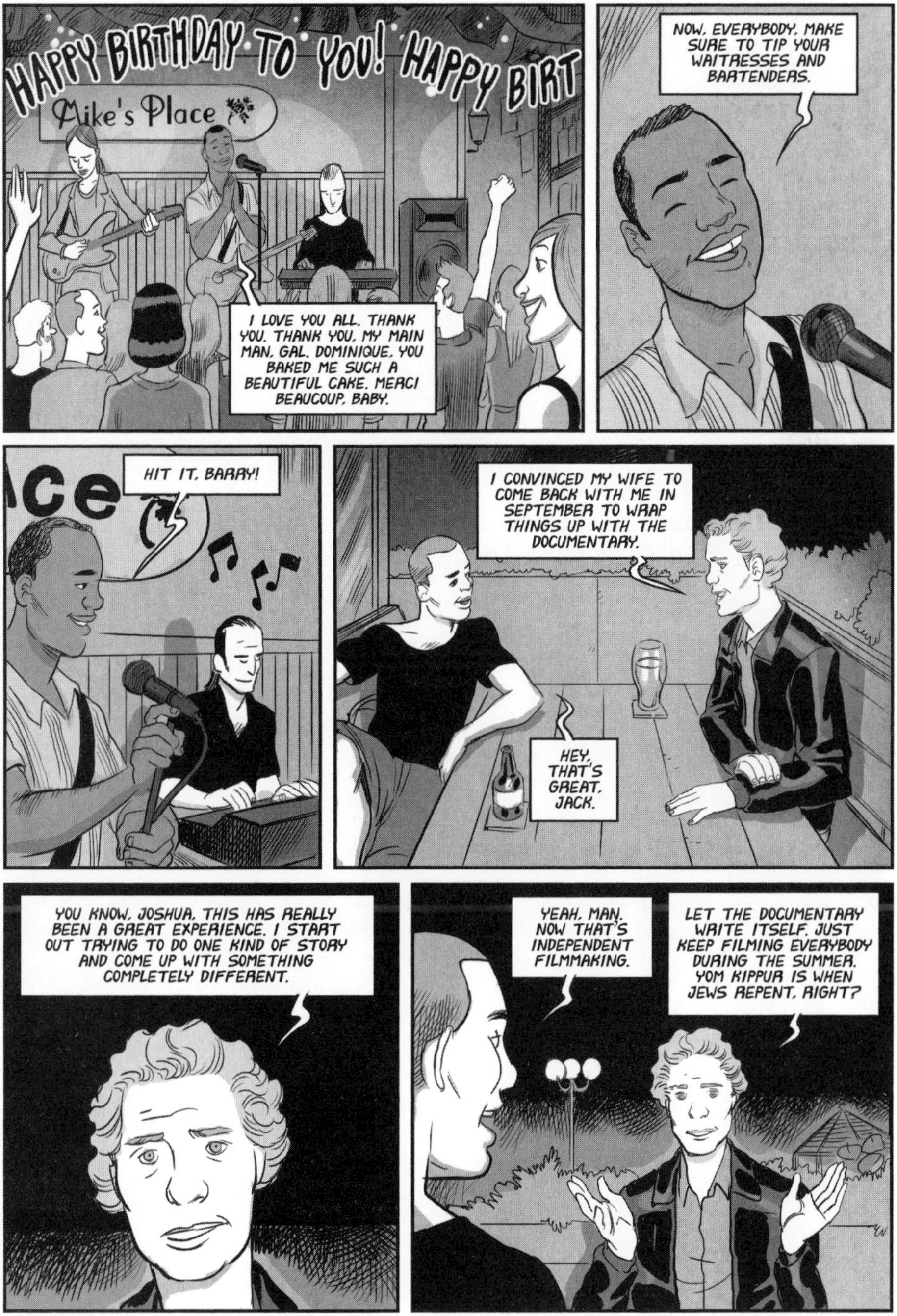
HAPPY BIRTHDAY TO YOU! HAPPY BIRT
Mike's Place
I LOVE YOU ALL. THANK YOU. THANK YOU. MY MAIN MAN, GAL. DOMINIQUE, YOU BAKED ME SUCH A BEAUTIFUL CAKE. MERCI BEAUCOUP, BABY.
NOW, EVERYBODY, MAKE SURE TO TIP YOUR WAITRESSES AND BARTENDERS.
HIT IT, BARRY!
I CONVINCED MY WIFE TO COME BACK WITH ME IN SEPTEMBER TO WRAP THINGS UP WITH THE DOCUMENTARY.
HEY, THAT'S GREAT, JACK.
YOU KNOW, JOSHUA, THIS HAS REALLY BEEN A GREAT EXPERIENCE. I START OUT TRYING TO DO ONE KIND OF STORY AND COME UP WITH SOMETHING COMPLETELY DIFFERENT.
YEAH, MAN. NOW THAT'S INDEPENDENT FILMMAKING.
LET THE DOCUMENTARY WRITE ITSELF. JUST KEEP FILMING EVERYBODY DURING THE SUMMER. YOM KIPPUR IS WHEN JEWS REPENT, RIGHT?

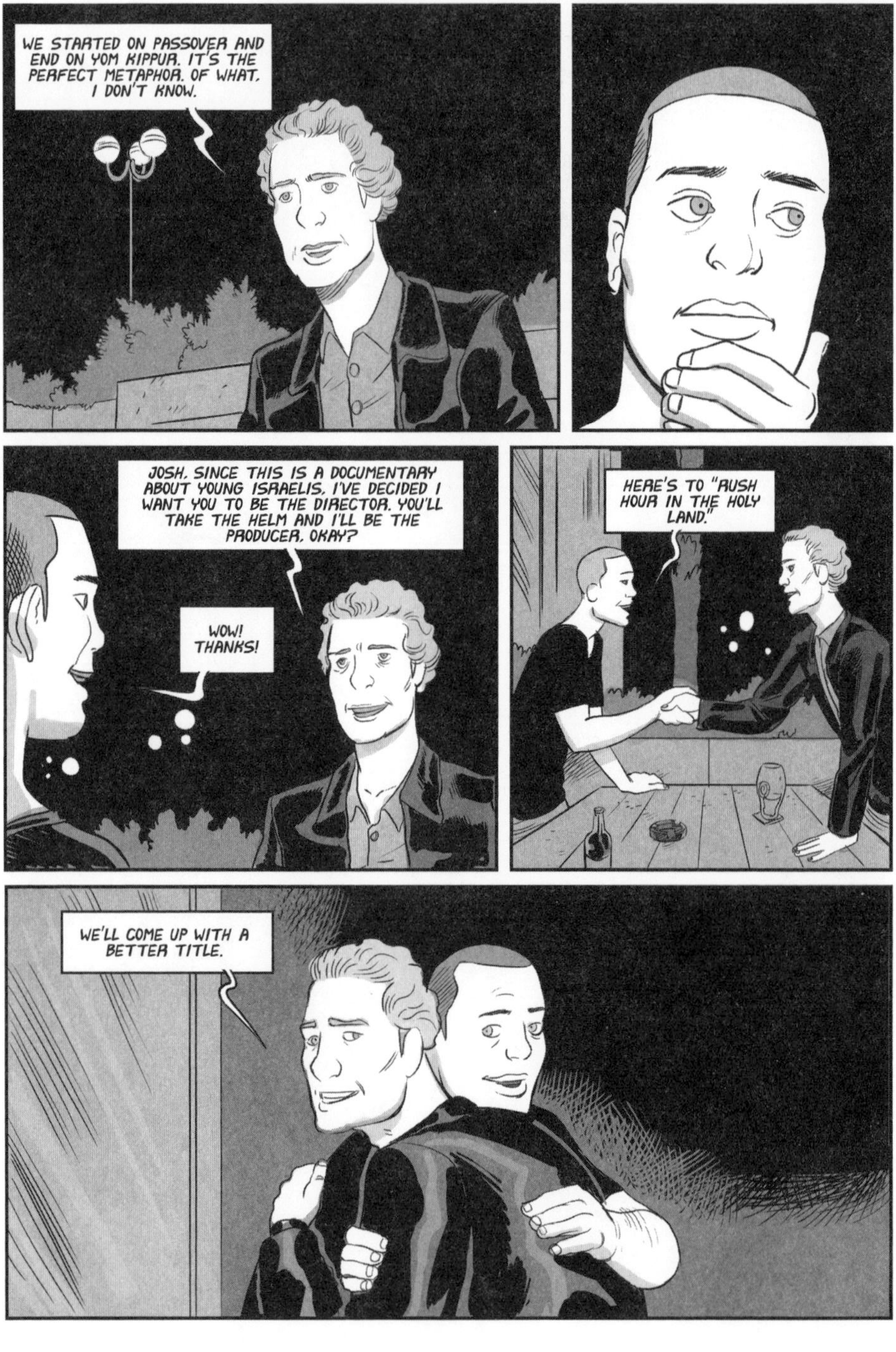
WE STARTED ON PASSOVER AND END ON YOM KIPPUR. IT'S THE PERFECT METAPHOR. OF WHAT, I DON'T KNOW.
JOSH, SINCE THIS IS A DOCUMENTARY ABOUT YOUNG ISRAELIS, I'VE DECIDED I WANT YOU TO BE THE DIRECTOR. YOU'LL TAKE THE HELM AND I'LL BE THE PRODUCER, OKAY?
WOW! THANKS!
HERE'S TO "RUSH HOUR IN THE HOLY LAND."
WE'LL COME UP WITH A BETTER TITLE.

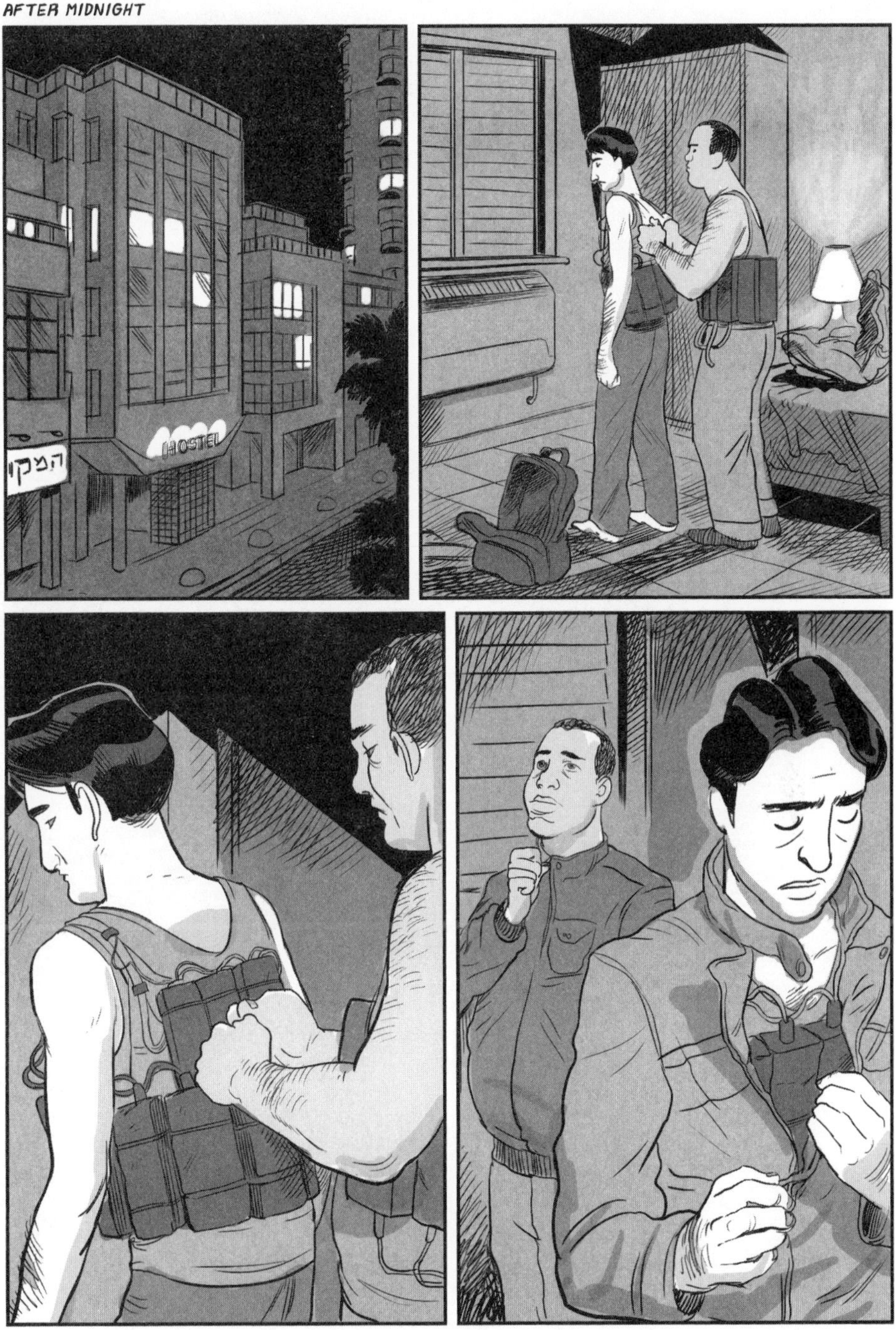
AFTER MIDNIGHT
HOSTEL

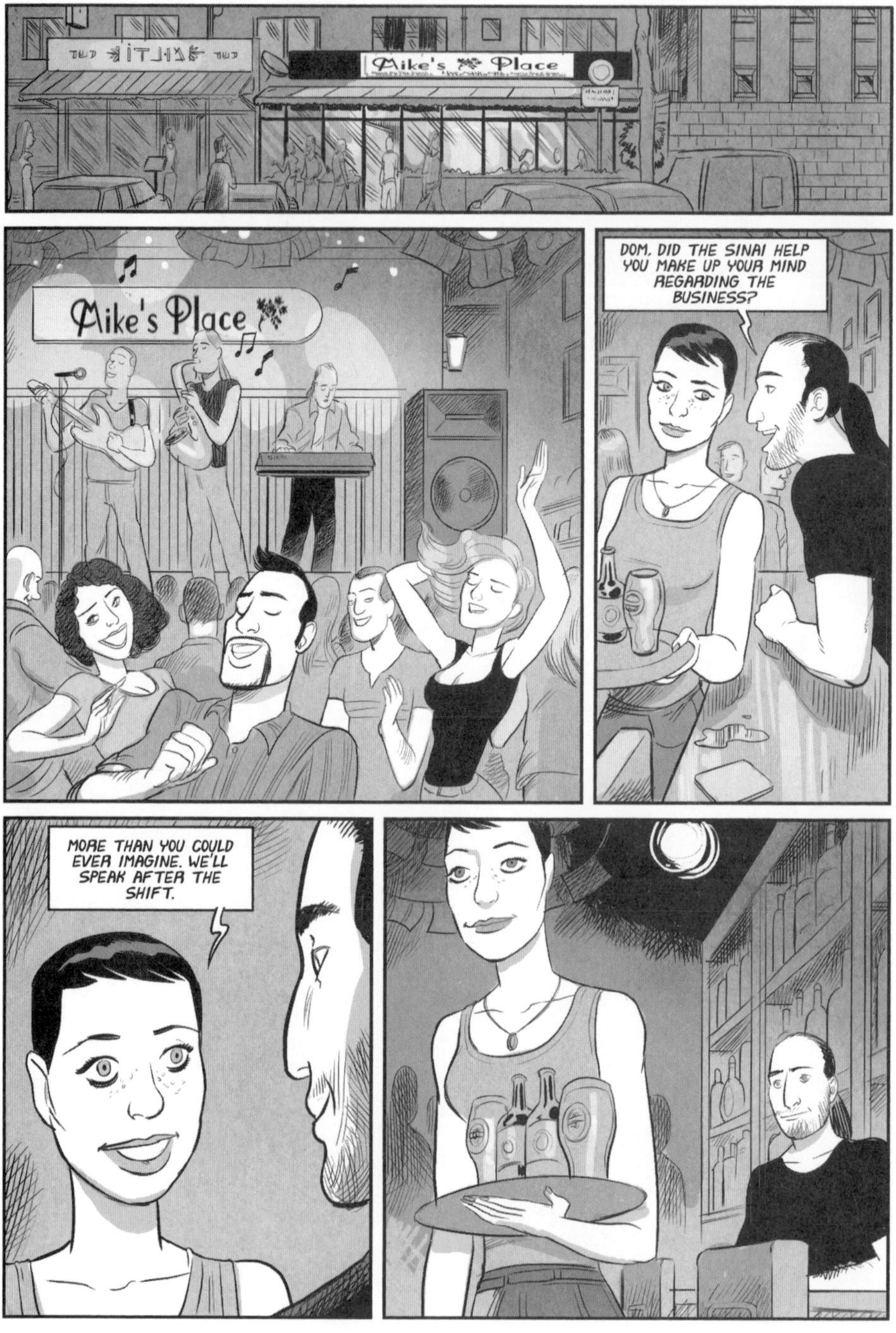
Mike's Place
Mike's Place
DOM, DID THE SINAI HELP YOU MAKE UP YOUR MIND REGARDING THE BUSINESS?
MORE THAN YOU COULD EVER IMAGINE. WE'LL SPEAK AFTER THE SHIFT.

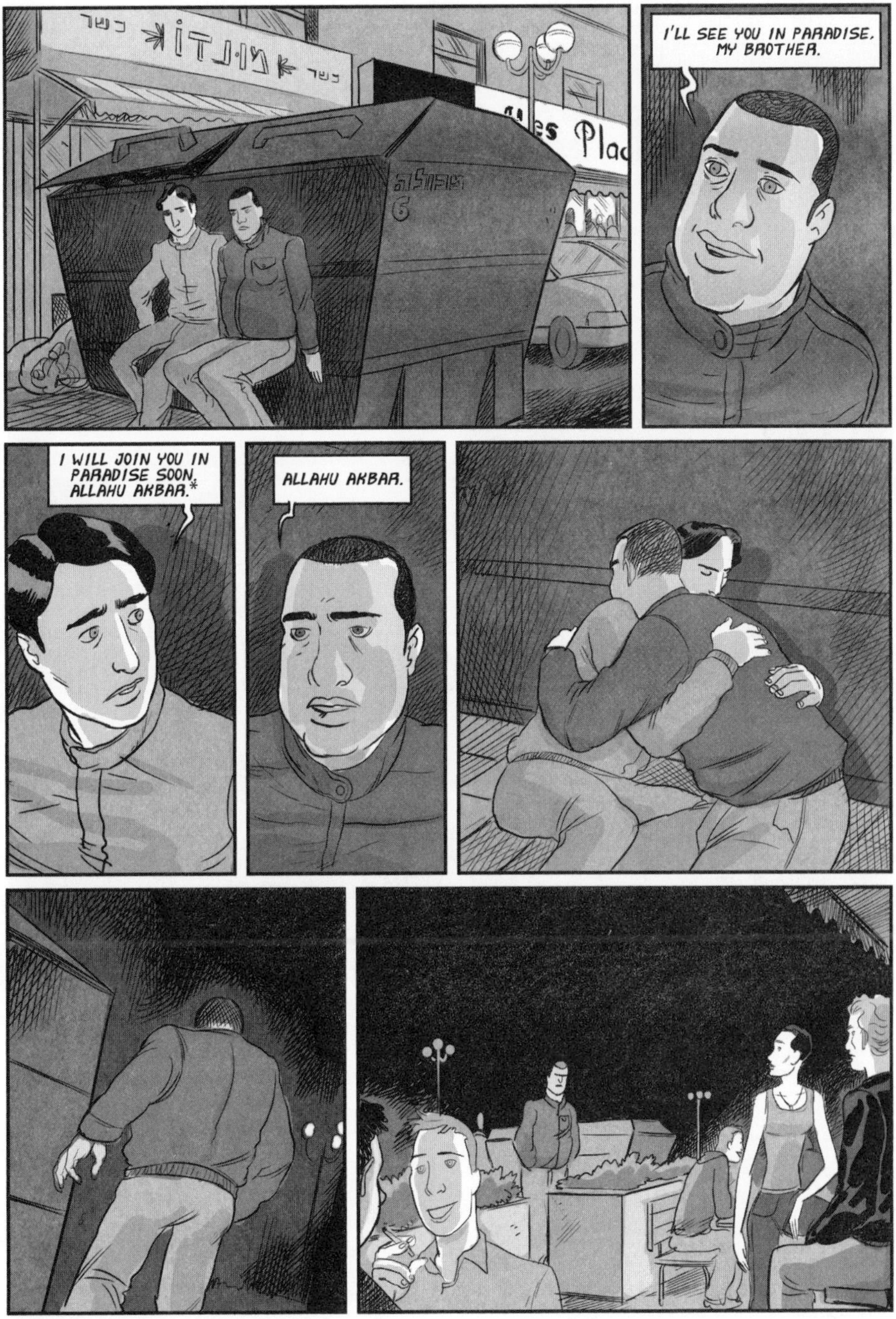
I'LL SEE YOU IN PARADISE, MY BROTHER.
I WILL JOIN YOU IN PARADISE SOON. ALLAHU AKBAR.*
ALLAHU AKBAR.

*GOD IS GREATEST.

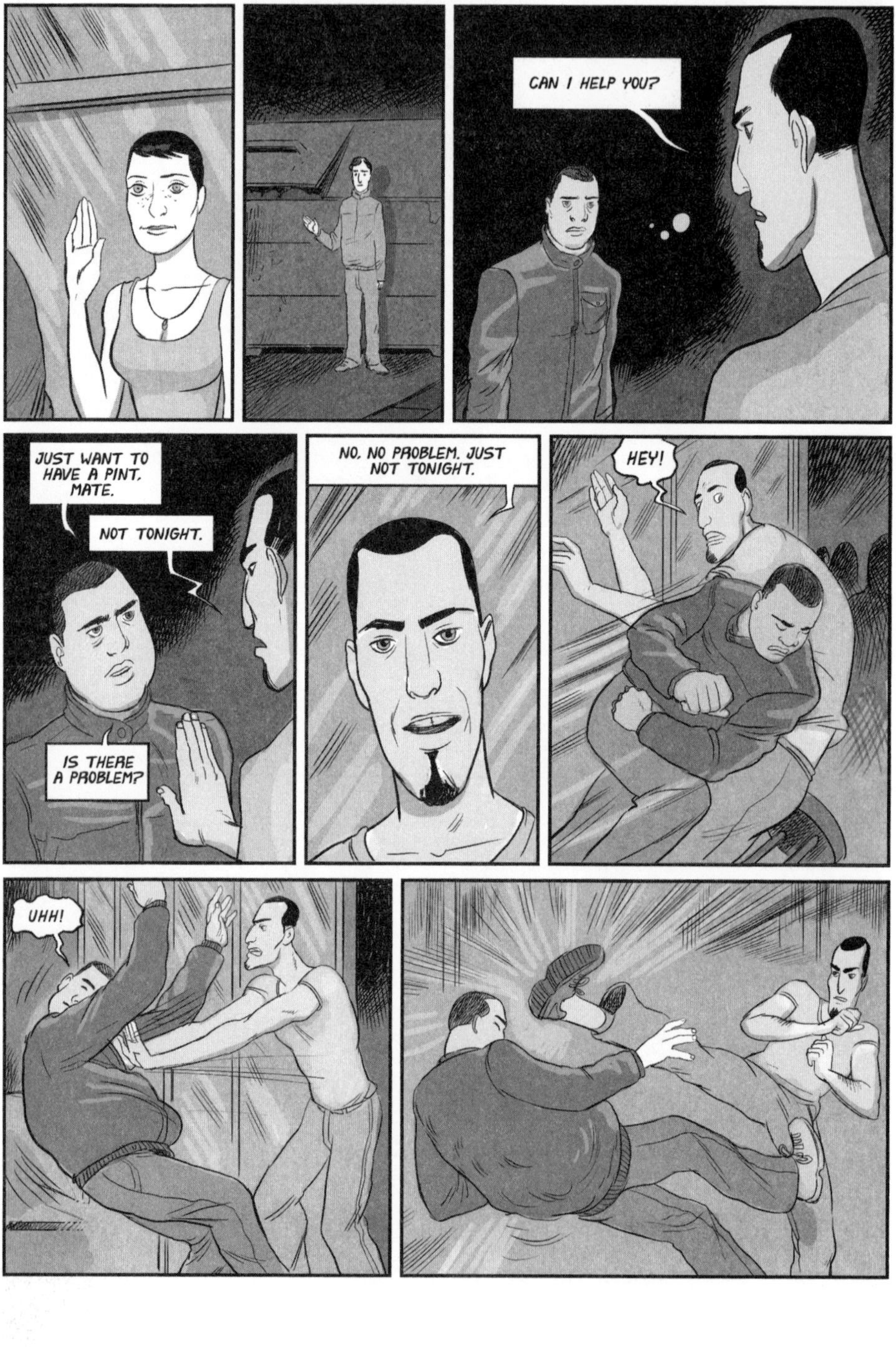
CAN I HELP YOU?
JUST WANT TO HAVE A PINT, MATE.
NOT TONIGHT.
IS THERE A PROBLEM?
NO, NO PROBLEM. JUST NOT TONIGHT.
HEY!
UHH!

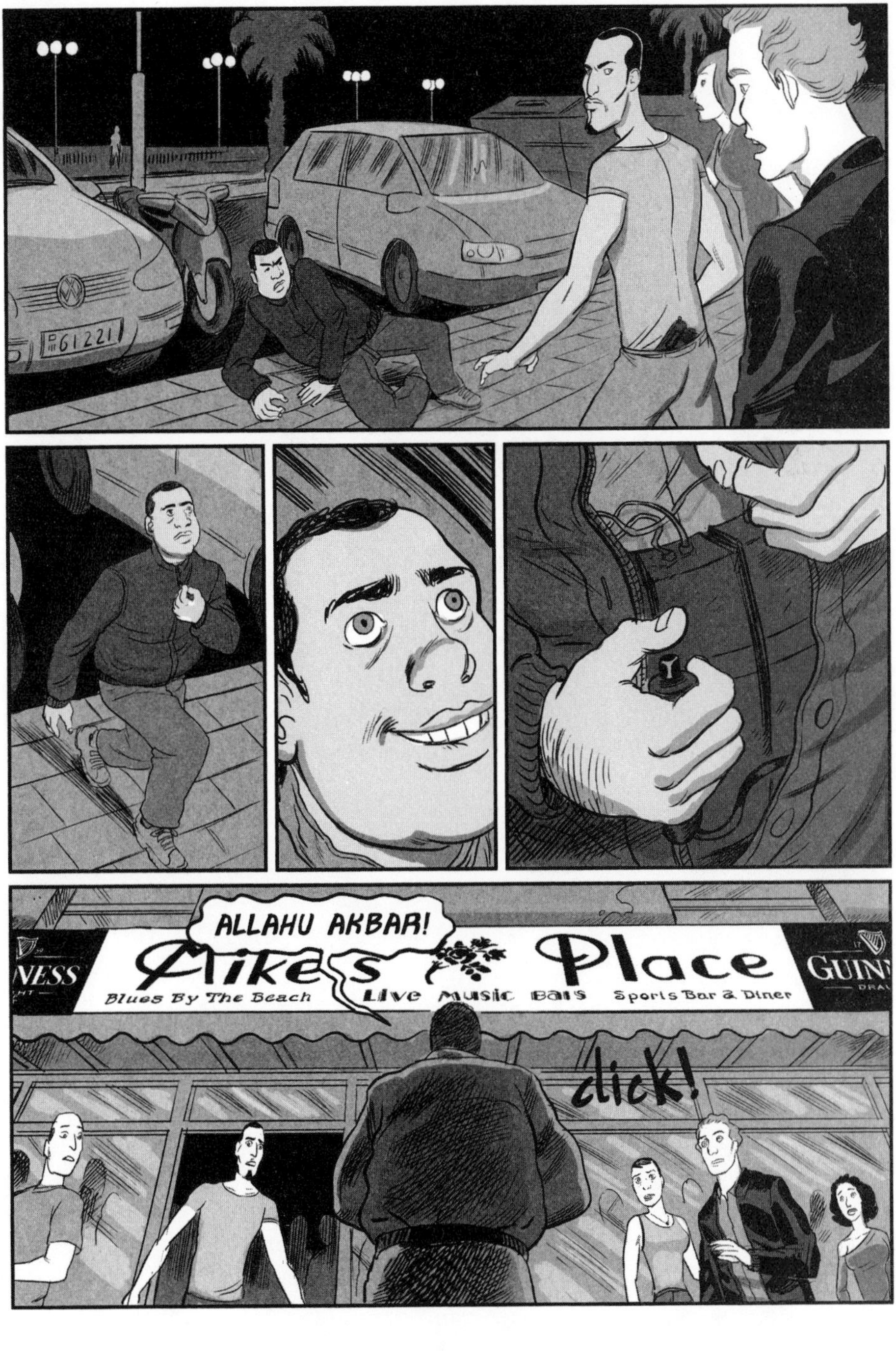
ALLAHU AKBAR!
Mike's Place
Blues By The Beach
Live Music Bars
Sports Bar & Diner
GUINNESS
click!

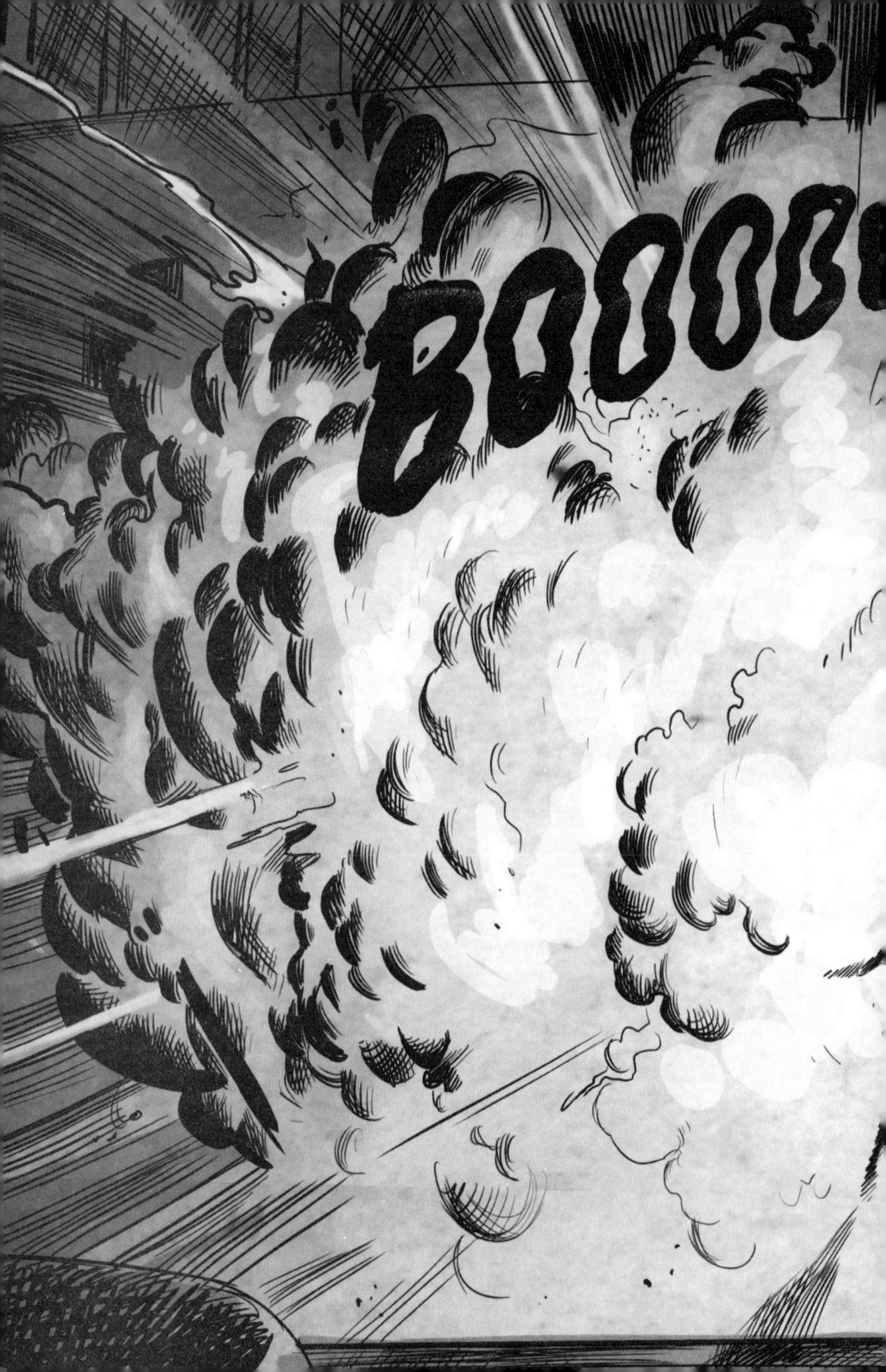
BOOOOB

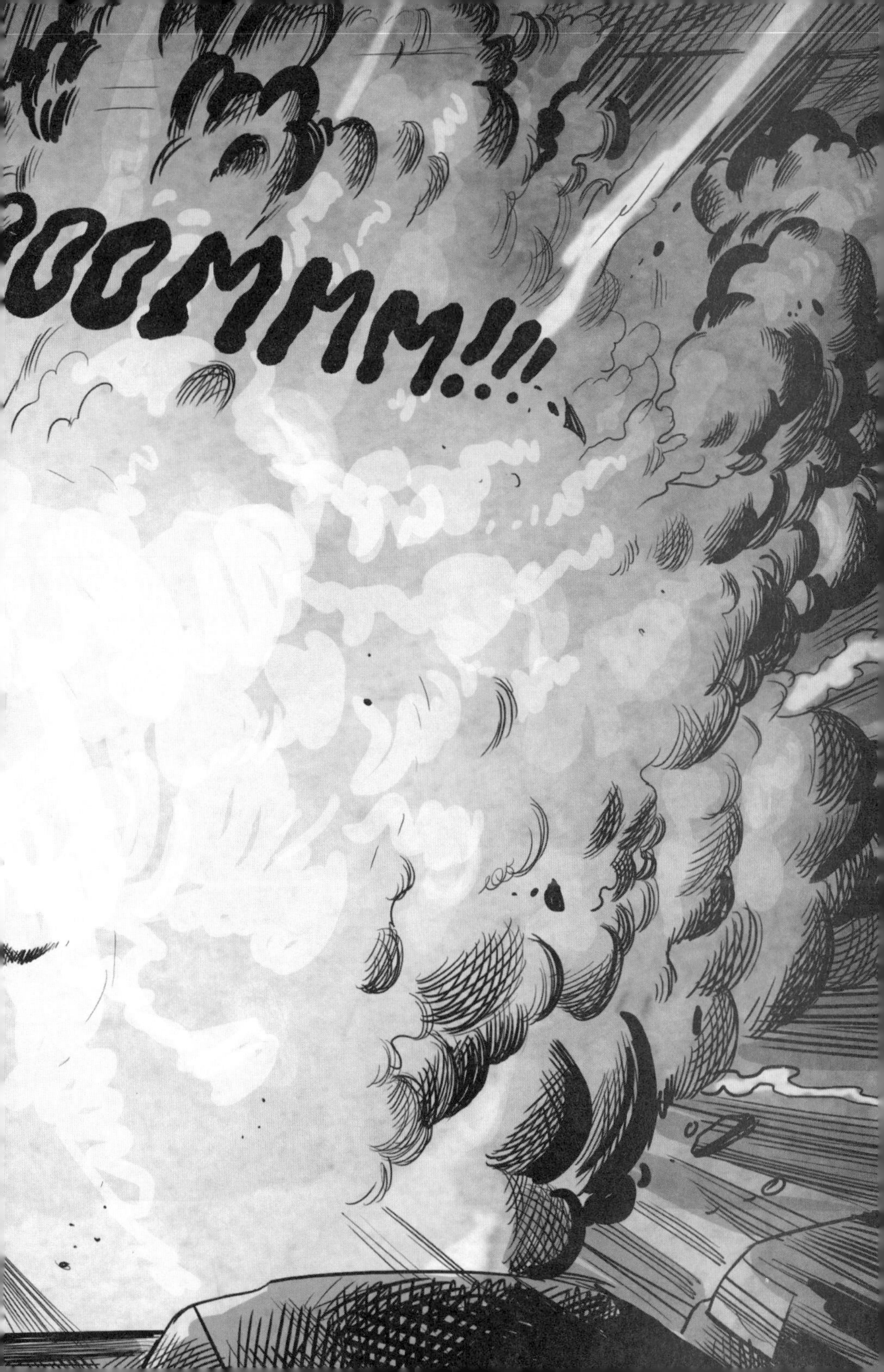
OOMMM!!!

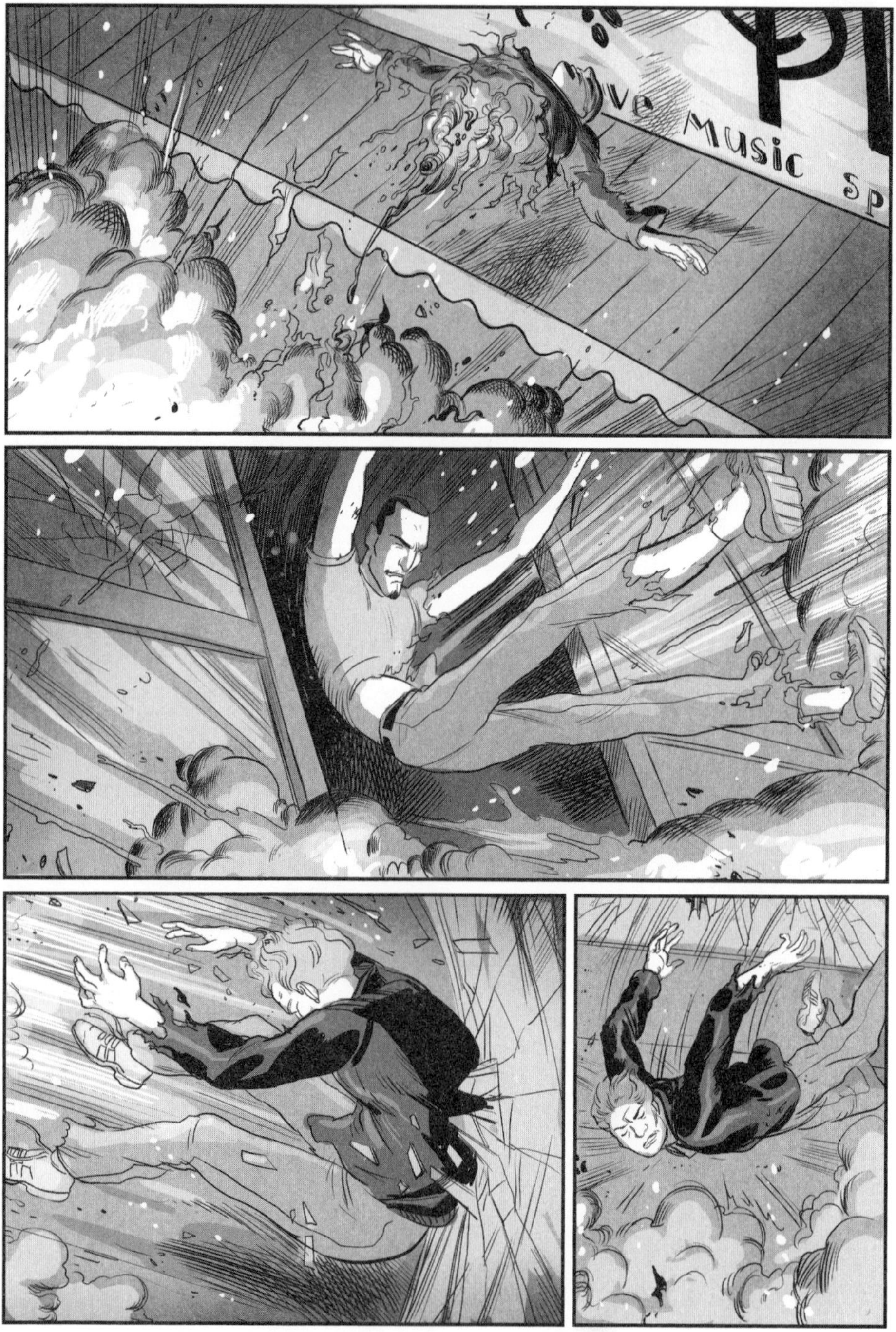
ve Music Sp

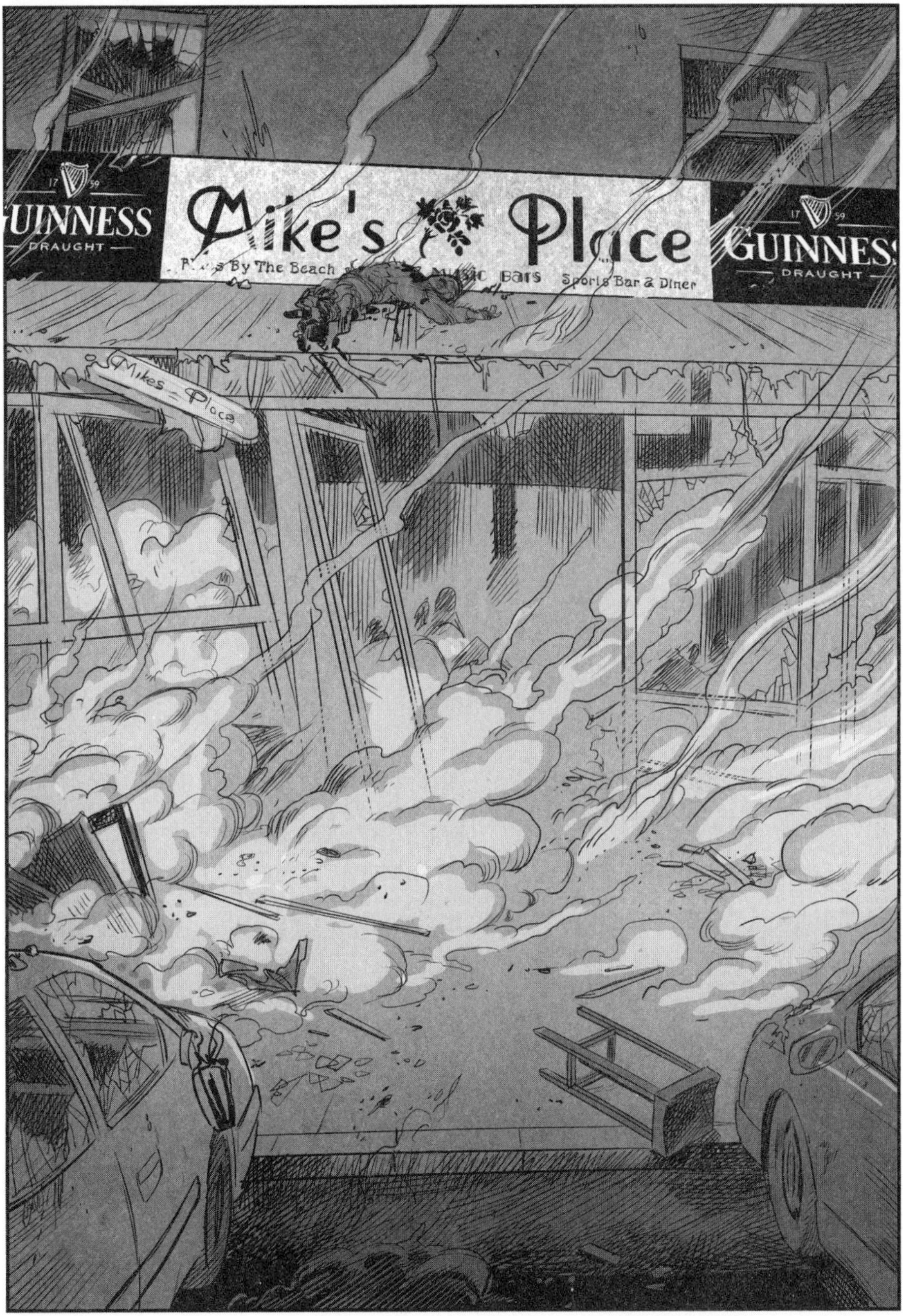

Mike's Place
By The Beach
Bars
Sports Bar & Diner
Mikes Place

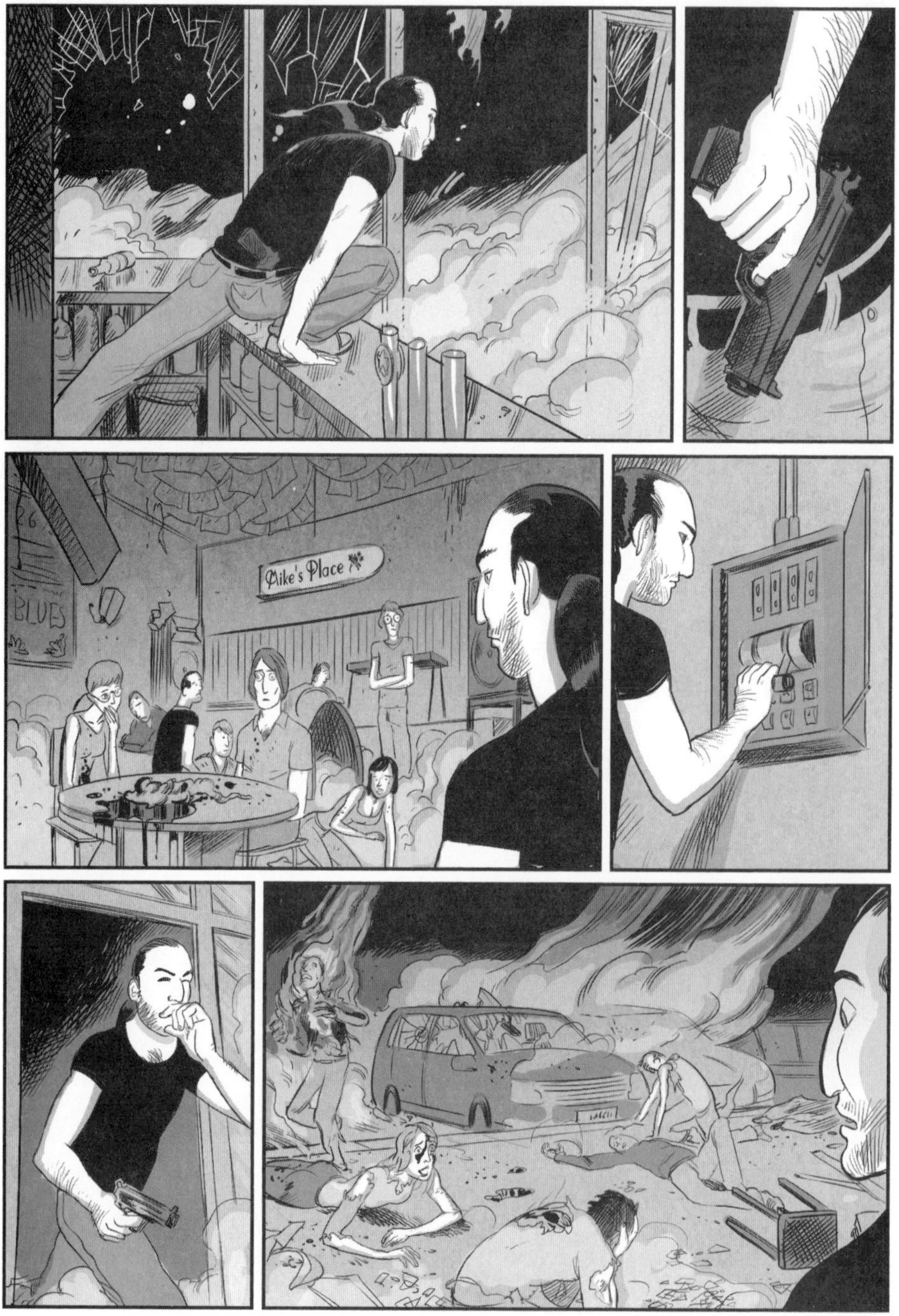
Mike's Place
BLUES

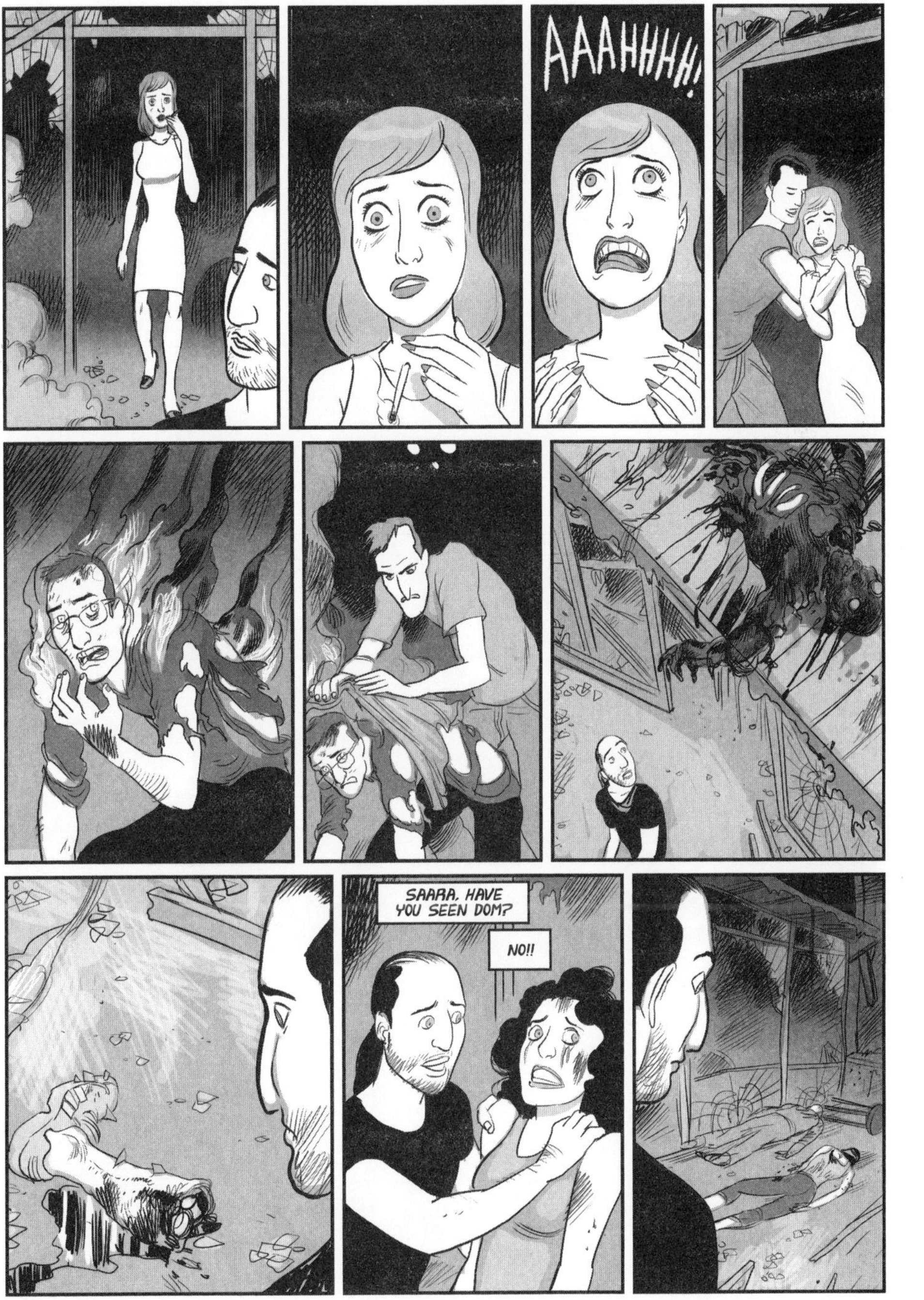
AAAHHHH!
SAARA, HAVE YOU SEEN DOM?
NO!!

DOM!

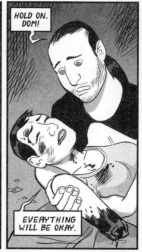

HOLD ON, DOM!

EVERYTHING WILL BE OKAY.

86

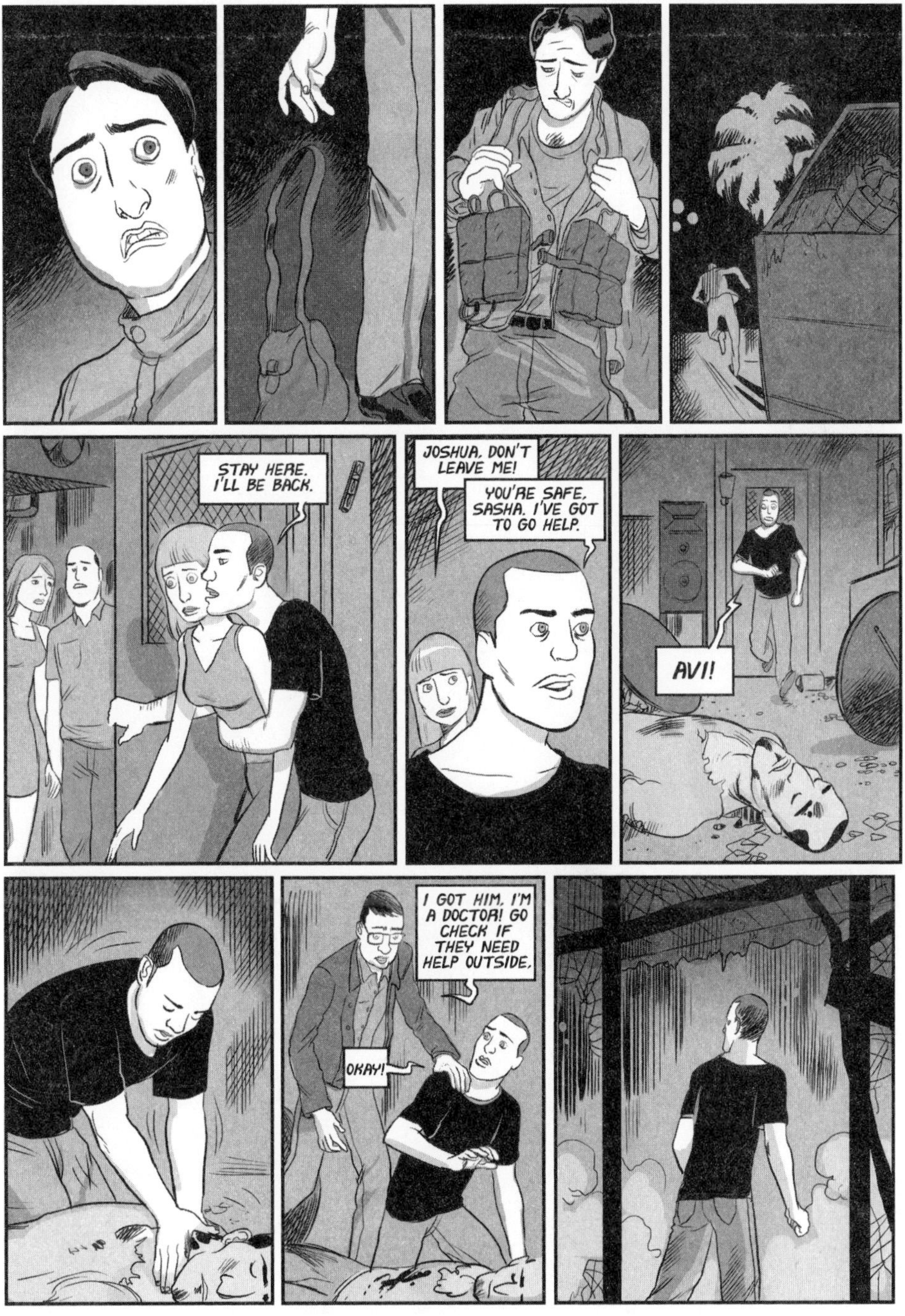
STAY HERE. I'LL BE BACK.
JOSHUA. DON'T LEAVE ME!
YOU'RE SAFE, SASHA. I'VE GOT TO GO HELP.
AVI!
I GOT HIM. I'M A DOCTOR! GO CHECK IF THEY NEED HELP OUTSIDE.
OKAY!

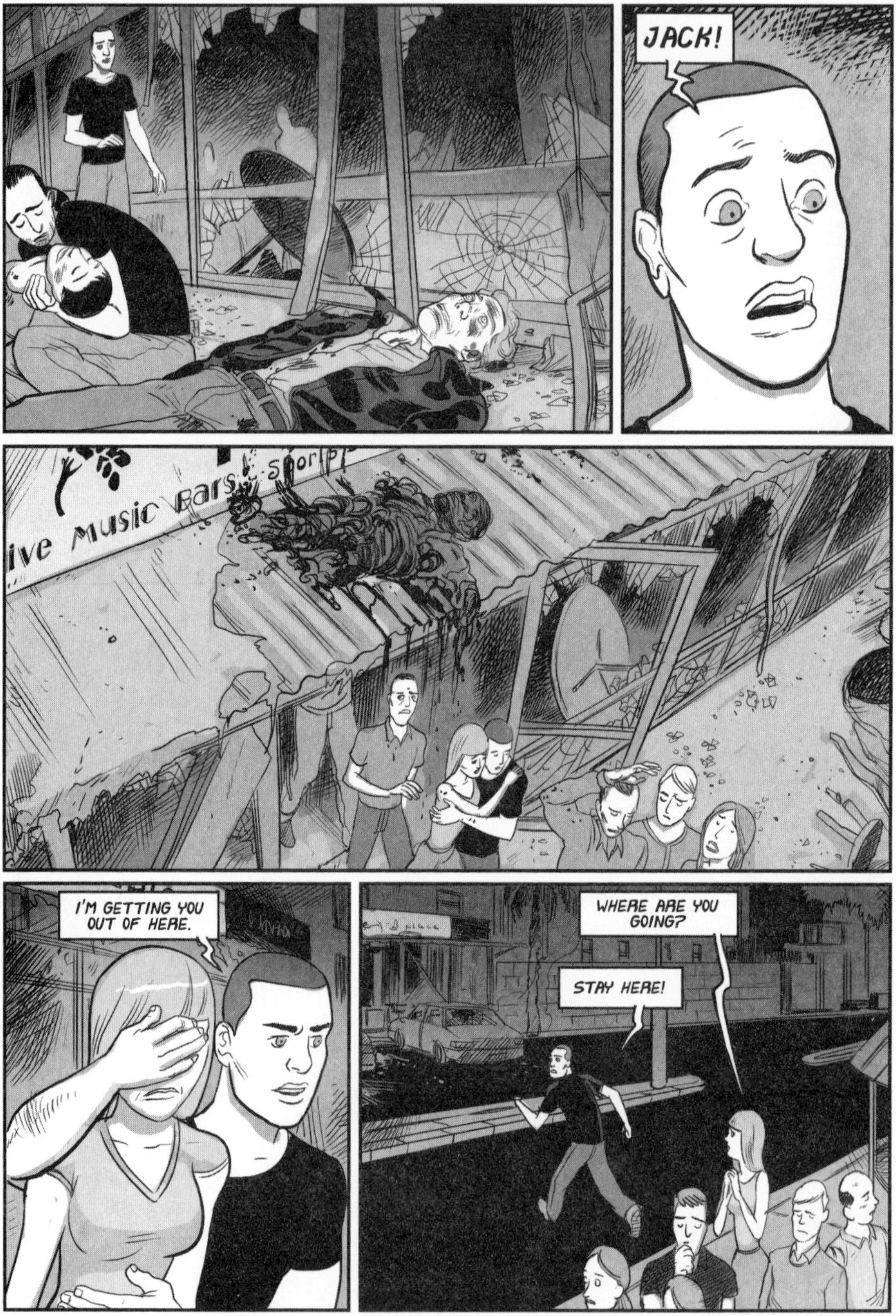
JACK!
ive Music Bars
I'M GETTING YOU OUT OF HERE.
WHERE ARE YOU GOING?
STAY HERE!

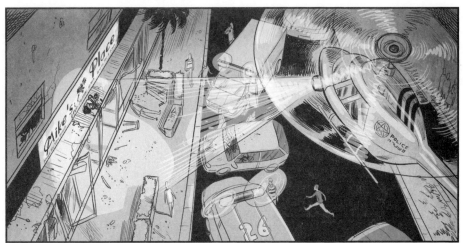

YARIV, WHAT ARE YOU DOING? GET THE HELL OUT OF HERE!

HEY, JOSHIE, WE'RE ALIVE, MAN.

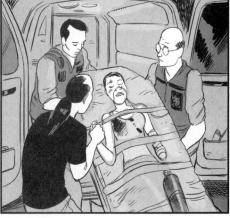

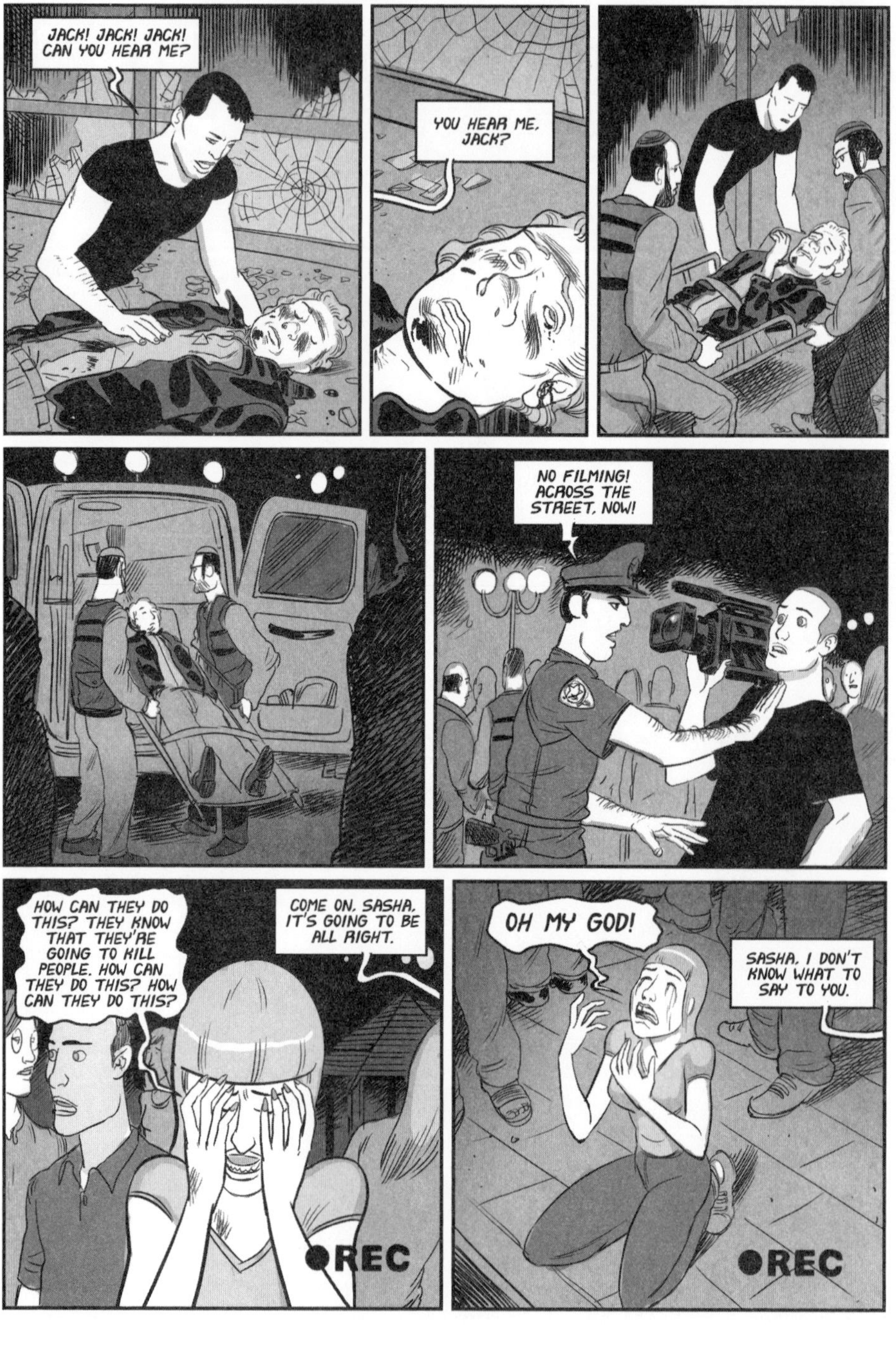
JACK! JACK! JACK! CAN YOU HEAR ME?
YOU HEAR ME, JACK?
NO FILMING! ACROSS THE STREET, NOW!
HOW CAN THEY DO THIS? THEY KNOW THAT THEY'RE GOING TO KILL PEOPLE. HOW CAN THEY DO THIS? HOW CAN THEY DO THIS?
COME ON, SASHA, IT'S GOING TO BE ALL RIGHT.
REC
OH MY GOD!
SASHA, I DON'T KNOW WHAT TO SAY TO YOU.
REC

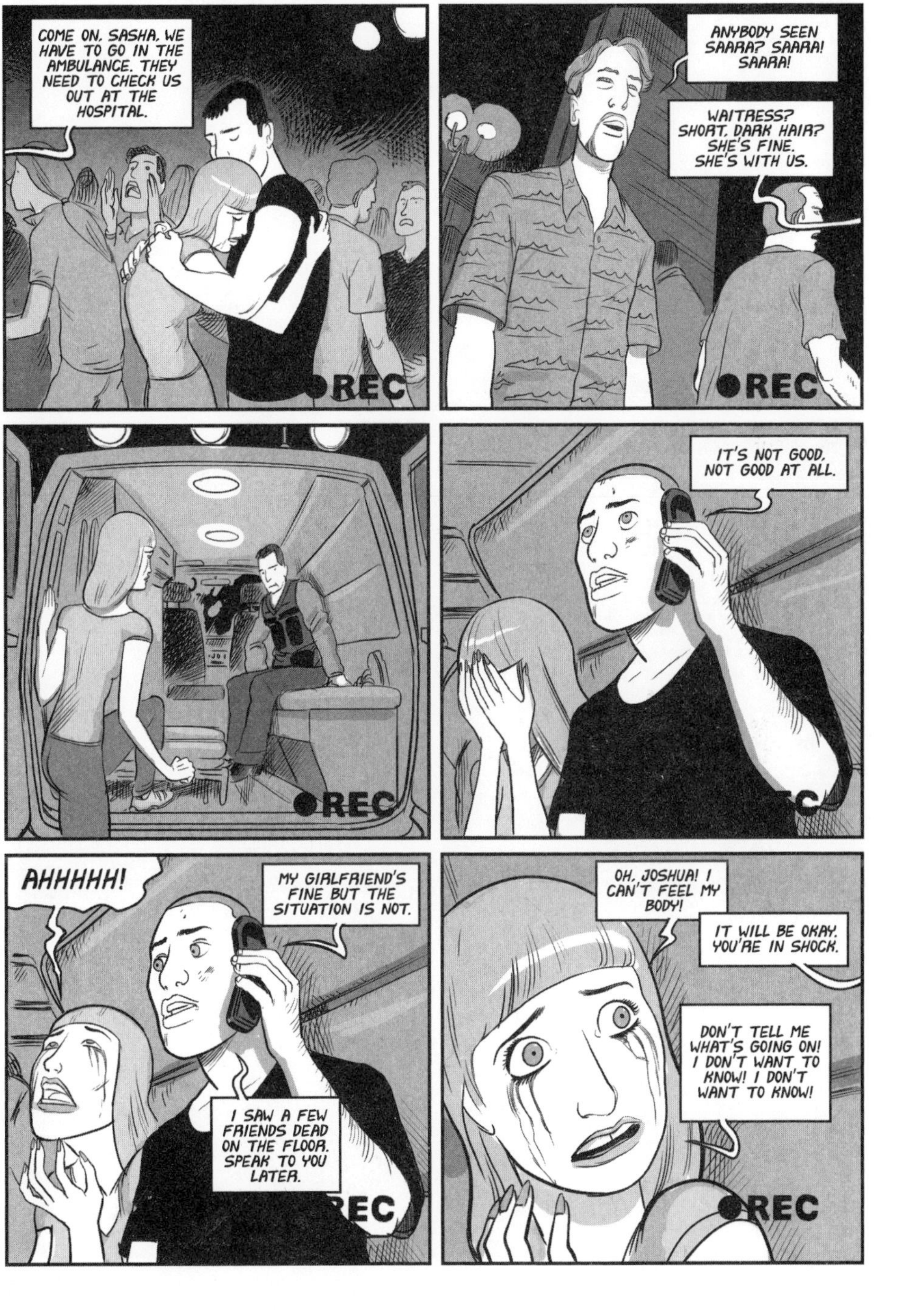

COME ON, SASHA. WE HAVE TO GO IN THE AMBULANCE. THEY NEED TO CHECK US OUT AT THE HOSPITAL.
REC
ANYBODY SEEN SAARA? SAARA! SAARA!
WAITRESS? SHORT, DARK HAIR? SHE'S FINE. SHE'S WITH US.
REC
REC
IT'S NOT GOOD, NOT GOOD AT ALL.
AHHHHH!
MY GIRLFRIEND'S FINE BUT THE SITUATION IS NOT.
I SAW A FEW FRIENDS DEAD ON THE FLOOR. SPEAK TO YOU LATER.
OH, JOSHUA! I CAN'T FEEL MY BODY!
IT WILL BE OKAY. YOU'RE IN SHOCK.
DON'T TELL ME WHAT'S GOING ON! I DON'T WANT TO KNOW! I DON'T WANT TO KNOW!
REC

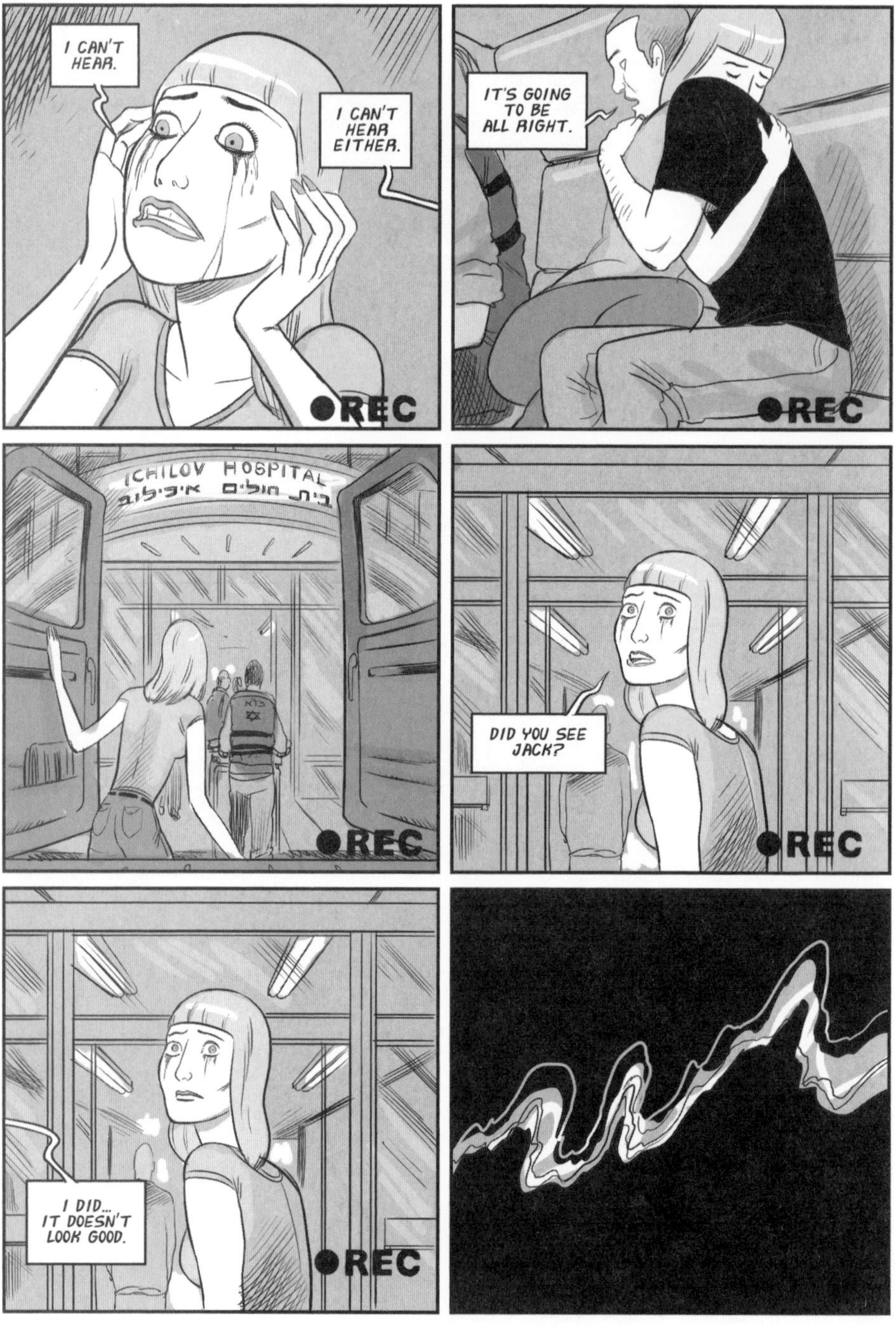
I CAN'T HEAR.
I CAN'T HEAR EITHER.
●REC
IT'S GOING TO BE ALL RIGHT.
●REC
ICHILOV HOSPITAL
בית חולים איכילוב
●REC
DID YOU SEE JACK?
●REC
I DID... IT DOESN'T LOOK GOOD.
●REC

IV

". . . Let them forgive and overlook, do you not wish that
Allah should forgive you?"

—Qur'an

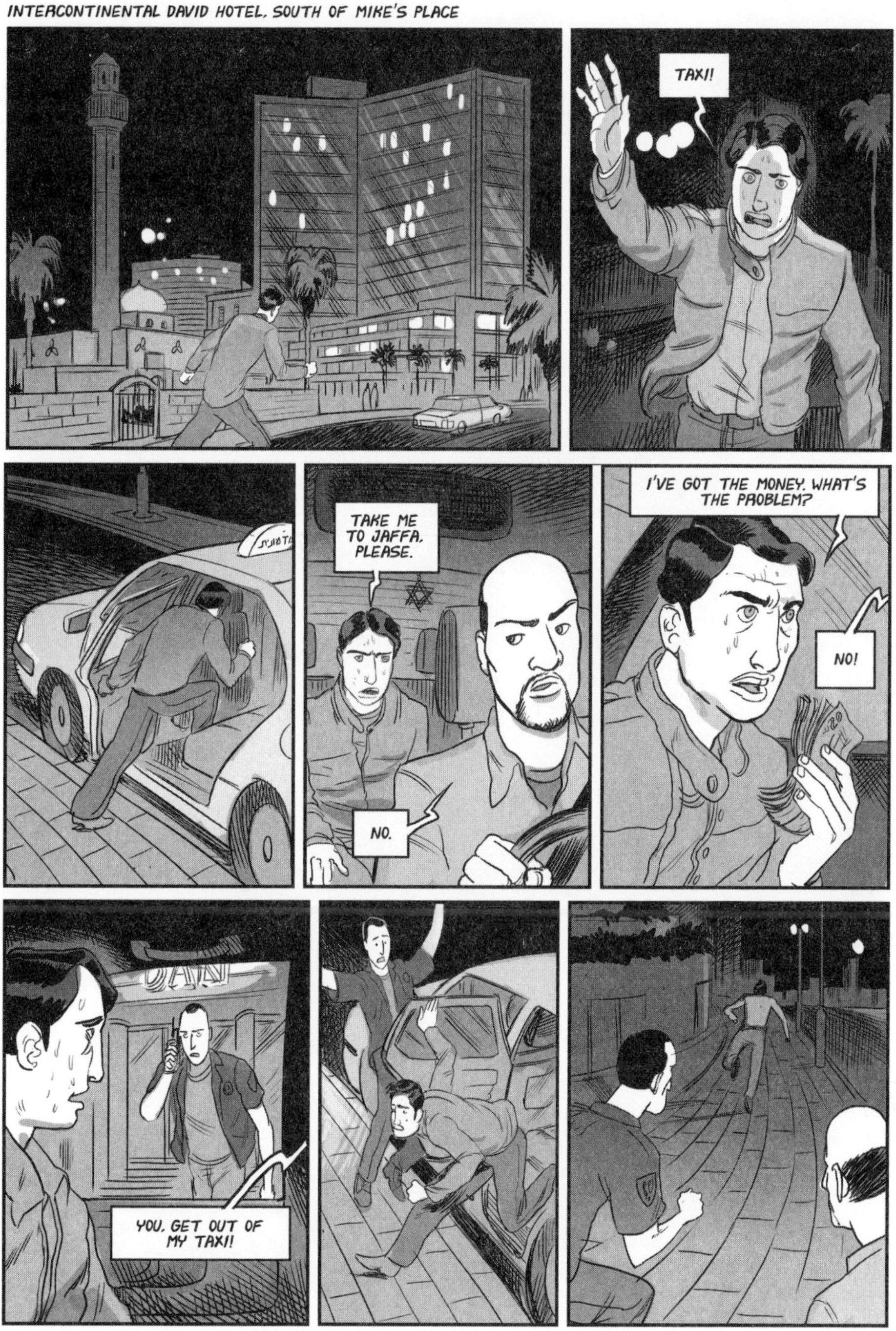

INTERCONTINENTAL DAVID HOTEL, SOUTH OF MIKE'S PLACE
TAXI!
TAKE ME TO JAFFA, PLEASE.
NO.
I'VE GOT THE MONEY. WHAT'S THE PROBLEM?
NO!
YOU, GET OUT OF MY TAXI!

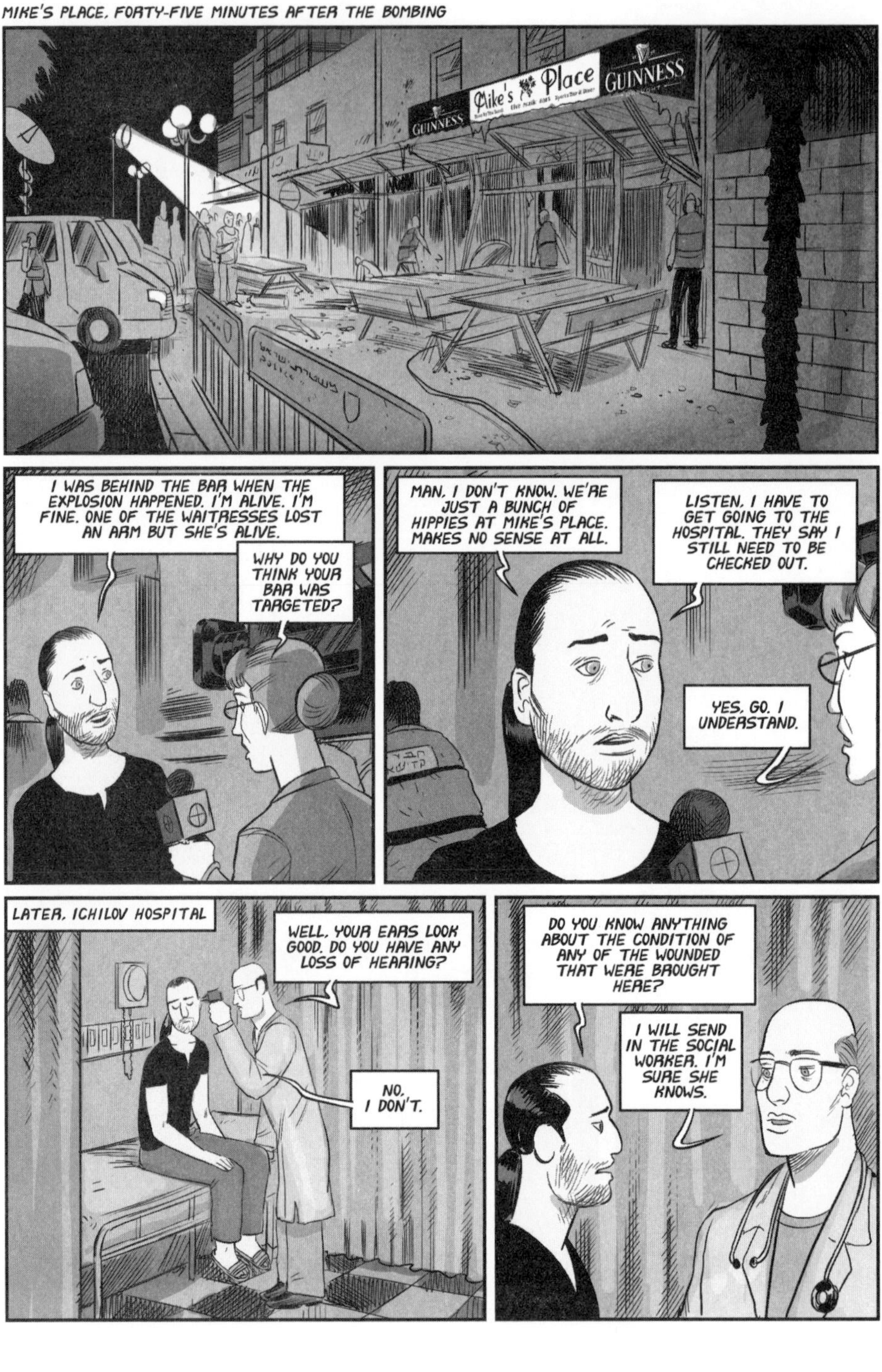
MIKE'S PLACE, FORTY-FIVE MINUTES AFTER THE BOMBING
GUINNESS
Mike's Place
GUINNESS
POLICE
I WAS BEHIND THE BAR WHEN THE EXPLOSION HAPPENED. I'M ALIVE. I'M FINE. ONE OF THE WAITRESSES LOST AN ARM BUT SHE'S ALIVE.
WHY DO YOU THINK YOUR BAR WAS TARGETED?
MAN, I DON'T KNOW. WE'RE JUST A BUNCH OF HIPPIES AT MIKE'S PLACE. MAKES NO SENSE AT ALL.
LISTEN, I HAVE TO GET GOING TO THE HOSPITAL. THEY SAY I STILL NEED TO BE CHECKED OUT.
YES, GO. I UNDERSTAND.
LATER, ICHILOV HOSPITAL
WELL, YOUR EARS LOOK GOOD. DO YOU HAVE ANY LOSS OF HEARING?
NO, I DON'T.
DO YOU KNOW ANYTHING ABOUT THE CONDITION OF ANY OF THE WOUNDED THAT WERE BROUGHT HERE?
I WILL SEND IN THE SOCIAL WORKER. I'M SURE SHE KNOWS.

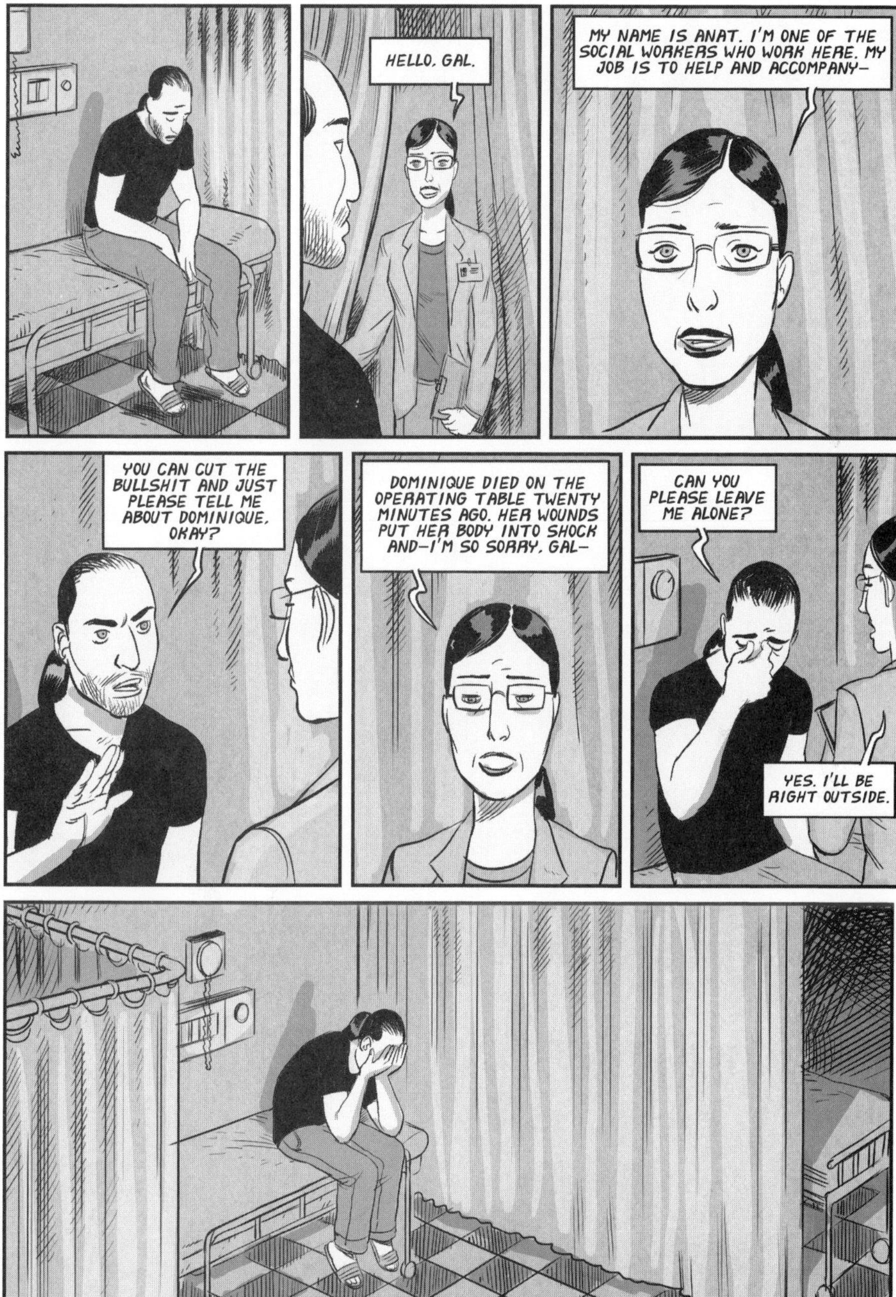
HELLO, GAL.
MY NAME IS ANAT. I'M ONE OF THE SOCIAL WORKERS WHO WORK HERE. MY JOB IS TO HELP AND ACCOMPANY–
YOU CAN CUT THE BULLSHIT AND JUST PLEASE TELL ME ABOUT DOMINIQUE, OKAY?
DOMINIQUE DIED ON THE OPERATING TABLE TWENTY MINUTES AGO. HER WOUNDS PUT HER BODY INTO SHOCK AND–I'M SO SORRY, GAL–
CAN YOU PLEASE LEAVE ME ALONE?
YES. I'LL BE RIGHT OUTSIDE.

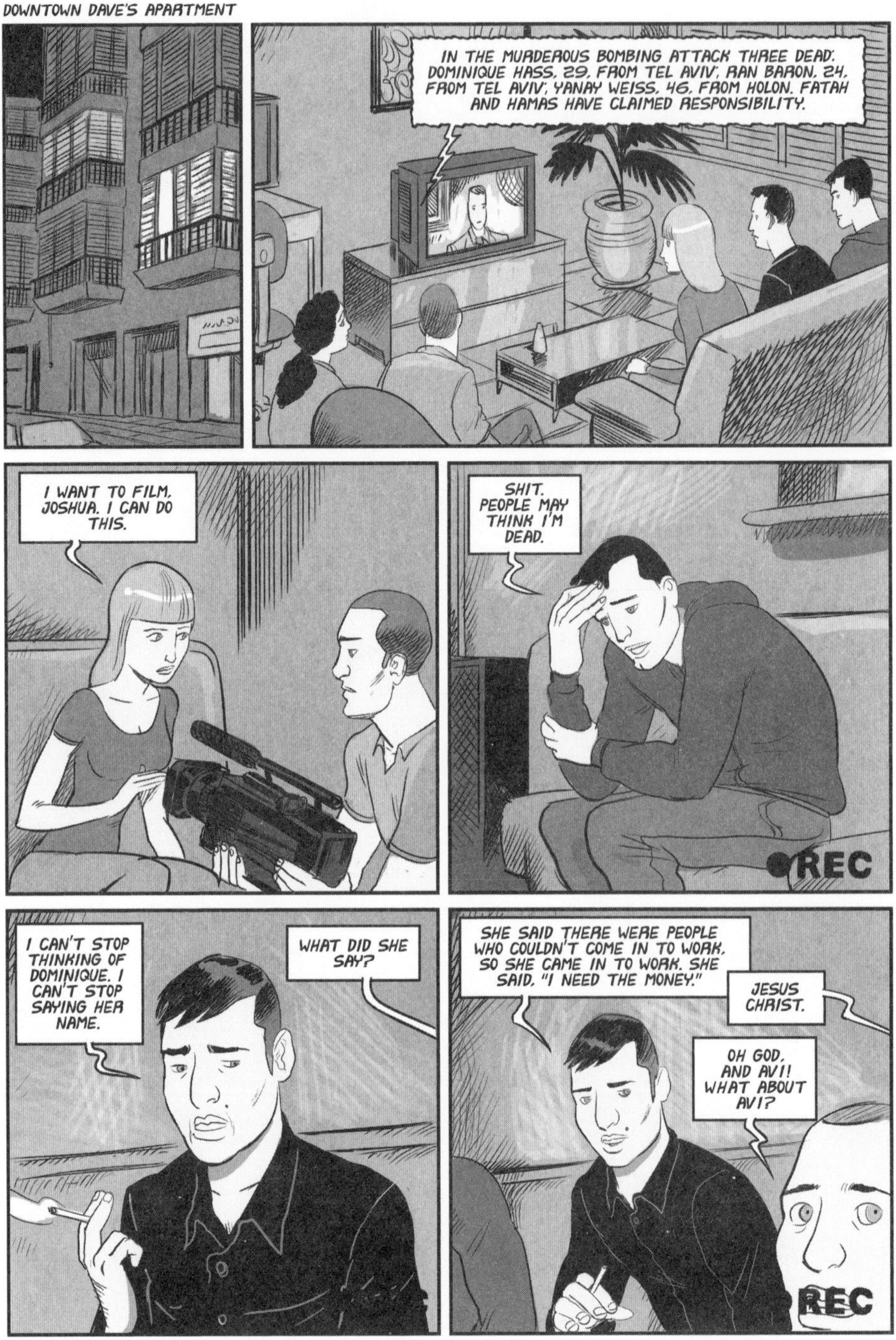
DOWNTOWN DAVE'S APARTMENT
IN THE MURDEROUS BOMBING ATTACK THREE DEAD: DOMINIQUE HASS, 29, FROM TEL AVIV; RAN BARON, 24, FROM TEL AVIV; YANAY WEISS, 46, FROM HOLON. FATAH AND HAMAS HAVE CLAIMED RESPONSIBILITY.
I WANT TO FILM, JOSHUA. I CAN DO THIS.
SHIT. PEOPLE MAY THINK I'M DEAD.
REC
I CAN'T STOP THINKING OF DOMINIQUE. I CAN'T STOP SAYING HER NAME.
WHAT DID SHE SAY?
SHE SAID THERE WERE PEOPLE WHO COULDN'T COME IN TO WORK, SO SHE CAME IN TO WORK. SHE SAID, "I NEED THE MONEY."
JESUS CHRIST.
OH GOD, AND AVI! WHAT ABOUT AVI?
REC

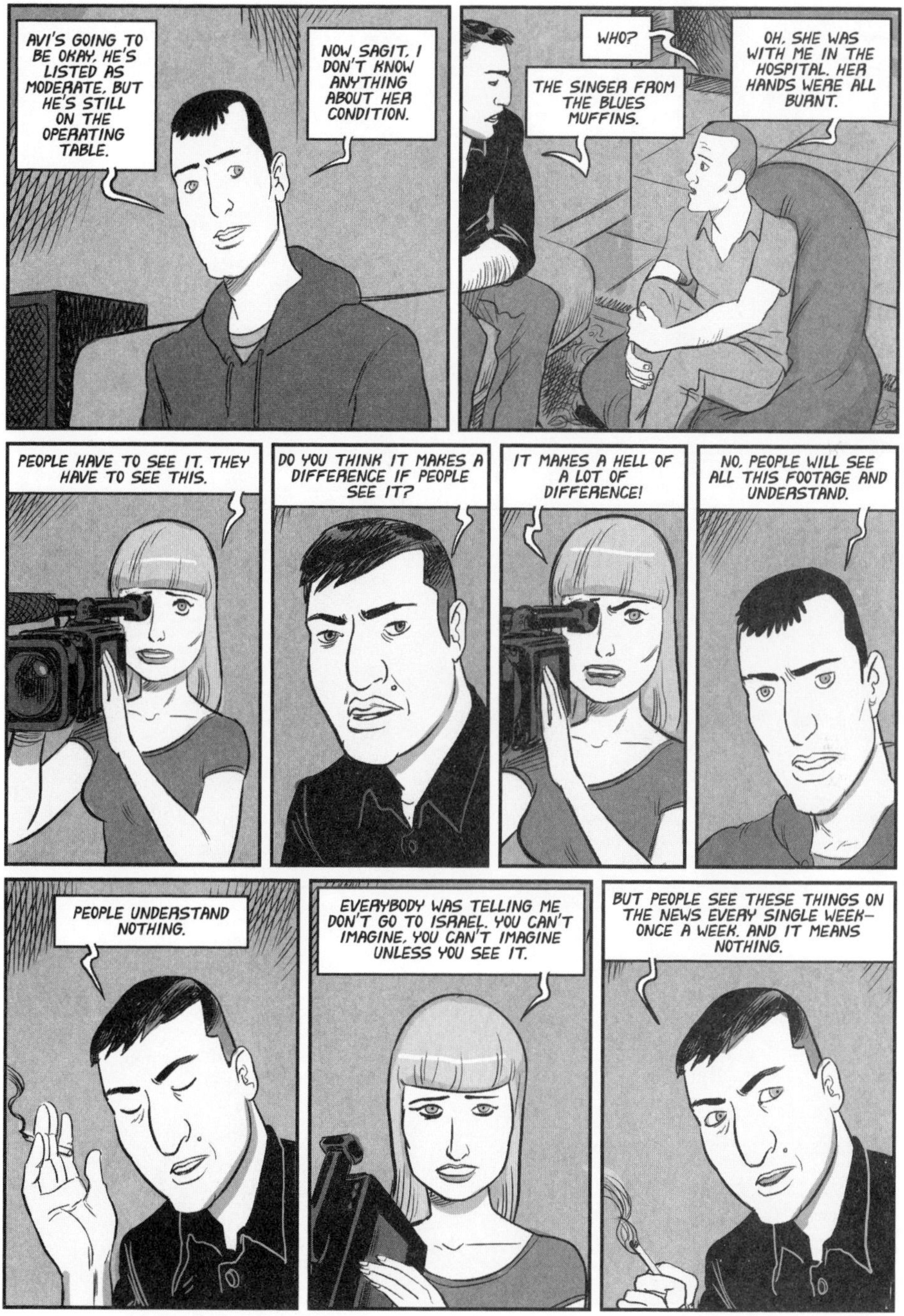
AVI'S GOING TO BE OKAY. HE'S LISTED AS MODERATE, BUT HE'S STILL ON THE OPERATING TABLE.
NOW SAGIT, I DON'T KNOW ANYTHING ABOUT HER CONDITION.
WHO?
THE SINGER FROM THE BLUES MUFFINS.
OH, SHE WAS WITH ME IN THE HOSPITAL. HER HANDS WERE ALL BURNT.
PEOPLE HAVE TO SEE IT. THEY HAVE TO SEE THIS.
DO YOU THINK IT MAKES A DIFFERENCE IF PEOPLE SEE IT?
IT MAKES A HELL OF A LOT OF DIFFERENCE!
NO, PEOPLE WILL SEE ALL THIS FOOTAGE AND UNDERSTAND.
PEOPLE UNDERSTAND NOTHING.
EVERYBODY WAS TELLING ME DON'T GO TO ISRAEL. YOU CAN'T IMAGINE, YOU CAN'T IMAGINE UNLESS YOU SEE IT.
BUT PEOPLE SEE THESE THINGS ON THE NEWS EVERY SINGLE WEEK—ONCE A WEEK. AND IT MEANS NOTHING.

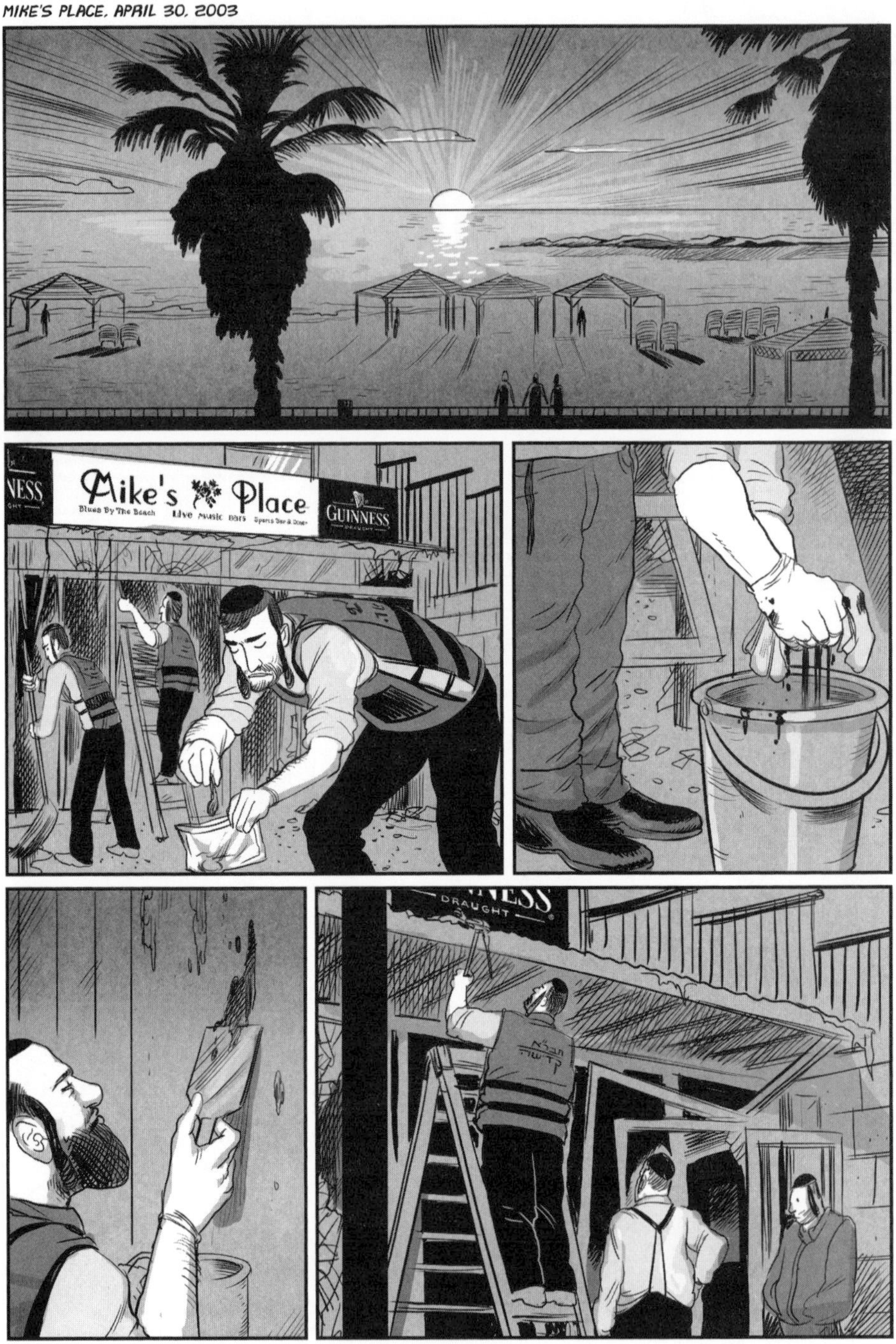
MIKE'S PLACE, APRIL 30, 2003
Mike's Place
Blues By The Beach
Live Music Bars
GUINNESS
DRAUGHT

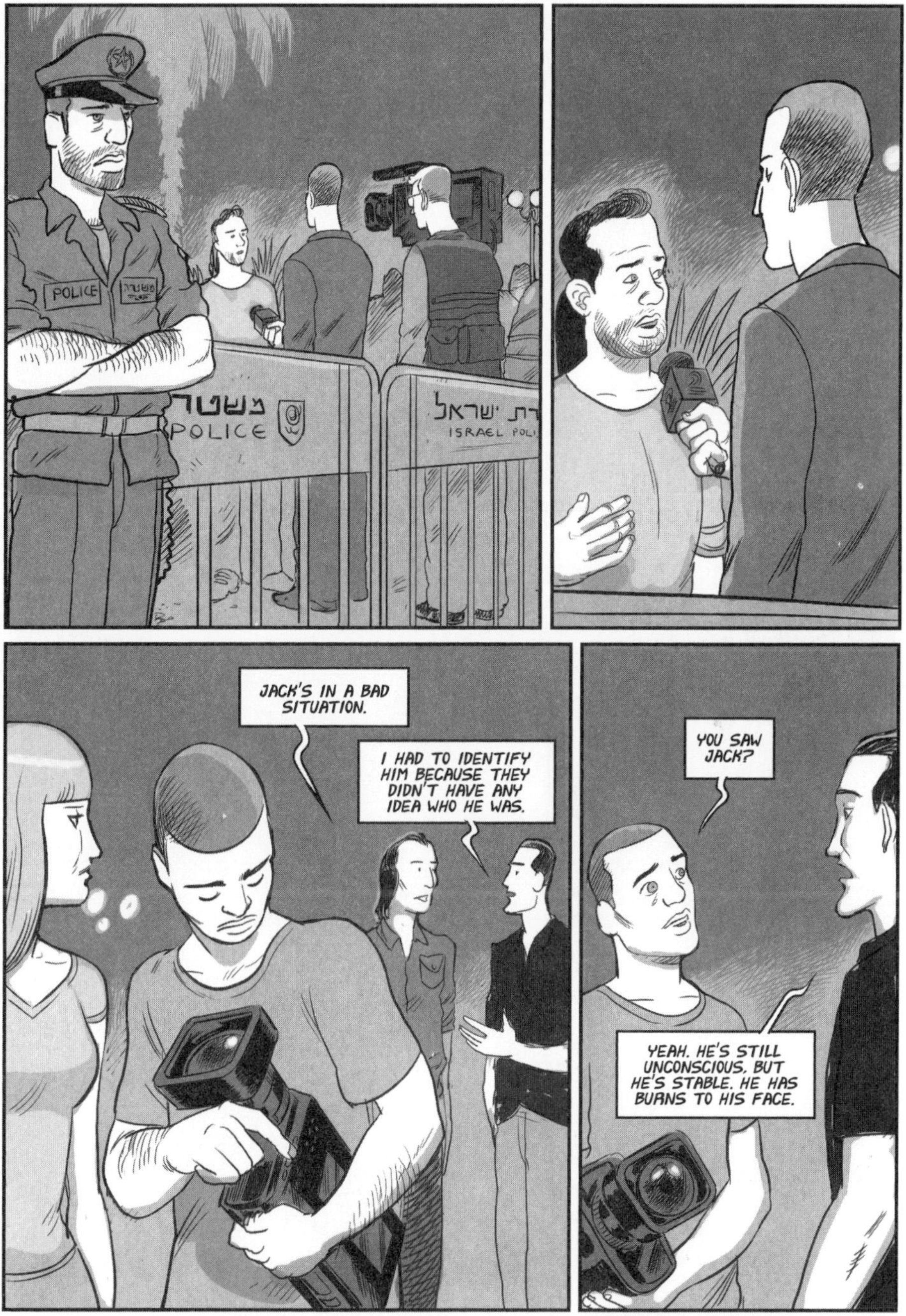
POLICE
משטר
POLICE
JACK'S IN A BAD SITUATION.
I HAD TO IDENTIFY HIM BECAUSE THEY DIDN'T HAVE ANY IDEA WHO HE WAS.
YOU SAW JACK?
YEAH. HE'S STILL UNCONSCIOUS, BUT HE'S STABLE. HE HAS BURNS TO HIS FACE.

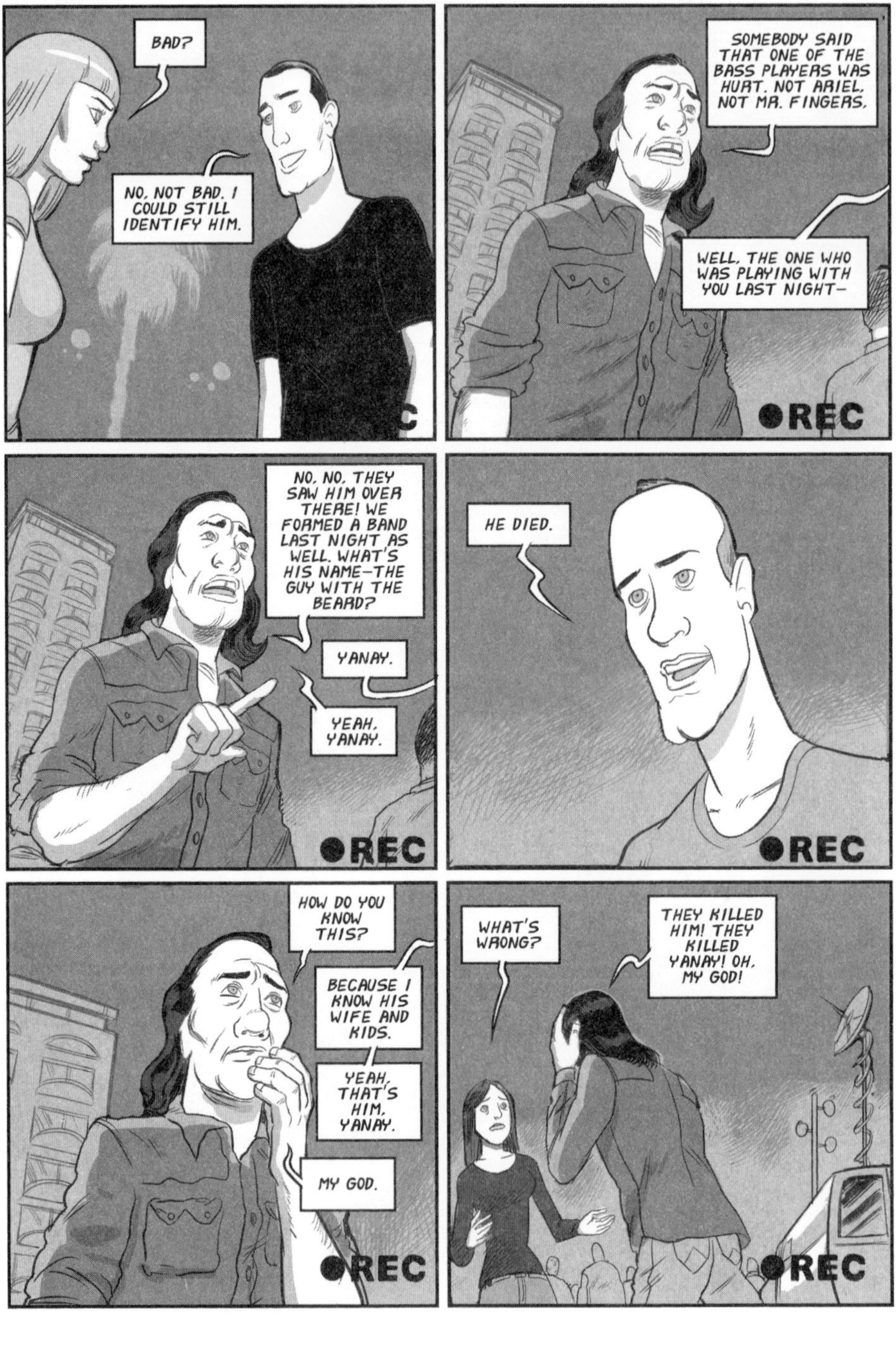
BAD?
NO, NOT BAD. I COULD STILL IDENTIFY HIM.
SOMEBODY SAID THAT ONE OF THE BASS PLAYERS WAS HURT. NOT ARIEL, NOT MR. FINGERS.
WELL, THE ONE WHO WAS PLAYING WITH YOU LAST NIGHT—
REC
NO, NO, THEY SAW HIM OVER THERE! WE FORMED A BAND LAST NIGHT AS WELL. WHAT'S HIS NAME—THE GUY WITH THE BEARD?
YANAY.
YEAH, YANAY.
REC
HE DIED.
REC
HOW DO YOU KNOW THIS?
BECAUSE I KNOW HIS WIFE AND KIDS.
YEAH, THAT'S HIM, YANAY.
MY GOD.
REC
WHAT'S WRONG?
THEY KILLED HIM! THEY KILLED YANAY! OH, MY GOD!
REC

GAL'S APARTMENT, MORNING

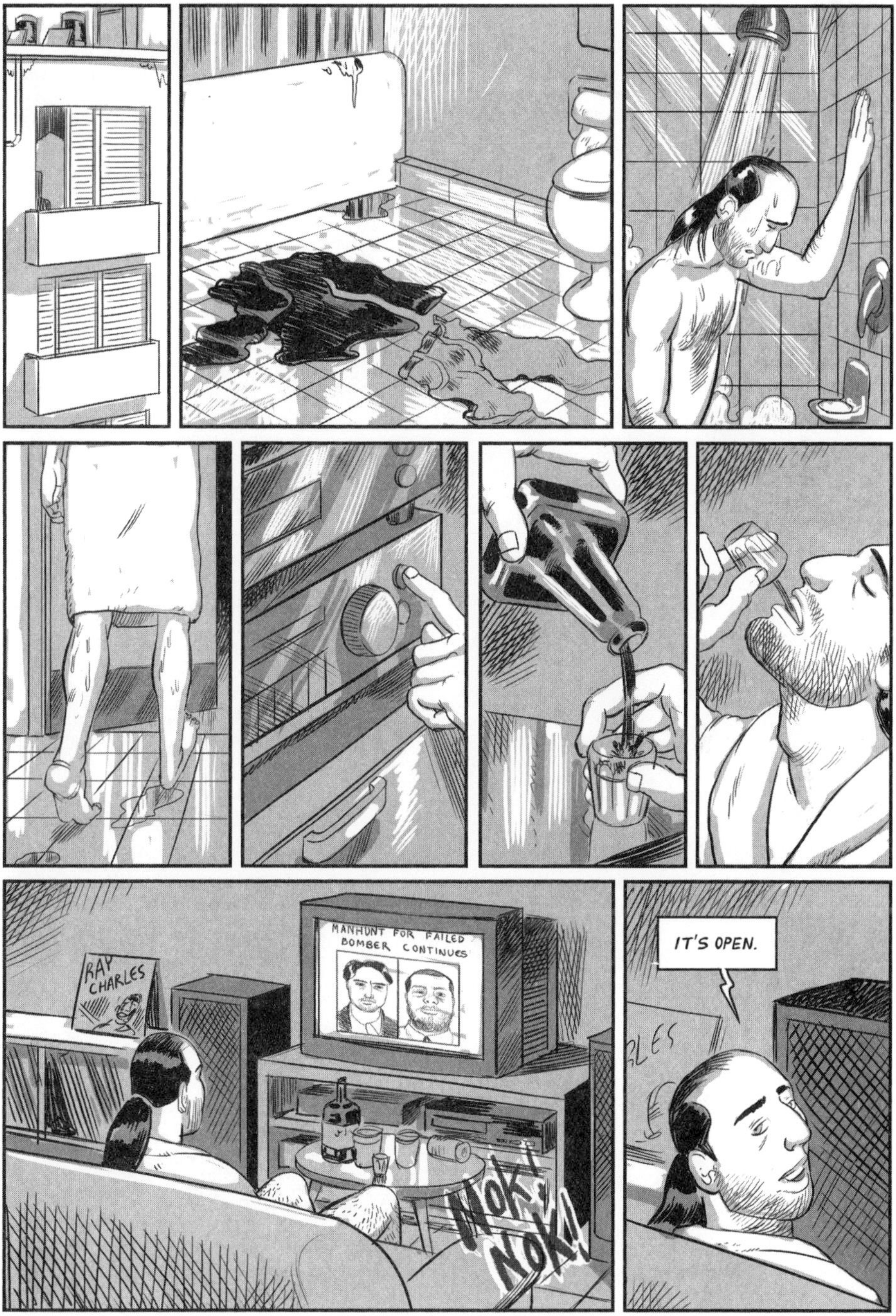

MANHUNT FOR FAILED BOMBER CONTINUES
RAY CHARLES
NOK! NOK!
IT'S OPEN.

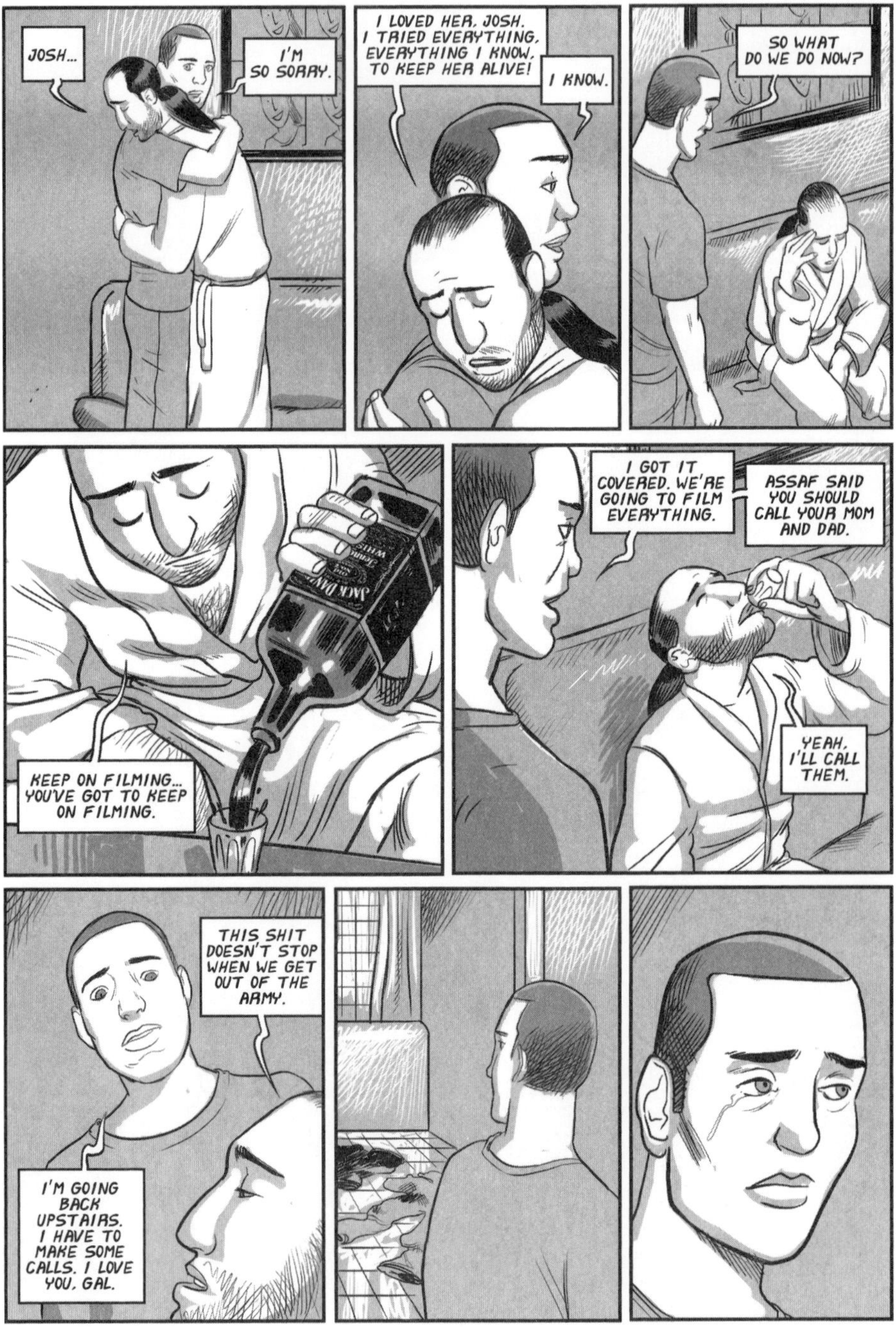
JOSH...
I'M SO SORRY.
I LOVED HER, JOSH. I TRIED EVERYTHING, EVERYTHING I KNOW, TO KEEP HER ALIVE!
I KNOW.
SO WHAT DO WE DO NOW?
KEEP ON FILMING... YOU'VE GOT TO KEEP ON FILMING.
I GOT IT COVERED. WE'RE GOING TO FILM EVERYTHING.
ASSAF SAID YOU SHOULD CALL YOUR MOM AND DAD.
YEAH, I'LL CALL THEM.
THIS SHIT DOESN'T STOP WHEN WE GET OUT OF THE ARMY.
I'M GOING BACK UPSTAIRS. I HAVE TO MAKE SOME CALLS. I LOVE YOU, GAL.

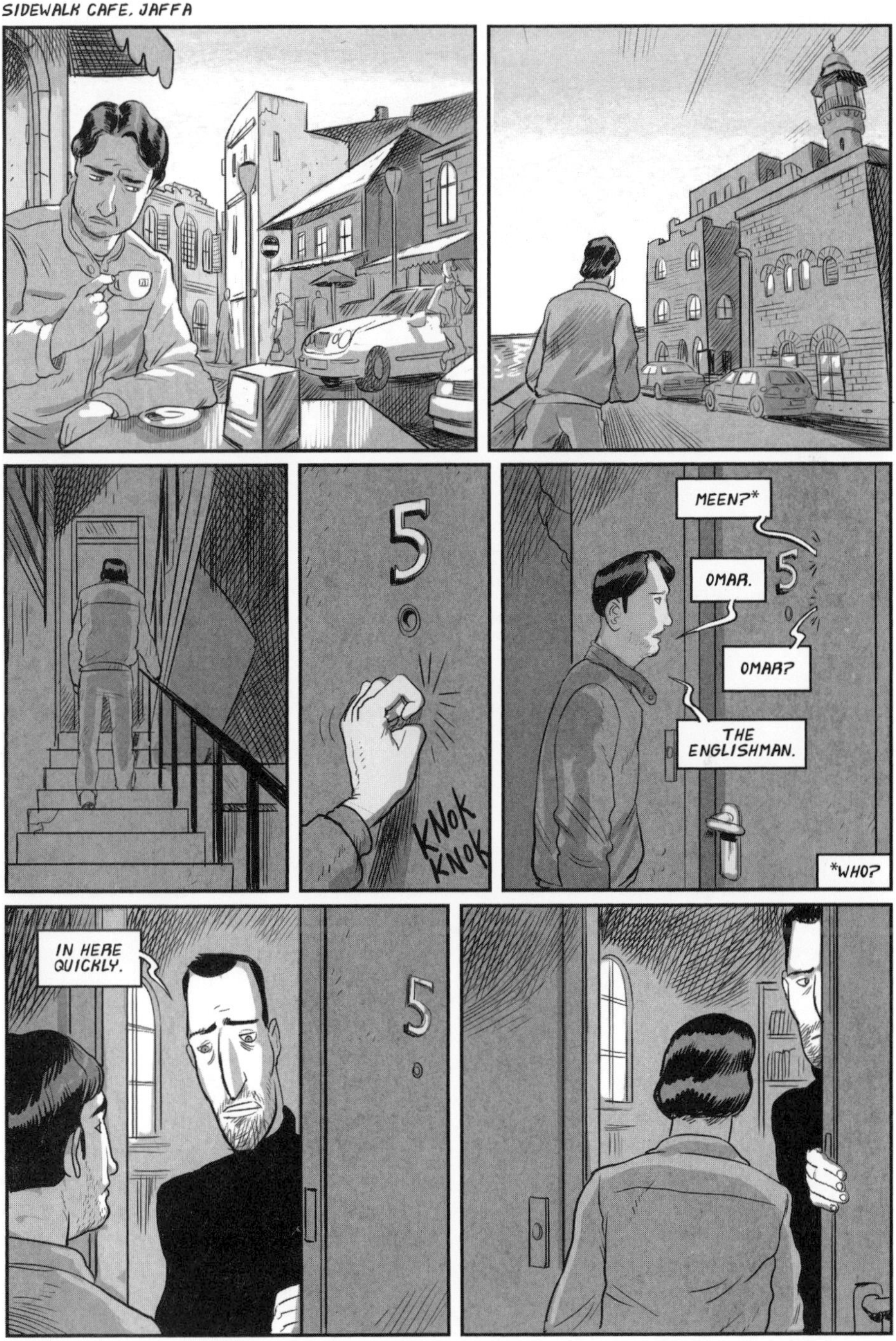
SIDEWALK CAFE, JAFFA
5
KNOK KNOK
MEEN?*
OMAR.
OMAR?
THE ENGLISHMAN.
*WHO?
IN HERE QUICKLY.
5

ICHILOV HOSPITAL, EMERGENCY TRAUMA WARD

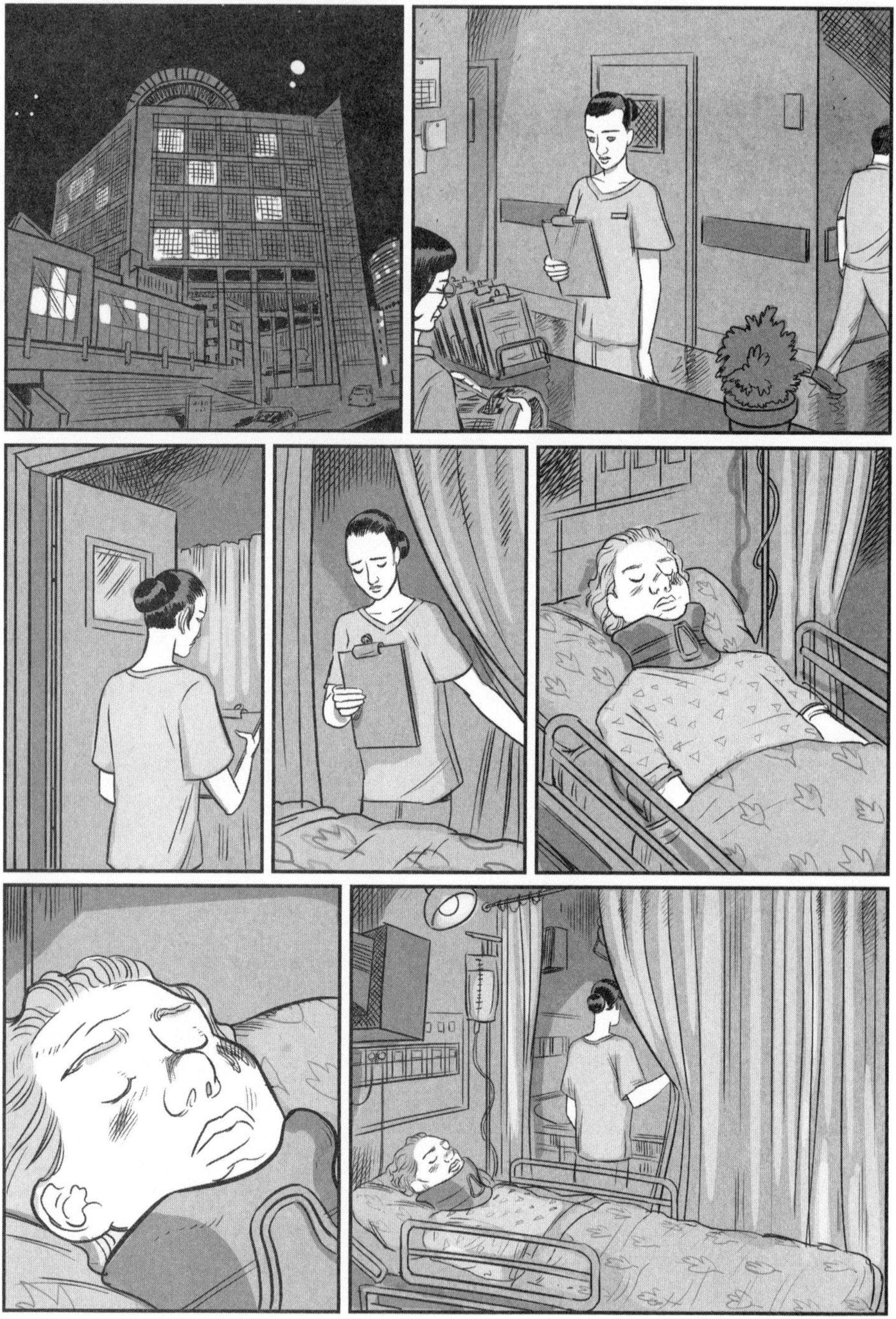

QUEEN ALIA AIRPORT, AMMAN, JORDAN

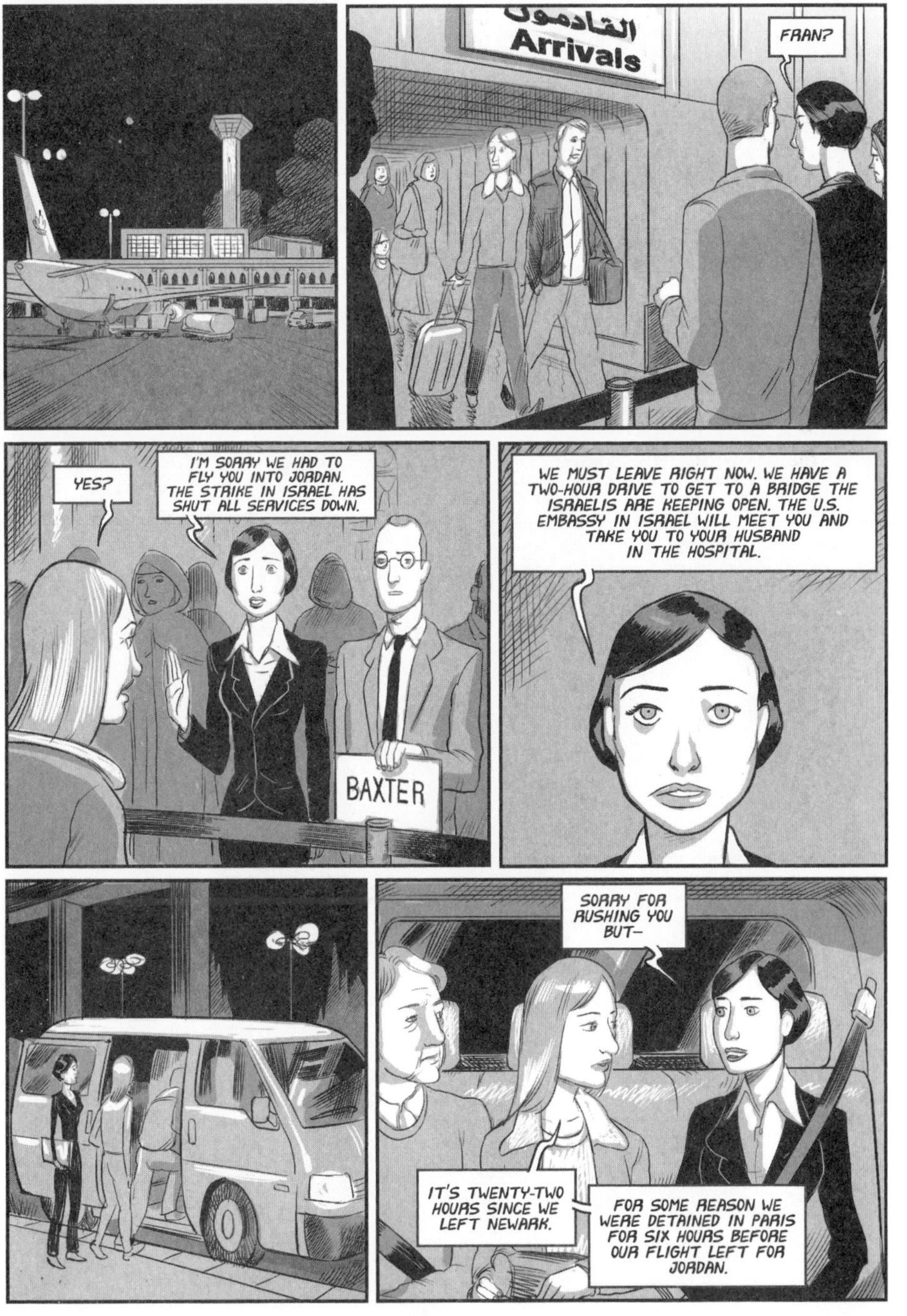
القادمون
Arrivals
FRAN?
YES?
I'M SORRY WE HAD TO FLY YOU INTO JORDAN. THE STRIKE IN ISRAEL HAS SHUT ALL SERVICES DOWN.
BAXTER
WE MUST LEAVE RIGHT NOW. WE HAVE A TWO-HOUR DRIVE TO GET TO A BRIDGE THE ISRAELIS ARE KEEPING OPEN. THE U.S. EMBASSY IN ISRAEL WILL MEET YOU AND TAKE YOU TO YOUR HUSBAND IN THE HOSPITAL.
SORRY FOR RUSHING YOU BUT—
IT'S TWENTY-TWO HOURS SINCE WE LEFT NEWARK.
FOR SOME REASON WE WERE DETAINED IN PARIS FOR SIX HOURS BEFORE OUR FLIGHT LEFT FOR JORDAN.

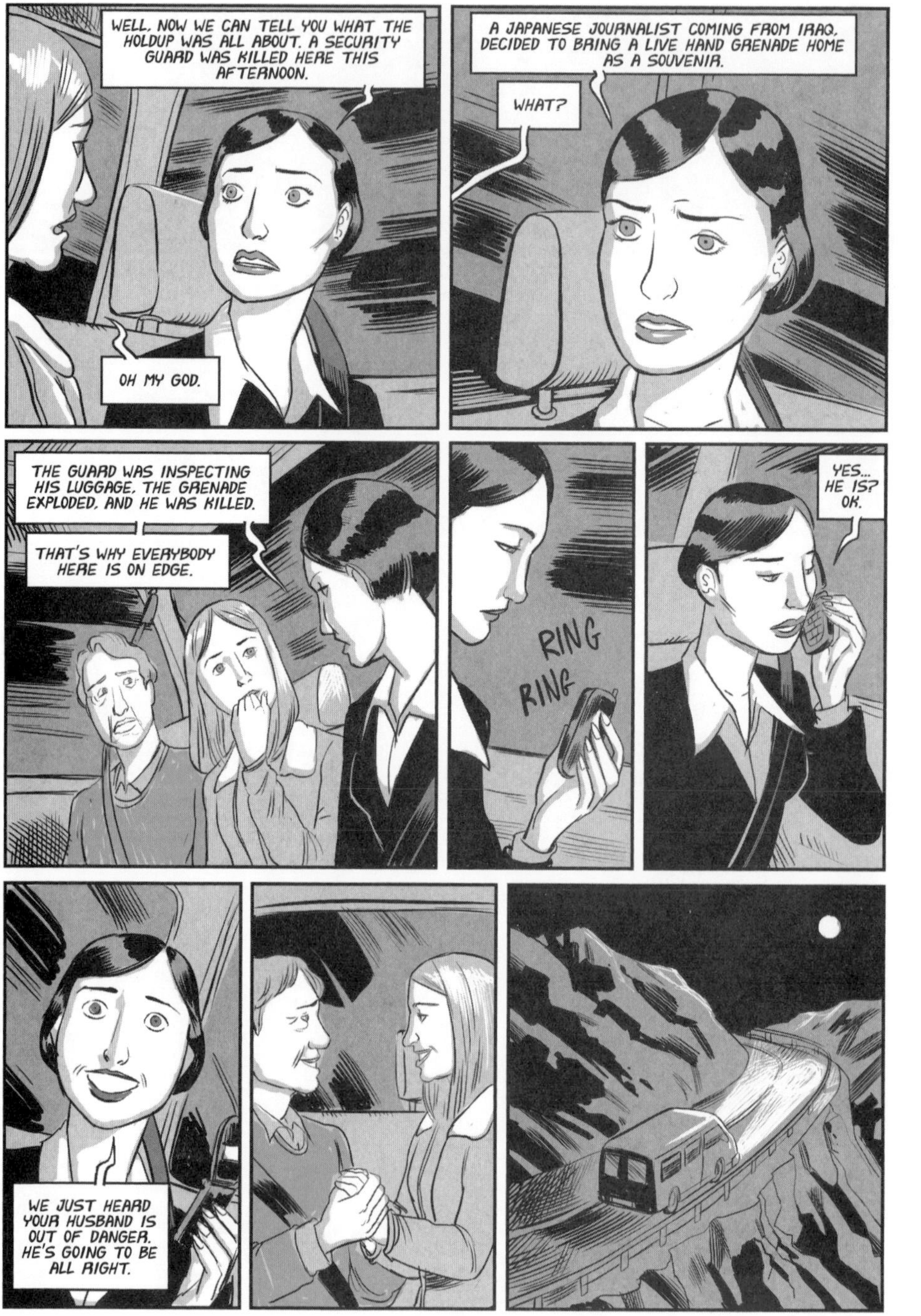
WELL, NOW WE CAN TELL YOU WHAT THE HOLDUP WAS ALL ABOUT. A SECURITY GUARD WAS KILLED HERE THIS AFTERNOON.
OH MY GOD.
A JAPANESE JOURNALIST COMING FROM IRAQ, DECIDED TO BRING A LIVE HAND GRENADE HOME AS A SOUVENIR.
WHAT?
THE GUARD WAS INSPECTING HIS LUGGAGE, THE GRENADE EXPLODED, AND HE WAS KILLED.
THAT'S WHY EVERYBODY HERE IS ON EDGE.
RING
RING
YES... HE IS? OK.
WE JUST HEARD YOUR HUSBAND IS OUT OF DANGER. HE'S GOING TO BE ALL RIGHT.

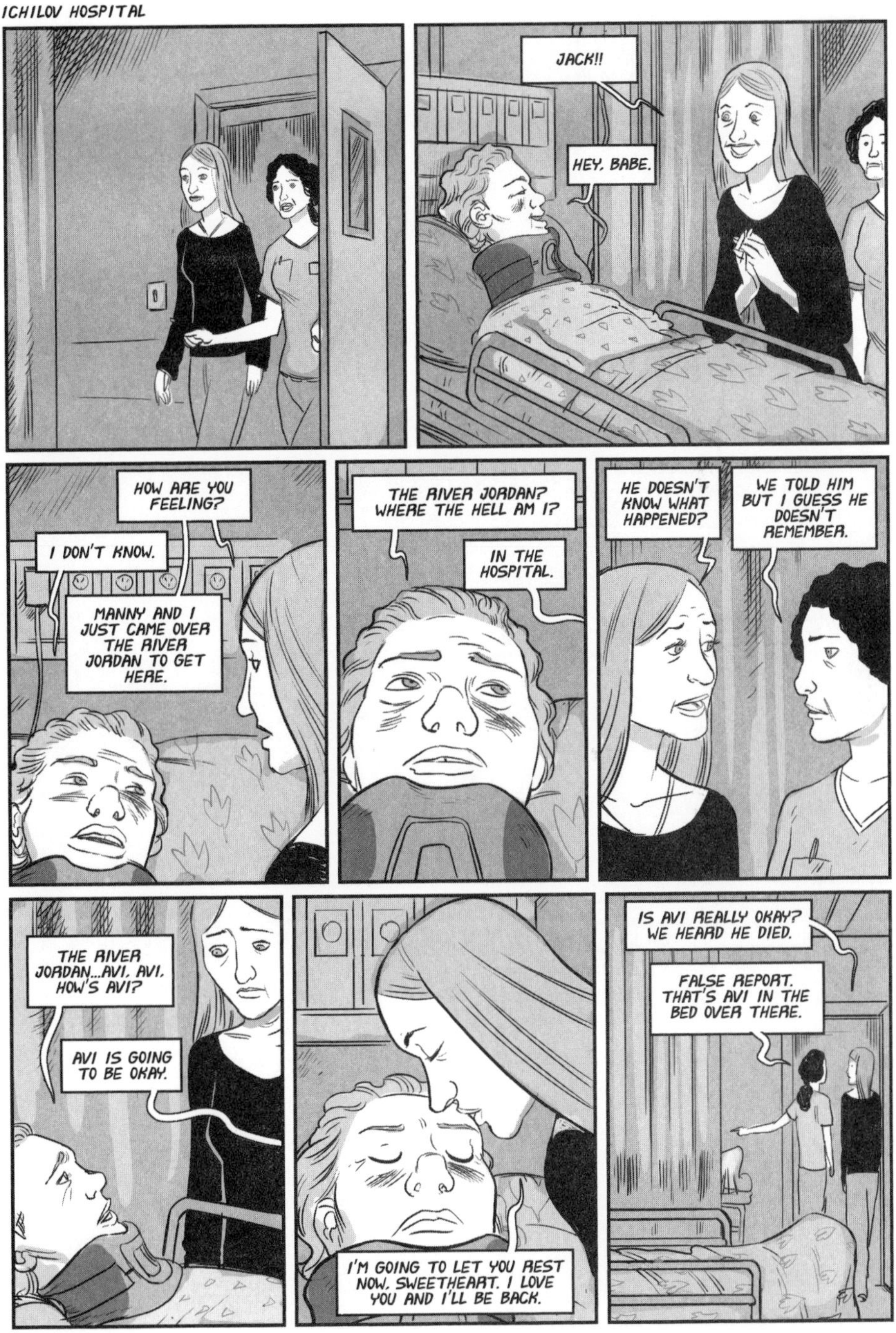
ICHILOV HOSPITAL
JACK!!
HEY, BABE.
HOW ARE YOU FEELING?
I DON'T KNOW.
MANNY AND I JUST CAME OVER THE RIVER JORDAN TO GET HERE.
THE RIVER JORDAN? WHERE THE HELL AM I?
IN THE HOSPITAL.
HE DOESN'T KNOW WHAT HAPPENED?
WE TOLD HIM BUT I GUESS HE DOESN'T REMEMBER.
THE RIVER JORDAN...AVI, AVI. HOW'S AVI?
AVI IS GOING TO BE OKAY.
I'M GOING TO LET YOU REST NOW, SWEETHEART. I LOVE YOU AND I'LL BE BACK.
IS AVI REALLY OKAY? WE HEARD HE DIED.
FALSE REPORT. THAT'S AVI IN THE BED OVER THERE.

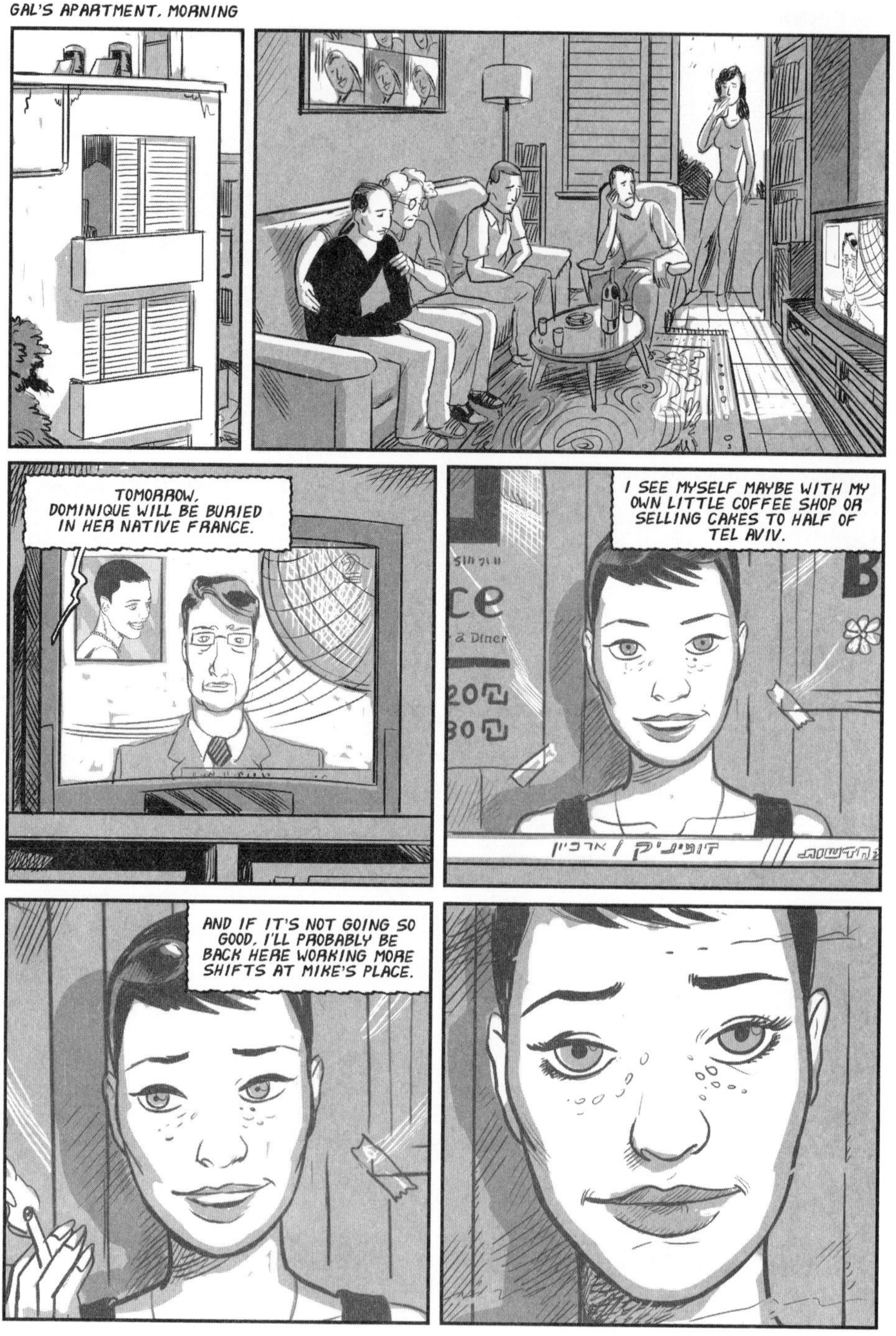
GAL'S APARTMENT, MORNING
TOMORROW, DOMINIQUE WILL BE BURIED IN HER NATIVE FRANCE.
I SEE MYSELF MAYBE WITH MY OWN LITTLE COFFEE SHOP OR SELLING CAKES TO HALF OF TEL AVIV.
AND IF IT'S NOT GOING SO GOOD, I'LL PROBABLY BE BACK HERE WORKING MORE SHIFTS AT MIKE'S PLACE.

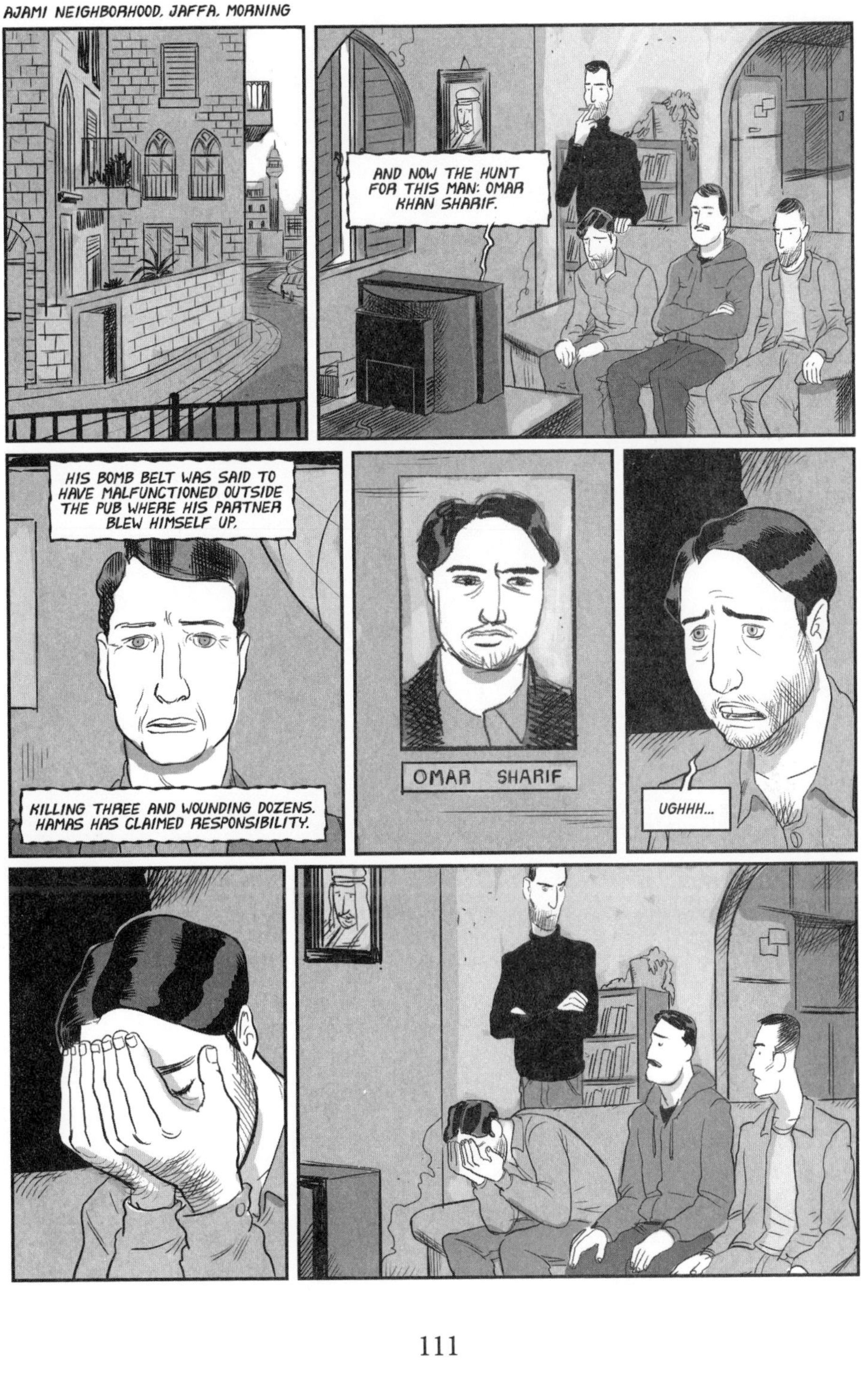
AJAMI NEIGHBORHOOD, JAFFA, MORNING
AND NOW THE HUNT FOR THIS MAN: OMAR KHAN SHARIF.
HIS BOMB BELT WAS SAID TO HAVE MALFUNCTIONED OUTSIDE THE PUB WHERE HIS PARTNER BLEW HIMSELF UP,
KILLING THREE AND WOUNDING DOZENS. HAMAS HAS CLAIMED RESPONSIBILITY.
OMAR SHARIF
UGHHH...

JOSHUA'S APARTMENT

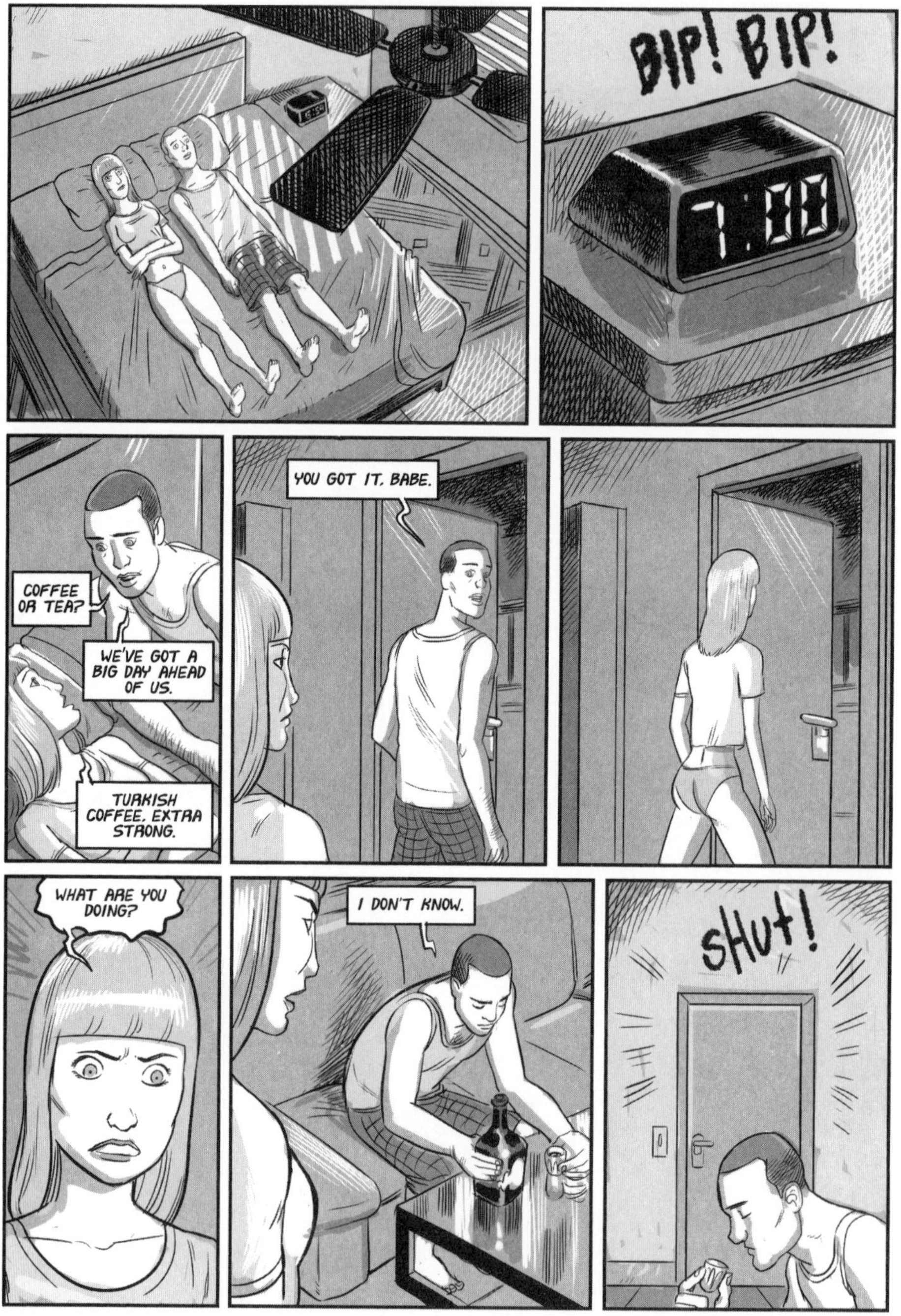

BIP! BIP!
7:00
COFFEE OR TEA?
WE'VE GOT A BIG DAY AHEAD OF US.
TURKISH COFFEE. EXTRA STRONG.
YOU GOT IT, BABE.
WHAT ARE YOU DOING?
I DON'T KNOW.
SHUT!

DOWNTOWN DAVE'S APARTMENT

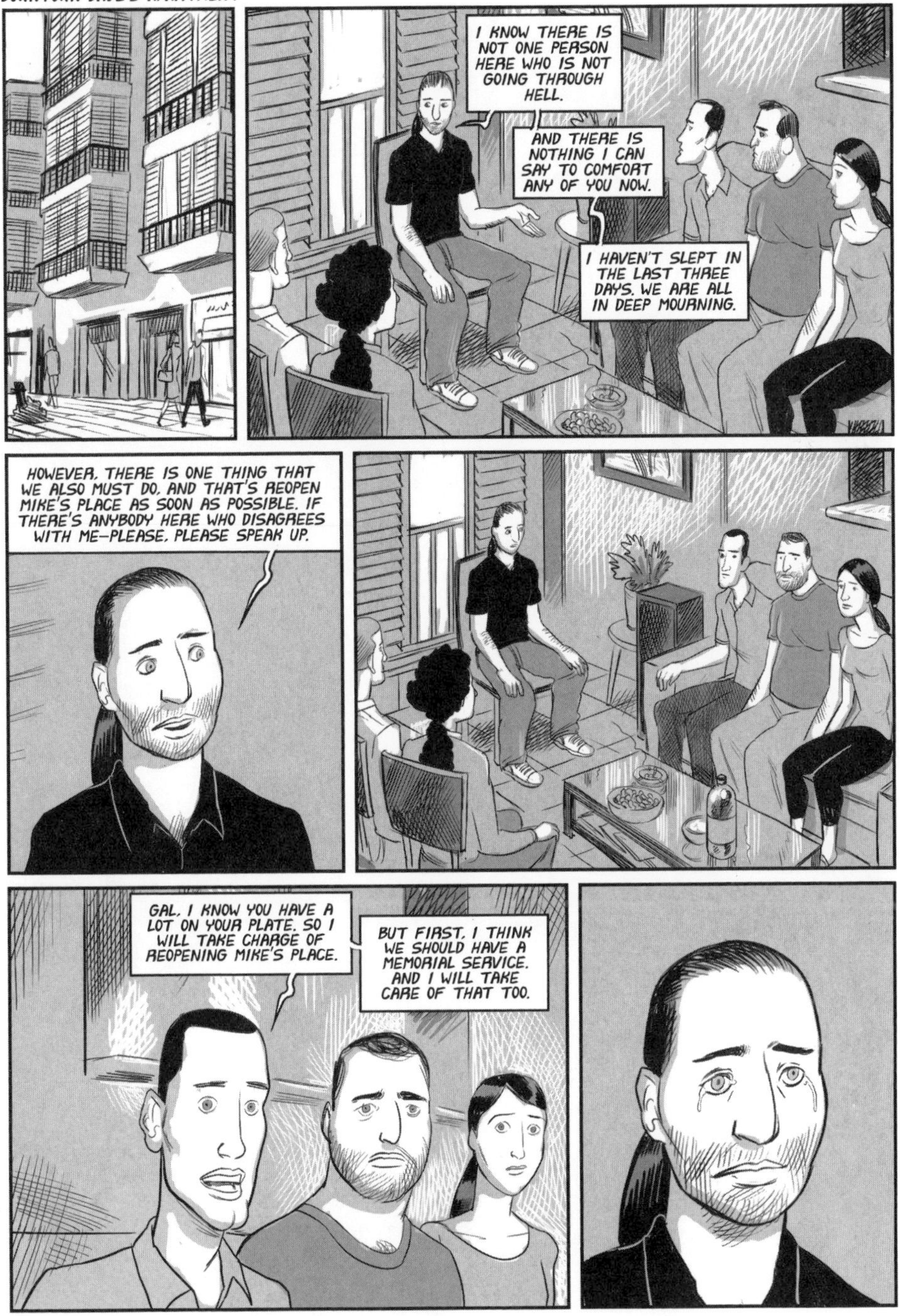
I KNOW THERE IS NOT ONE PERSON HERE WHO IS NOT GOING THROUGH HELL.
AND THERE IS NOTHING I CAN SAY TO COMFORT ANY OF YOU NOW.
I HAVEN'T SLEPT IN THE LAST THREE DAYS. WE ARE ALL IN DEEP MOURNING.
HOWEVER, THERE IS ONE THING THAT WE ALSO MUST DO, AND THAT'S REOPEN MIKE'S PLACE AS SOON AS POSSIBLE. IF THERE'S ANYBODY HERE WHO DISAGREES WITH ME—PLEASE, PLEASE SPEAK UP.
GAL, I KNOW YOU HAVE A LOT ON YOUR PLATE, SO I WILL TAKE CHARGE OF REOPENING MIKE'S PLACE.
BUT FIRST, I THINK WE SHOULD HAVE A MEMORIAL SERVICE. AND I WILL TAKE CARE OF THAT TOO.

ICHILOV HOSPITAL, LATE AFTERNOON

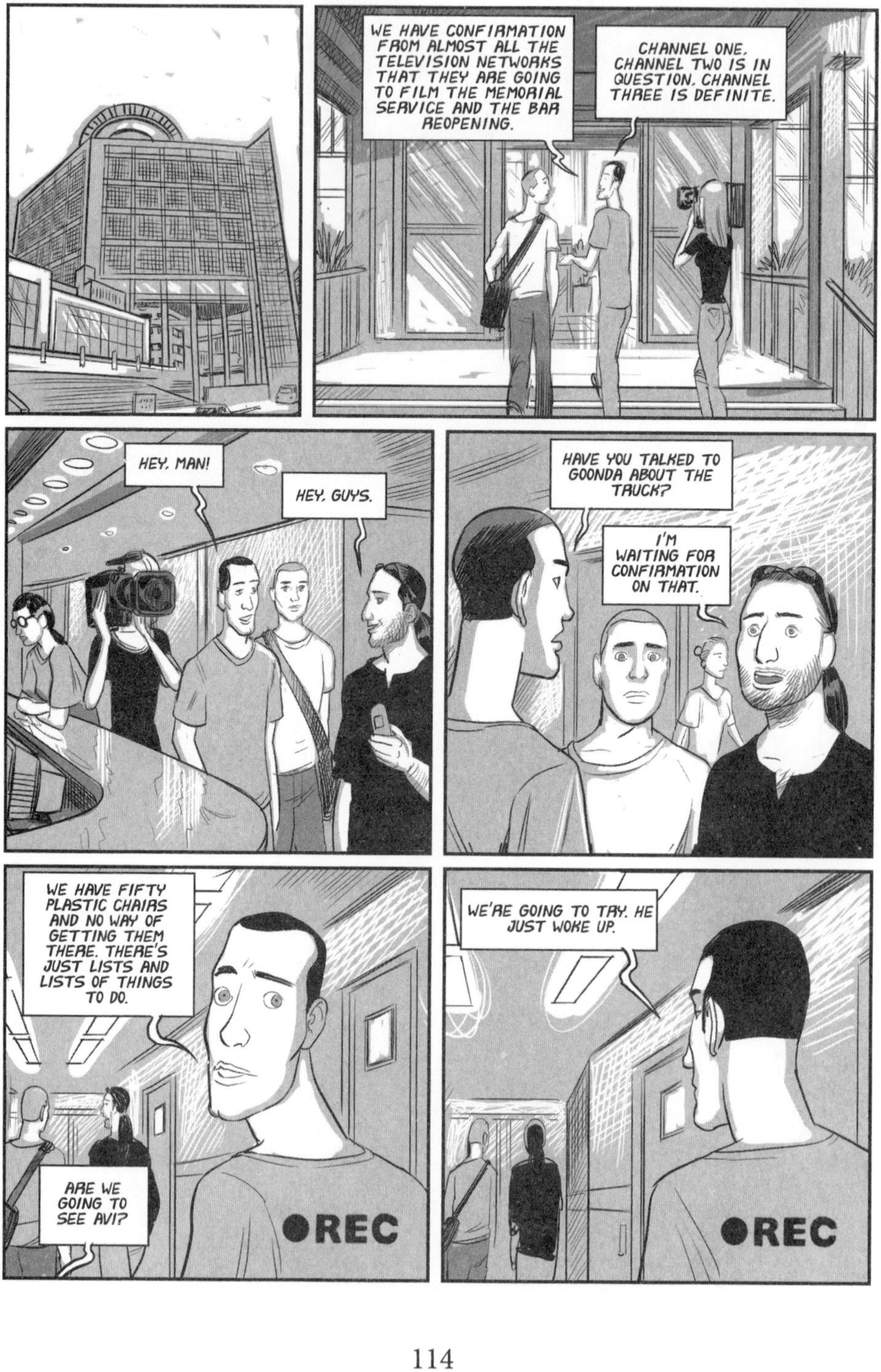

WE HAVE CONFIRMATION FROM ALMOST ALL THE TELEVISION NETWORKS THAT THEY ARE GOING TO FILM THE MEMORIAL SERVICE AND THE BAR REOPENING.
CHANNEL ONE, CHANNEL TWO IS IN QUESTION, CHANNEL THREE IS DEFINITE.
HEY, MAN!
HEY, GUYS.
HAVE YOU TALKED TO GOONDA ABOUT THE TRUCK?
I'M WAITING FOR CONFIRMATION ON THAT.
WE HAVE FIFTY PLASTIC CHAIRS AND NO WAY OF GETTING THEM THERE. THERE'S JUST LISTS AND LISTS OF THINGS TO DO.
ARE WE GOING TO SEE AVI?
●REC
WE'RE GOING TO TRY. HE JUST WOKE UP.
●REC

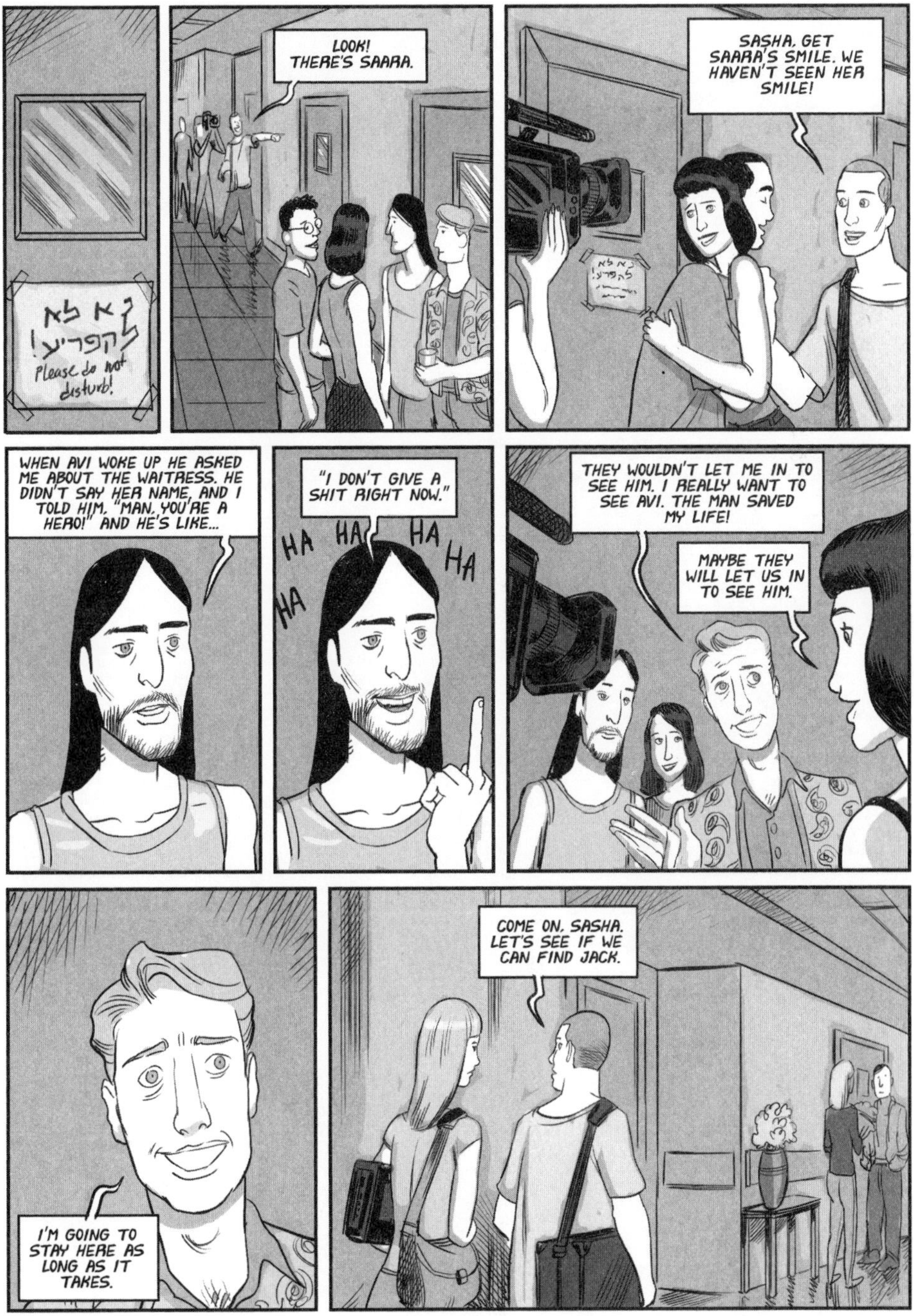
נא לא להפריע!
Please do not disturb!
LOOK! THERE'S SAARA.
SASHA, GET SAARA'S SMILE. WE HAVEN'T SEEN HER SMILE!
WHEN AVI WOKE UP HE ASKED ME ABOUT THE WAITRESS. HE DIDN'T SAY HER NAME, AND I TOLD HIM, "MAN, YOU'RE A HERO!" AND HE'S LIKE...
"I DON'T GIVE A SHIT RIGHT NOW."
HA HA HA HA HA
THEY WOULDN'T LET ME IN TO SEE HIM. I REALLY WANT TO SEE AVI. THE MAN SAVED MY LIFE!
MAYBE THEY WILL LET US IN TO SEE HIM.
I'M GOING TO STAY HERE AS LONG AS IT TAKES.
COME ON, SASHA. LET'S SEE IF WE CAN FIND JACK.

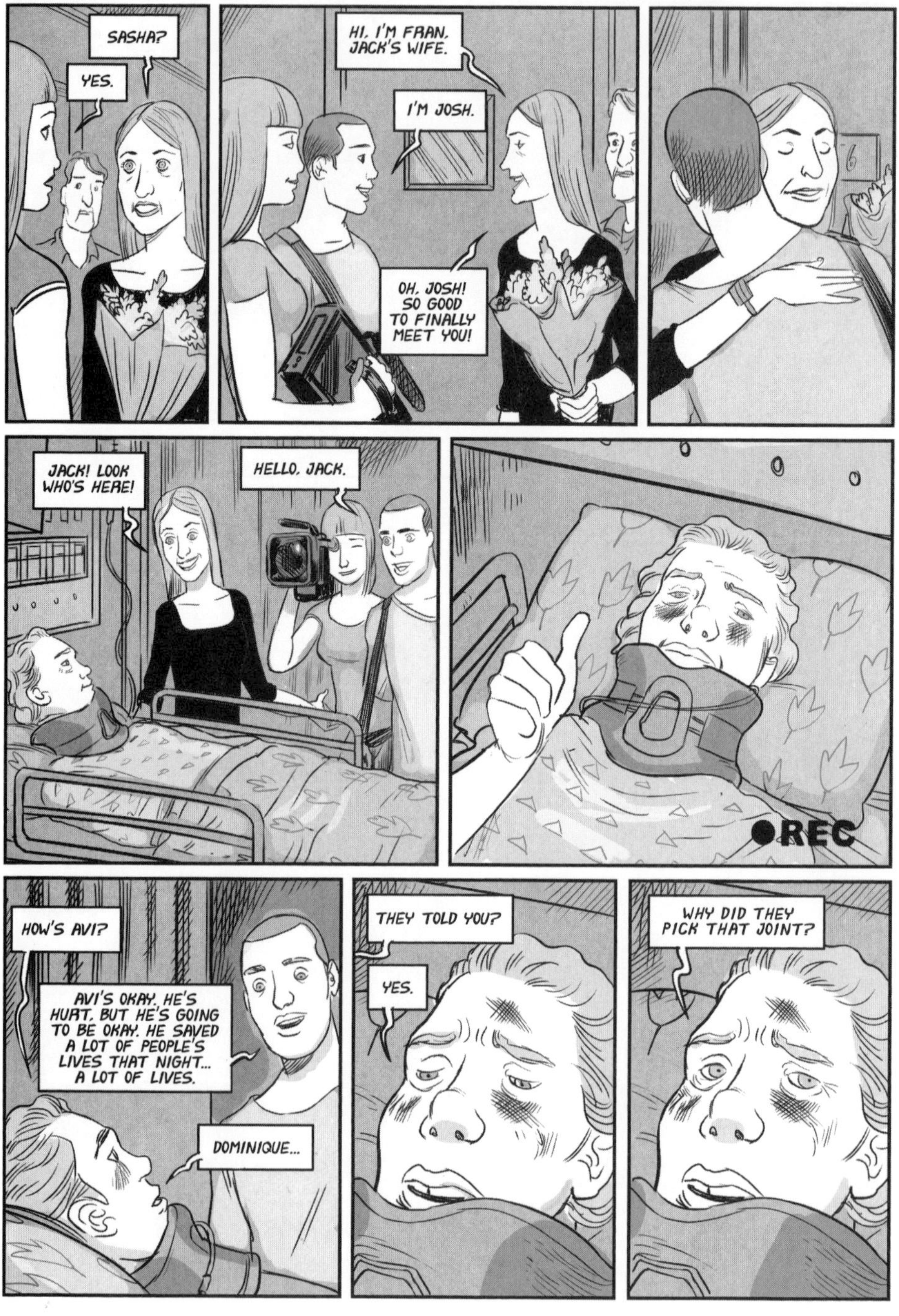
SASHA?
YES.
HI, I'M FRAN, JACK'S WIFE.
I'M JOSH.
OH, JOSH! SO GOOD TO FINALLY MEET YOU!
JACK! LOOK WHO'S HERE!
HELLO, JACK.
REC
HOW'S AVI?
AVI'S OKAY. HE'S HURT, BUT HE'S GOING TO BE OKAY. HE SAVED A LOT OF PEOPLE'S LIVES THAT NIGHT... A LOT OF LIVES.
DOMINIQUE...
THEY TOLD YOU?
YES.
WHY DID THEY PICK THAT JOINT?

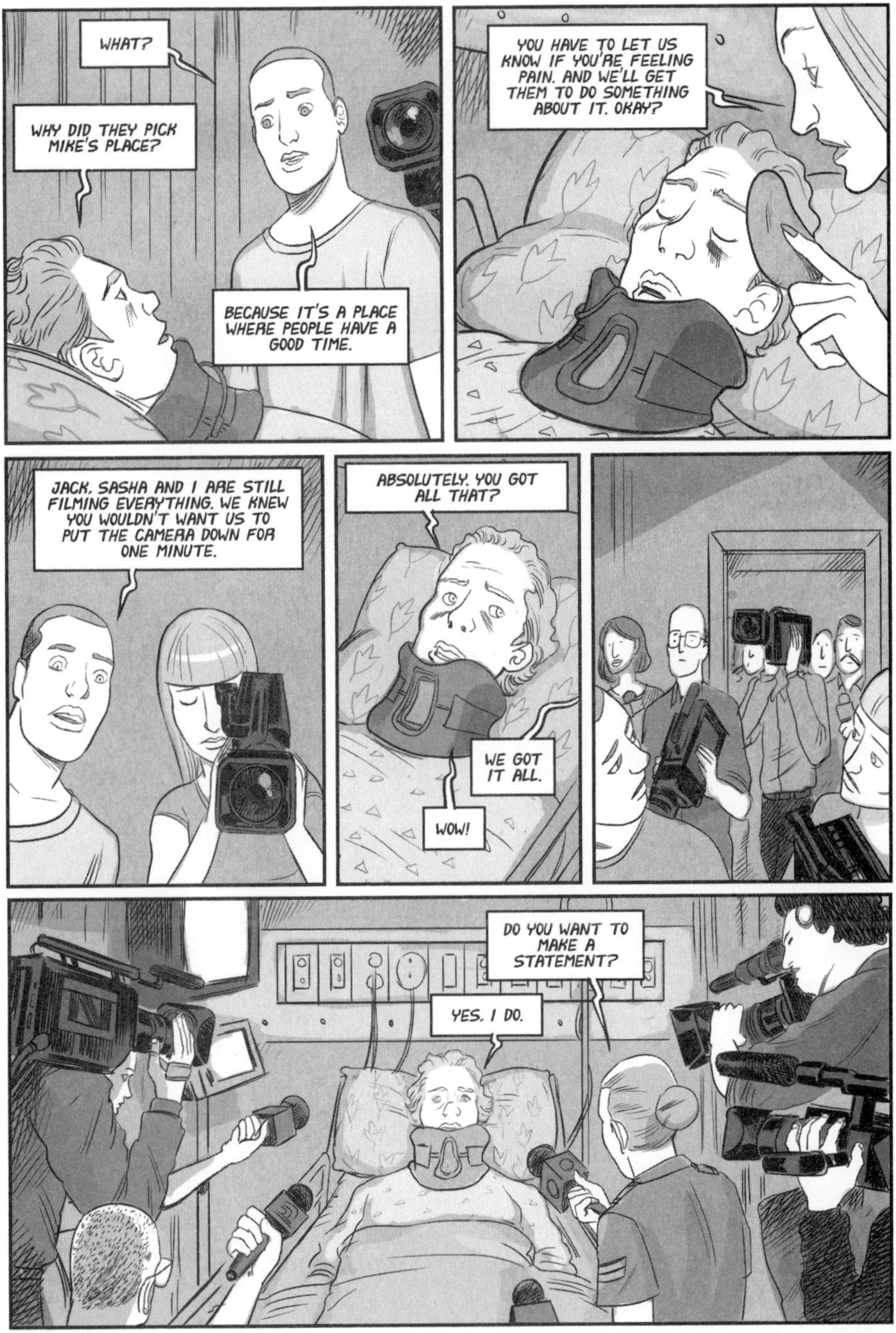
WHAT?
WHY DID THEY PICK MIKE'S PLACE?
BECAUSE IT'S A PLACE WHERE PEOPLE HAVE A GOOD TIME.
YOU HAVE TO LET US KNOW IF YOU'RE FEELING PAIN. AND WE'LL GET THEM TO DO SOMETHING ABOUT IT. OKAY?
JACK, SASHA AND I ARE STILL FILMING EVERYTHING. WE KNEW YOU WOULDN'T WANT US TO PUT THE CAMERA DOWN FOR ONE MINUTE.
ABSOLUTELY. YOU GOT ALL THAT?
WE GOT IT ALL.
WOW!
DO YOU WANT TO MAKE A STATEMENT?
YES, I DO.

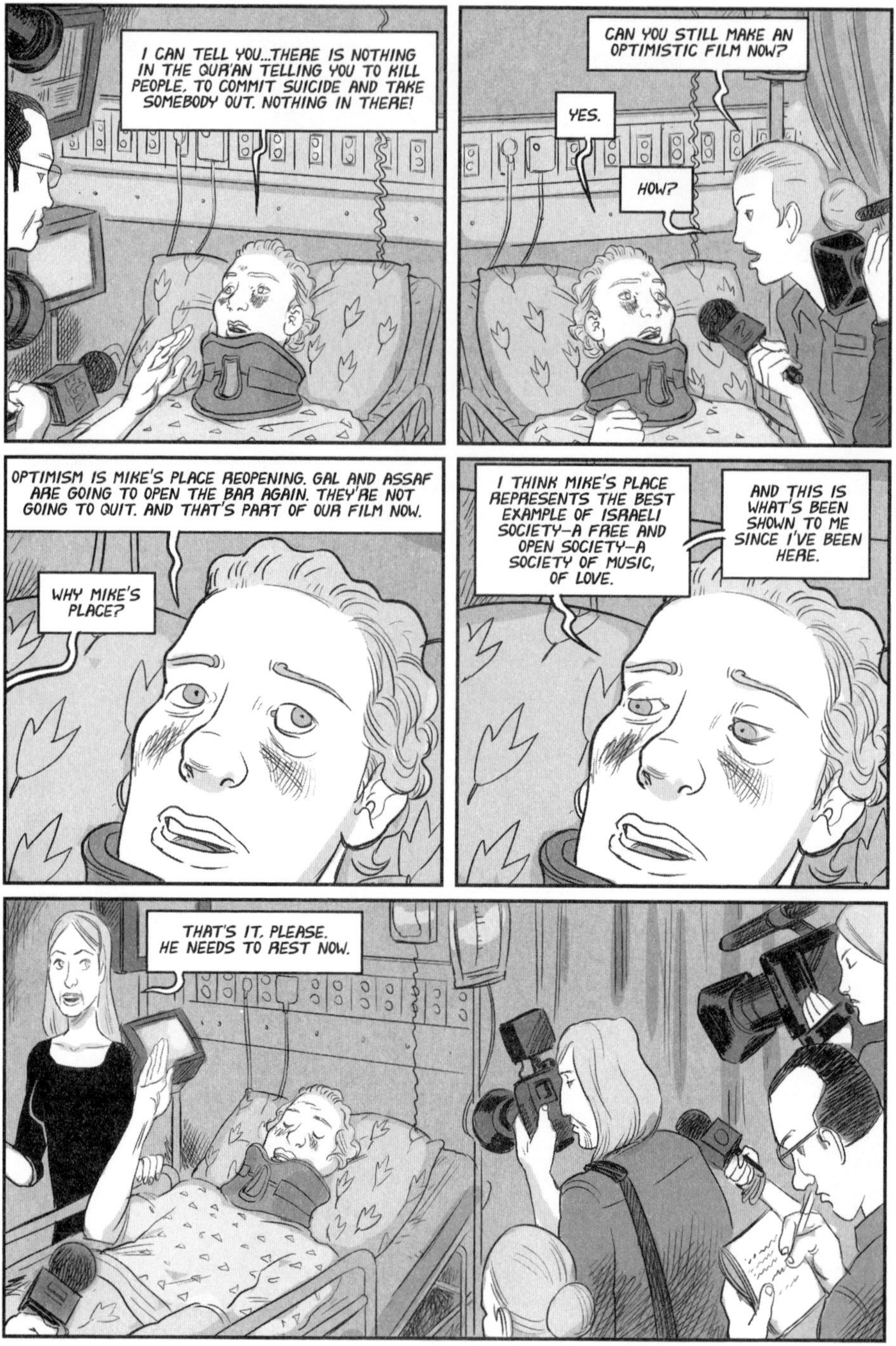
I CAN TELL YOU...THERE IS NOTHING IN THE QUR'AN TELLING YOU TO KILL PEOPLE, TO COMMIT SUICIDE AND TAKE SOMEBODY OUT. NOTHING IN THERE!
CAN YOU STILL MAKE AN OPTIMISTIC FILM NOW?
YES.
HOW?
OPTIMISM IS MIKE'S PLACE REOPENING. GAL AND ASSAF ARE GOING TO OPEN THE BAR AGAIN. THEY'RE NOT GOING TO QUIT. AND THAT'S PART OF OUR FILM NOW.
WHY MIKE'S PLACE?
I THINK MIKE'S PLACE REPRESENTS THE BEST EXAMPLE OF ISRAELI SOCIETY—A FREE AND OPEN SOCIETY—A SOCIETY OF MUSIC, OF LOVE.
AND THIS IS WHAT'S BEEN SHOWN TO ME SINCE I'VE BEEN HERE.
THAT'S IT, PLEASE. HE NEEDS TO REST NOW.

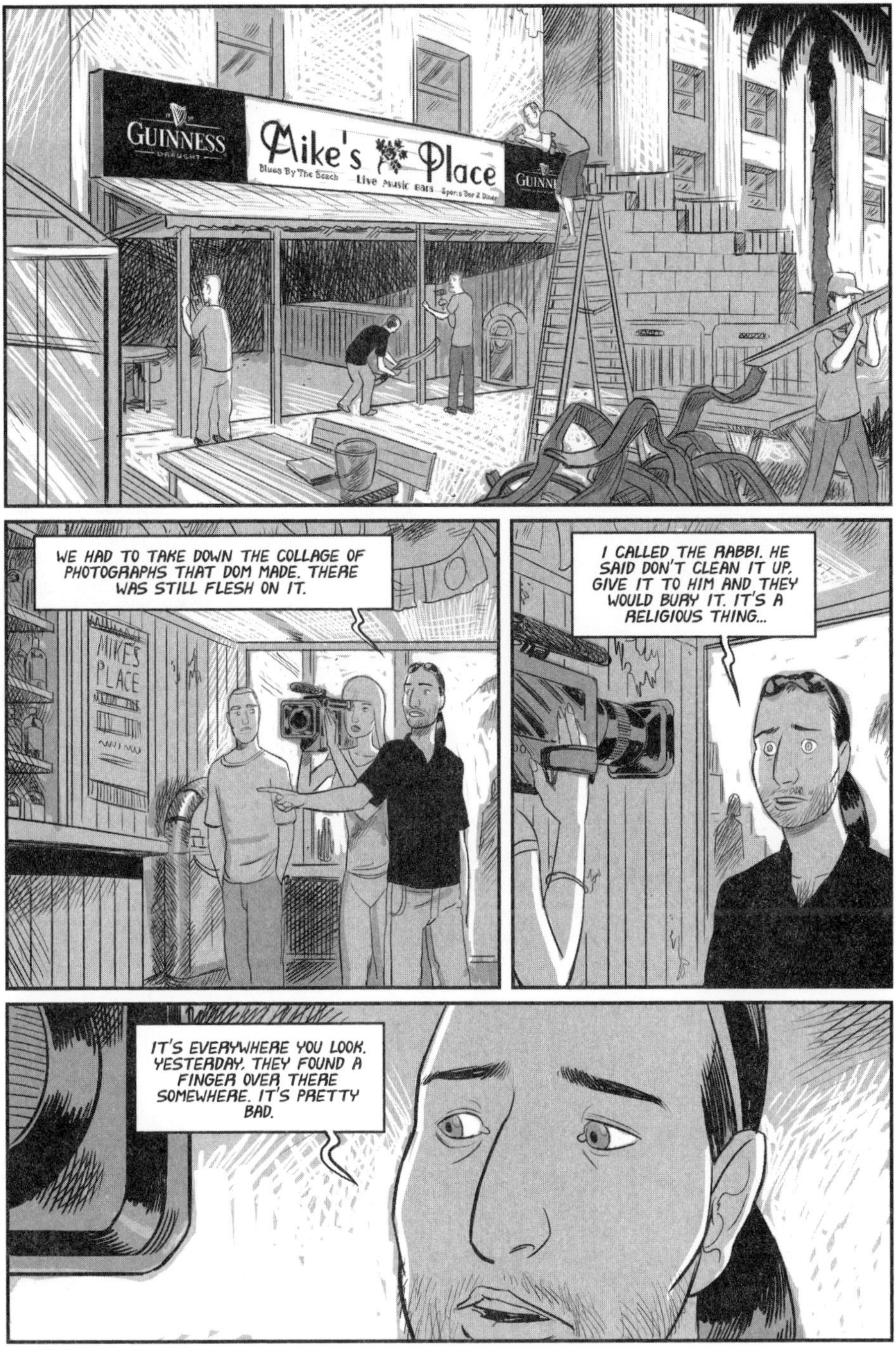
GUINNESS
Mike's Place
Blues By The Beach
Live Music Bars
GUINNESS
WE HAD TO TAKE DOWN THE COLLAGE OF PHOTOGRAPHS THAT DOM MADE. THERE WAS STILL FLESH ON IT.
MIKE'S PLACE
I CALLED THE RABBI. HE SAID DON'T CLEAN IT UP, GIVE IT TO HIM AND THEY WOULD BURY IT. IT'S A RELIGIOUS THING...
IT'S EVERYWHERE YOU LOOK. YESTERDAY, THEY FOUND A FINGER OVER THERE SOMEWHERE. IT'S PRETTY BAD.

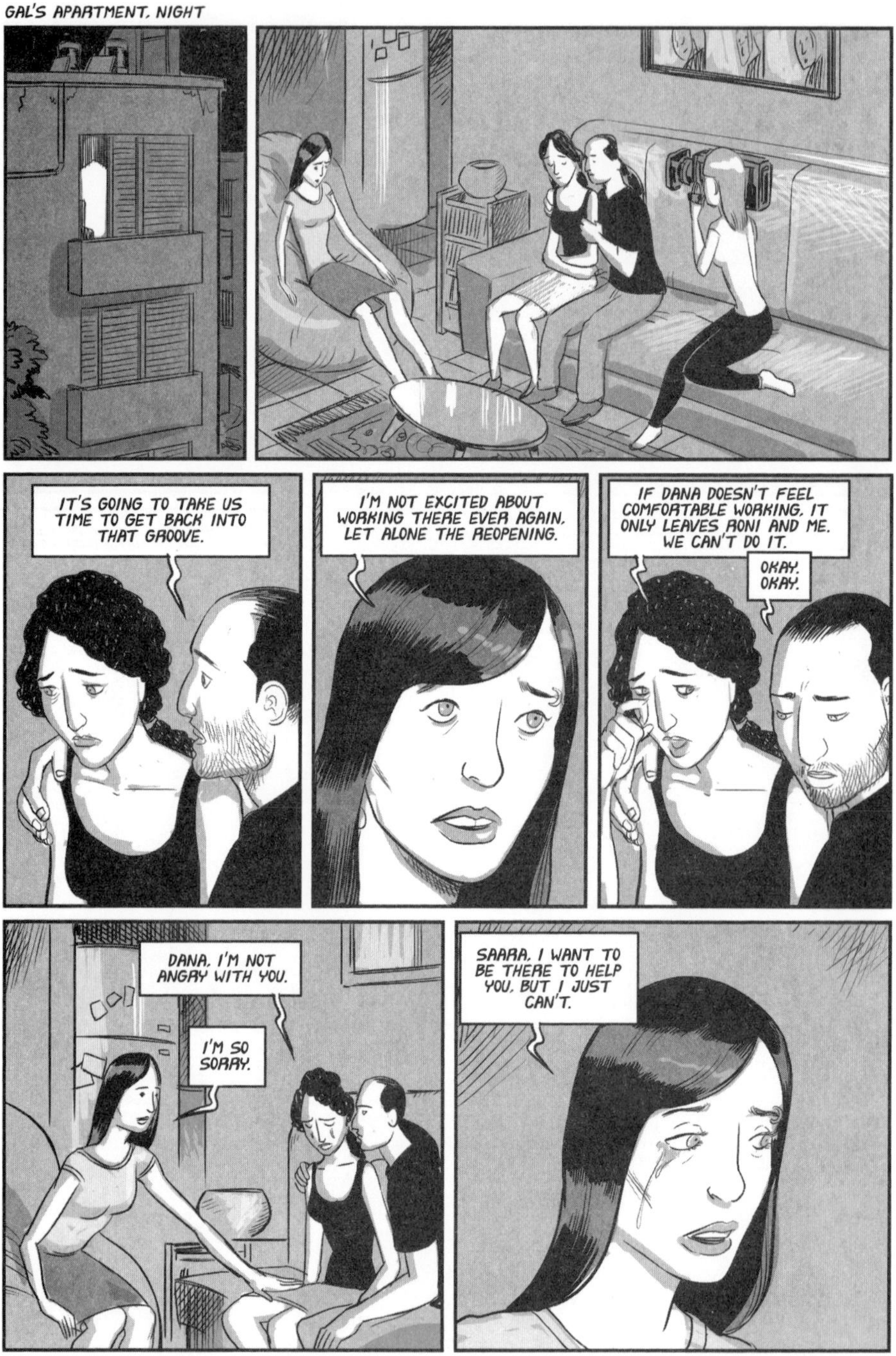
GAL'S APARTMENT, NIGHT
IT'S GOING TO TAKE US TIME TO GET BACK INTO THAT GROOVE.
I'M NOT EXCITED ABOUT WORKING THERE EVER AGAIN, LET ALONE THE REOPENING.
IF DANA DOESN'T FEEL COMFORTABLE WORKING, IT ONLY LEAVES RONI AND ME. WE CAN'T DO IT.
OKAY. OKAY.
DANA, I'M NOT ANGRY WITH YOU.
I'M SO SORRY.
SARRA, I WANT TO BE THERE TO HELP YOU, BUT I JUST CAN'T.

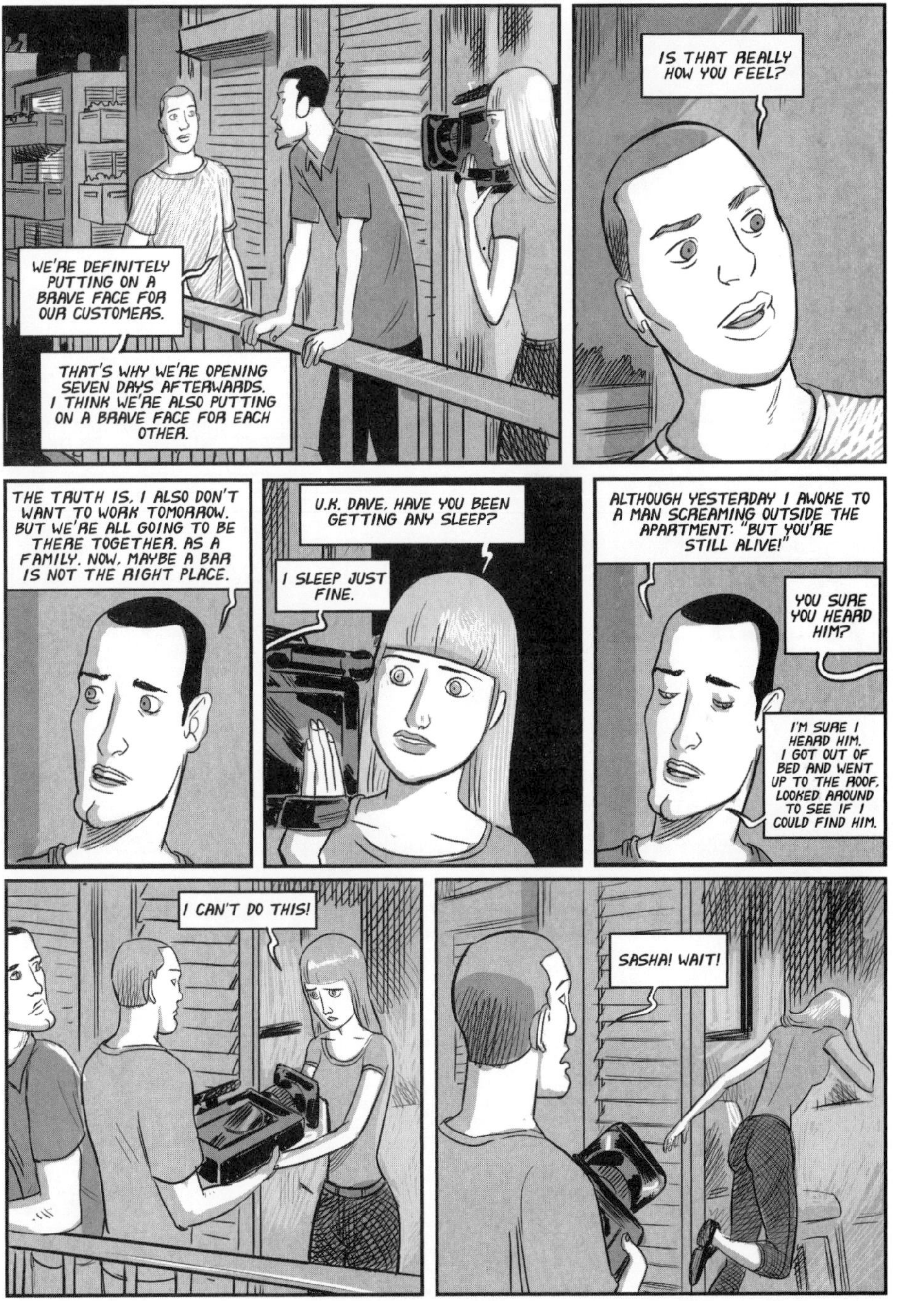
WE'RE DEFINITELY PUTTING ON A BRAVE FACE FOR OUR CUSTOMERS.
THAT'S WHY WE'RE OPENING SEVEN DAYS AFTERWARDS. I THINK WE'RE ALSO PUTTING ON A BRAVE FACE FOR EACH OTHER.
IS THAT REALLY HOW YOU FEEL?
THE TRUTH IS, I ALSO DON'T WANT TO WORK TOMORROW. BUT WE'RE ALL GOING TO BE THERE TOGETHER. AS A FAMILY. NOW, MAYBE A BAR IS NOT THE RIGHT PLACE.
U.K. DAVE, HAVE YOU BEEN GETTING ANY SLEEP?
I SLEEP JUST FINE.
ALTHOUGH YESTERDAY I AWOKE TO A MAN SCREAMING OUTSIDE THE APARTMENT: "BUT YOU'RE STILL ALIVE!"
YOU SURE YOU HEARD HIM?
I'M SURE I HEARD HIM. I GOT OUT OF BED AND WENT UP TO THE ROOF, LOOKED AROUND TO SEE IF I COULD FIND HIM.
I CAN'T DO THIS!
SASHA! WAIT!

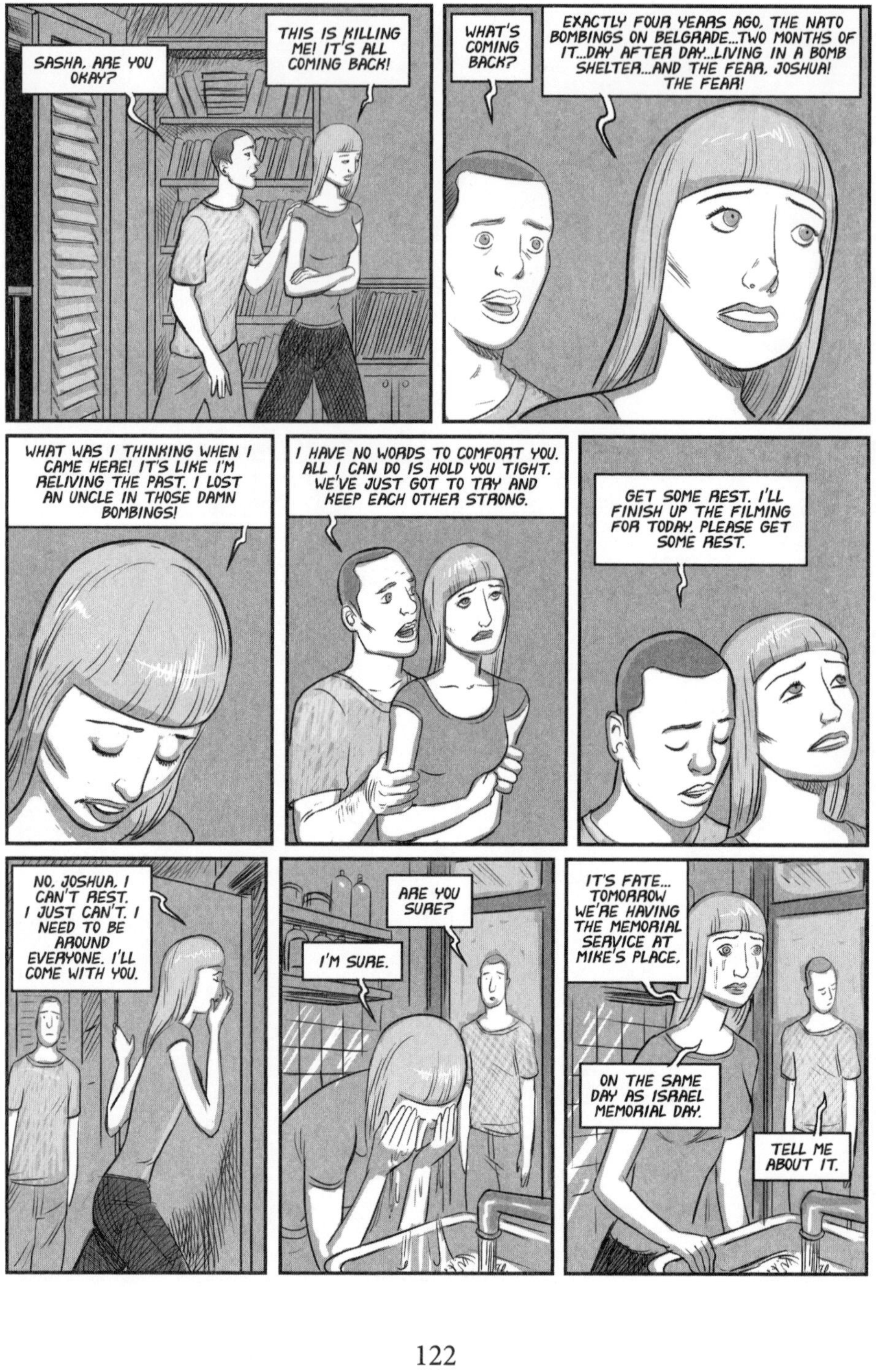
SASHA, ARE YOU OKAY?
THIS IS KILLING ME! IT'S ALL COMING BACK!
WHAT'S COMING BACK?
EXACTLY FOUR YEARS AGO, THE NATO BOMBINGS ON BELGRADE...TWO MONTHS OF IT...DAY AFTER DAY...LIVING IN A BOMB SHELTER...AND THE FEAR, JOSHUA! THE FEAR!
WHAT WAS I THINKING WHEN I CAME HERE! IT'S LIKE I'M RELIVING THE PAST. I LOST AN UNCLE IN THOSE DAMN BOMBINGS!
I HAVE NO WORDS TO COMFORT YOU. ALL I CAN DO IS HOLD YOU TIGHT. WE'VE JUST GOT TO TRY AND KEEP EACH OTHER STRONG.
GET SOME REST. I'LL FINISH UP THE FILMING FOR TODAY. PLEASE GET SOME REST.
NO, JOSHUA, I CAN'T REST. I JUST CAN'T. I NEED TO BE AROUND EVERYONE. I'LL COME WITH YOU.
ARE YOU SURE?
I'M SURE.
IT'S FATE... TOMORROW WE'RE HAVING THE MEMORIAL SERVICE AT MIKE'S PLACE,
ON THE SAME DAY AS ISRAEL MEMORIAL DAY.
TELL ME ABOUT IT.

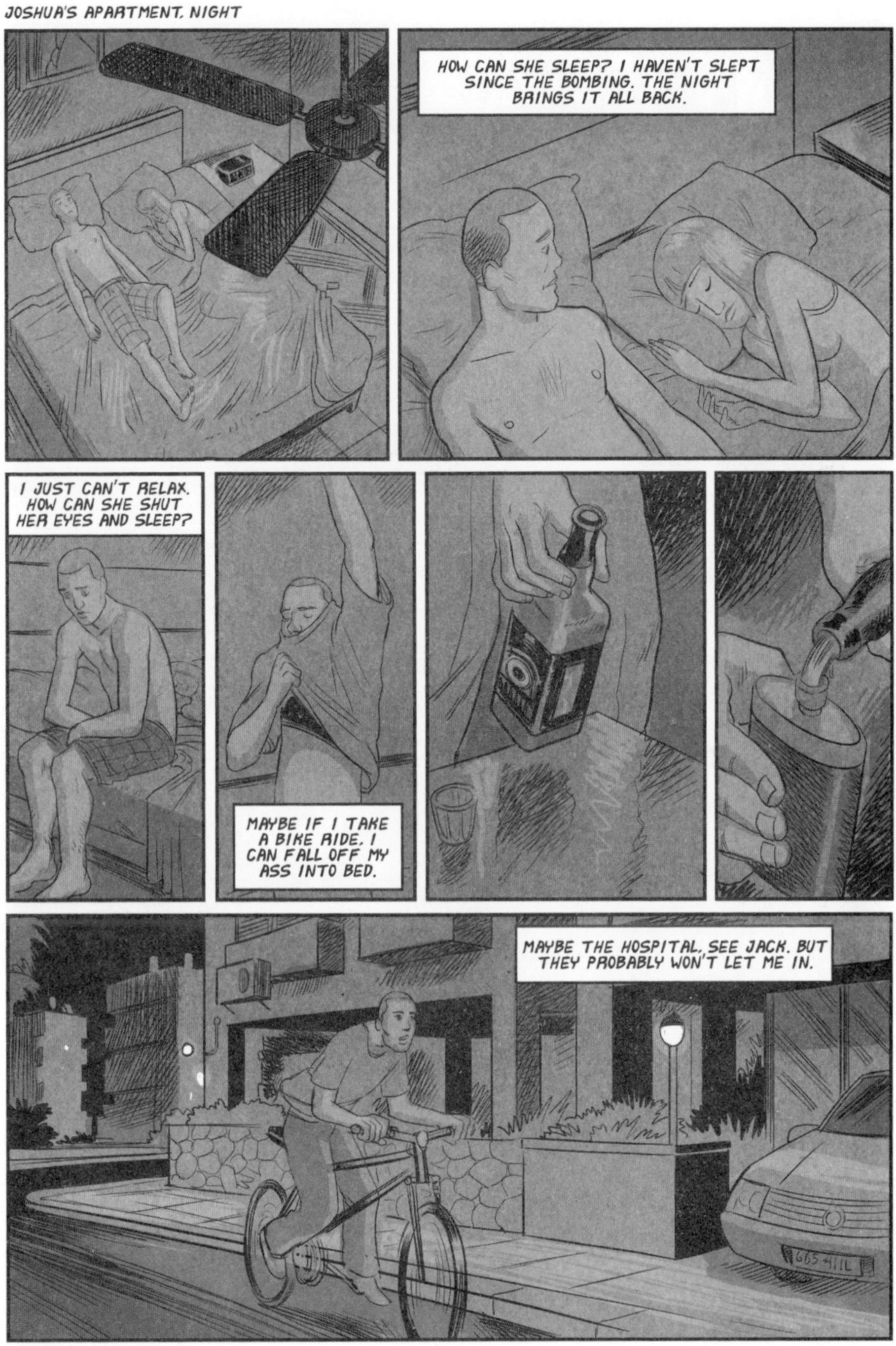
JOSHUA'S APARTMENT, NIGHT
HOW CAN SHE SLEEP? I HAVEN'T SLEPT SINCE THE BOMBING. THE NIGHT BRINGS IT ALL BACK.
I JUST CAN'T RELAX. HOW CAN SHE SHUT HER EYES AND SLEEP?
MAYBE IF I TAKE A BIKE RIDE, I CAN FALL OFF MY ASS INTO BED.
MAYBE THE HOSPITAL, SEE JACK. BUT THEY PROBABLY WON'T LET ME IN.

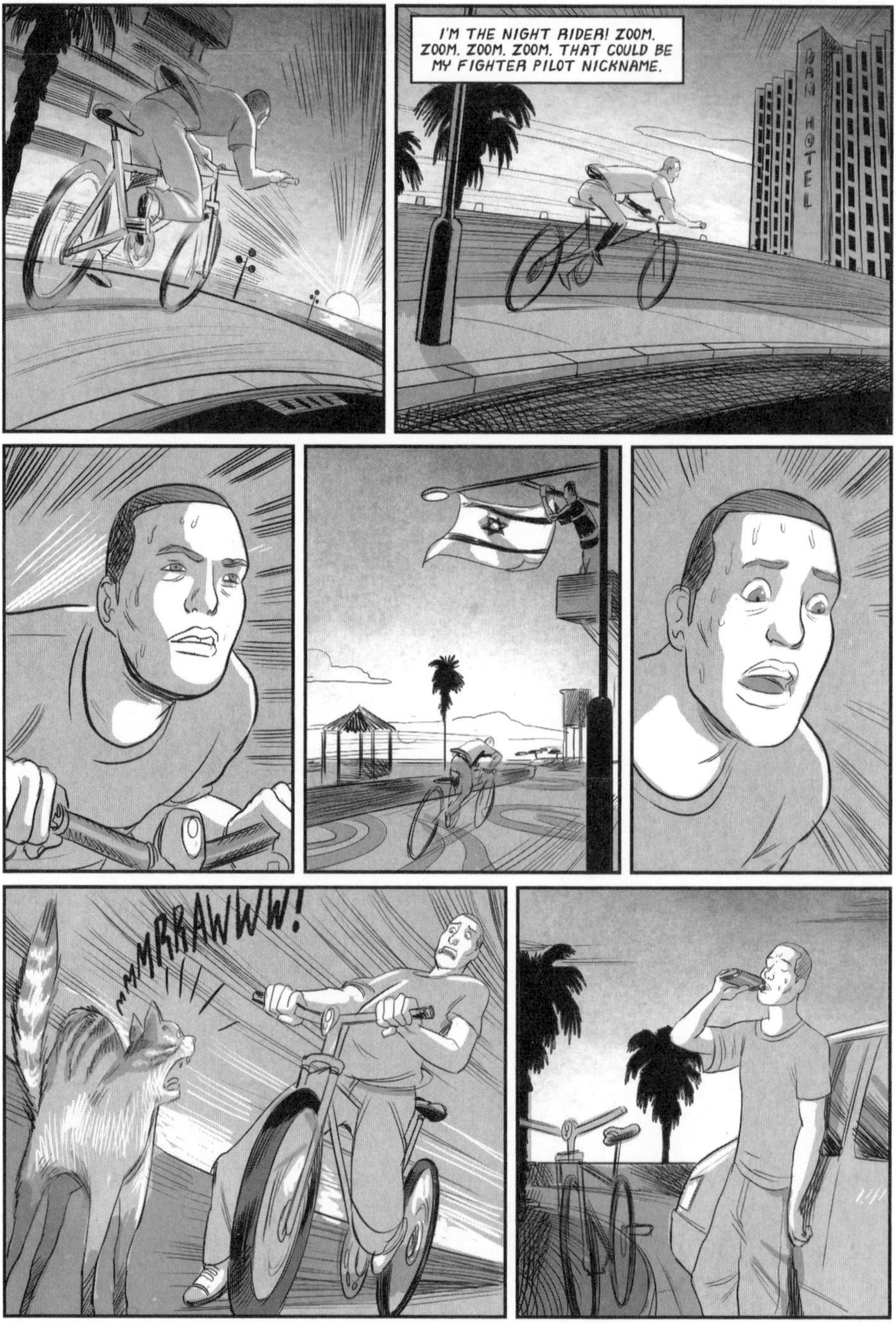
I'M THE NIGHT RIDER! ZOOM. ZOOM. ZOOM. ZOOM. THAT COULD BE MY FIGHTER PILOT NICKNAME.
DAN HOTEL
MMRRAWWW!

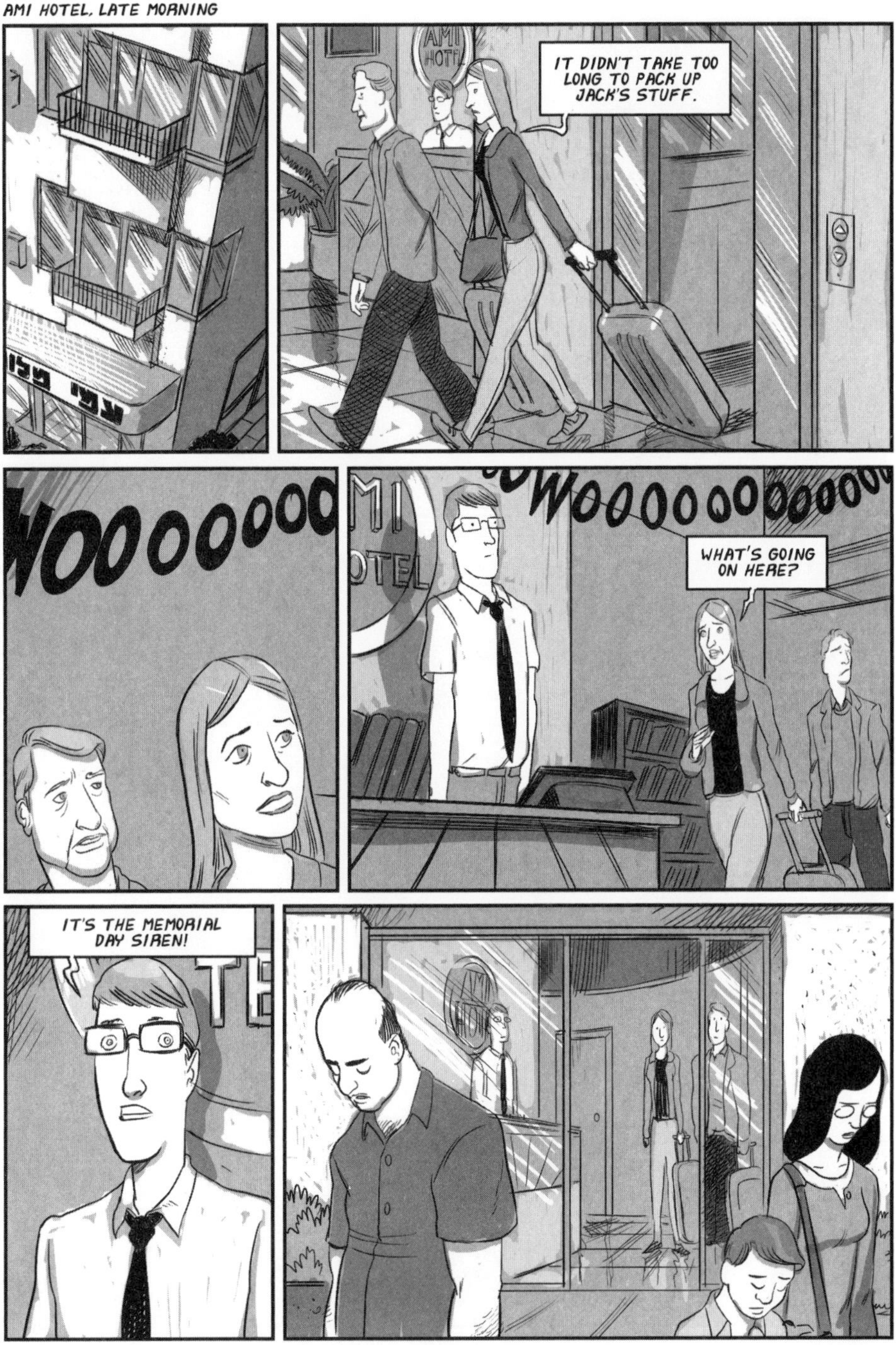
AMI HOTEL, LATE MORNING
IT DIDN'T TAKE TOO LONG TO PACK UP JACK'S STUFF.
WOOOOOOO
WOOOOOOOOOOOOOO
WHAT'S GOING ON HERE?
IT'S THE MEMORIAL DAY SIREN!

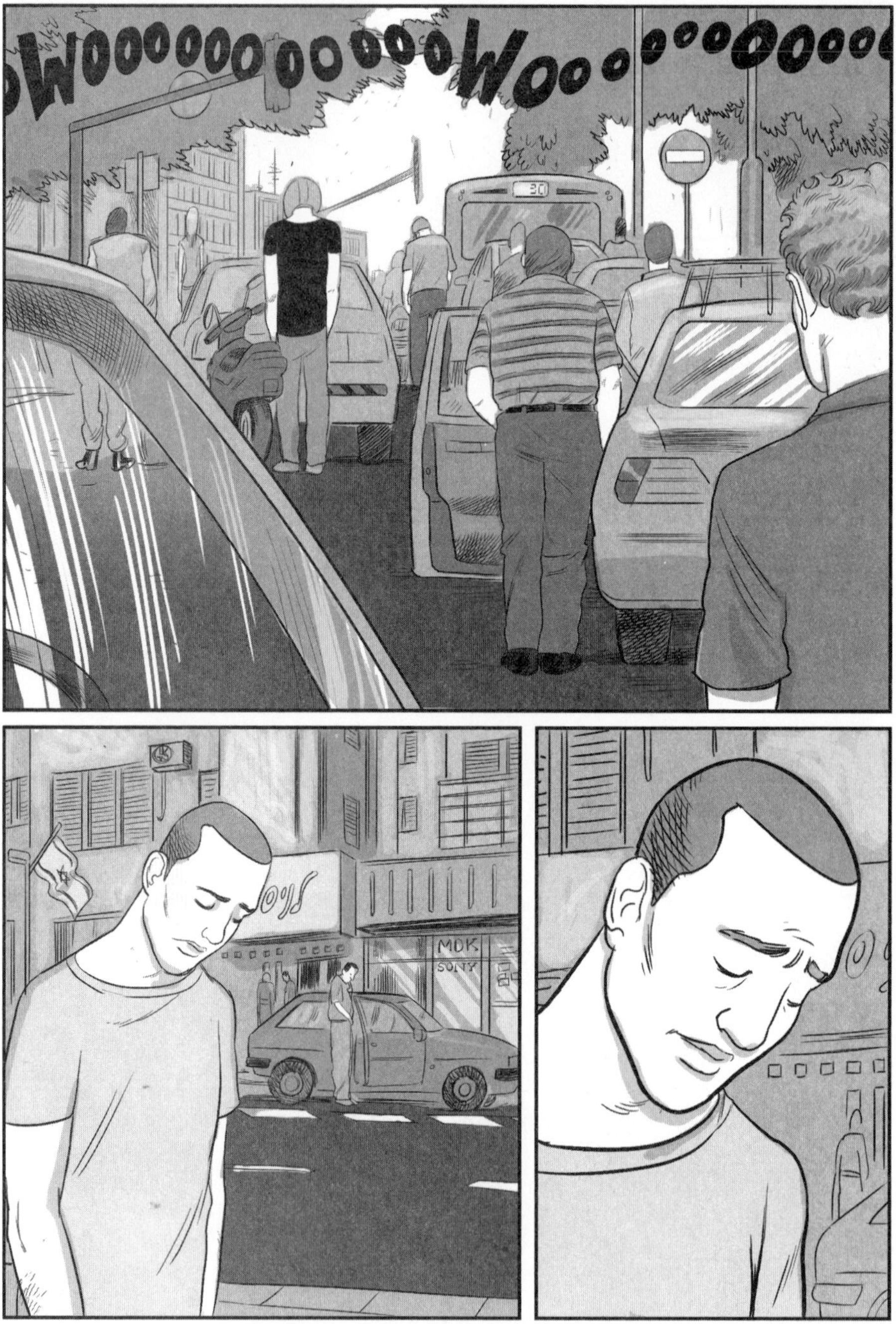
oWoooooooooooWooooooooooo
30
MDK
SONY

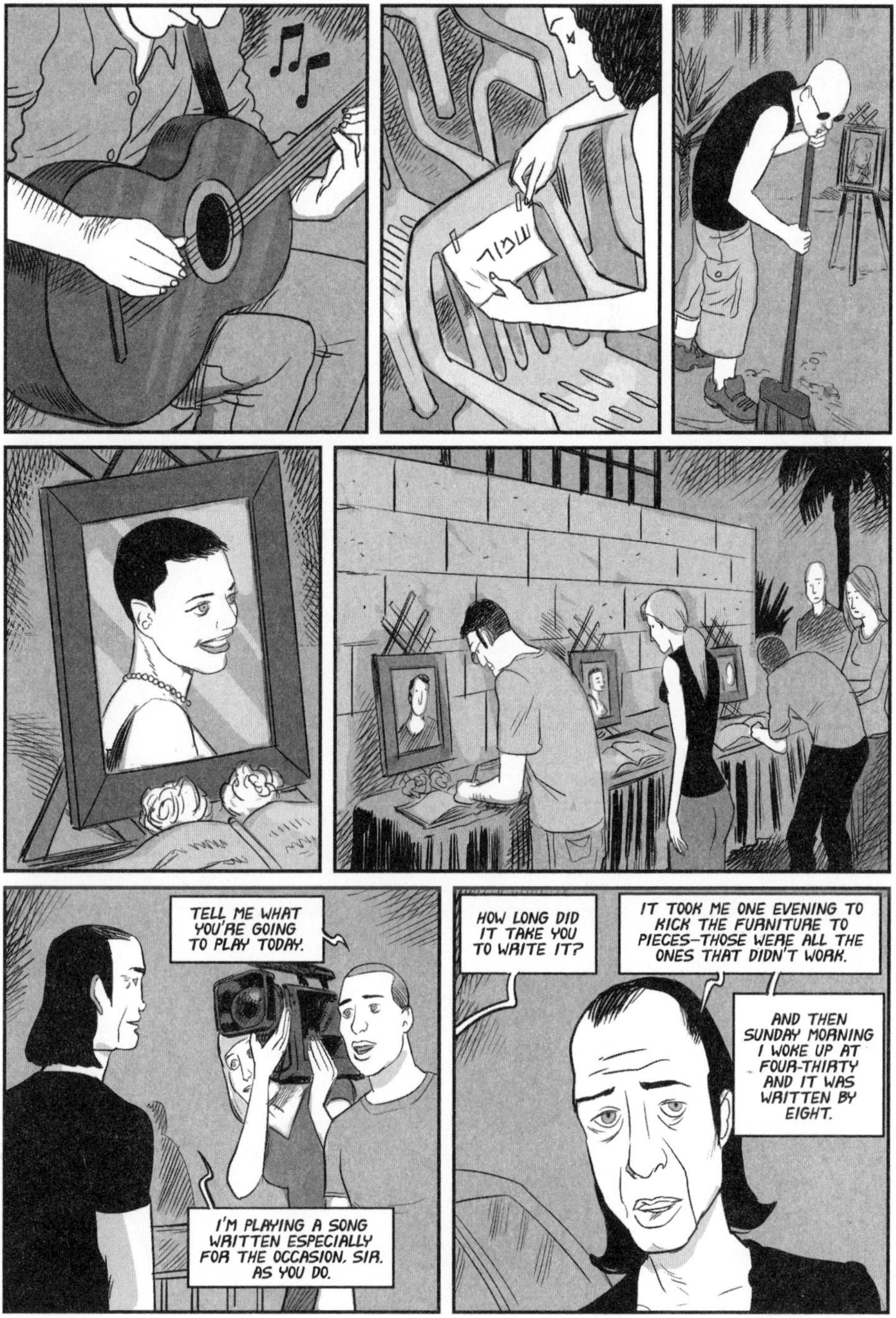
שמור
TELL ME WHAT YOU'RE GOING TO PLAY TODAY.
I'M PLAYING A SONG WRITTEN ESPECIALLY FOR THE OCCASION, SIR. AS YOU DO.
HOW LONG DID IT TAKE YOU TO WRITE IT?
IT TOOK ME ONE EVENING TO KICK THE FURNITURE TO PIECES—THOSE WERE ALL THE ONES THAT DIDN'T WORK.
AND THEN SUNDAY MORNING I WOKE UP AT FOUR-THIRTY AND IT WAS WRITTEN BY EIGHT.

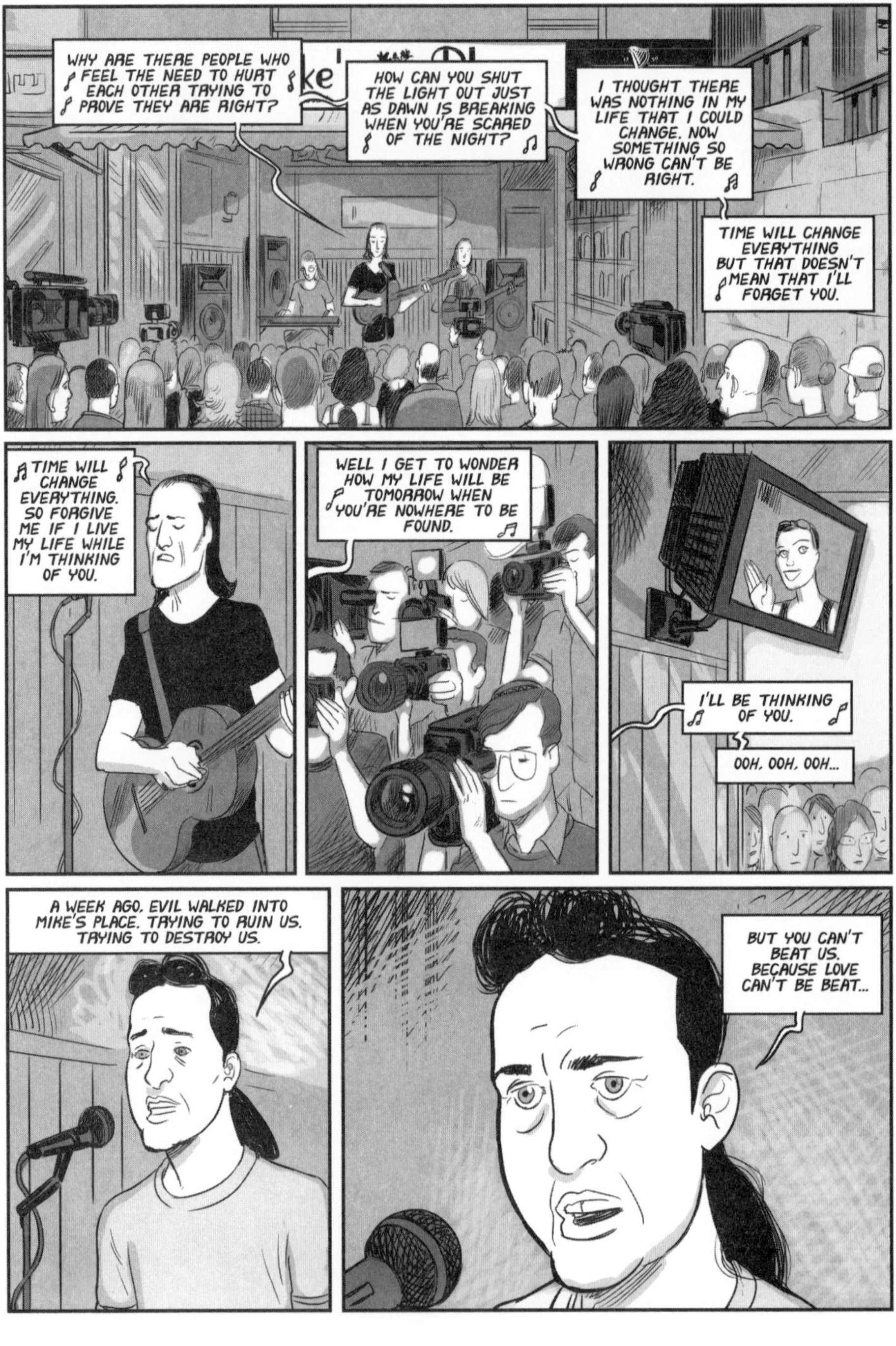

WHY ARE THERE PEOPLE WHO FEEL THE NEED TO HURT EACH OTHER TRYING TO PROVE THEY ARE RIGHT?
HOW CAN YOU SHUT THE LIGHT OUT JUST AS DAWN IS BREAKING WHEN YOU'RE SCARED OF THE NIGHT?
I THOUGHT THERE WAS NOTHING IN MY LIFE THAT I COULD CHANGE. NOW SOMETHING SO WRONG CAN'T BE RIGHT.
TIME WILL CHANGE EVERYTHING BUT THAT DOESN'T MEAN THAT I'LL FORGET YOU.
TIME WILL CHANGE EVERYTHING. SO FORGIVE ME IF I LIVE MY LIFE WHILE I'M THINKING OF YOU.
WELL I GET TO WONDER HOW MY LIFE WILL BE TOMORROW WHEN YOU'RE NOWHERE TO BE FOUND.
I'LL BE THINKING OF YOU.
OOH, OOH, OOH...
A WEEK AGO, EVIL WALKED INTO MIKE'S PLACE. TRYING TO RUIN US. TRYING TO DESTROY US.
BUT YOU CAN'T BEAT US. BECAUSE LOVE CAN'T BE BEAT...

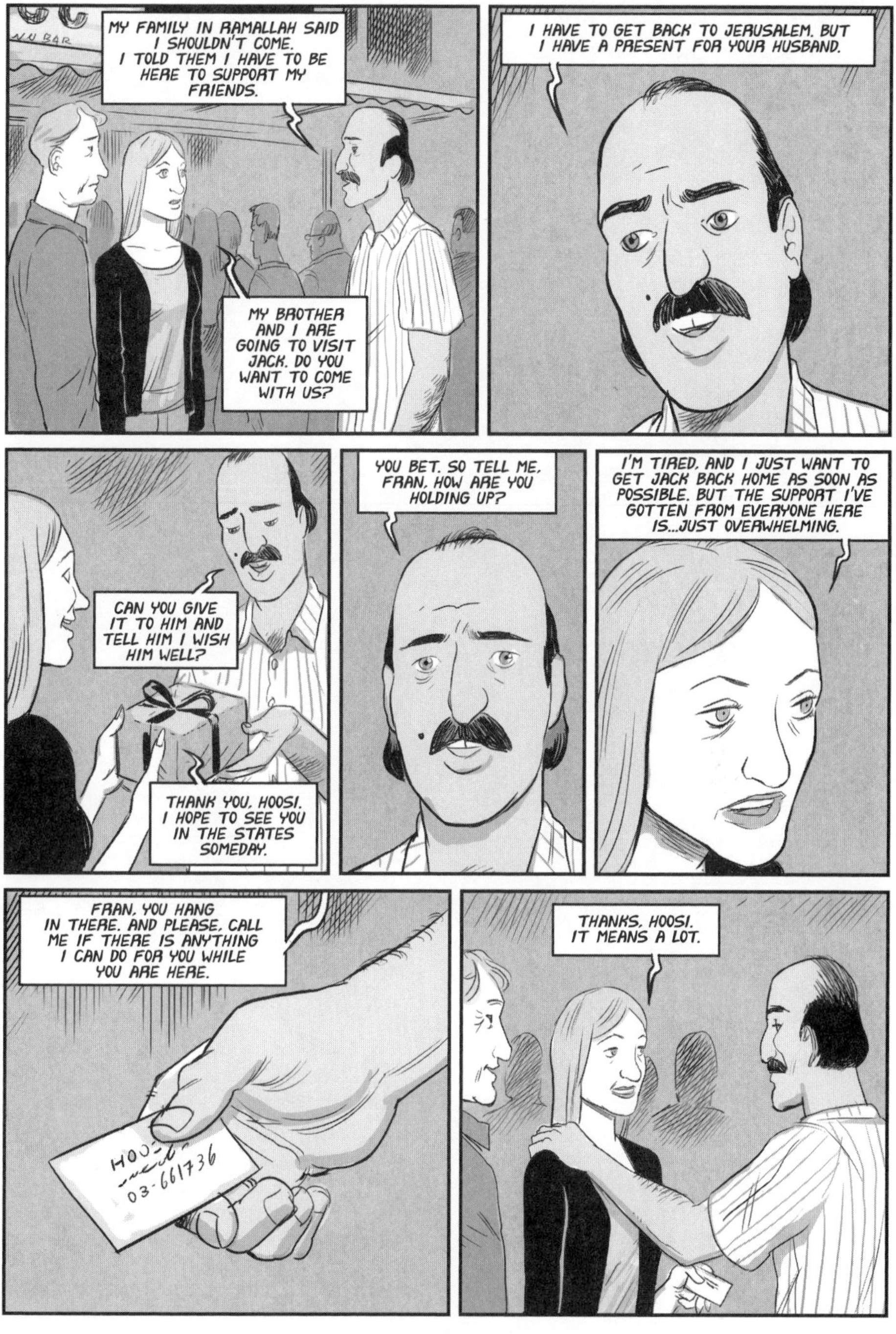

MY FAMILY IN RAMALLAH SAID I SHOULDN'T COME. I TOLD THEM I HAVE TO BE HERE TO SUPPORT MY FRIENDS.
MY BROTHER AND I ARE GOING TO VISIT JACK. DO YOU WANT TO COME WITH US?
I HAVE TO GET BACK TO JERUSALEM. BUT I HAVE A PRESENT FOR YOUR HUSBAND.
CAN YOU GIVE IT TO HIM AND TELL HIM I WISH HIM WELL?
THANK YOU, HOOSI. I HOPE TO SEE YOU IN THE STATES SOMEDAY.
YOU BET. SO TELL ME, FRAN, HOW ARE YOU HOLDING UP?
I'M TIRED, AND I JUST WANT TO GET JACK BACK HOME AS SOON AS POSSIBLE. BUT THE SUPPORT I'VE GOTTEN FROM EVERYONE HERE IS...JUST OVERWHELMING.
FRAN, YOU HANG IN THERE. AND PLEASE, CALL ME IF THERE IS ANYTHING I CAN DO FOR YOU WHILE YOU ARE HERE.
03-661736
THANKS, HOOSI. IT MEANS A LOT.

ICHILOV HOSPITAL

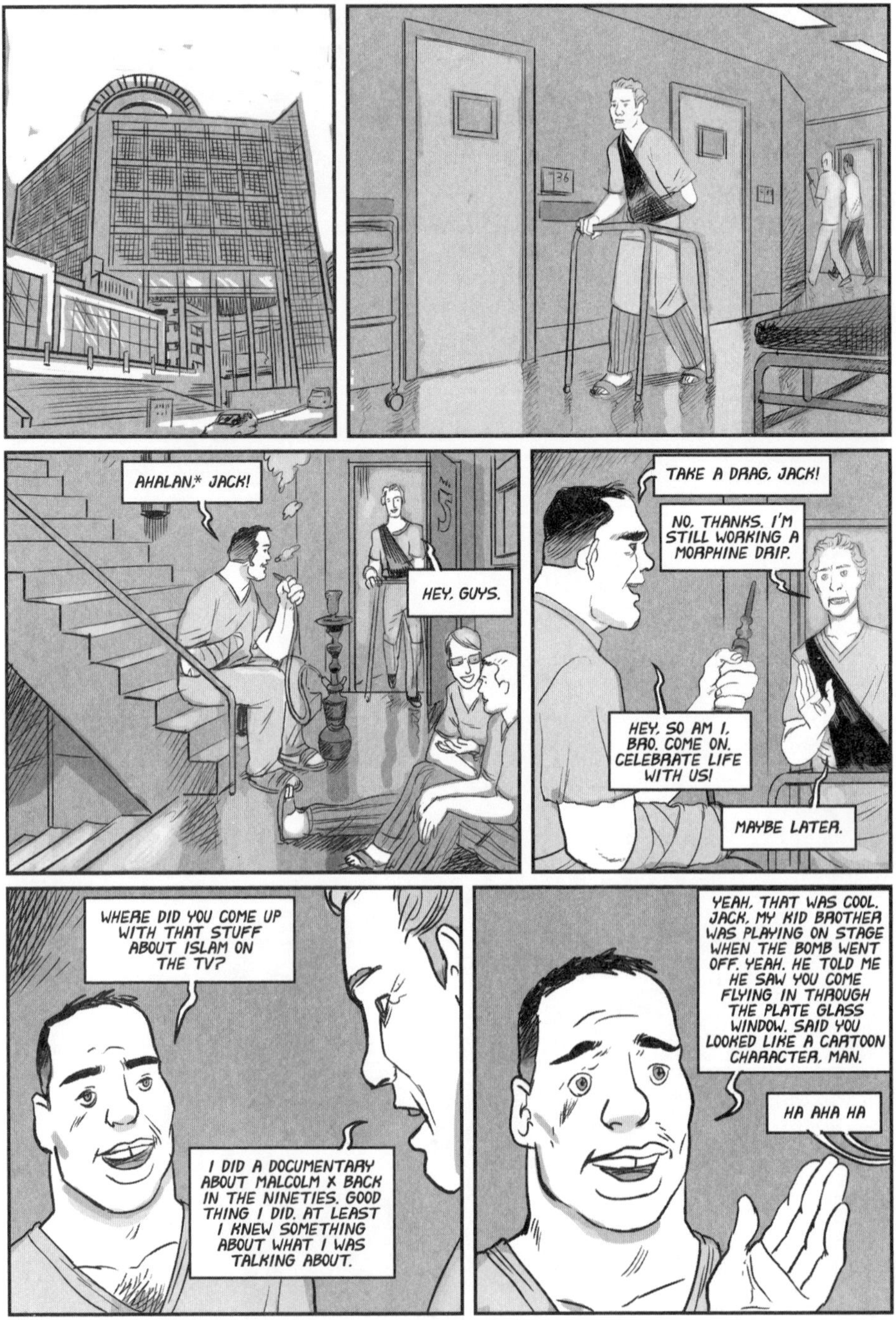
AHALAN,* JACK!
HEY, GUYS.
TAKE A DRAG, JACK!
NO, THANKS. I'M STILL WORKING A MORPHINE DRIP.
HEY, SO AM I, BRO. COME ON. CELEBRATE LIFE WITH US!
MAYBE LATER.
WHERE DID YOU COME UP WITH THAT STUFF ABOUT ISLAM ON THE TV?
I DID A DOCUMENTARY ABOUT MALCOLM X BACK IN THE NINETIES. GOOD THING I DID. AT LEAST I KNEW SOMETHING ABOUT WHAT I WAS TALKING ABOUT.
YEAH, THAT WAS COOL, JACK. MY KID BROTHER WAS PLAYING ON STAGE WHEN THE BOMB WENT OFF. YEAH, HE TOLD ME HE SAW YOU COME FLYING IN THROUGH THE PLATE GLASS WINDOW. SAID YOU LOOKED LIKE A CARTOON CHARACTER, MAN.
HA AHA HA

*WELCOME

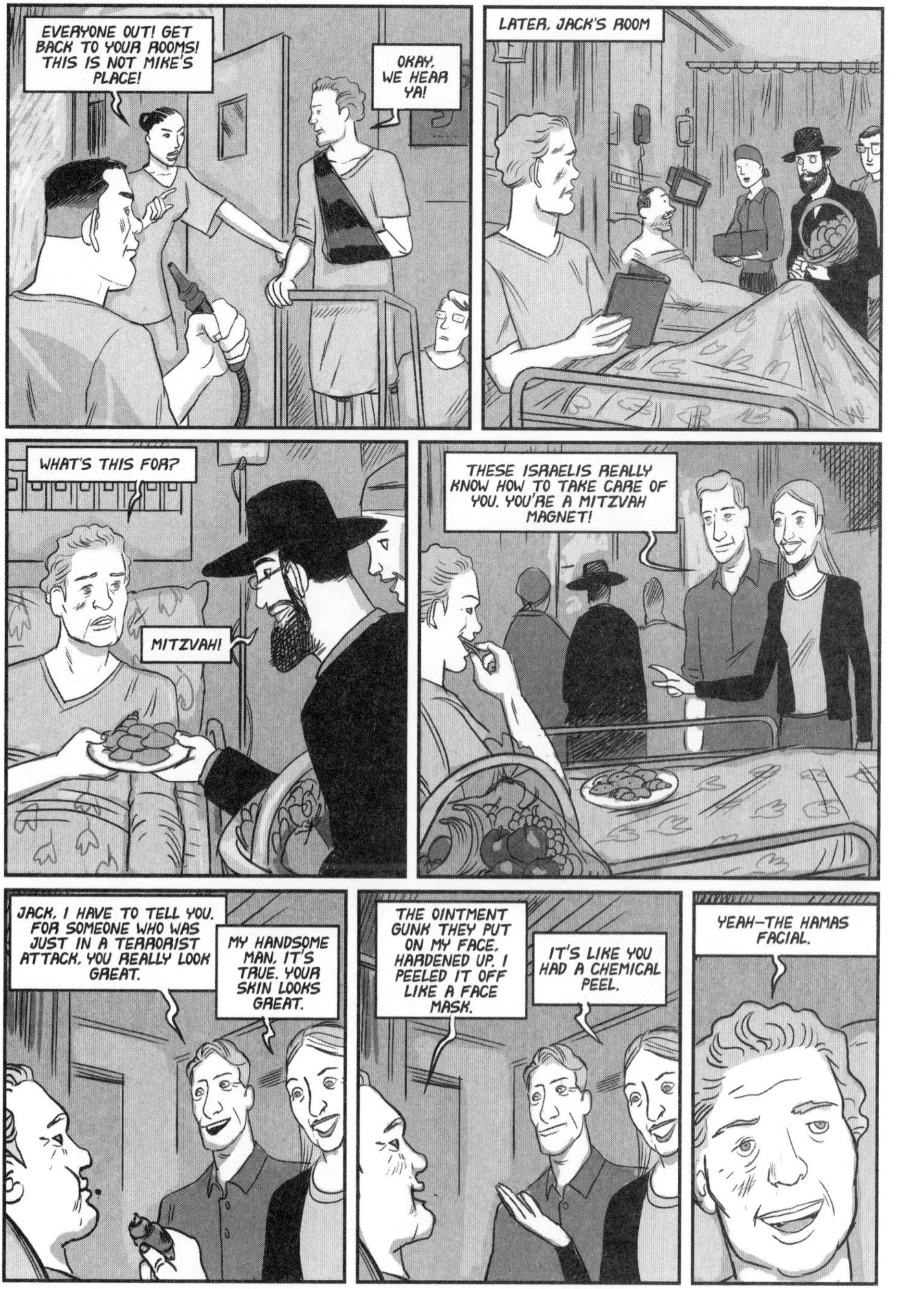
EVERYONE OUT! GET BACK TO YOUR ROOMS! THIS IS NOT MIKE'S PLACE!
OKAY, WE HEAR YA!
LATER, JACK'S ROOM
WHAT'S THIS FOR?
MITZVAH!
THESE ISRAELIS REALLY KNOW HOW TO TAKE CARE OF YOU. YOU'RE A MITZVAH MAGNET!
JACK, I HAVE TO TELL YOU. FOR SOMEONE WHO WAS JUST IN A TERRORIST ATTACK, YOU REALLY LOOK GREAT.
MY HANDSOME MAN, IT'S TRUE. YOUR SKIN LOOKS GREAT.
THE OINTMENT GUNK THEY PUT ON MY FACE, HARDENED UP. I PEELED IT OFF LIKE A FACE MASK.
IT'S LIKE YOU HAD A CHEMICAL PEEL.
YEAH—THE HAMAS FACIAL.

OLD JAFFA

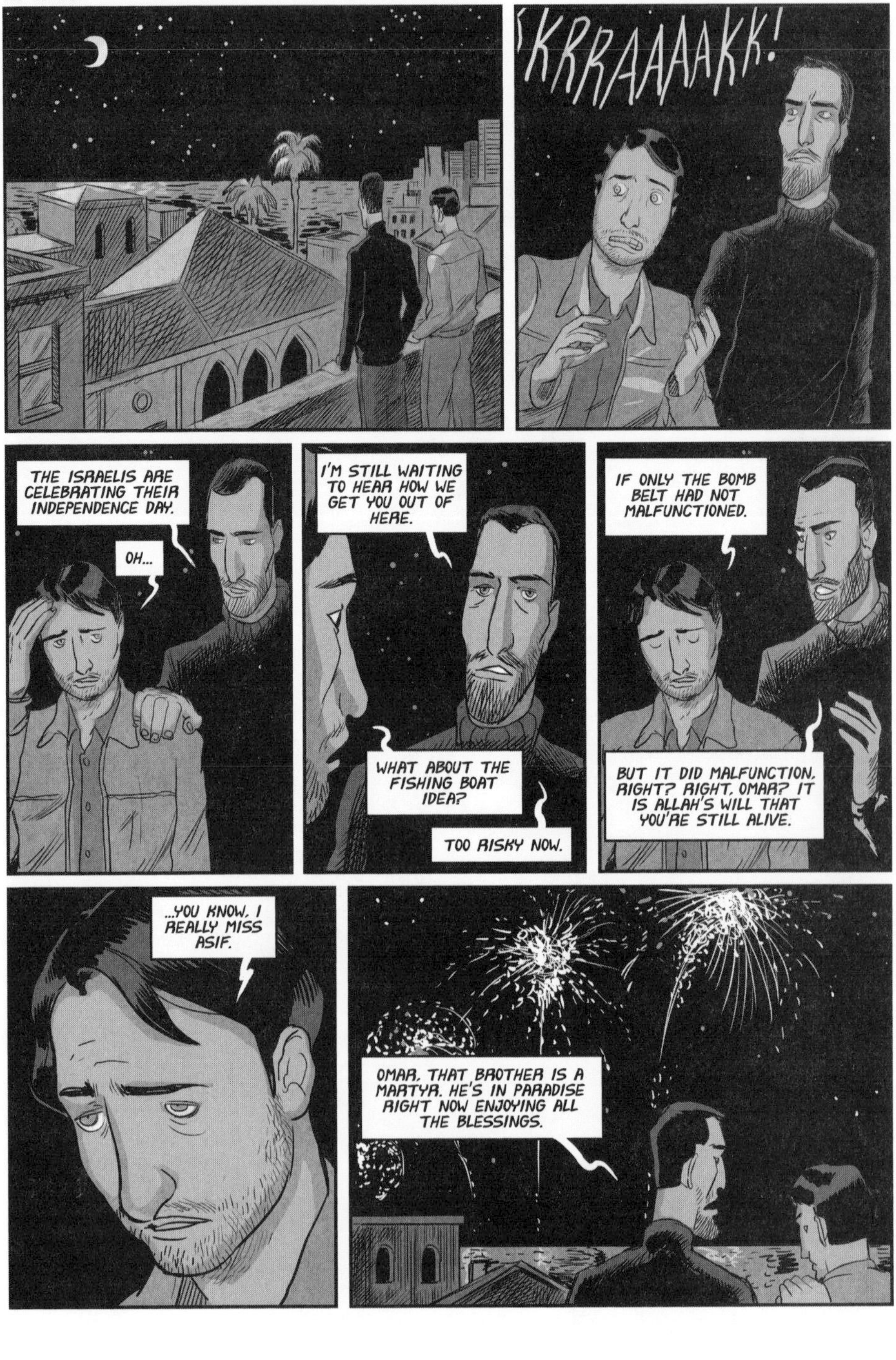

KRRAAAAKK!
THE ISRAELIS ARE CELEBRATING THEIR INDEPENDENCE DAY.
OH...
I'M STILL WAITING TO HEAR HOW WE GET YOU OUT OF HERE.
WHAT ABOUT THE FISHING BOAT IDEA?
TOO RISKY NOW.
IF ONLY THE BOMB BELT HAD NOT MALFUNCTIONED.
BUT IT DID MALFUNCTION, RIGHT? RIGHT, OMAR? IT IS ALLAH'S WILL THAT YOU'RE STILL ALIVE.
...YOU KNOW, I REALLY MISS ASIF.
OMAR, THAT BROTHER IS A MARTYR. HE'S IN PARADISE RIGHT NOW ENJOYING ALL THE BLESSINGS.

MIKE'S PLACE, ISRAEL INDEPENDENCE DAY EVE (SAME TIME)

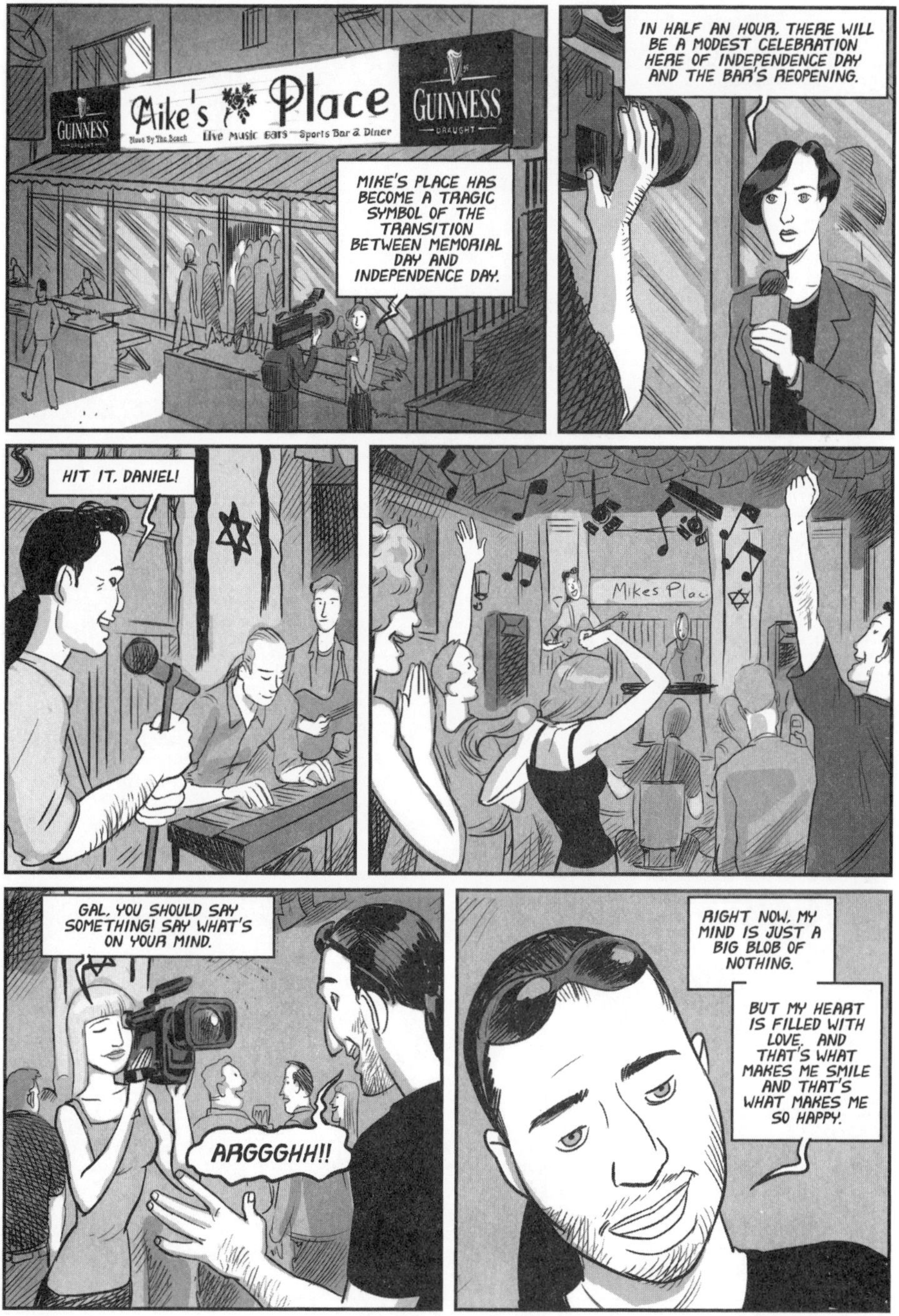
Mike's Place
GUINNESS
Blues By The Beach
Live Music Bars
Sports Bar & Diner
GUINNESS
MIKE'S PLACE HAS BECOME A TRAGIC SYMBOL OF THE TRANSITION BETWEEN MEMORIAL DAY AND INDEPENDENCE DAY.
IN HALF AN HOUR, THERE WILL BE A MODEST CELEBRATION HERE OF INDEPENDENCE DAY AND THE BAR'S REOPENING.
HIT IT, DANIEL!
Mikes Plac
GAL, YOU SHOULD SAY SOMETHING! SAY WHAT'S ON YOUR MIND.
ARGGGHH!!
RIGHT NOW, MY MIND IS JUST A BIG BLOB OF NOTHING.
BUT MY HEART IS FILLED WITH LOVE. AND THAT'S WHAT MAKES ME SMILE AND THAT'S WHAT MAKES ME SO HAPPY.

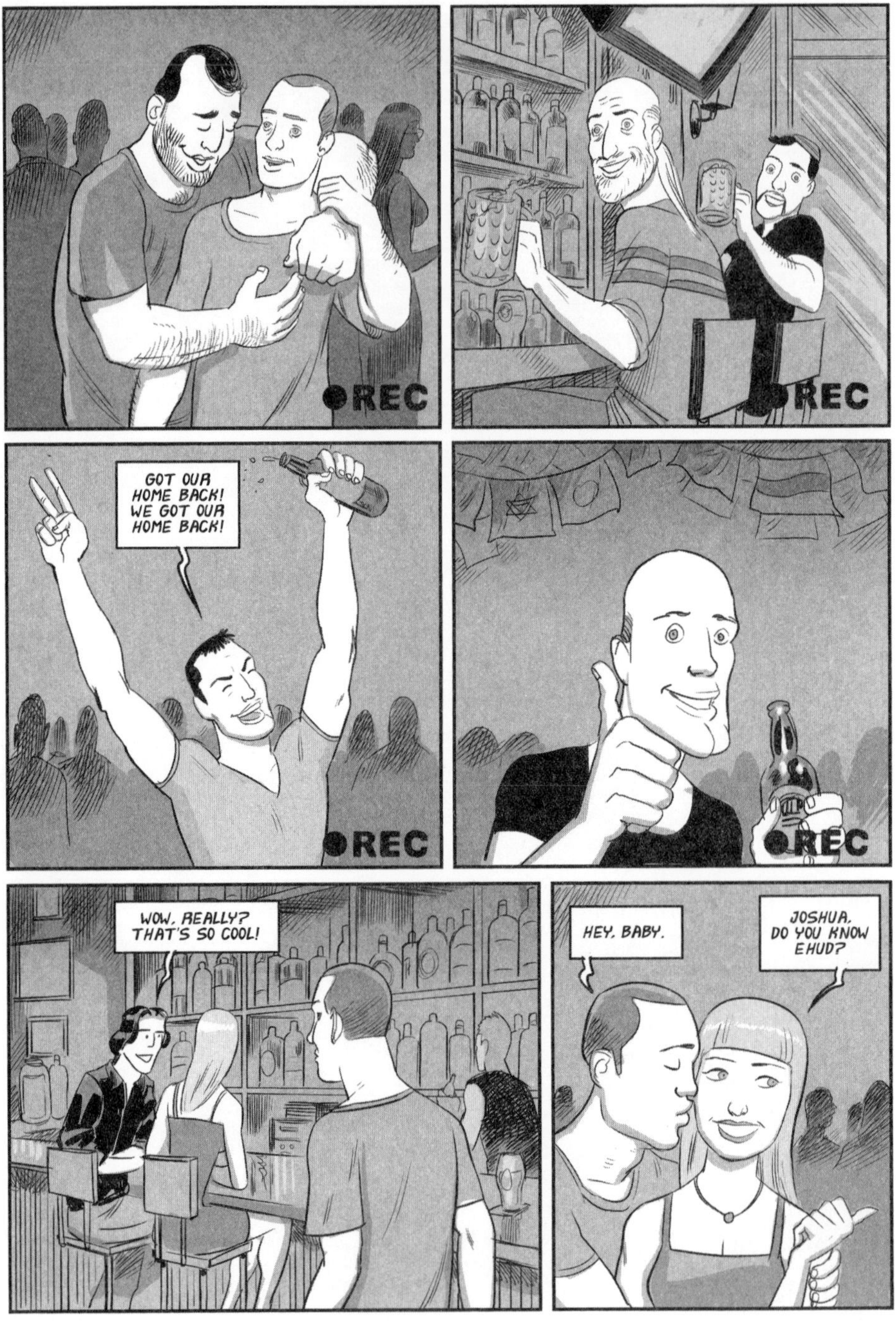
●REC
●REC
GOT OUR HOME BACK! WE GOT OUR HOME BACK!
●REC
●REC
WOW, REALLY? THAT'S SO COOL!
HEY, BABY.
JOSHUA, DO YOU KNOW EHUD?

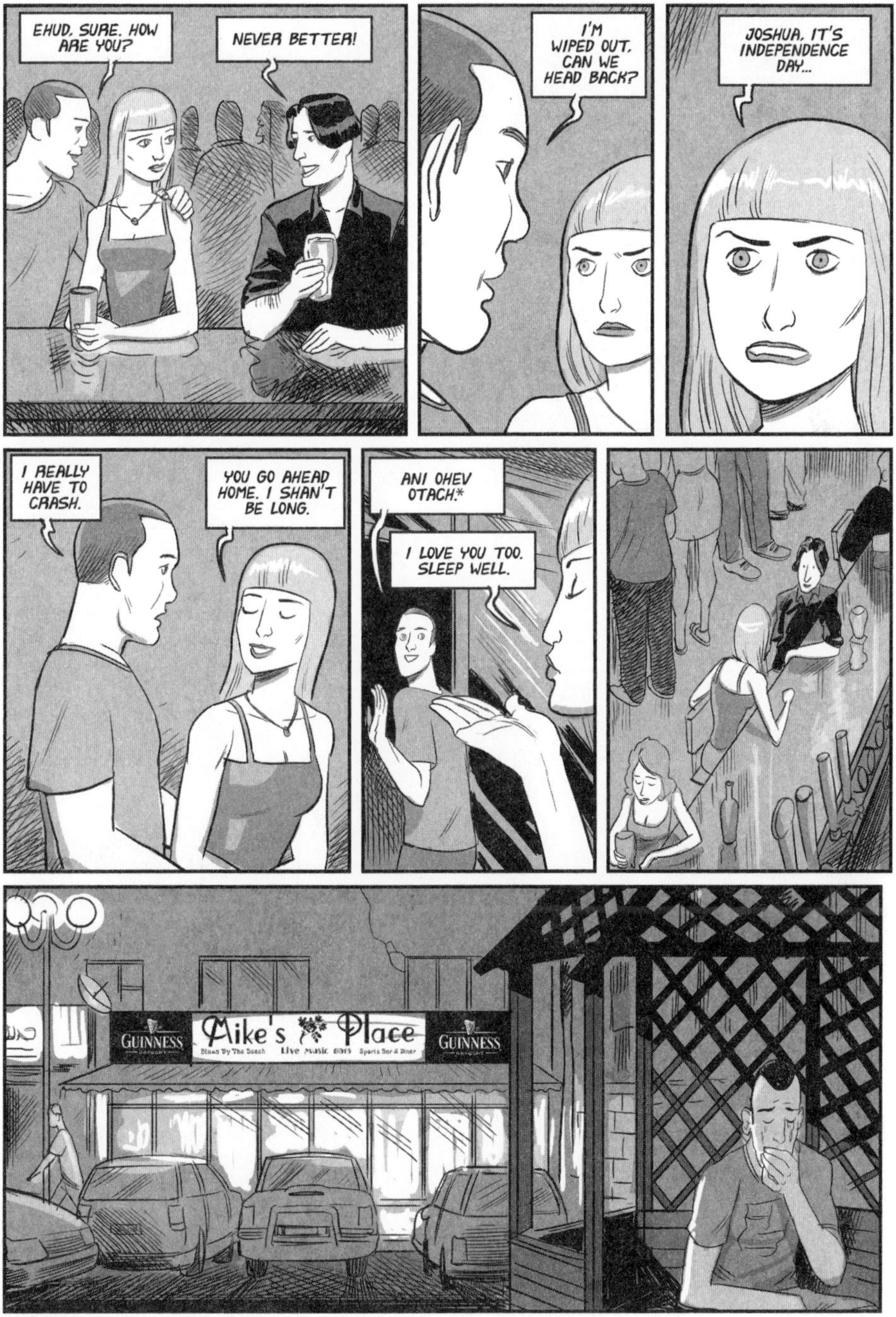
EHUD, SURE. HOW ARE YOU?
NEVER BETTER!
I'M WIPED OUT. CAN WE HEAD BACK?
JOSHUA, IT'S INDEPENDENCE DAY...
I REALLY HAVE TO CRASH.
YOU GO AHEAD HOME. I SHAN'T BE LONG.
ANI OHEV OTACH.*
I LOVE YOU TOO. SLEEP WELL.
GUINNESS
Mike's Place
Blues By The Beach Live Music Sports Bar & Diner
GUINNESS

*I LOVE YOU

ICHILOV HOSPITAL

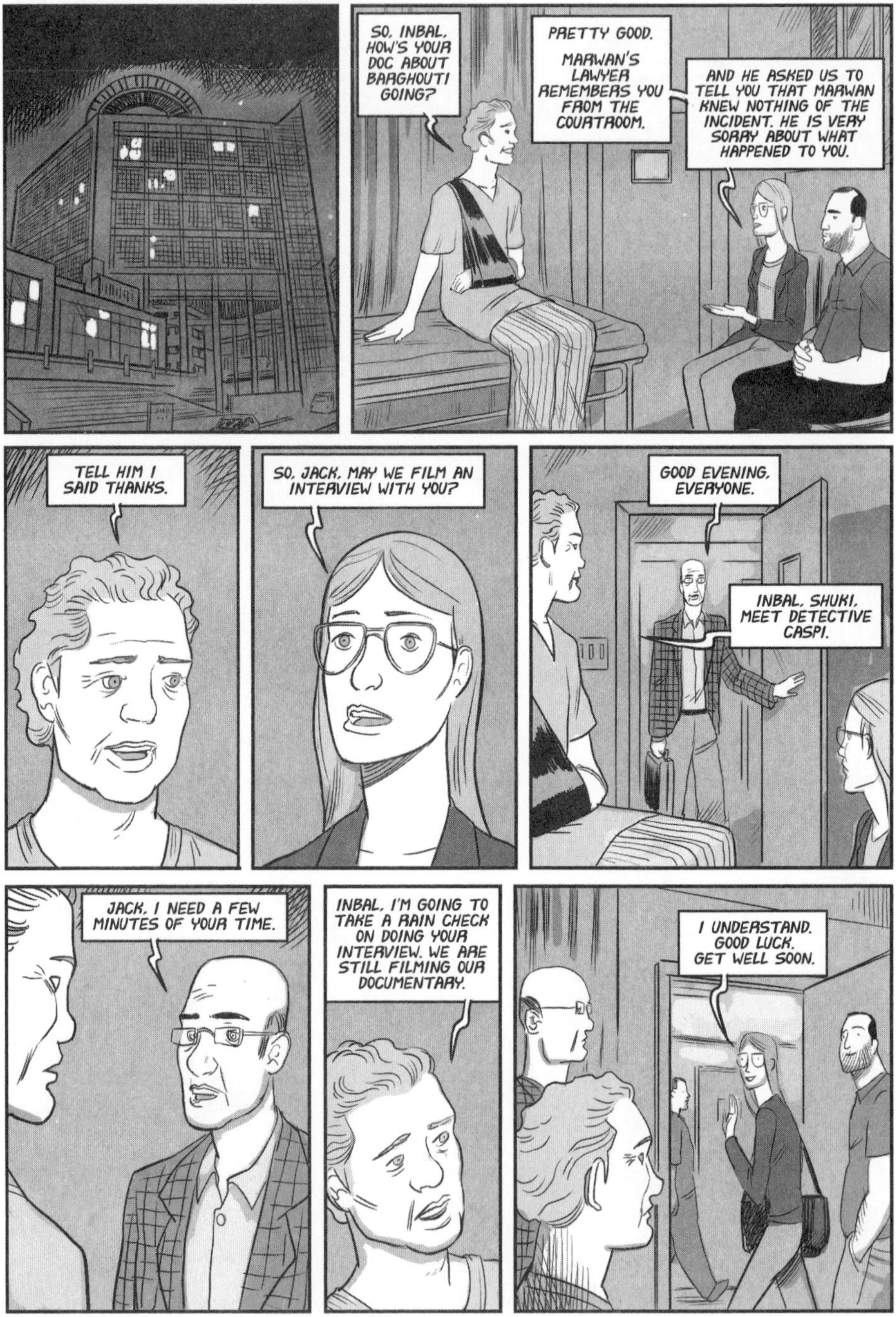
SO, INBAL, HOW'S YOUR DOC ABOUT BARGHOUTI GOING?
PRETTY GOOD.
MARWAN'S LAWYER REMEMBERS YOU FROM THE COURTROOM.
AND HE ASKED US TO TELL YOU THAT MARWAN KNEW NOTHING OF THE INCIDENT. HE IS VERY SORRY ABOUT WHAT HAPPENED TO YOU.
TELL HIM I SAID THANKS.
SO, JACK, MAY WE FILM AN INTERVIEW WITH YOU?
GOOD EVENING, EVERYONE.
INBAL, SHUKI, MEET DETECTIVE CASPI.
JACK, I NEED A FEW MINUTES OF YOUR TIME.
INBAL, I'M GOING TO TAKE A RAIN CHECK ON DOING YOUR INTERVIEW. WE ARE STILL FILMING OUR DOCUMENTARY.
I UNDERSTAND. GOOD LUCK. GET WELL SOON.

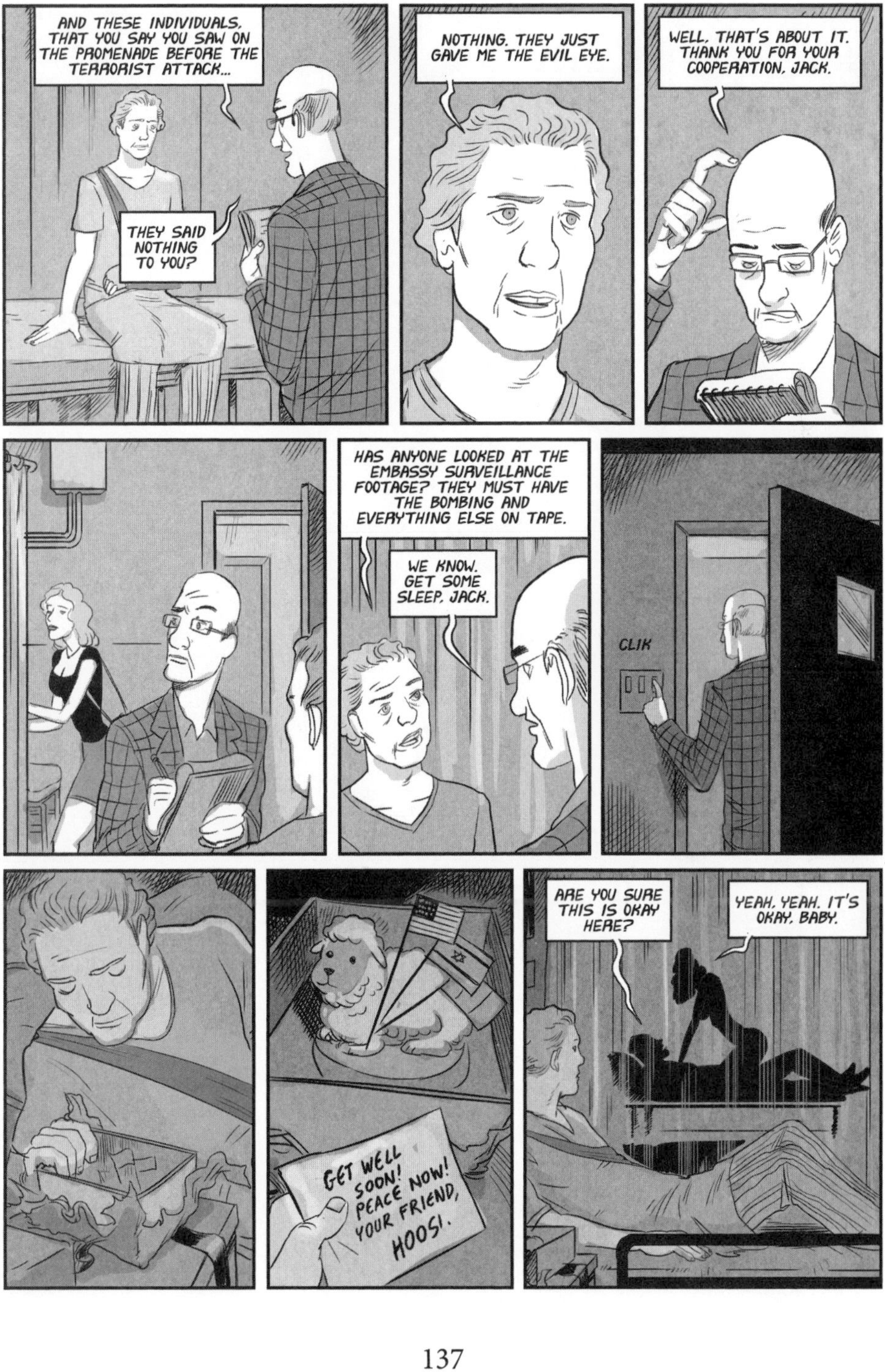
AND THESE INDIVIDUALS, THAT YOU SAY YOU SAW ON THE PROMENADE BEFORE THE TERRORIST ATTACK...
THEY SAID NOTHING TO YOU?
NOTHING. THEY JUST GAVE ME THE EVIL EYE.
WELL, THAT'S ABOUT IT. THANK YOU FOR YOUR COOPERATION, JACK.
HAS ANYONE LOOKED AT THE EMBASSY SURVEILLANCE FOOTAGE? THEY MUST HAVE THE BOMBING AND EVERYTHING ELSE ON TAPE.
WE KNOW. GET SOME SLEEP, JACK.
CLIK
GET WELL SOON! PEACE NOW! YOUR FRIEND, HOOSI.
ARE YOU SURE THIS IS OKAY HERE?
YEAH. YEAH. IT'S OKAY, BABY.

PSYCHIC ON ALLENBY STREET

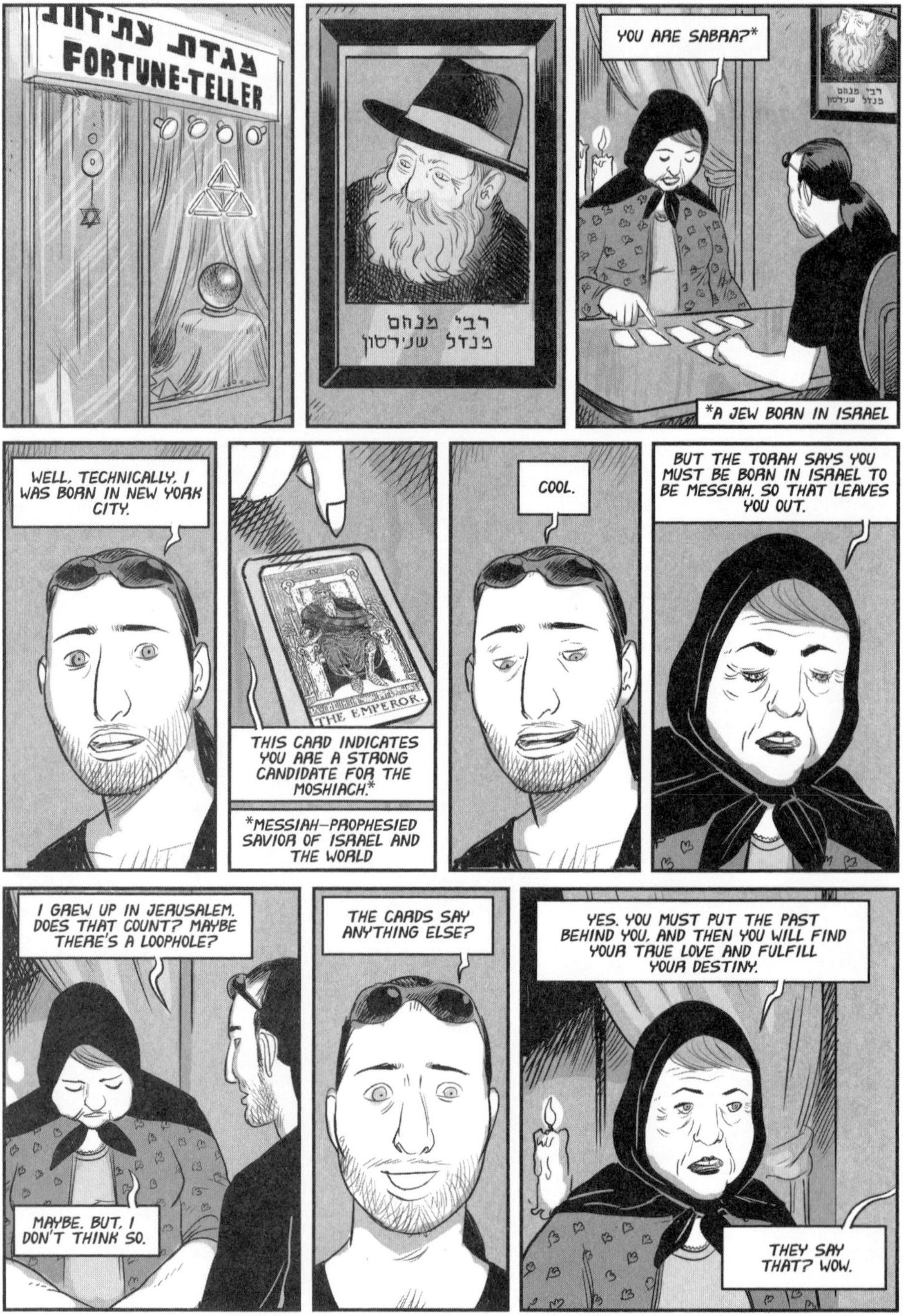

מגדת עתידות
FORTUNE-TELLER
רבי מנחם
מנדל שנירסון
YOU ARE SABRA?*
*A JEW BORN IN ISRAEL
WELL, TECHNICALLY, I WAS BORN IN NEW YORK CITY.
THE EMPEROR.
THIS CARD INDICATES YOU ARE A STRONG CANDIDATE FOR THE MOSHIACH.*
*MESSIAH—PROPHESIED SAVIOR OF ISRAEL AND THE WORLD
COOL.
BUT THE TORAH SAYS YOU MUST BE BORN IN ISRAEL TO BE MESSIAH. SO THAT LEAVES YOU OUT.
I GREW UP IN JERUSALEM. DOES THAT COUNT? MAYBE THERE'S A LOOPHOLE?
MAYBE. BUT, I DON'T THINK SO.
THE CARDS SAY ANYTHING ELSE?
YES. YOU MUST PUT THE PAST BEHIND YOU, AND THEN YOU WILL FIND YOUR TRUE LOVE AND FULFILL YOUR DESTINY.
THEY SAY THAT? WOW.

BEACHFRONT CONDOMINIUM, TEL AVIV

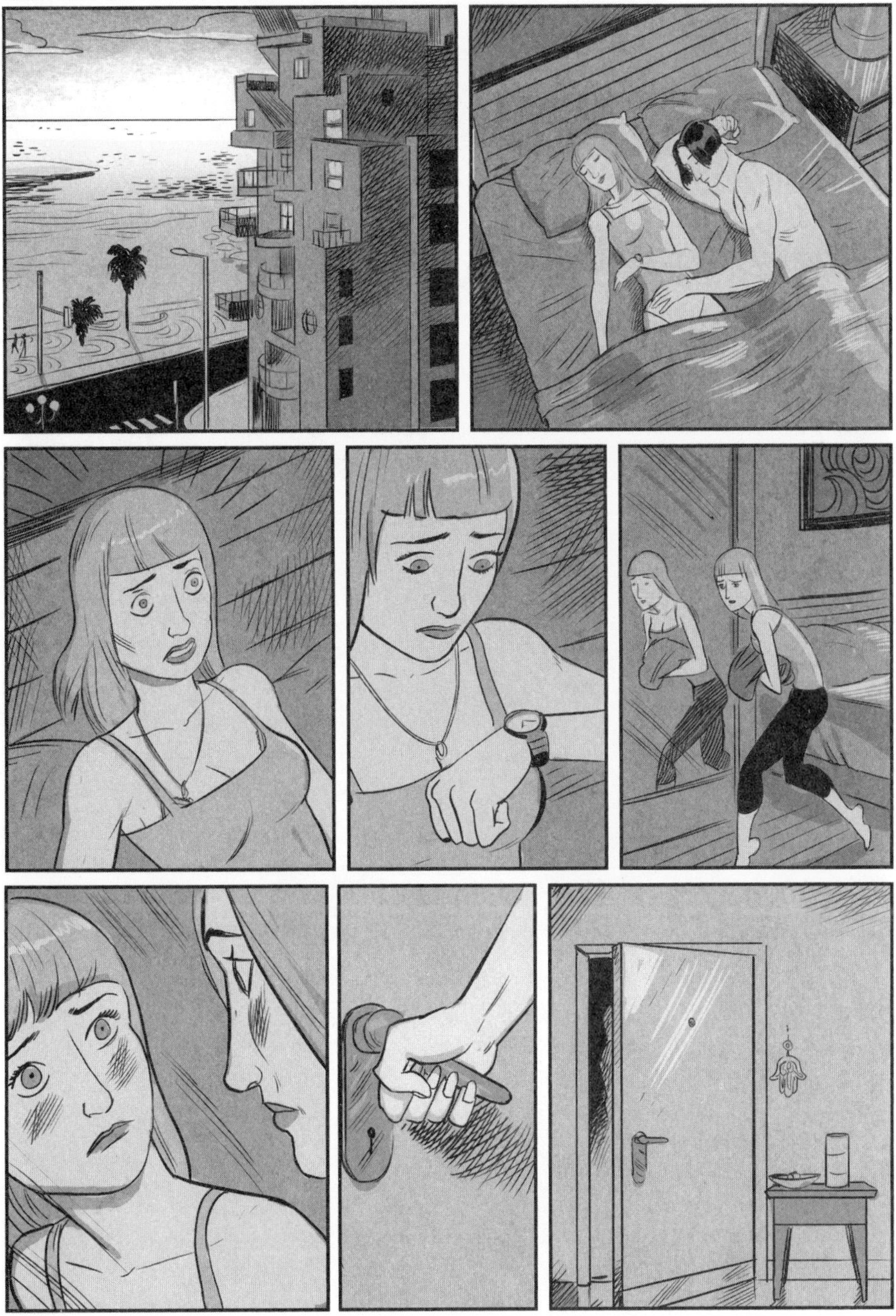

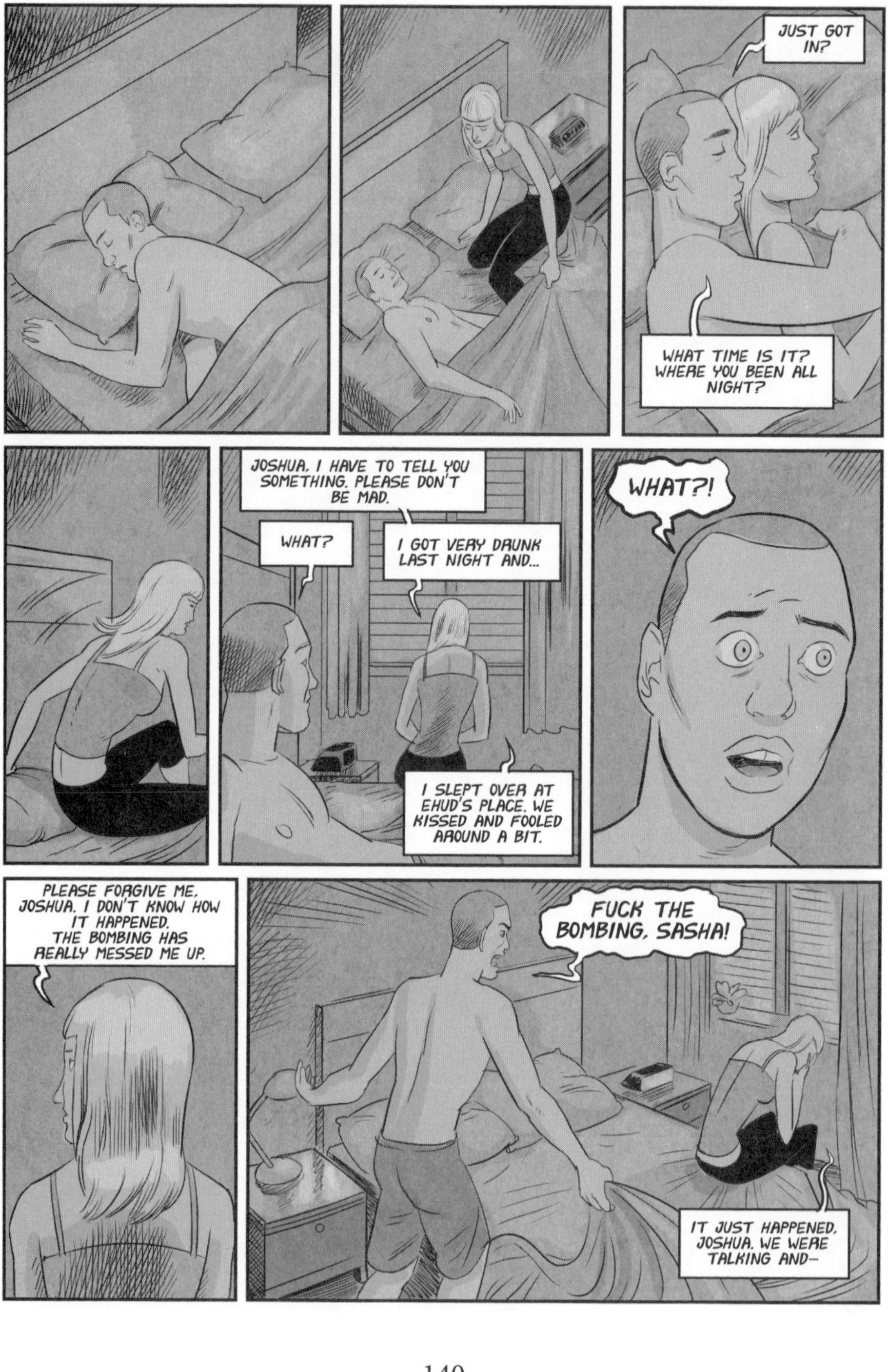
JUST GOT IN?
WHAT TIME IS IT? WHERE YOU BEEN ALL NIGHT?
JOSHUA, I HAVE TO TELL YOU SOMETHING. PLEASE DON'T BE MAD.
WHAT?
I GOT VERY DRUNK LAST NIGHT AND...
I SLEPT OVER AT EHUD'S PLACE. WE KISSED AND FOOLED AROUND A BIT.
WHAT?!
PLEASE FORGIVE ME, JOSHUA. I DON'T KNOW HOW IT HAPPENED. THE BOMBING HAS REALLY MESSED ME UP.
FUCK THE BOMBING, SASHA!
IT JUST HAPPENED, JOSHUA. WE WERE TALKING AND–

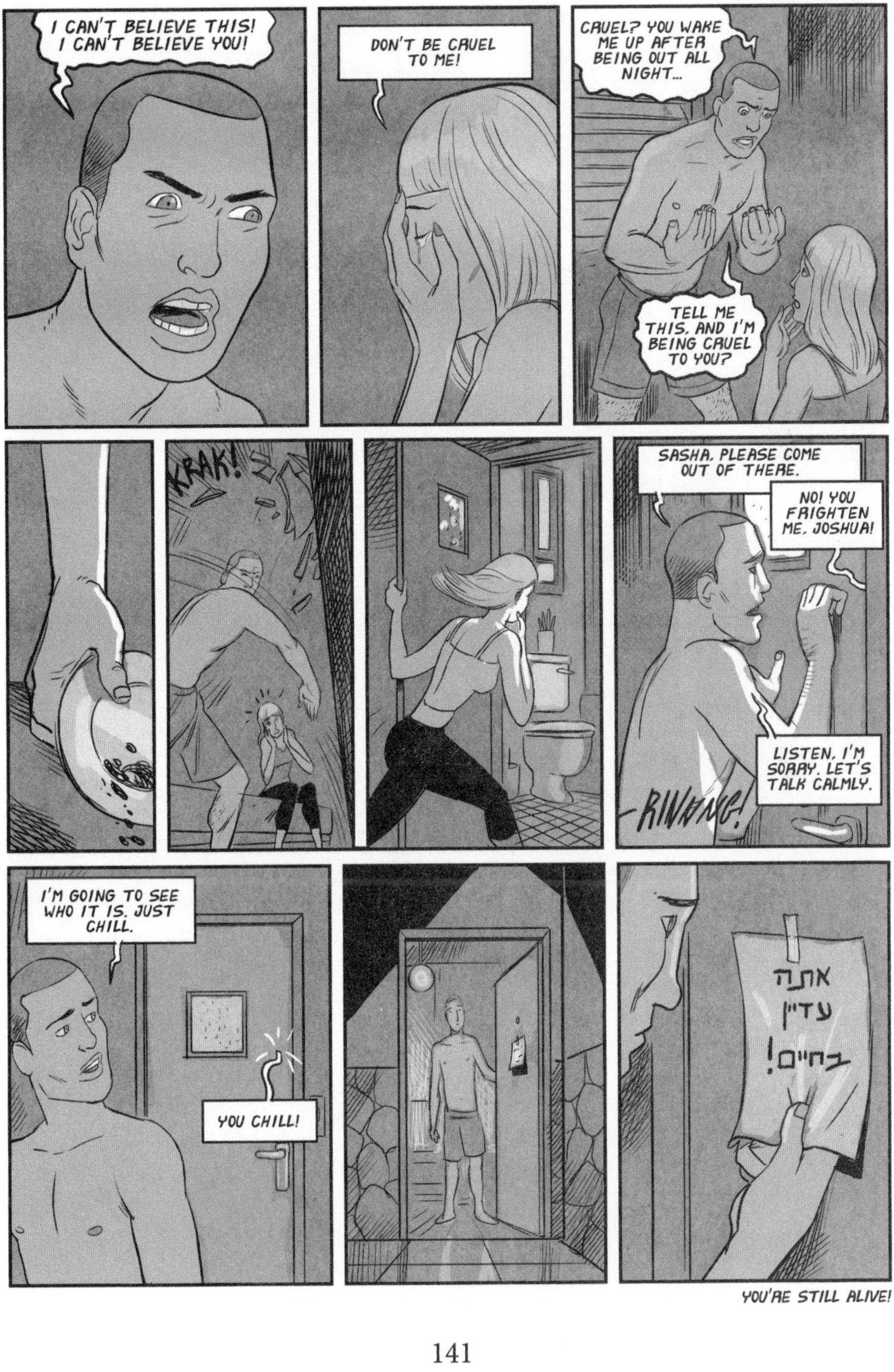
I CAN'T BELIEVE THIS! I CAN'T BELIEVE YOU!
DON'T BE CRUEL TO ME!
CRUEL? YOU WAKE ME UP AFTER BEING OUT ALL NIGHT...
TELL ME THIS, AND I'M BEING CRUEL TO YOU?
KRAK!
SASHA, PLEASE COME OUT OF THERE.
NO! YOU FRIGHTEN ME, JOSHUA!
LISTEN, I'M SORRY. LET'S TALK CALMLY.
RINNNG!
I'M GOING TO SEE WHO IT IS. JUST CHILL.
YOU CHILL!
אתה
עדיין
בחיים!
YOU'RE STILL ALIVE!

ICHILOV HOSPITAL, AFTERNOON

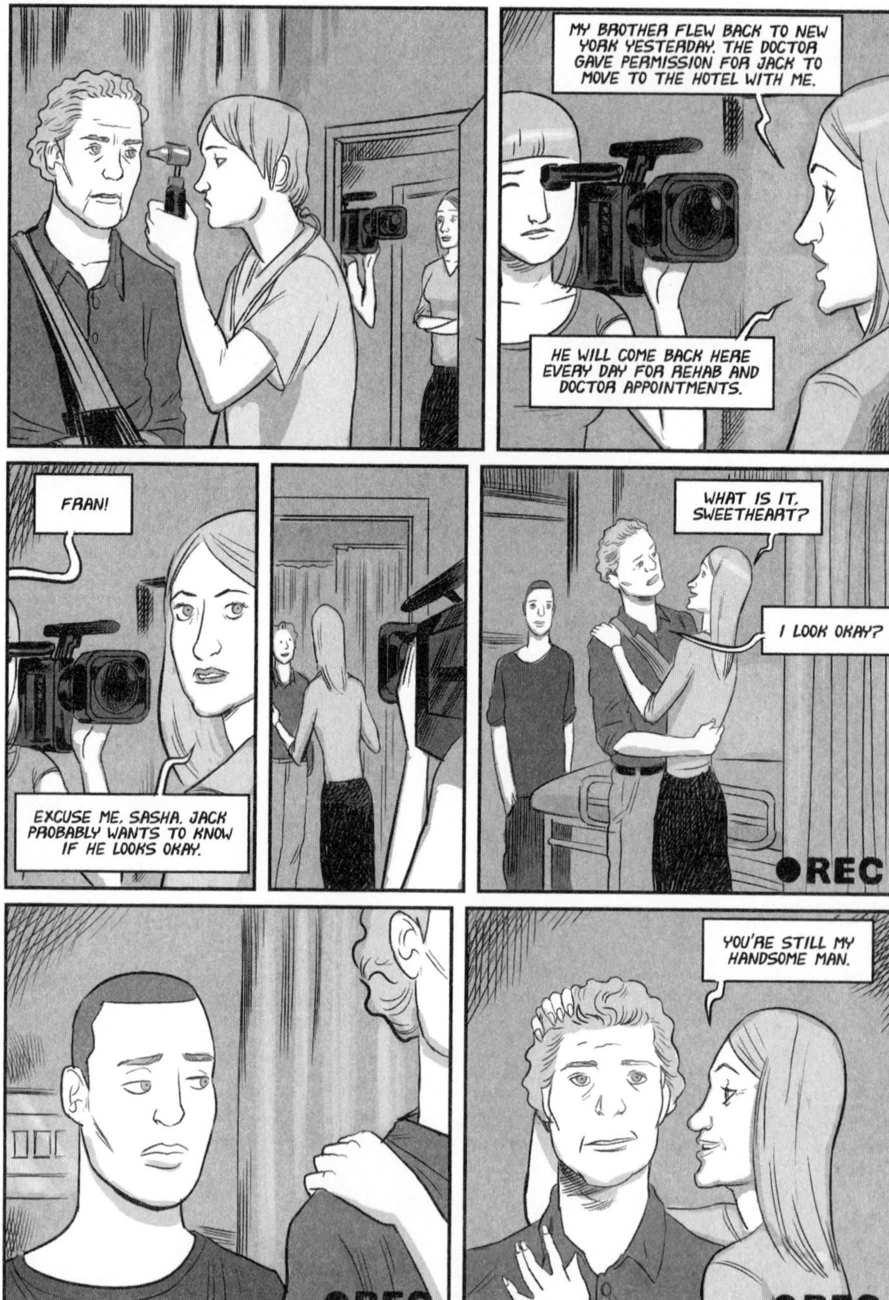

MY BROTHER FLEW BACK TO NEW YORK YESTERDAY. THE DOCTOR GAVE PERMISSION FOR JACK TO MOVE TO THE HOTEL WITH ME.
HE WILL COME BACK HERE EVERY DAY FOR REHAB AND DOCTOR APPOINTMENTS.
FRAN!
EXCUSE ME, SASHA. JACK PROBABLY WANTS TO KNOW IF HE LOOKS OKAY.
WHAT IS IT, SWEETHEART?
I LOOK OKAY?
REC
REC
YOU'RE STILL MY HANDSOME MAN.
REC

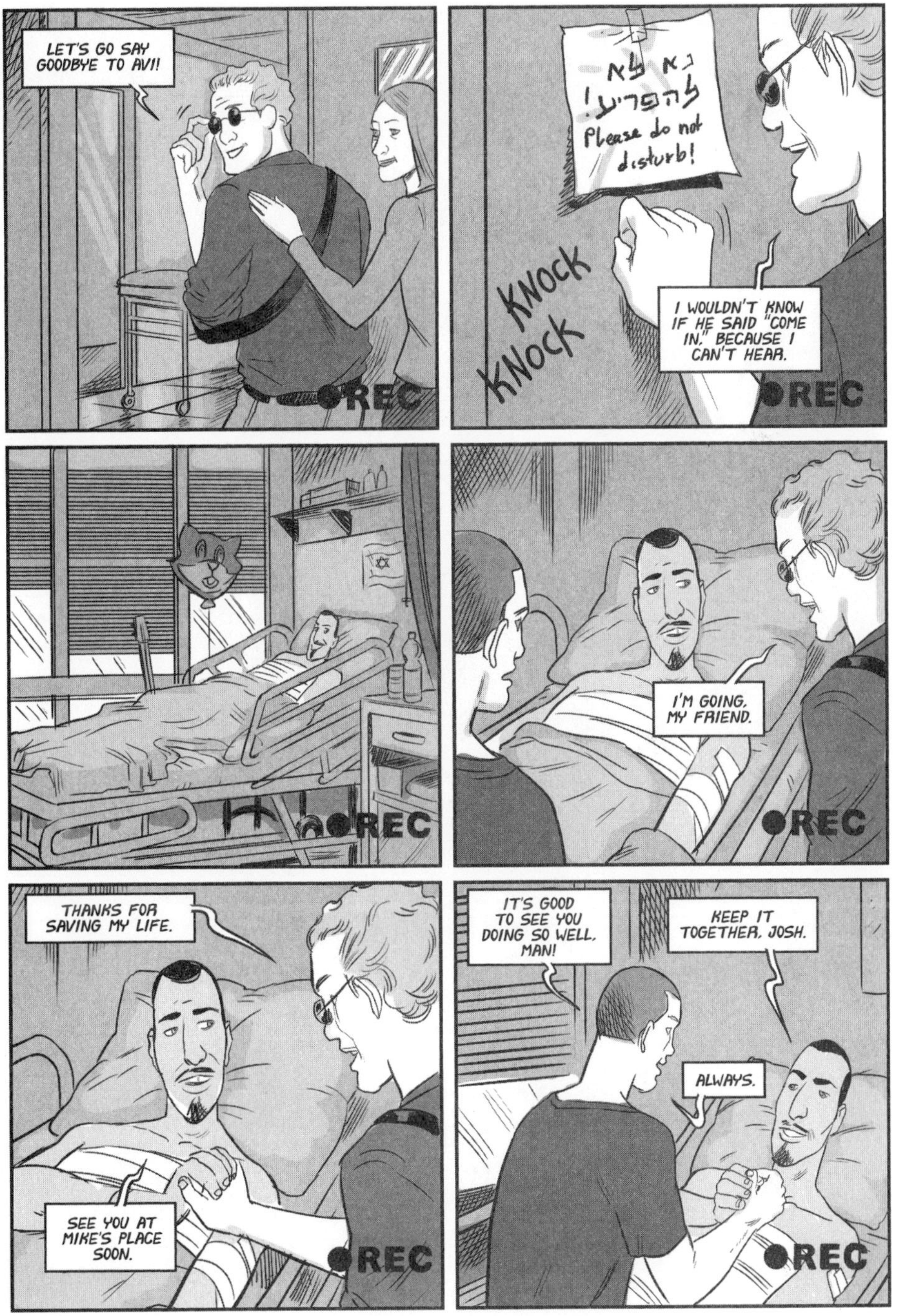
LET'S GO SAY GOODBYE TO AVI!
REC
בא לא להפריע!
Please do not disturb!
KNOCK KNOCK
I WOULDN'T KNOW IF HE SAID "COME IN." BECAUSE I CAN'T HEAR.
REC
REC
I'M GOING, MY FRIEND.
REC
THANKS FOR SAVING MY LIFE.
SEE YOU AT MIKE'S PLACE SOON.
REC
IT'S GOOD TO SEE YOU DOING SO WELL, MAN!
KEEP IT TOGETHER, JOSH.
ALWAYS.
REC

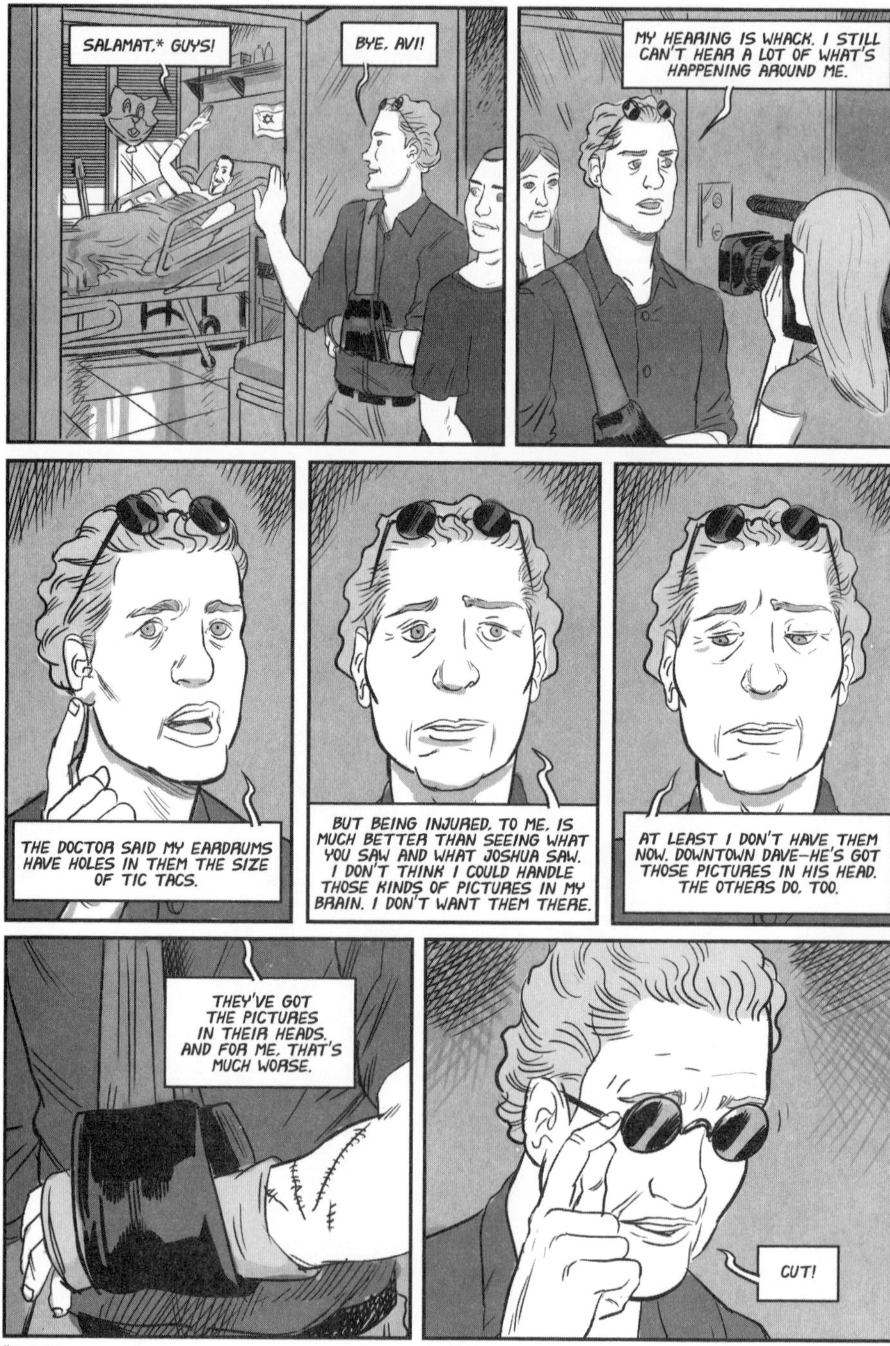
SALAMAT,* GUYS!
BYE, AVI!
MY HEARING IS WHACK. I STILL CAN'T HEAR A LOT OF WHAT'S HAPPENING AROUND ME.
THE DOCTOR SAID MY EARDRUMS HAVE HOLES IN THEM THE SIZE OF TIC TACS.
BUT BEING INJURED, TO ME, IS MUCH BETTER THAN SEEING WHAT YOU SAW AND WHAT JOSHUA SAW. I DON'T THINK I COULD HANDLE THOSE KINDS OF PICTURES IN MY BRAIN. I DON'T WANT THEM THERE.
AT LEAST I DON'T HAVE THEM NOW. DOWNTOWN DAVE—HE'S GOT THOSE PICTURES IN HIS HEAD. THE OTHERS DO, TOO.
THEY'VE GOT THE PICTURES IN THEIR HEADS. AND FOR ME, THAT'S MUCH WORSE.
CUT!

*PEACE

V

"It may be that Allah will grant love (and friendship) between you and those whom you (now) hold as enemies."

— Qur'an

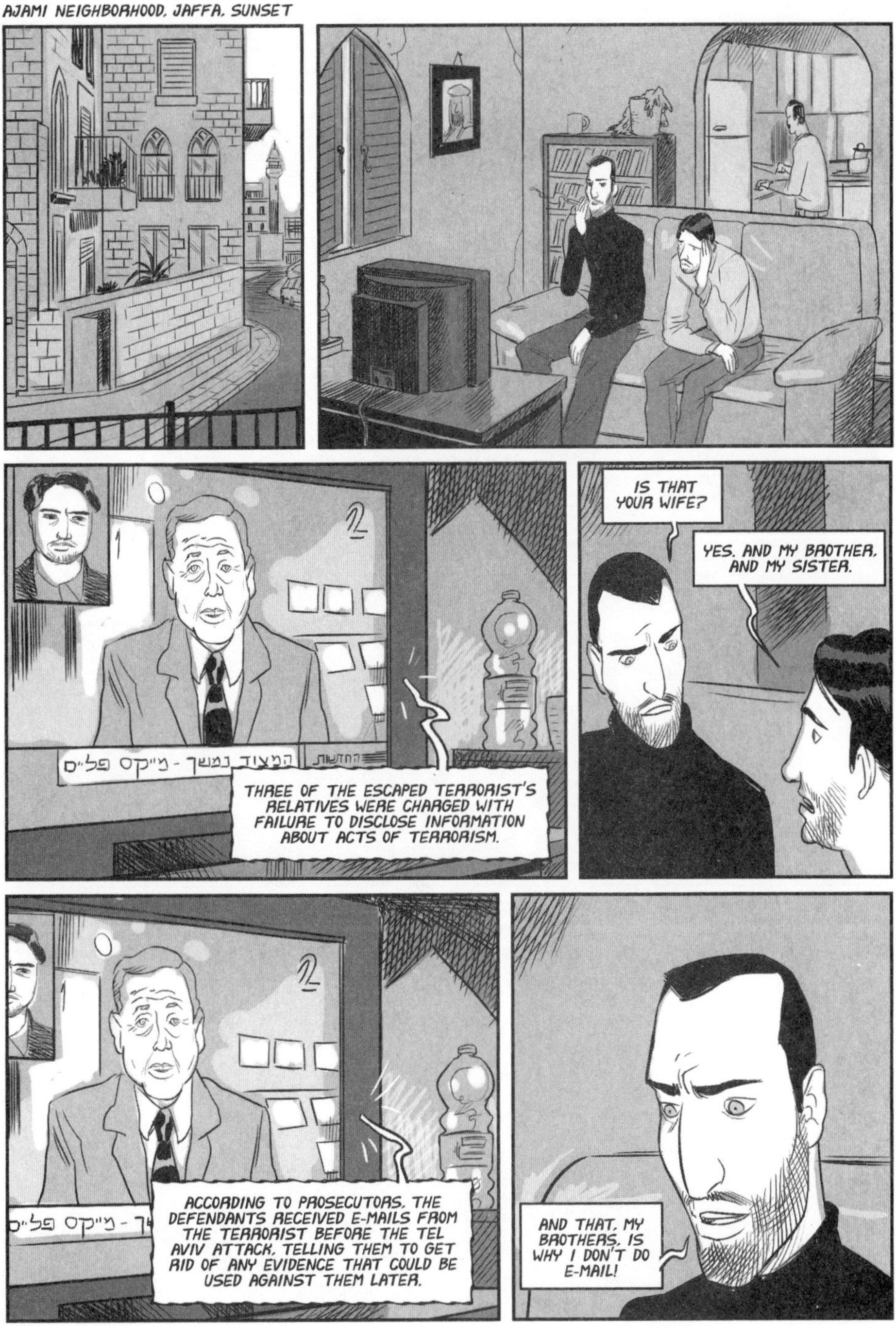
AJAMI NEIGHBORHOOD, JAFFA, SUNSET
THREE OF THE ESCAPED TERRORIST'S RELATIVES WERE CHARGED WITH FAILURE TO DISCLOSE INFORMATION ABOUT ACTS OF TERRORISM.
IS THAT YOUR WIFE?
YES. AND MY BROTHER, AND MY SISTER.
ACCORDING TO PROSECUTORS, THE DEFENDANTS RECEIVED E-MAILS FROM THE TERRORIST BEFORE THE TEL AVIV ATTACK, TELLING THEM TO GET RID OF ANY EVIDENCE THAT COULD BE USED AGAINST THEM LATER.
AND THAT, MY BROTHERS, IS WHY I DON'T DO E-MAIL!

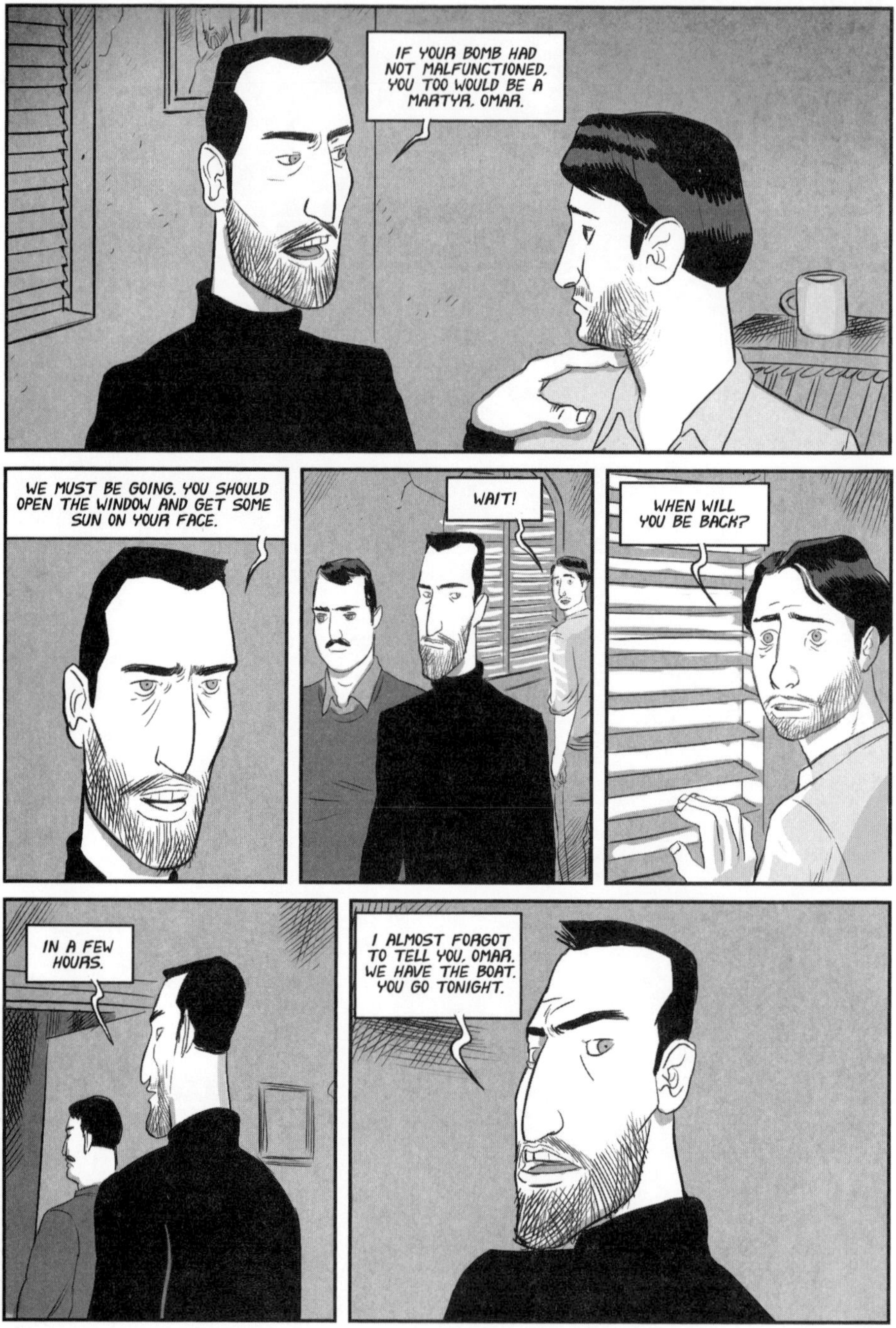
IF YOUR BOMB HAD NOT MALFUNCTIONED, YOU TOO WOULD BE A MARTYR, OMAR.
WE MUST BE GOING. YOU SHOULD OPEN THE WINDOW AND GET SOME SUN ON YOUR FACE.
WAIT!
WHEN WILL YOU BE BACK?
IN A FEW HOURS.
I ALMOST FORGOT TO TELL YOU, OMAR. WE HAVE THE BOAT. YOU GO TONIGHT.

TEL AVIV BEACHFRONT, SUNDOWN

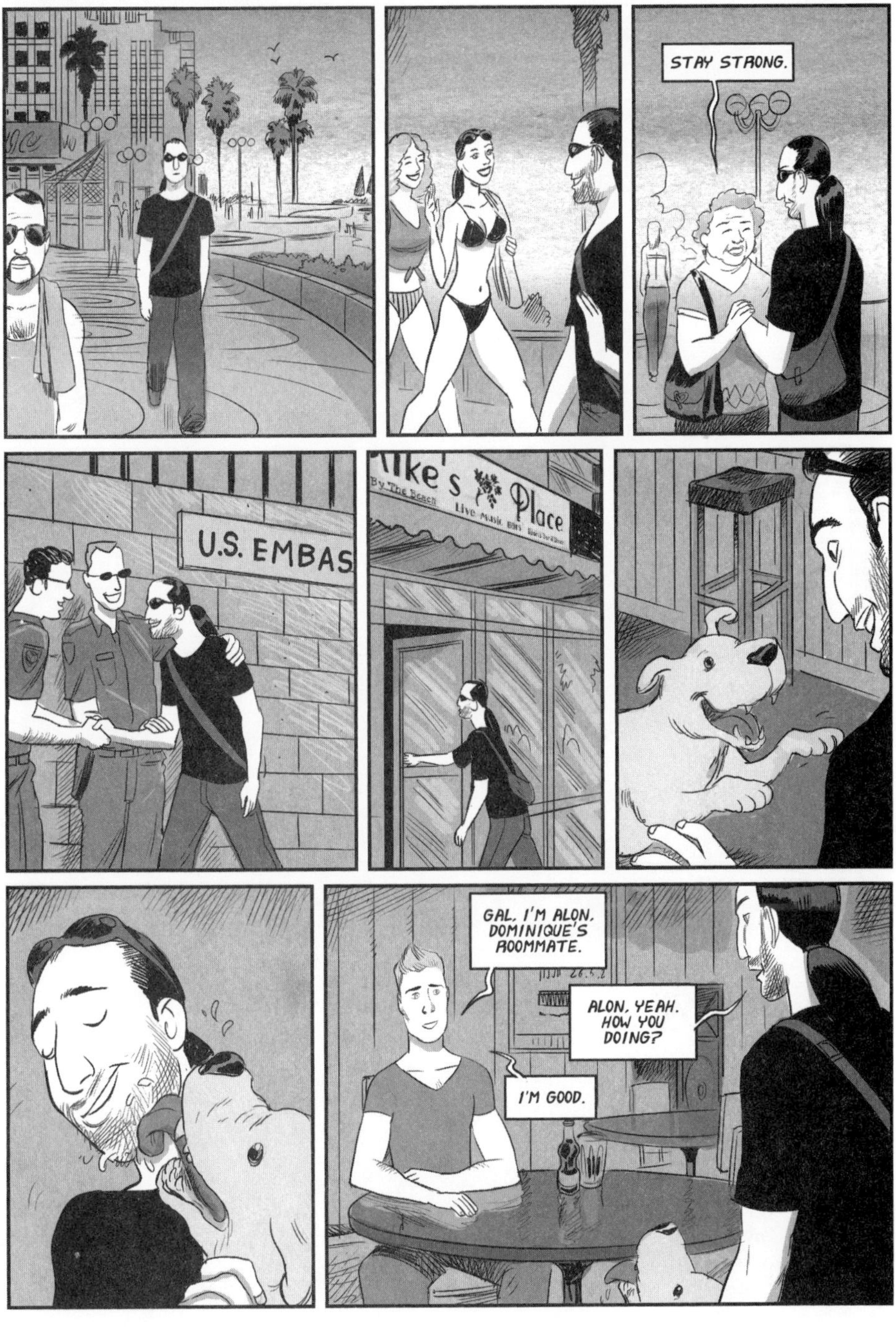
STAY STRONG.
U.S. EMBAS
By The Beach
Live Music
GAL, I'M ALON, DOMINIQUE'S ROOMMATE.
ALON, YEAH. HOW YOU DOING?
I'M GOOD.

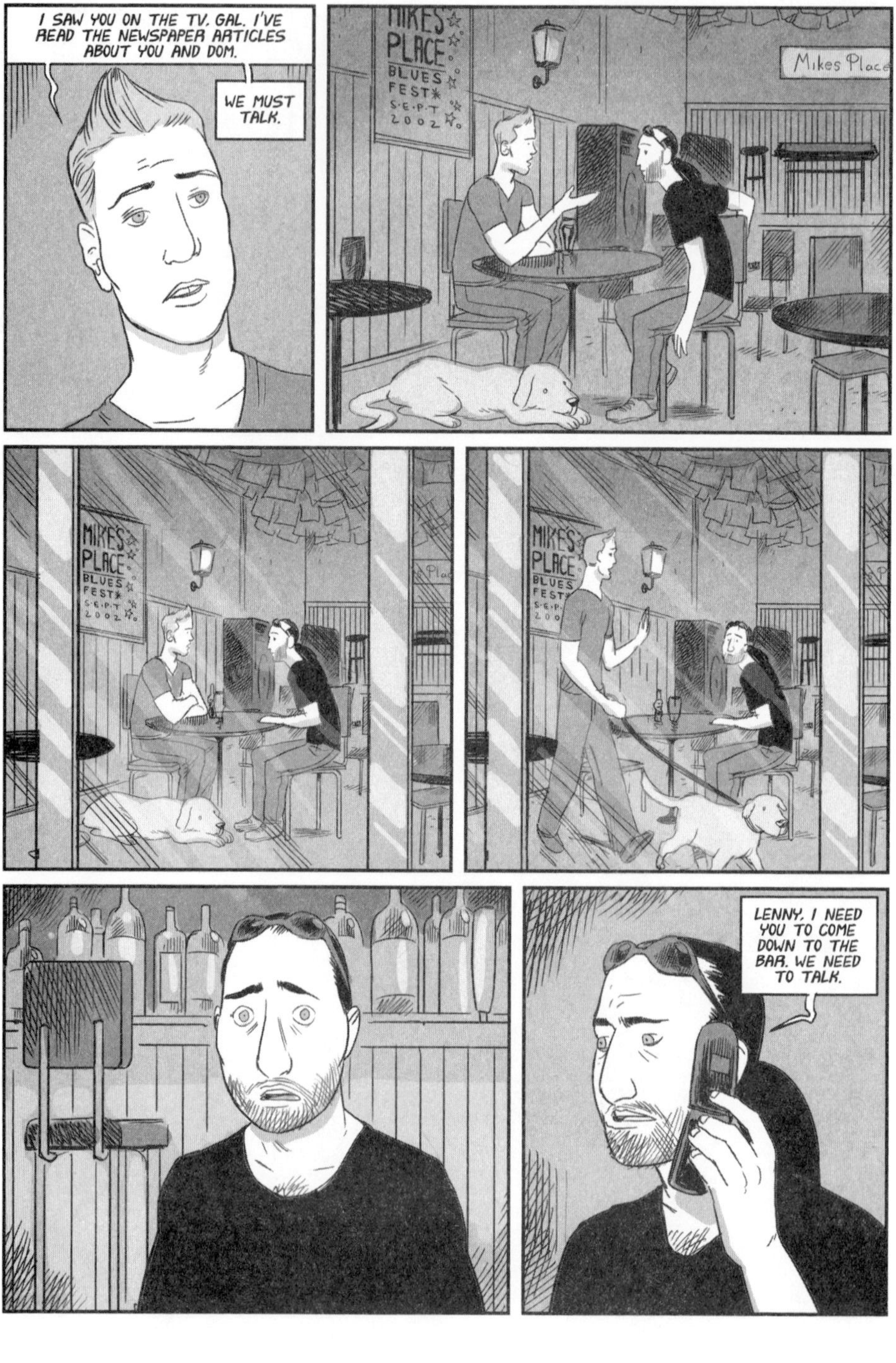
I SAW YOU ON THE TV, GAL. I'VE READ THE NEWSPAPER ARTICLES ABOUT YOU AND DOM.
WE MUST TALK.
MIKES' PLACE BLUES FEST S·E·P·T 2002
Mikes Place
MIKES' PLACE BLUES FEST S·E·P·T 2002
MIKES' PLACE BLUES FEST
LENNY, I NEED YOU TO COME DOWN TO THE BAR. WE NEED TO TALK.

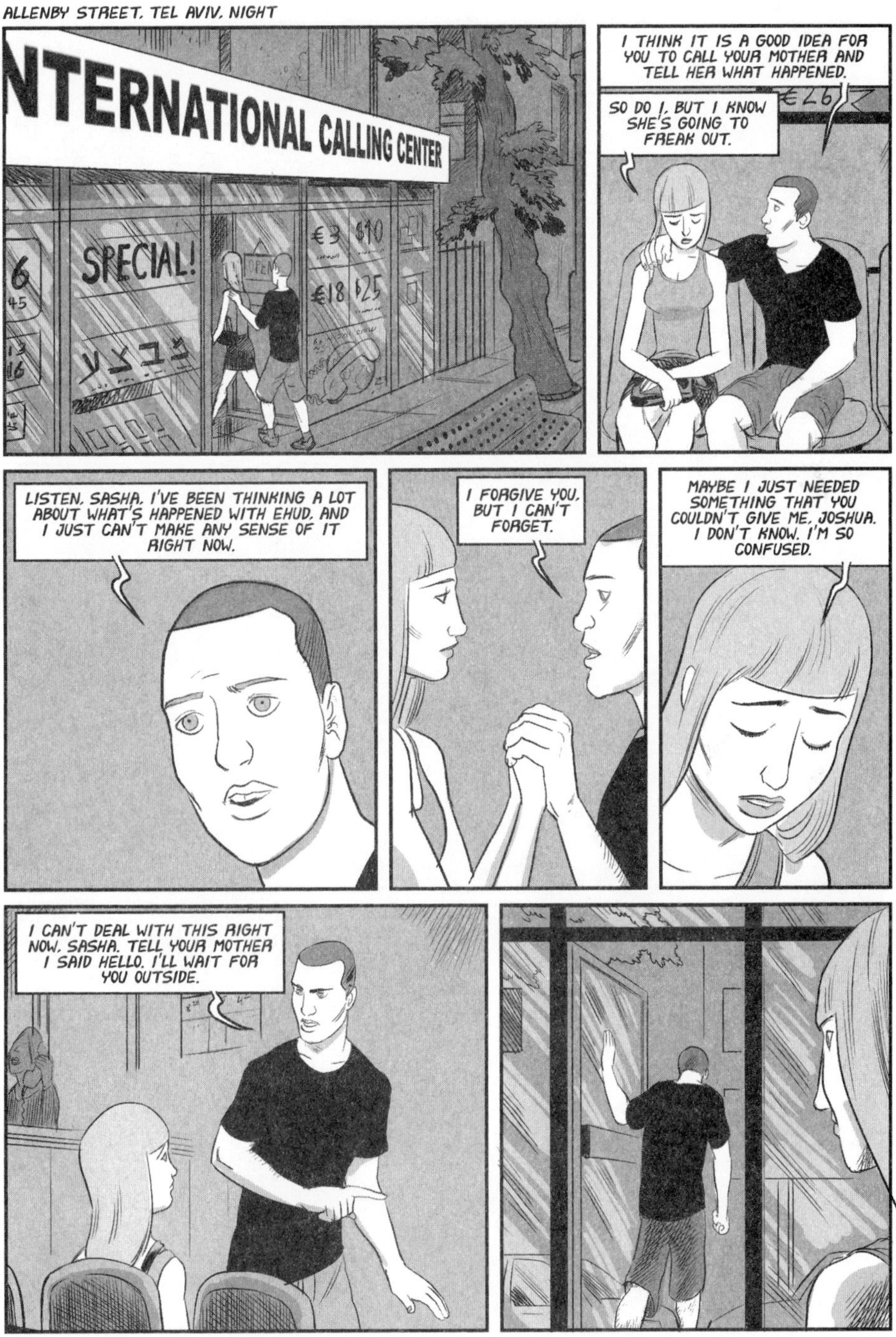
ALLENBY STREET, TEL AVIV, NIGHT
INTERNATIONAL CALLING CENTER
SPECIAL!
€3 $10
€18 $25
OPEN
I THINK IT IS A GOOD IDEA FOR YOU TO CALL YOUR MOTHER AND TELL HER WHAT HAPPENED.
SO DO I, BUT I KNOW SHE'S GOING TO FREAK OUT.
LISTEN, SASHA, I'VE BEEN THINKING A LOT ABOUT WHAT'S HAPPENED WITH EHUD, AND I JUST CAN'T MAKE ANY SENSE OF IT RIGHT NOW.
I FORGIVE YOU, BUT I CAN'T FORGET.
MAYBE I JUST NEEDED SOMETHING THAT YOU COULDN'T GIVE ME, JOSHUA. I DON'T KNOW. I'M SO CONFUSED.
I CAN'T DEAL WITH THIS RIGHT NOW, SASHA. TELL YOUR MOTHER I SAID HELLO. I'LL WAIT FOR YOU OUTSIDE.

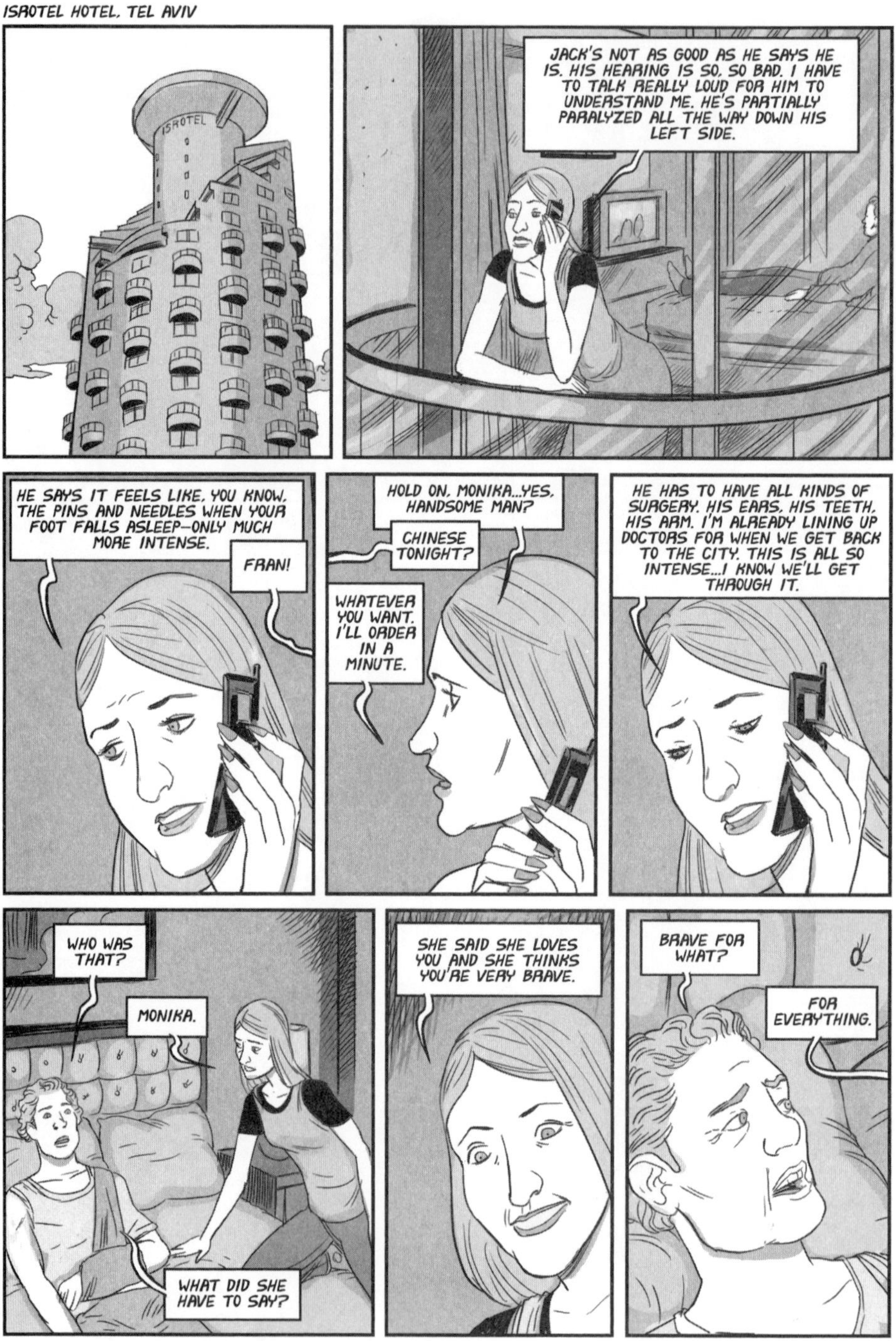
ISROTEL HOTEL, TEL AVIV
ISROTEL
JACK'S NOT AS GOOD AS HE SAYS HE IS. HIS HEARING IS SO, SO BAD. I HAVE TO TALK REALLY LOUD FOR HIM TO UNDERSTAND ME. HE'S PARTIALLY PARALYZED ALL THE WAY DOWN HIS LEFT SIDE.
HE SAYS IT FEELS LIKE, YOU KNOW, THE PINS AND NEEDLES WHEN YOUR FOOT FALLS ASLEEP—ONLY MUCH MORE INTENSE.
FRAN!
HOLD ON, MONIKA...YES, HANDSOME MAN?
CHINESE TONIGHT?
WHATEVER YOU WANT. I'LL ORDER IN A MINUTE.
HE HAS TO HAVE ALL KINDS OF SURGERY. HIS EARS, HIS TEETH, HIS ARM. I'M ALREADY LINING UP DOCTORS FOR WHEN WE GET BACK TO THE CITY. THIS IS ALL SO INTENSE...I KNOW WE'LL GET THROUGH IT.
WHO WAS THAT?
MONIKA.
WHAT DID SHE HAVE TO SAY?
SHE SAID SHE LOVES YOU AND SHE THINKS YOU'RE VERY BRAVE.
BRAVE FOR WHAT?
FOR EVERYTHING.

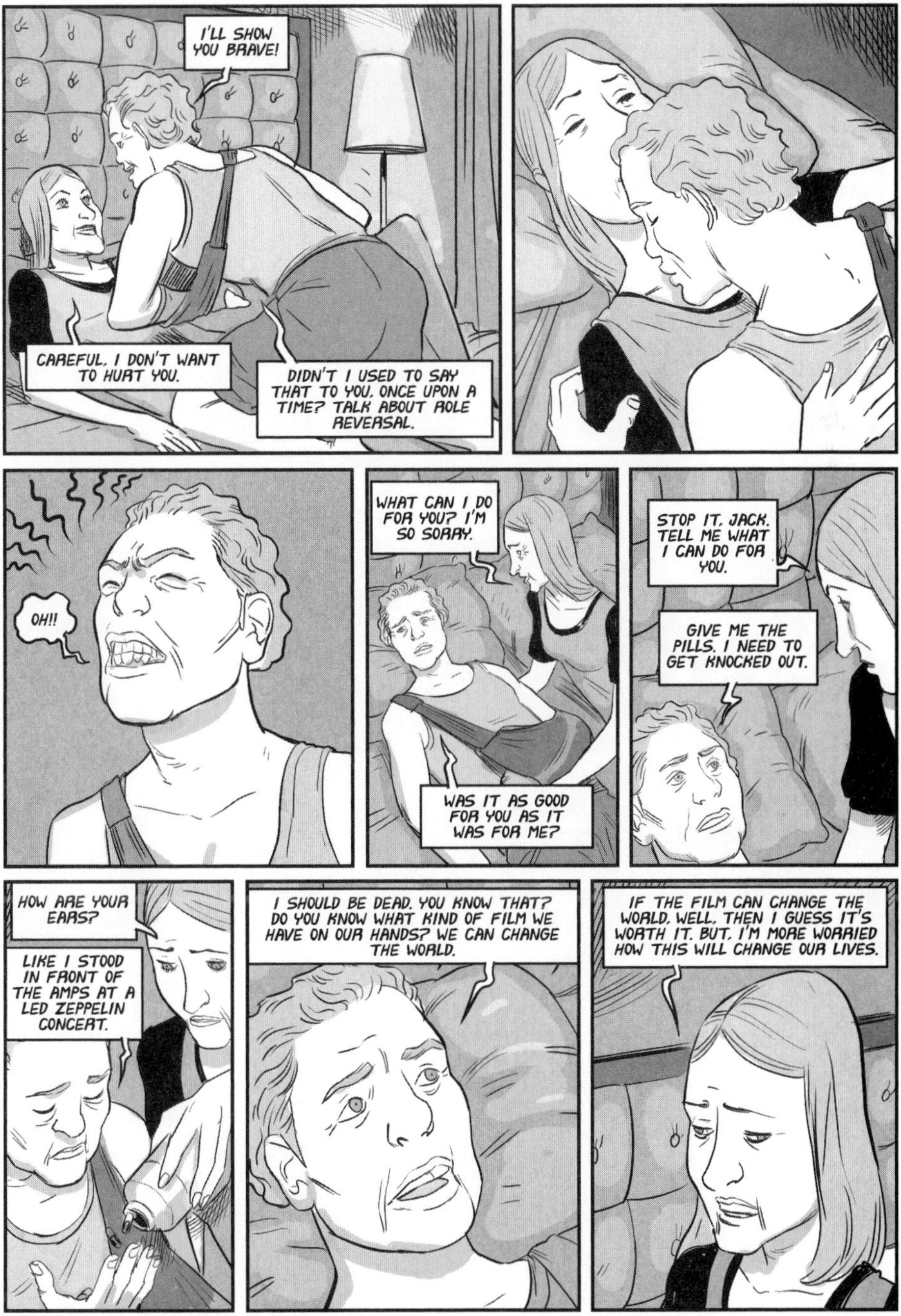
I'LL SHOW YOU BRAVE!
CAREFUL. I DON'T WANT TO HURT YOU.
DIDN'T I USED TO SAY THAT TO YOU, ONCE UPON A TIME? TALK ABOUT ROLE REVERSAL.
OH!!
WHAT CAN I DO FOR YOU? I'M SO SORRY.
WAS IT AS GOOD FOR YOU AS IT WAS FOR ME?
STOP IT, JACK. TELL ME WHAT I CAN DO FOR YOU.
GIVE ME THE PILLS. I NEED TO GET KNOCKED OUT.
HOW ARE YOUR EARS?
LIKE I STOOD IN FRONT OF THE AMPS AT A LED ZEPPELIN CONCERT.
I SHOULD BE DEAD. YOU KNOW THAT? DO YOU KNOW WHAT KIND OF FILM WE HAVE ON OUR HANDS? WE CAN CHANGE THE WORLD.
IF THE FILM CAN CHANGE THE WORLD, WELL, THEN I GUESS IT'S WORTH IT. BUT, I'M MORE WORRIED HOW THIS WILL CHANGE OUR LIVES.

AJAMI APARTMENT BUILDING, JAFFA, NIGHT

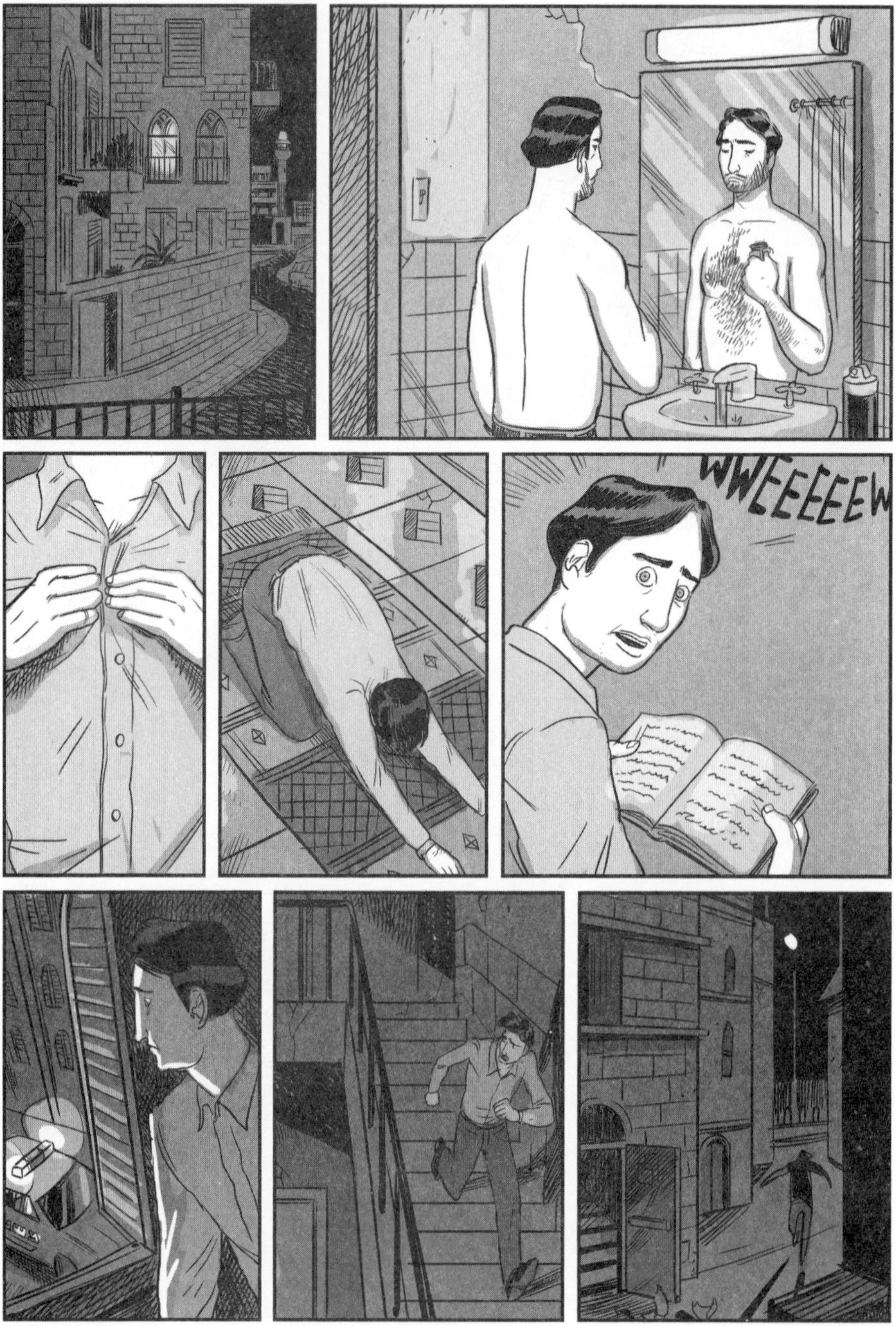
WWEEEEEW

LATER, JAFFA BEACH

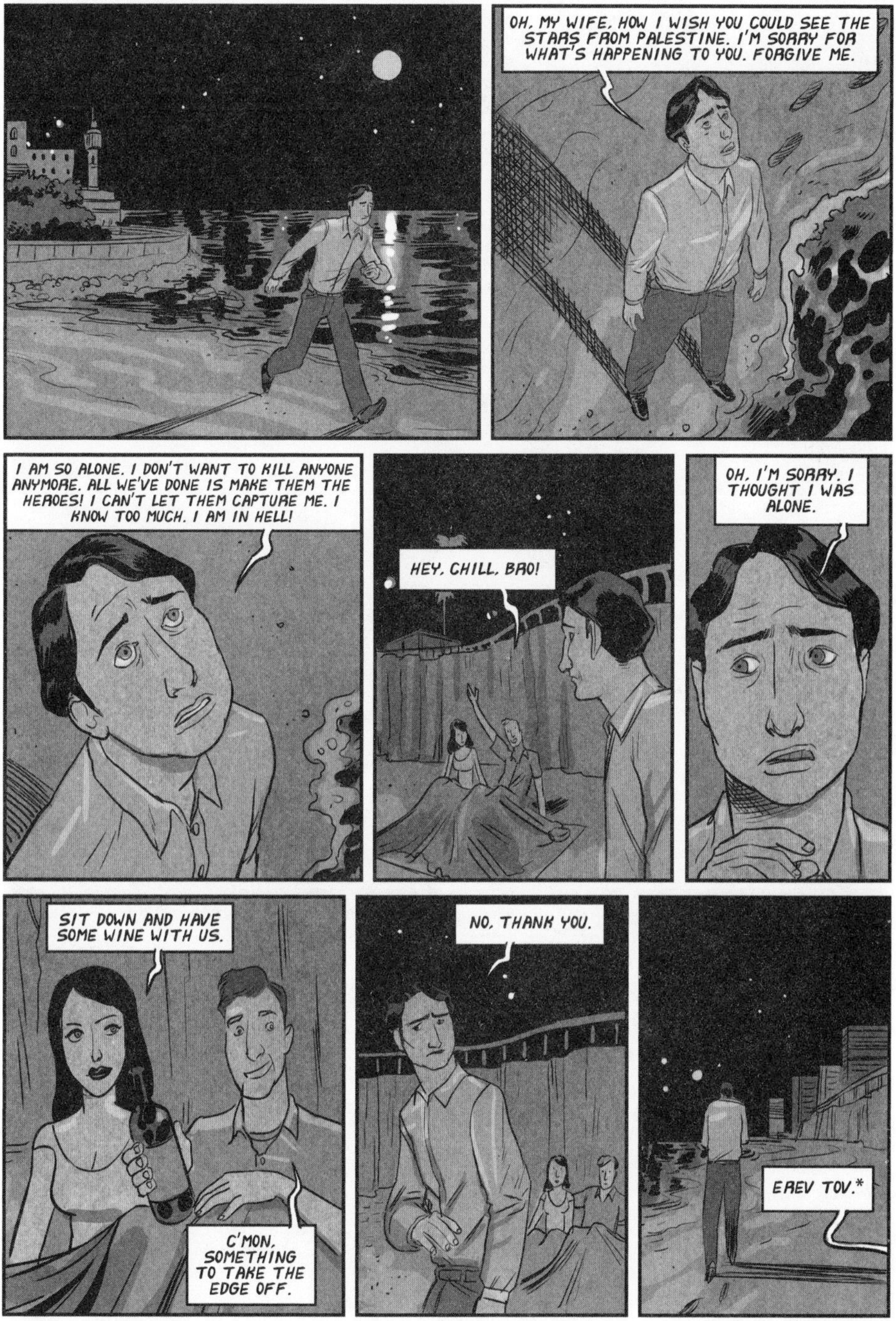
OH, MY WIFE, HOW I WISH YOU COULD SEE THE STARS FROM PALESTINE. I'M SORRY FOR WHAT'S HAPPENING TO YOU. FORGIVE ME.
I AM SO ALONE. I DON'T WANT TO KILL ANYONE ANYMORE. ALL WE'VE DONE IS MAKE THEM THE HEROES! I CAN'T LET THEM CAPTURE ME. I KNOW TOO MUCH. I AM IN HELL!
HEY, CHILL, BRO!
OH, I'M SORRY. I THOUGHT I WAS ALONE.
SIT DOWN AND HAVE SOME WINE WITH US.
C'MON, SOMETHING TO TAKE THE EDGE OFF.
NO, THANK YOU.
EREV TOV.*

*GOOD NIGHT.

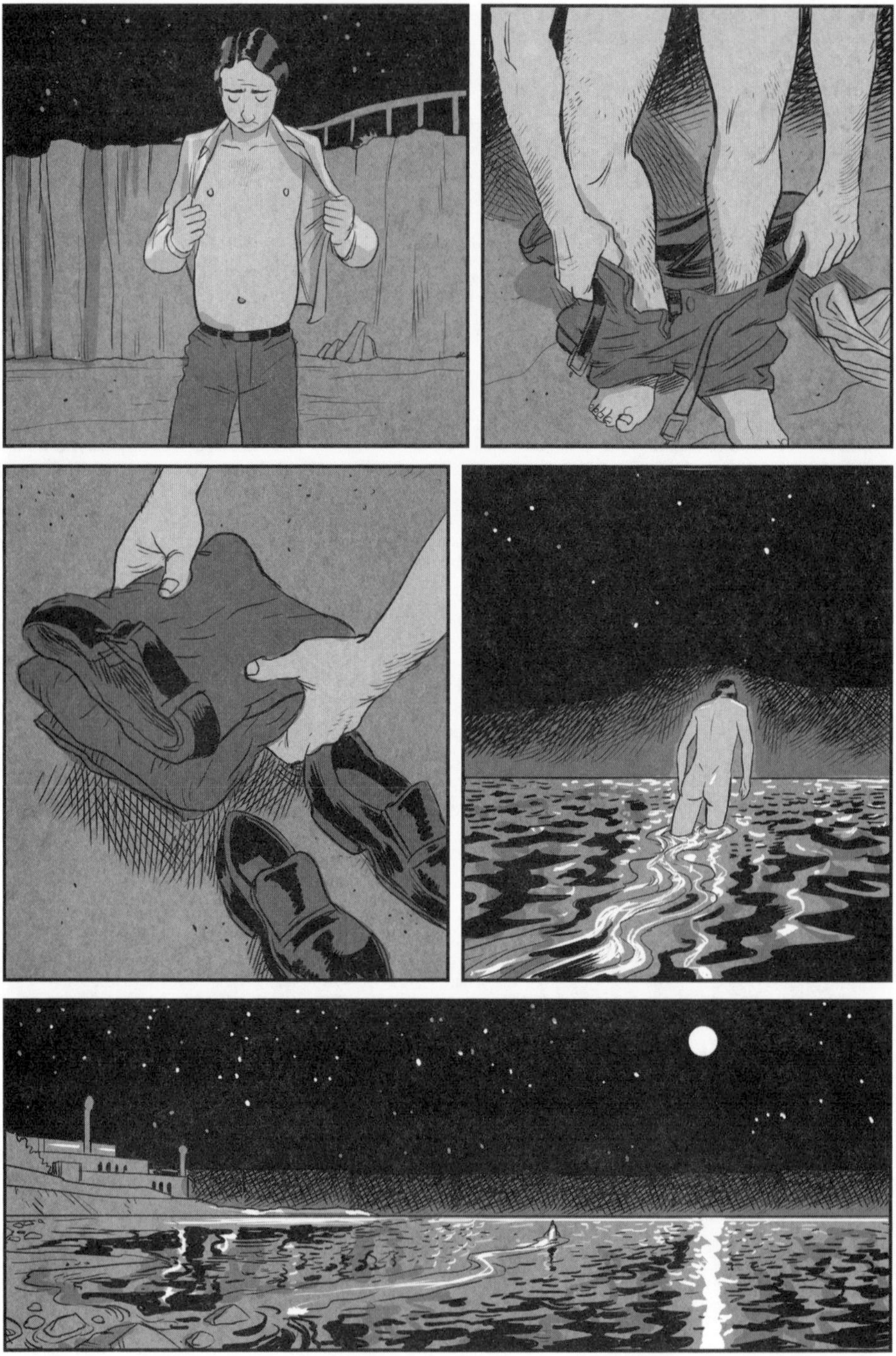

MIKE'S PLACE, NIGHT

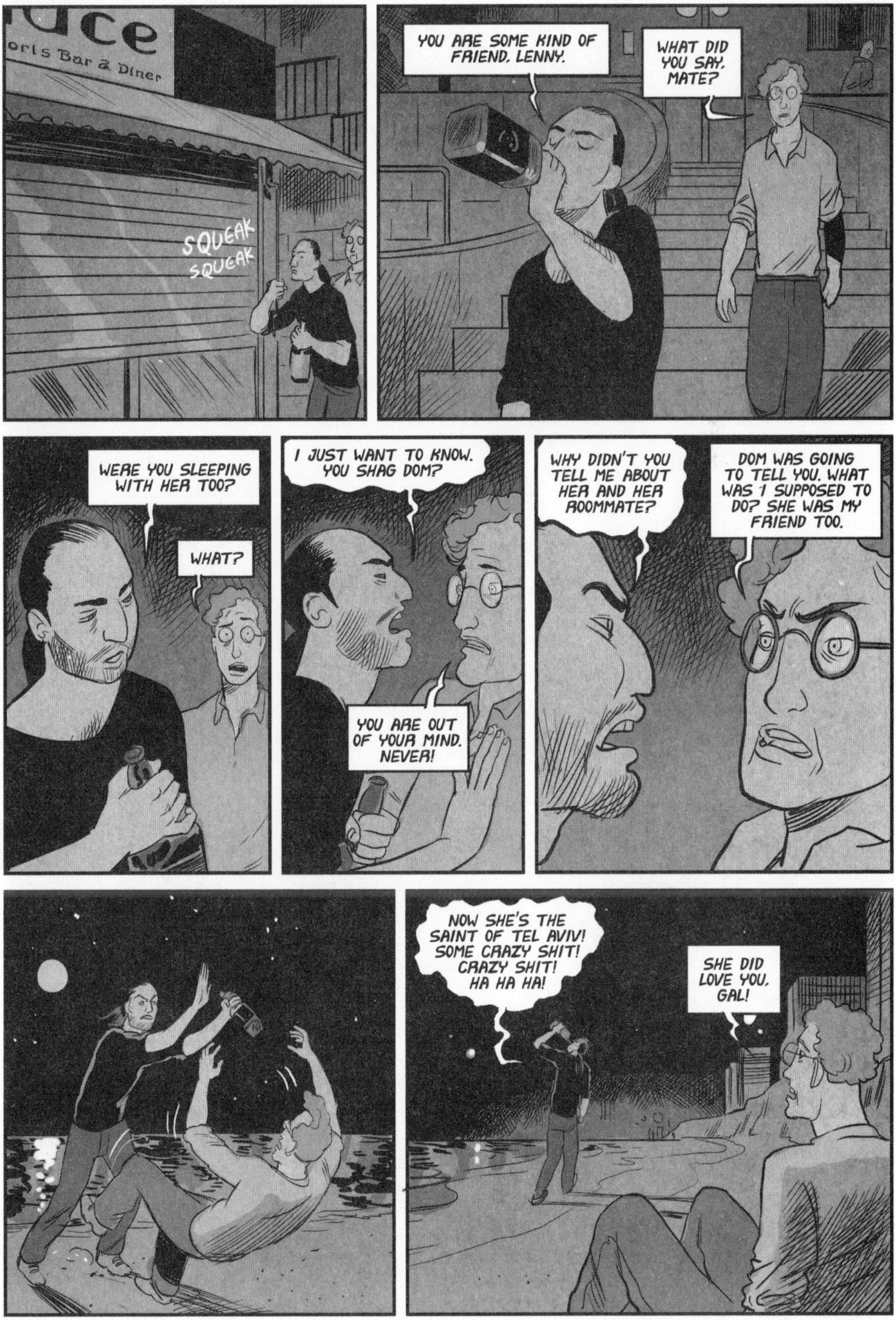

Bar & Diner
SQUEAK
SQUEAK
YOU ARE SOME KIND OF FRIEND, LENNY.
WHAT DID YOU SAY, MATE?
WERE YOU SLEEPING WITH HER TOO?
WHAT?
I JUST WANT TO KNOW. YOU SHAG DOM?
YOU ARE OUT OF YOUR MIND. NEVER!
WHY DIDN'T YOU TELL ME ABOUT HER AND HER ROOMMATE?
DOM WAS GOING TO TELL YOU. WHAT WAS I SUPPOSED TO DO? SHE WAS MY FRIEND TOO.
NOW SHE'S THE SAINT OF TEL AVIV! SOME CRAZY SHIT! CRAZY SHIT! HA HA HA!
SHE DID LOVE YOU, GAL!

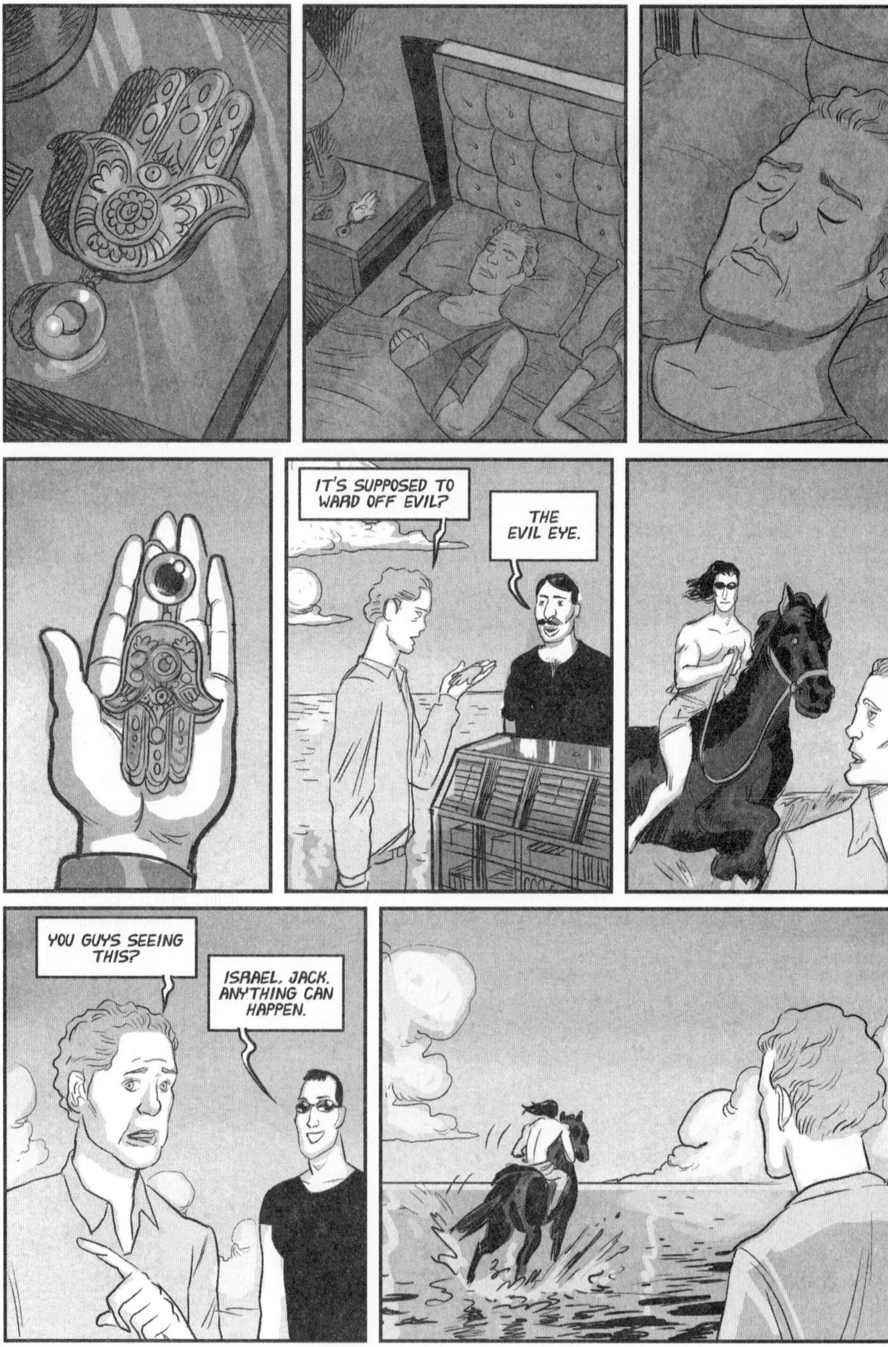
IT'S SUPPOSED TO WARD OFF EVIL?
THE EVIL EYE.
YOU GUYS SEEING THIS?
ISRAEL, JACK. ANYTHING CAN HAPPEN.

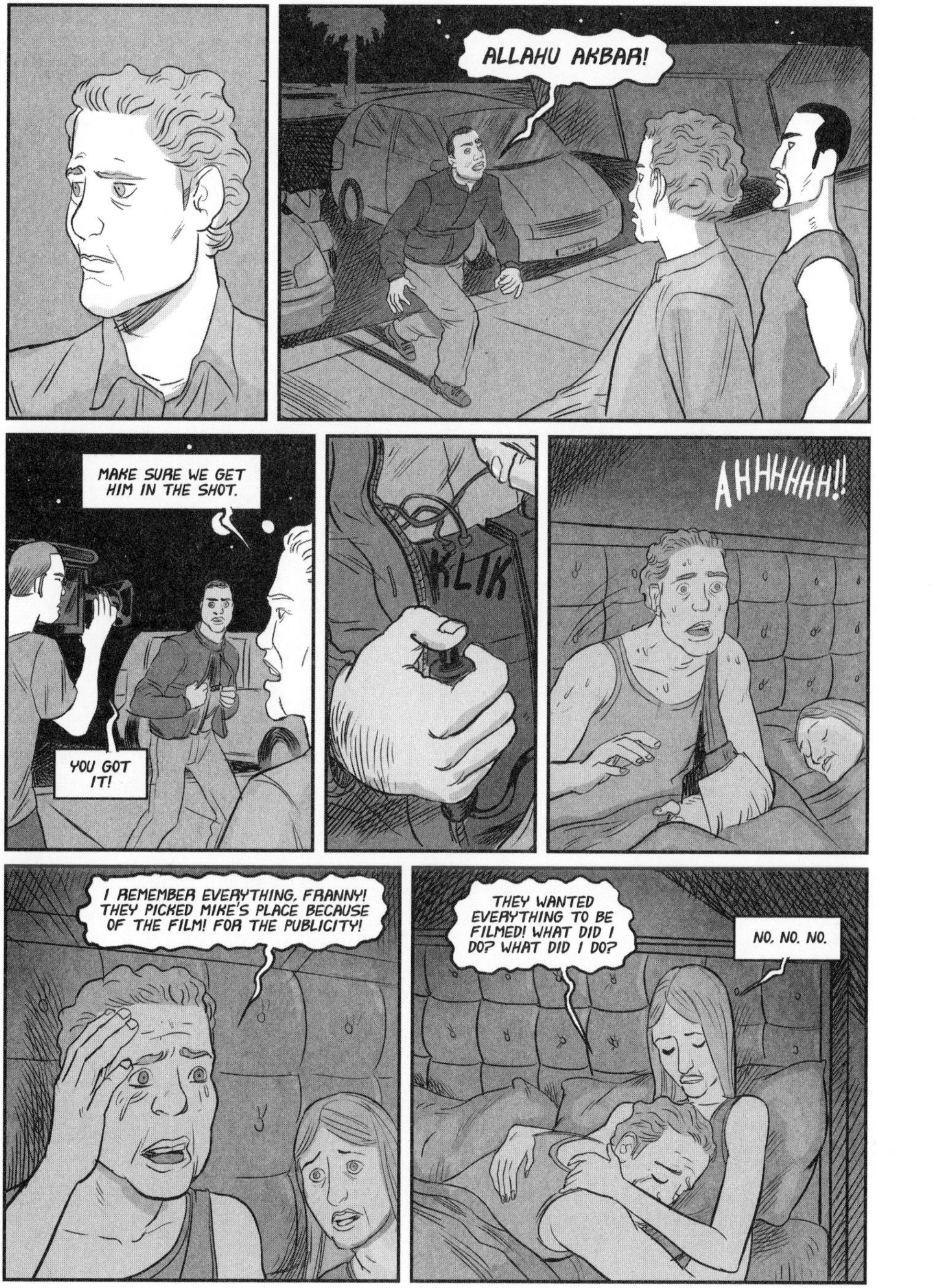
ALLAHU AKBAR!
MAKE SURE WE GET HIM IN THE SHOT.
YOU GOT IT!
KLIK
AHHHHHH!!
I REMEMBER EVERYTHING, FRANNY! THEY PICKED MIKE'S PLACE BECAUSE OF THE FILM! FOR THE PUBLICITY!
THEY WANTED EVERYTHING TO BE FILMED! WHAT DID I DO? WHAT DID I DO?
NO, NO. NO.

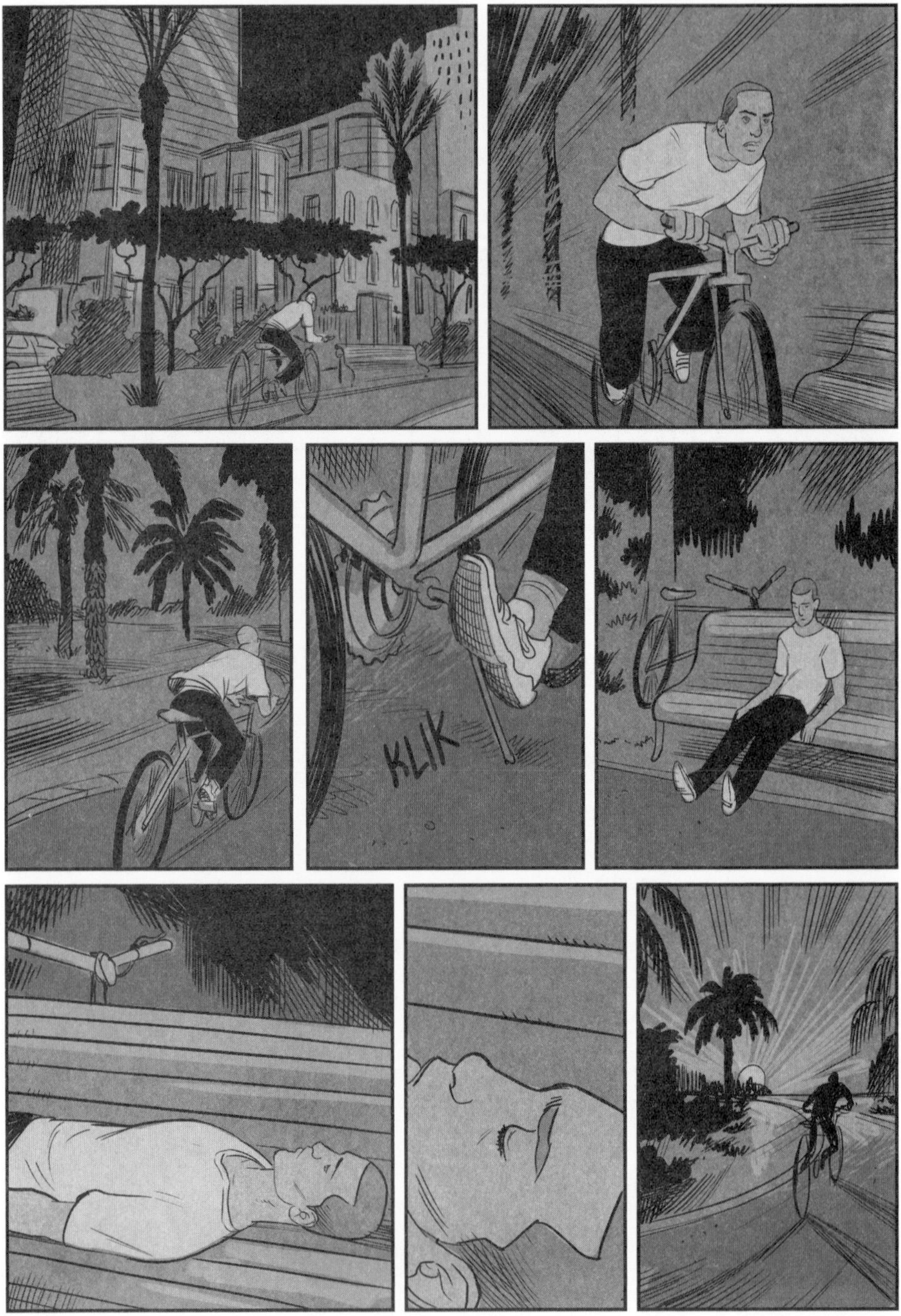
KLIK

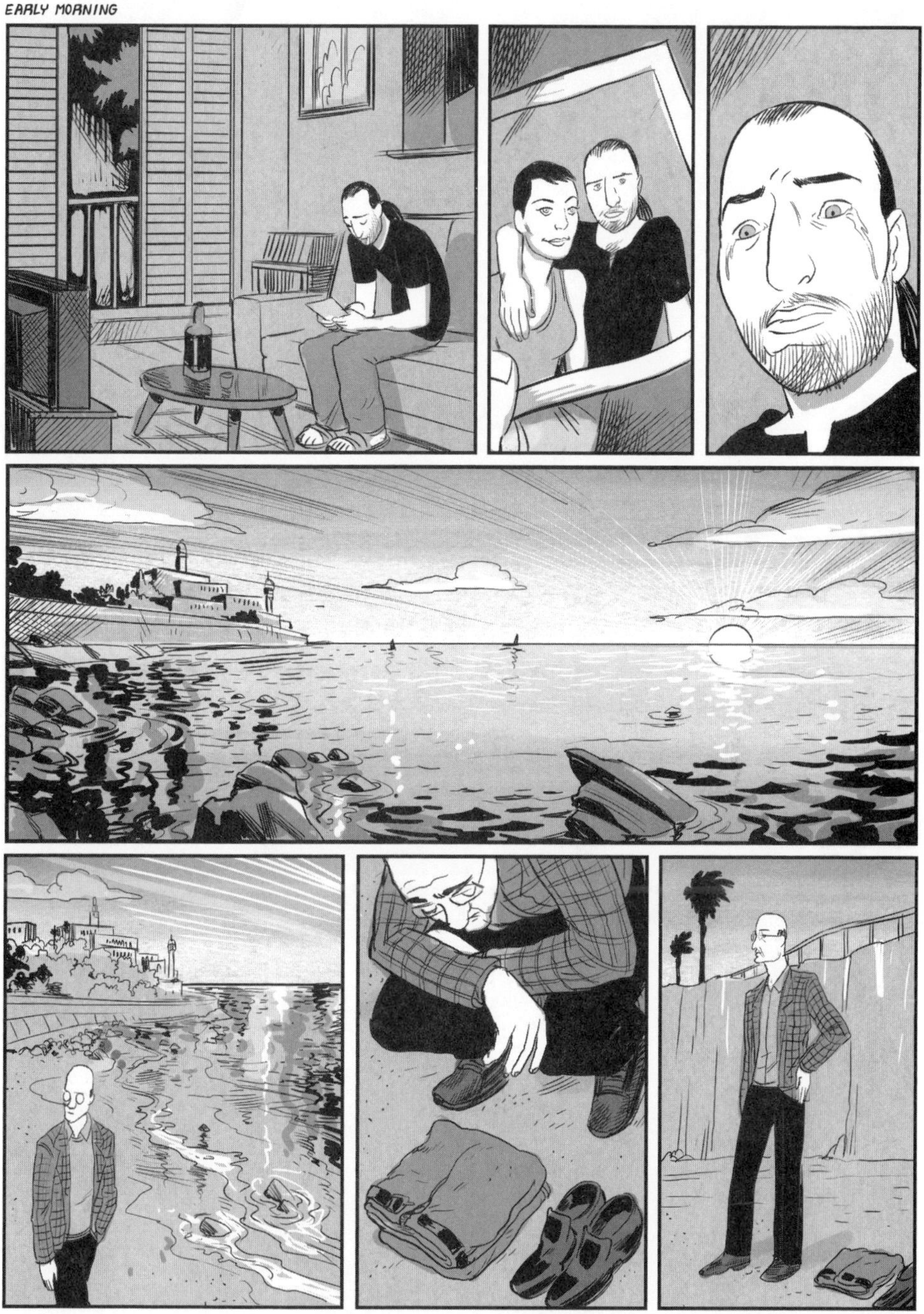
EARLY MORNING

MIKE'S PLACE, DAY

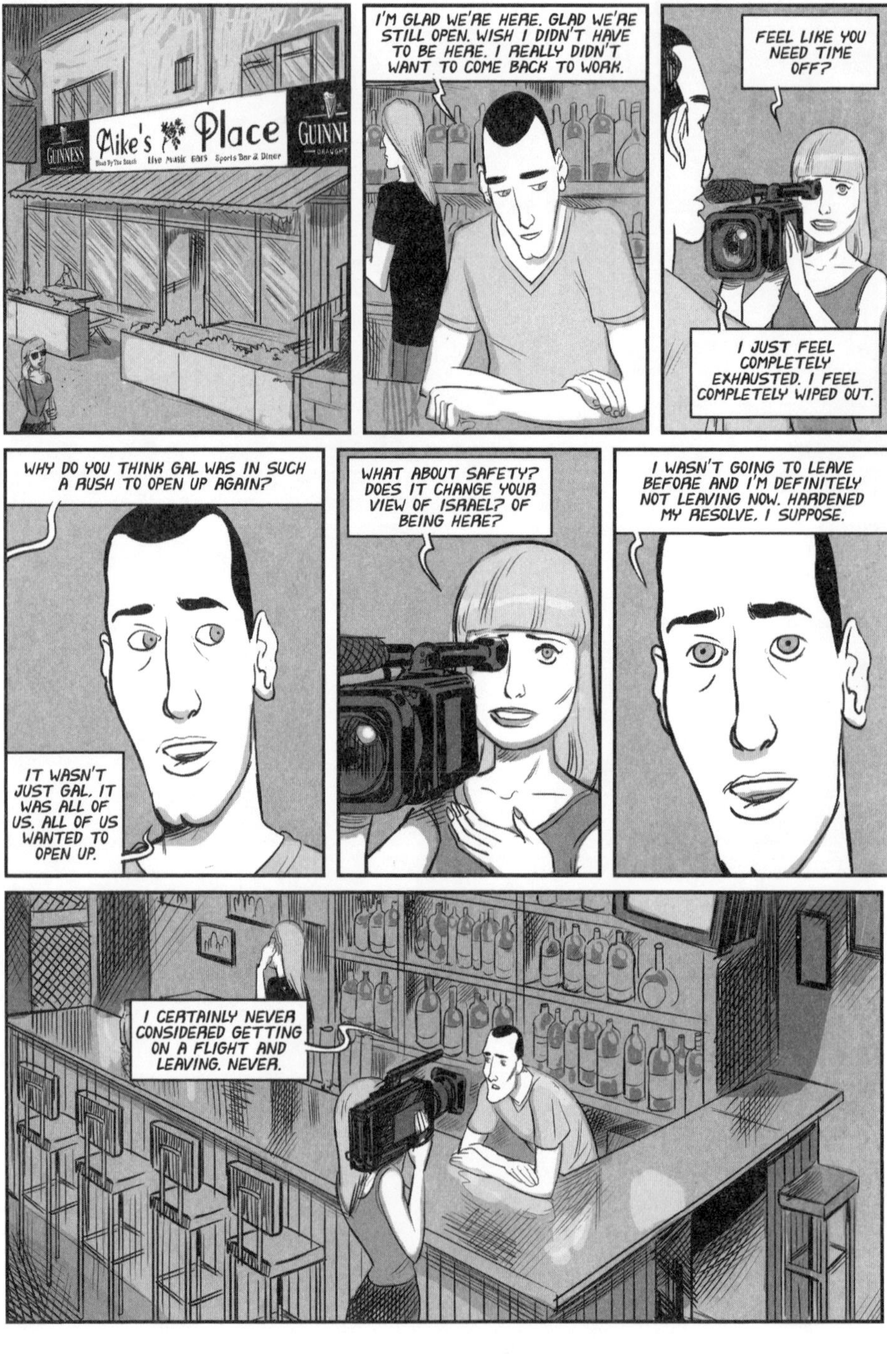

Mike's Place
GUINNESS
Blues By The Beach Live Music Bars Sports Bar & Diner
I'M GLAD WE'RE HERE. GLAD WE'RE STILL OPEN. WISH I DIDN'T HAVE TO BE HERE. I REALLY DIDN'T WANT TO COME BACK TO WORK.
FEEL LIKE YOU NEED TIME OFF?
I JUST FEEL COMPLETELY EXHAUSTED. I FEEL COMPLETELY WIPED OUT.
WHY DO YOU THINK GAL WAS IN SUCH A RUSH TO OPEN UP AGAIN?
IT WASN'T JUST GAL, IT WAS ALL OF US. ALL OF US WANTED TO OPEN UP.
WHAT ABOUT SAFETY? DOES IT CHANGE YOUR VIEW OF ISRAEL? OF BEING HERE?
I WASN'T GOING TO LEAVE BEFORE AND I'M DEFINITELY NOT LEAVING NOW. HARDENED MY RESOLVE, I SUPPOSE.
I CERTAINLY NEVER CONSIDERED GETTING ON A FLIGHT AND LEAVING. NEVER.

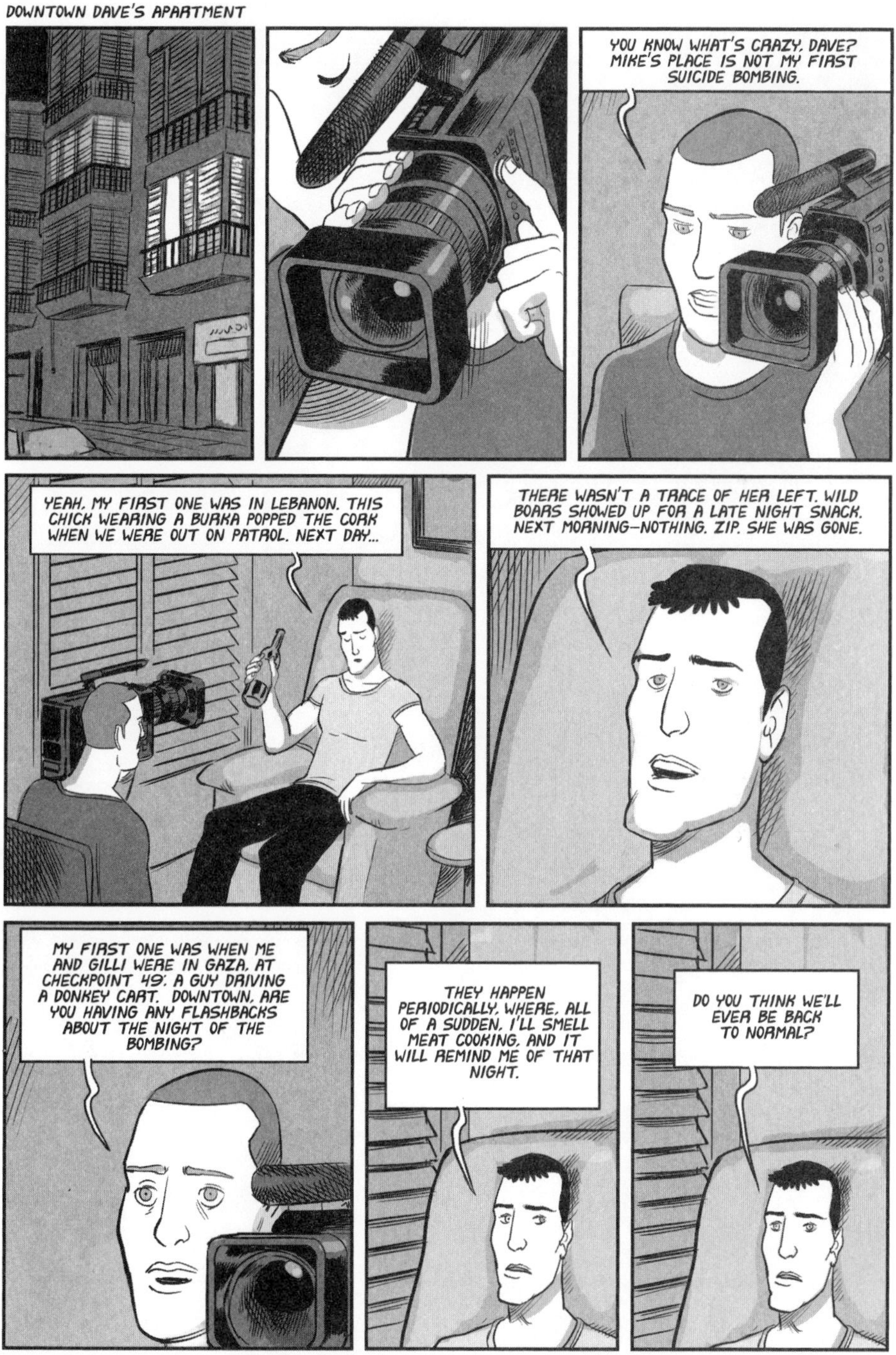
DOWNTOWN DAVE'S APARTMENT
YOU KNOW WHAT'S CRAZY, DAVE? MIKE'S PLACE IS NOT MY FIRST SUICIDE BOMBING.
YEAH, MY FIRST ONE WAS IN LEBANON. THIS CHICK WEARING A BURKA POPPED THE CORK WHEN WE WERE OUT ON PATROL. NEXT DAY...
THERE WASN'T A TRACE OF HER LEFT. WILD BOARS SHOWED UP FOR A LATE NIGHT SNACK. NEXT MORNING—NOTHING. ZIP. SHE WAS GONE.
MY FIRST ONE WAS WHEN ME AND GILLI WERE IN GAZA, AT CHECKPOINT 49: A GUY DRIVING A DONKEY CART. DOWNTOWN, ARE YOU HAVING ANY FLASHBACKS ABOUT THE NIGHT OF THE BOMBING?
THEY HAPPEN PERIODICALLY, WHERE, ALL OF A SUDDEN, I'LL SMELL MEAT COOKING, AND IT WILL REMIND ME OF THAT NIGHT.
DO YOU THINK WE'LL EVER BE BACK TO NORMAL?

MIKE'S PLACE, NIGHT

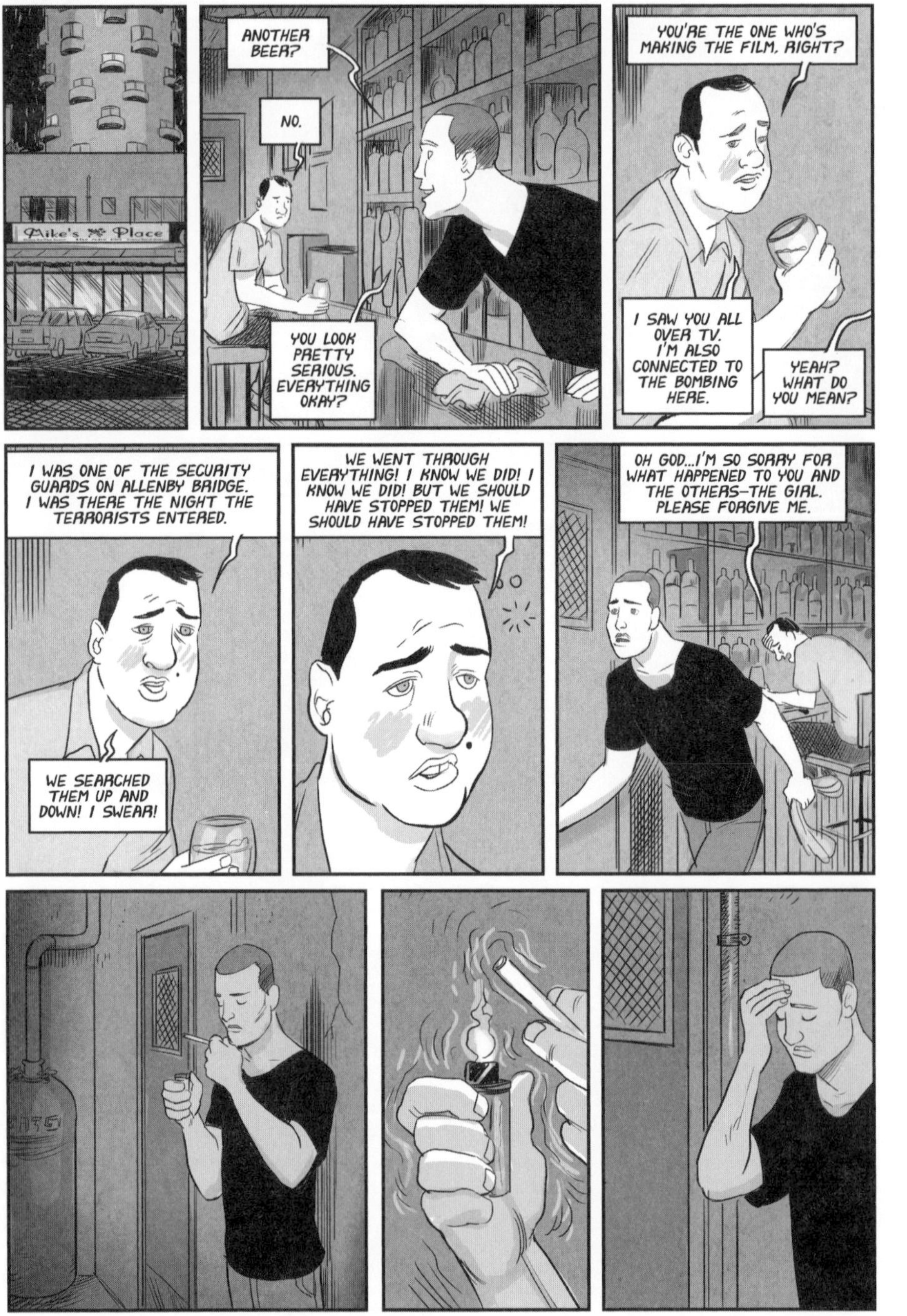
Mike's Place
ANOTHER BEER?
NO.
YOU LOOK PRETTY SERIOUS. EVERYTHING OKAY?
YOU'RE THE ONE WHO'S MAKING THE FILM, RIGHT?
I SAW YOU ALL OVER TV. I'M ALSO CONNECTED TO THE BOMBING HERE.
YEAH? WHAT DO YOU MEAN?
I WAS ONE OF THE SECURITY GUARDS ON ALLENBY BRIDGE. I WAS THERE THE NIGHT THE TERRORISTS ENTERED.
WE SEARCHED THEM UP AND DOWN! I SWEAR!
WE WENT THROUGH EVERYTHING! I KNOW WE DID! I KNOW WE DID! BUT WE SHOULD HAVE STOPPED THEM! WE SHOULD HAVE STOPPED THEM!
OH GOD...I'M SO SORRY FOR WHAT HAPPENED TO YOU AND THE OTHERS—THE GIRL. PLEASE FORGIVE ME.

FRAN AND JACK'S HOTEL ROOM, NIGHT

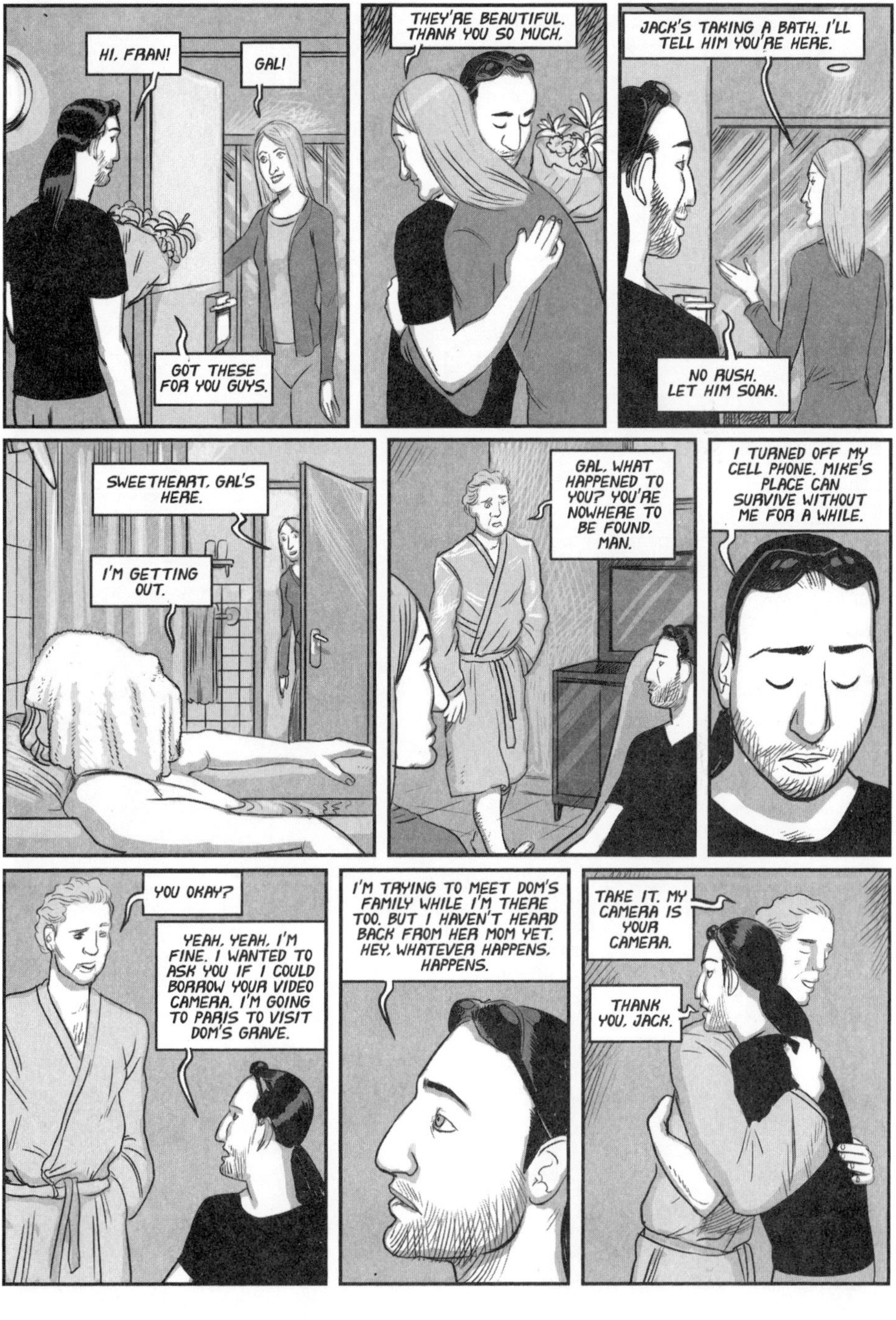
HI, FRAN!
GAL!
GOT THESE FOR YOU GUYS.
THEY'RE BEAUTIFUL. THANK YOU SO MUCH.
JACK'S TAKING A BATH. I'LL TELL HIM YOU'RE HERE.
NO RUSH. LET HIM SOAK.
SWEETHEART, GAL'S HERE.
I'M GETTING OUT.
GAL, WHAT HAPPENED TO YOU? YOU'RE NOWHERE TO BE FOUND, MAN.
I TURNED OFF MY CELL PHONE. MIKE'S PLACE CAN SURVIVE WITHOUT ME FOR A WHILE.
YOU OKAY?
YEAH, YEAH, I'M FINE. I WANTED TO ASK YOU IF I COULD BORROW YOUR VIDEO CAMERA. I'M GOING TO PARIS TO VISIT DOM'S GRAVE.
I'M TRYING TO MEET DOM'S FAMILY WHILE I'M THERE TOO. BUT I HAVEN'T HEARD BACK FROM HER MOM YET. HEY, WHATEVER HAPPENS, HAPPENS.
TAKE IT. MY CAMERA IS YOUR CAMERA.
THANK YOU, JACK.

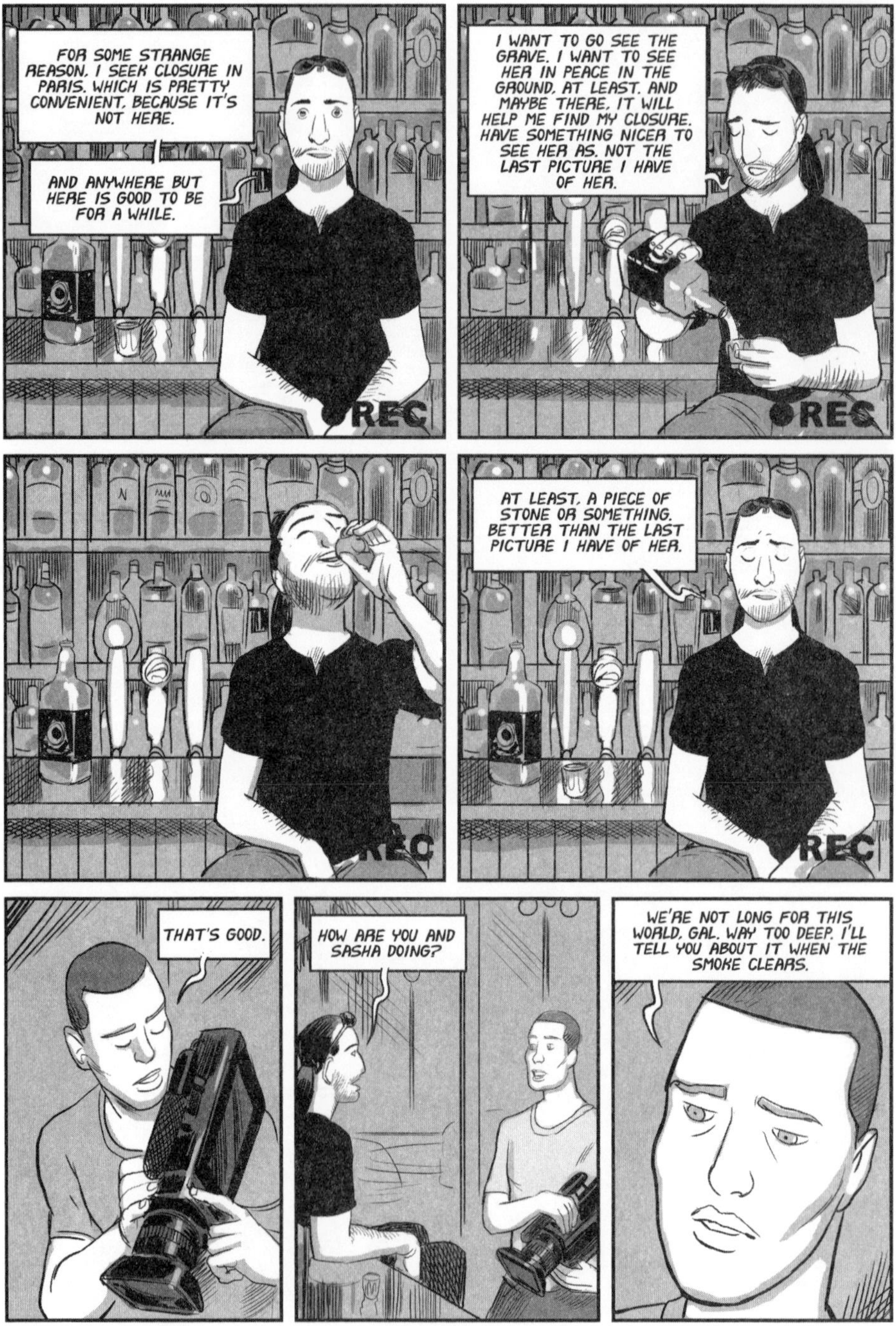
FOR SOME STRANGE REASON, I SEEK CLOSURE IN PARIS. WHICH IS PRETTY CONVENIENT, BECAUSE IT'S NOT HERE.
AND ANYWHERE BUT HERE IS GOOD TO BE FOR A WHILE.
REC
I WANT TO GO SEE THE GRAVE. I WANT TO SEE HER IN PEACE IN THE GROUND, AT LEAST. AND MAYBE THERE, IT WILL HELP ME FIND MY CLOSURE. HAVE SOMETHING NICER TO SEE HER AS. NOT THE LAST PICTURE I HAVE OF HER.
REC
REC
AT LEAST, A PIECE OF STONE OR SOMETHING. BETTER THAN THE LAST PICTURE I HAVE OF HER.
REC
THAT'S GOOD.
HOW ARE YOU AND SASHA DOING?
WE'RE NOT LONG FOR THIS WORLD, GAL. WAY TOO DEEP. I'LL TELL YOU ABOUT IT WHEN THE SMOKE CLEARS.

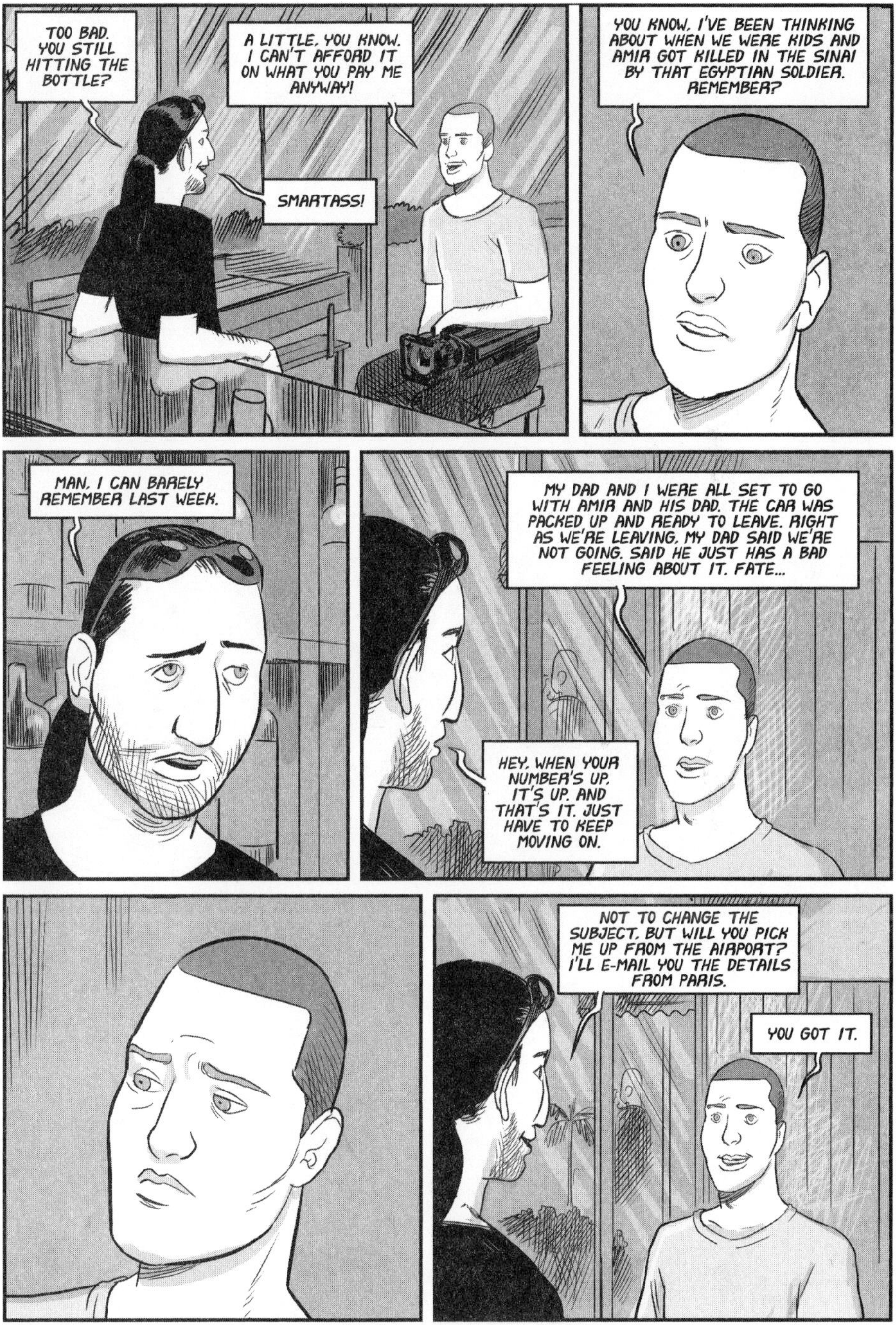
TOO BAD. YOU STILL HITTING THE BOTTLE?
A LITTLE, YOU KNOW. I CAN'T AFFORD IT ON WHAT YOU PAY ME ANYWAY!
SMARTASS!
YOU KNOW, I'VE BEEN THINKING ABOUT WHEN WE WERE KIDS AND AMIR GOT KILLED IN THE SINAI BY THAT EGYPTIAN SOLDIER. REMEMBER?
MAN, I CAN BARELY REMEMBER LAST WEEK.
MY DAD AND I WERE ALL SET TO GO WITH AMIR AND HIS DAD. THE CAR WAS PACKED UP AND READY TO LEAVE. RIGHT AS WE'RE LEAVING, MY DAD SAID WE'RE NOT GOING. SAID HE JUST HAS A BAD FEELING ABOUT IT. FATE...
HEY, WHEN YOUR NUMBER'S UP, IT'S UP. AND THAT'S IT. JUST HAVE TO KEEP MOVING ON.
NOT TO CHANGE THE SUBJECT, BUT WILL YOU PICK ME UP FROM THE AIRPORT? I'LL E-MAIL YOU THE DETAILS FROM PARIS.
YOU GOT IT.

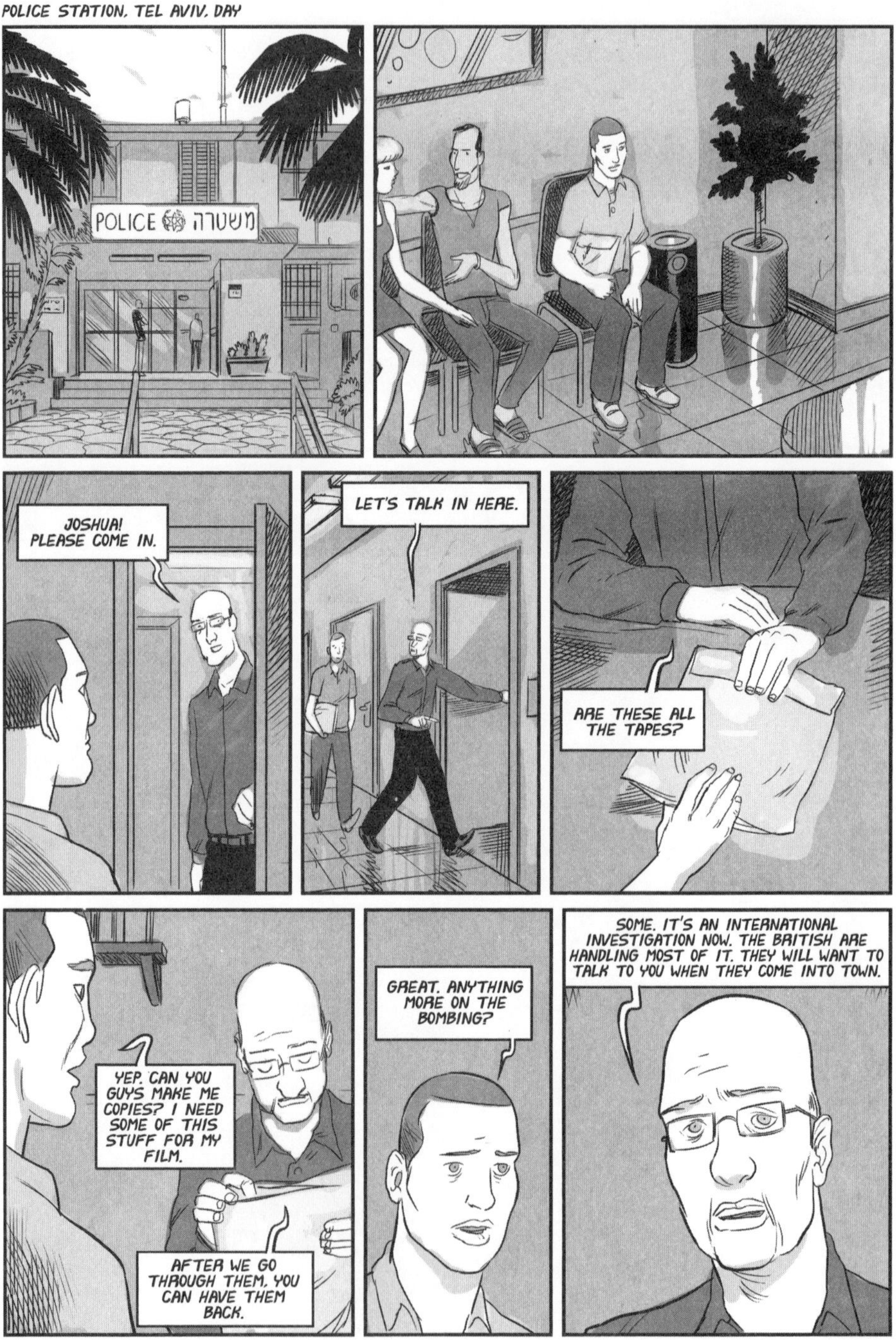
POLICE STATION, TEL AVIV, DAY
POLICE משטרה
JOSHUA! PLEASE COME IN.
LET'S TALK IN HERE.
ARE THESE ALL THE TAPES?
YEP. CAN YOU GUYS MAKE ME COPIES? I NEED SOME OF THIS STUFF FOR MY FILM.
AFTER WE GO THROUGH THEM, YOU CAN HAVE THEM BACK.
GREAT. ANYTHING MORE ON THE BOMBING?
SOME. IT'S AN INTERNATIONAL INVESTIGATION NOW. THE BRITISH ARE HANDLING MOST OF IT. THEY WILL WANT TO TALK TO YOU WHEN THEY COME INTO TOWN.

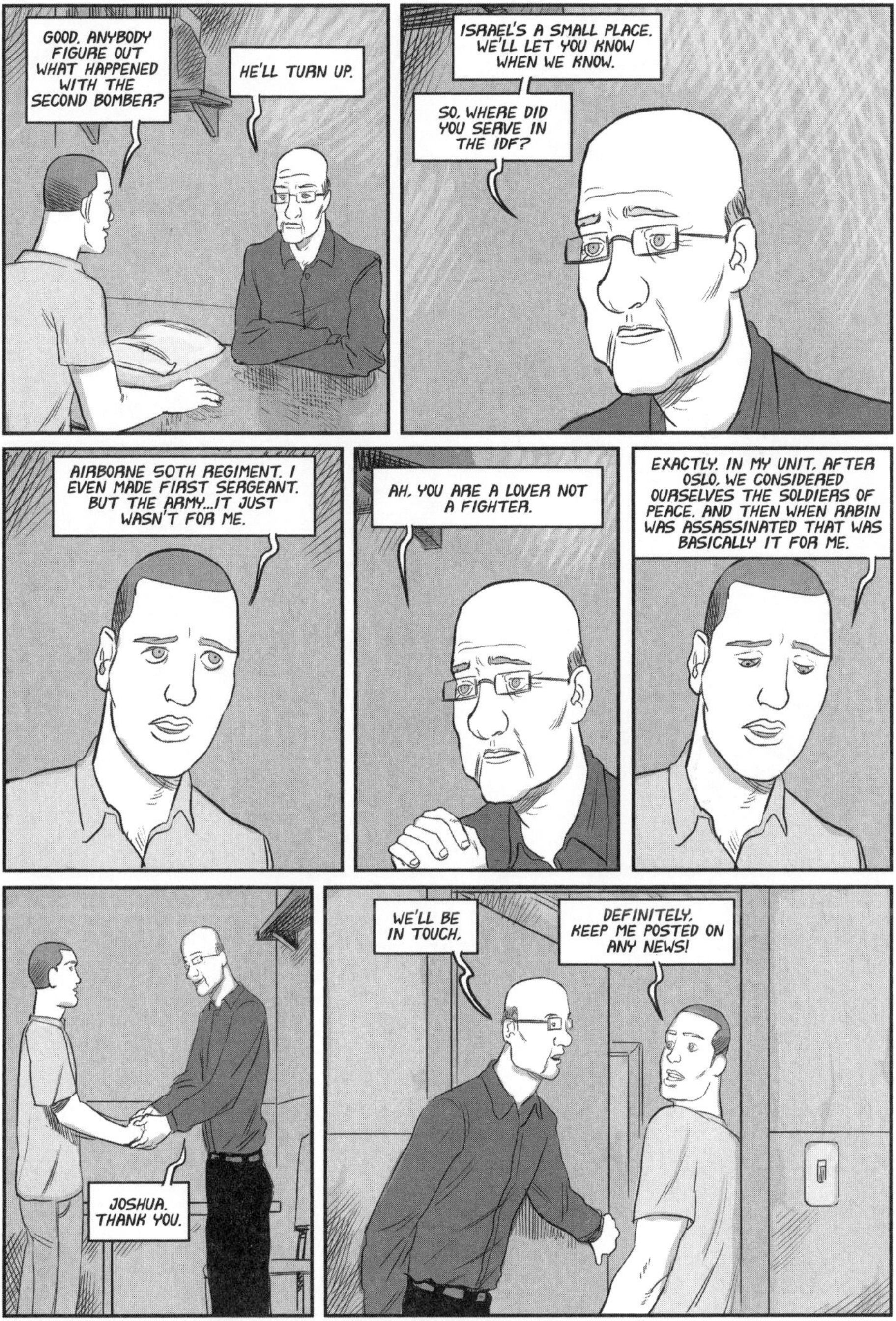
GOOD. ANYBODY FIGURE OUT WHAT HAPPENED WITH THE SECOND BOMBER?
HE'LL TURN UP.
ISRAEL'S A SMALL PLACE. WE'LL LET YOU KNOW WHEN WE KNOW.
SO, WHERE DID YOU SERVE IN THE IDF?
AIRBORNE 50TH REGIMENT. I EVEN MADE FIRST SERGEANT. BUT THE ARMY...IT JUST WASN'T FOR ME.
AH, YOU ARE A LOVER NOT A FIGHTER.
EXACTLY. IN MY UNIT. AFTER OSLO, WE CONSIDERED OURSELVES THE SOLDIERS OF PEACE. AND THEN WHEN RABIN WAS ASSASSINATED THAT WAS BASICALLY IT FOR ME.
JOSHUA. THANK YOU.
WE'LL BE IN TOUCH.
DEFINITELY. KEEP ME POSTED ON ANY NEWS!

OH, JEEZ, LOOK AT YOUR ARM!

THE DOCTOR SAID MY BODY WOULD ABSORB IT EVENTUALLY.

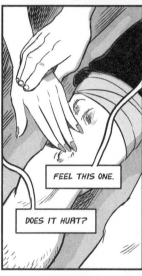

FEEL THIS ONE.

DOES IT HURT?

NAH, JUST FEELS WEIRD, THAT'S ALL. AVI TOLD ME HE'S GOT ORGANIC SHRAPNEL TOO.

PIECES OF THE BOMBER'S BODY. WONDER HOW LONG I'M GOING TO BE CARRYING THIS GUY AROUND IN ME.

UGH.

YOU KNOW, I NEVER WANTED YOU TO GO TO ISRAEL IN THE FIRST PLACE. BUT YOU WERE SO SET ON GOING I DIDN'T WANT TO STAND IN YOUR WAY!

BUT, IF WE HAD KIDS, I WOULDN'T HAVE LET YOU GO.

IF WE HAD KIDS, I PROBABLY WOULDN'T HAVE GONE.

170

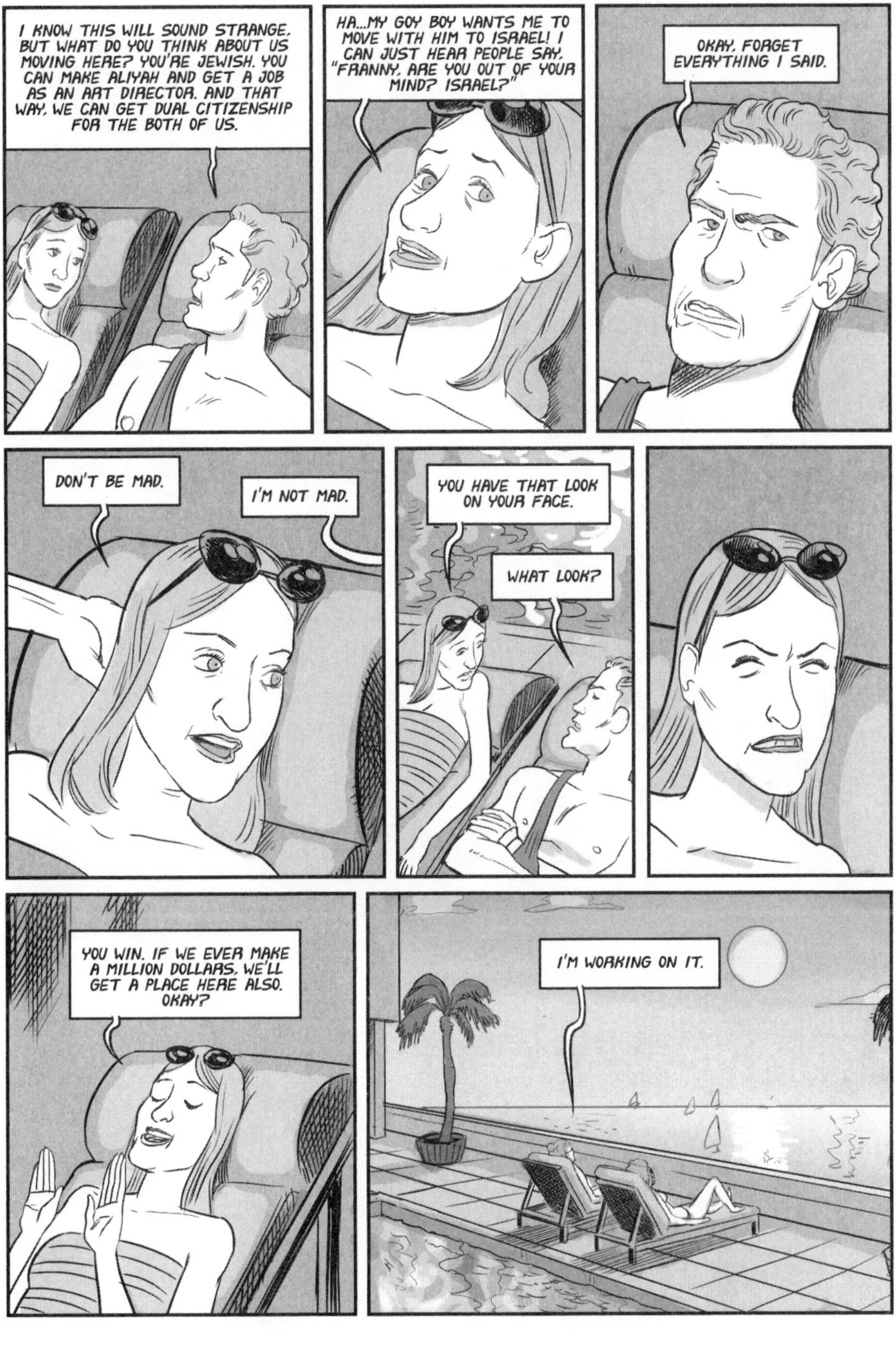
I KNOW THIS WILL SOUND STRANGE, BUT WHAT DO YOU THINK ABOUT US MOVING HERE? YOU'RE JEWISH. YOU CAN MAKE ALIYAH AND GET A JOB AS AN ART DIRECTOR. AND THAT WAY, WE CAN GET DUAL CITIZENSHIP FOR THE BOTH OF US.
HA...MY GOY BOY WANTS ME TO MOVE WITH HIM TO ISRAEL! I CAN JUST HEAR PEOPLE SAY, "FRANNY, ARE YOU OUT OF YOUR MIND? ISRAEL?"
OKAY, FORGET EVERYTHING I SAID.
DON'T BE MAD.
I'M NOT MAD.
YOU HAVE THAT LOOK ON YOUR FACE.
WHAT LOOK?
YOU WIN. IF WE EVER MAKE A MILLION DOLLARS, WE'LL GET A PLACE HERE ALSO. OKAY?
I'M WORKING ON IT.

CIMETIÈRE DE BAGNEUX, PARIS, FRANCE

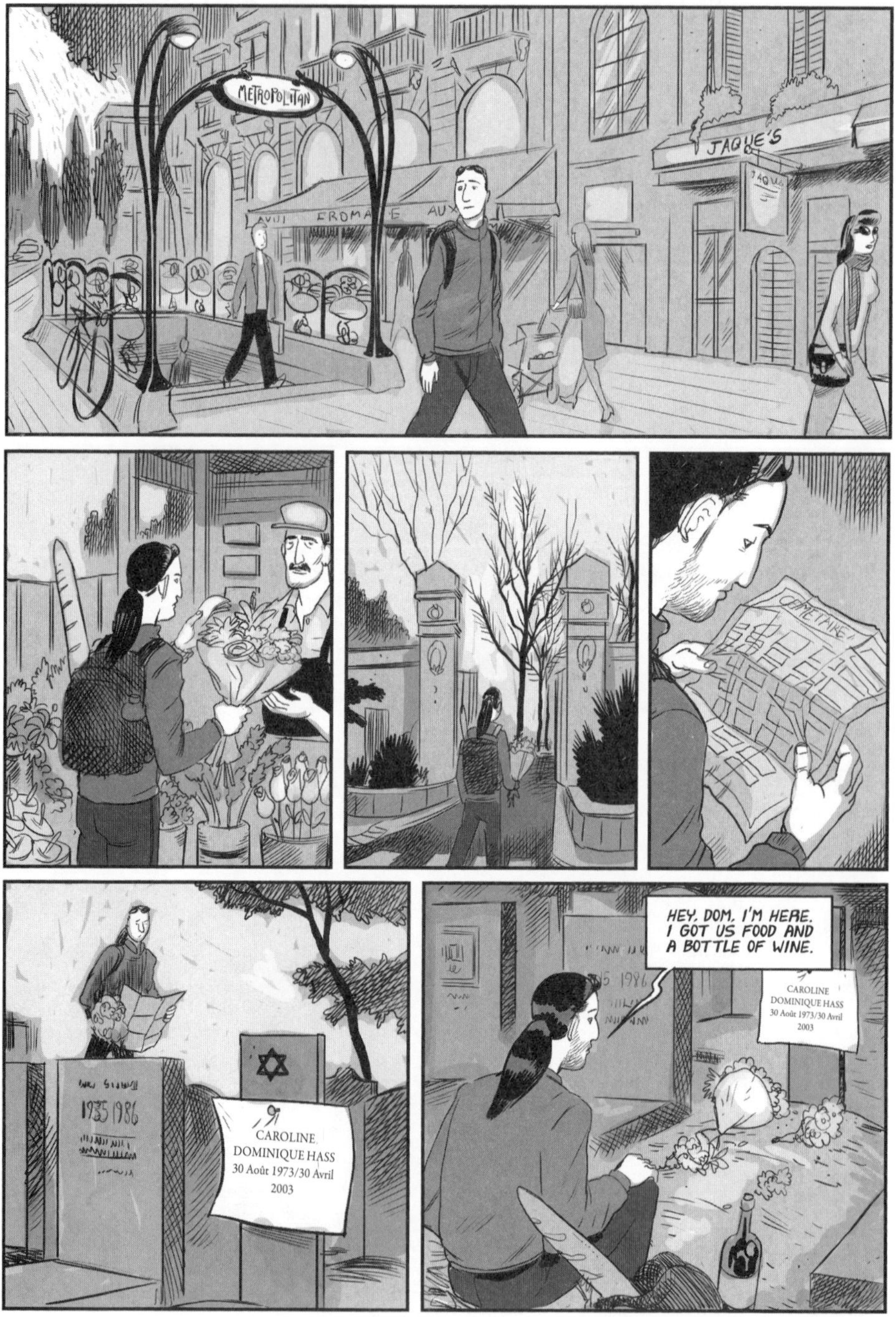
METROPOLITAN
JAQUE'S
1935 1986
CAROLINE DOMINIQUE HASS 30 Août 1973/30 Avril 2003
HEY, DOM, I'M HERE. I GOT US FOOD AND A BOTTLE OF WINE.
CAROLINE DOMINIQUE HASS 30 Août 1973/30 Avril 2003

HERE'S TO YOU, DOM. CHEERS.

DO WE KNOW HOW TO PARTY OR WHAT?

I GRABBED THESE SHOTS OFF THE WEBSITE. THEY HAD TO BURY THE ORIGINALS. BUT YOU KNOW THAT.

CAROLINE DOMINIQUE HASS
30 Août 1973/30 Avril 2003

I WAS SCRAPING PIECES OF GUM OFF THE FLOOR WHEN YOU CAME INTO THE BAR ASKING ME FOR A JOB. YOU WERE...THIS ANGEL.

YOU WERE SO DEDICATED, SO BRAVE. I LOVE YOU, DOM. I LOVE YOU...I KNOW WHAT YOU WERE GOING TO SAY TO ME AFTER PASSOVER. I LOVED YOU, DOM.

PLEASE, PLEASE FORGIVE ME— FORGIVE ME FOR ASKING YOU TO WORK THAT LAST NIGHT!

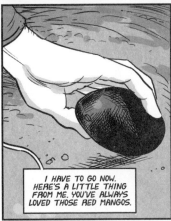

I HAVE TO GO NOW. HERE'S A LITTLE THING FROM ME. YOU'VE ALWAYS LOVED THOSE RED MANGOS.

CAROLINE DOMINIQUE HASS
30 Août 1973/30 Avril 2003

173

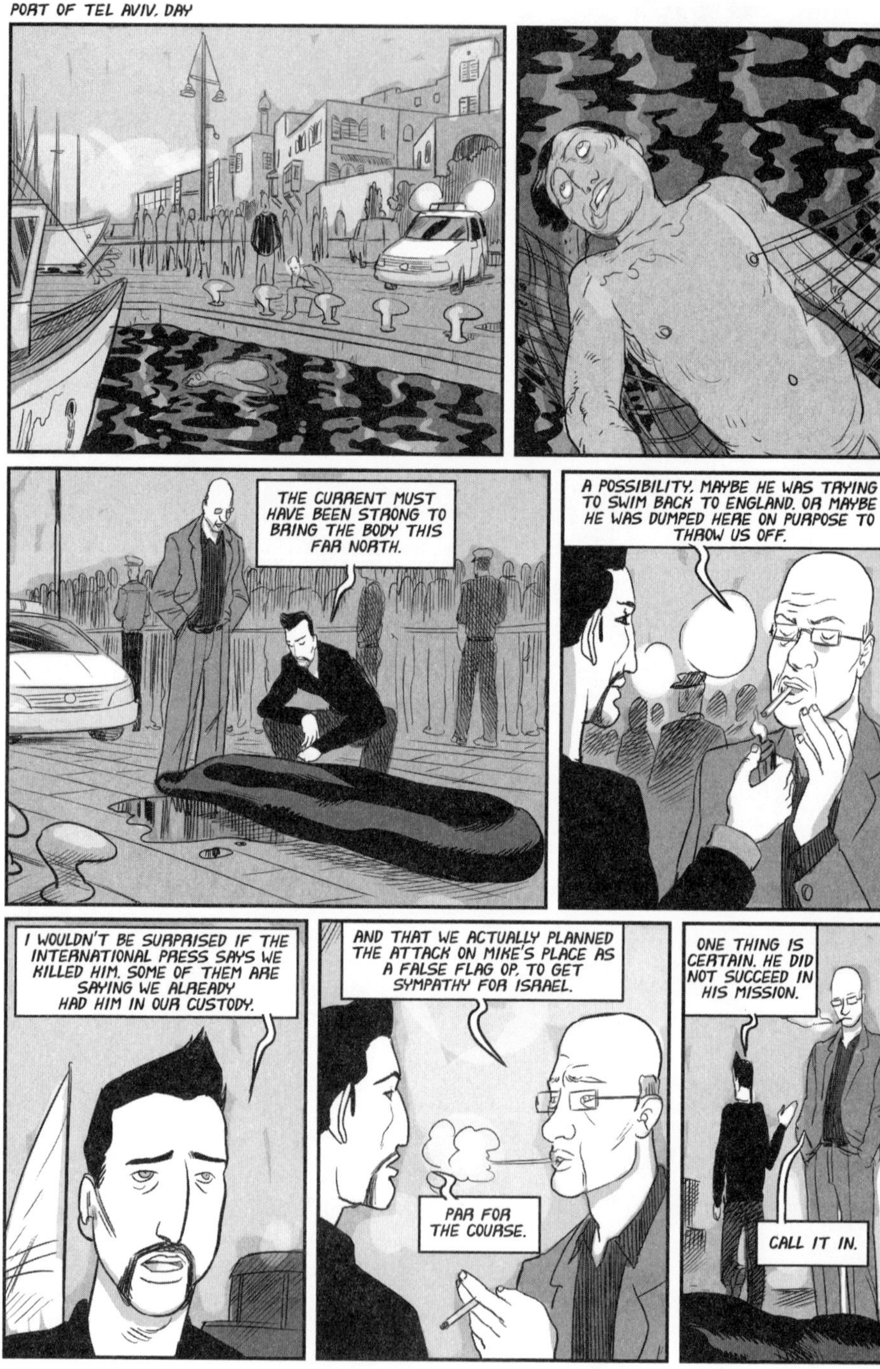
PORT OF TEL AVIV, DAY
THE CURRENT MUST HAVE BEEN STRONG TO BRING THE BODY THIS FAR NORTH.
A POSSIBILITY. MAYBE HE WAS TRYING TO SWIM BACK TO ENGLAND. OR MAYBE HE WAS DUMPED HERE ON PURPOSE TO THROW US OFF.
I WOULDN'T BE SURPRISED IF THE INTERNATIONAL PRESS SAYS WE KILLED HIM. SOME OF THEM ARE SAYING WE ALREADY HAD HIM IN OUR CUSTODY.
AND THAT WE ACTUALLY PLANNED THE ATTACK ON MIKE'S PLACE AS A FALSE FLAG OP, TO GET SYMPATHY FOR ISRAEL.
PAR FOR THE COURSE.
ONE THING IS CERTAIN. HE DID NOT SUCCEED IN HIS MISSION.
CALL IT IN.

VI

"... Take not life, which Allah hath made sacred, except by
way of justice and law ..."

—Qur'an

BEN YEHUDA STREET, EVENING

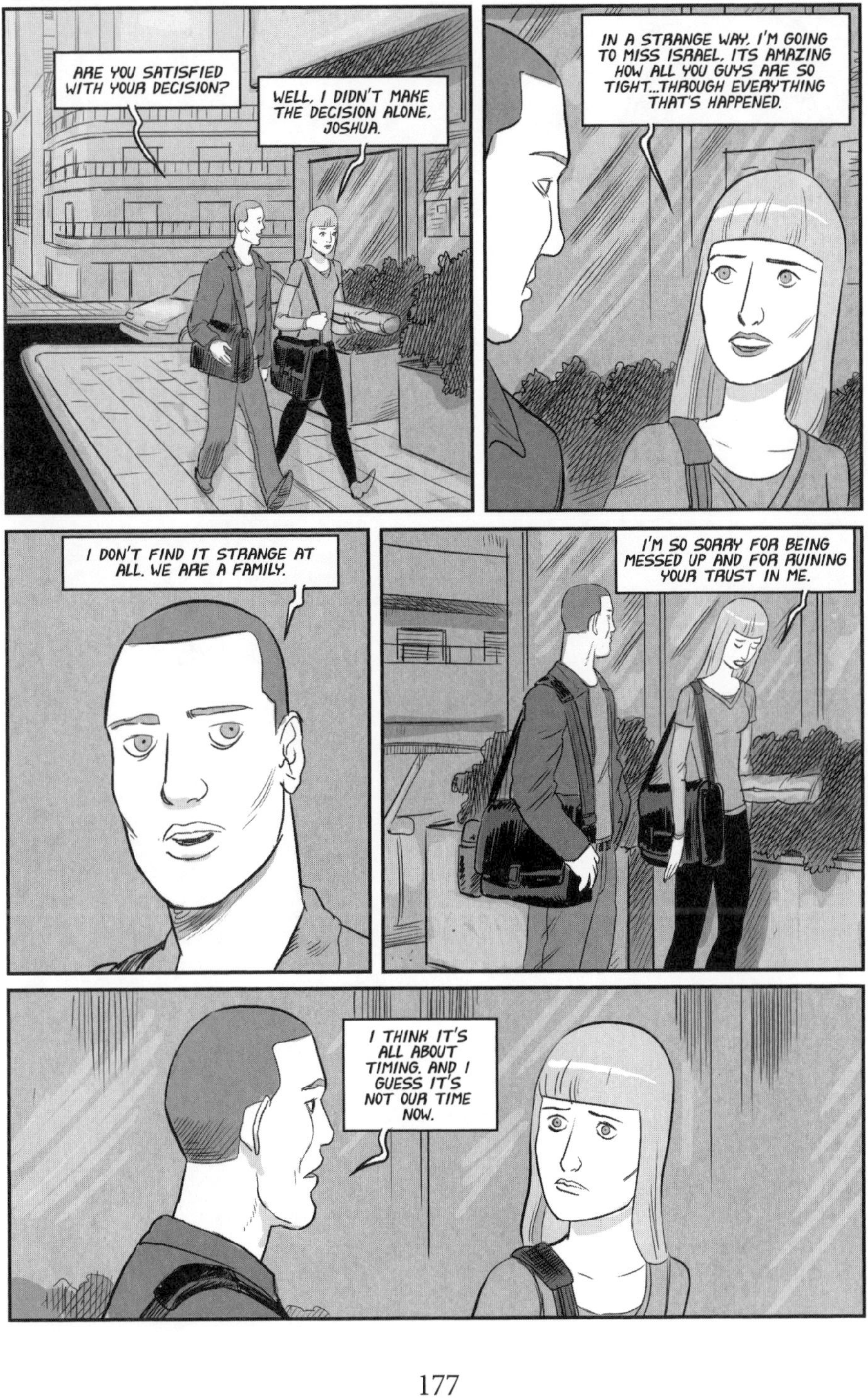
ARE YOU SATISFIED WITH YOUR DECISION?
WELL, I DIDN'T MAKE THE DECISION ALONE, JOSHUA.
IN A STRANGE WAY, I'M GOING TO MISS ISRAEL. ITS AMAZING HOW ALL YOU GUYS ARE SO TIGHT...THROUGH EVERYTHING THAT'S HAPPENED.
I DON'T FIND IT STRANGE AT ALL. WE ARE A FAMILY.
I'M SO SORRY FOR BEING MESSED UP AND FOR RUINING YOUR TRUST IN ME.
I THINK IT'S ALL ABOUT TIMING, AND I GUESS IT'S NOT OUR TIME NOW.

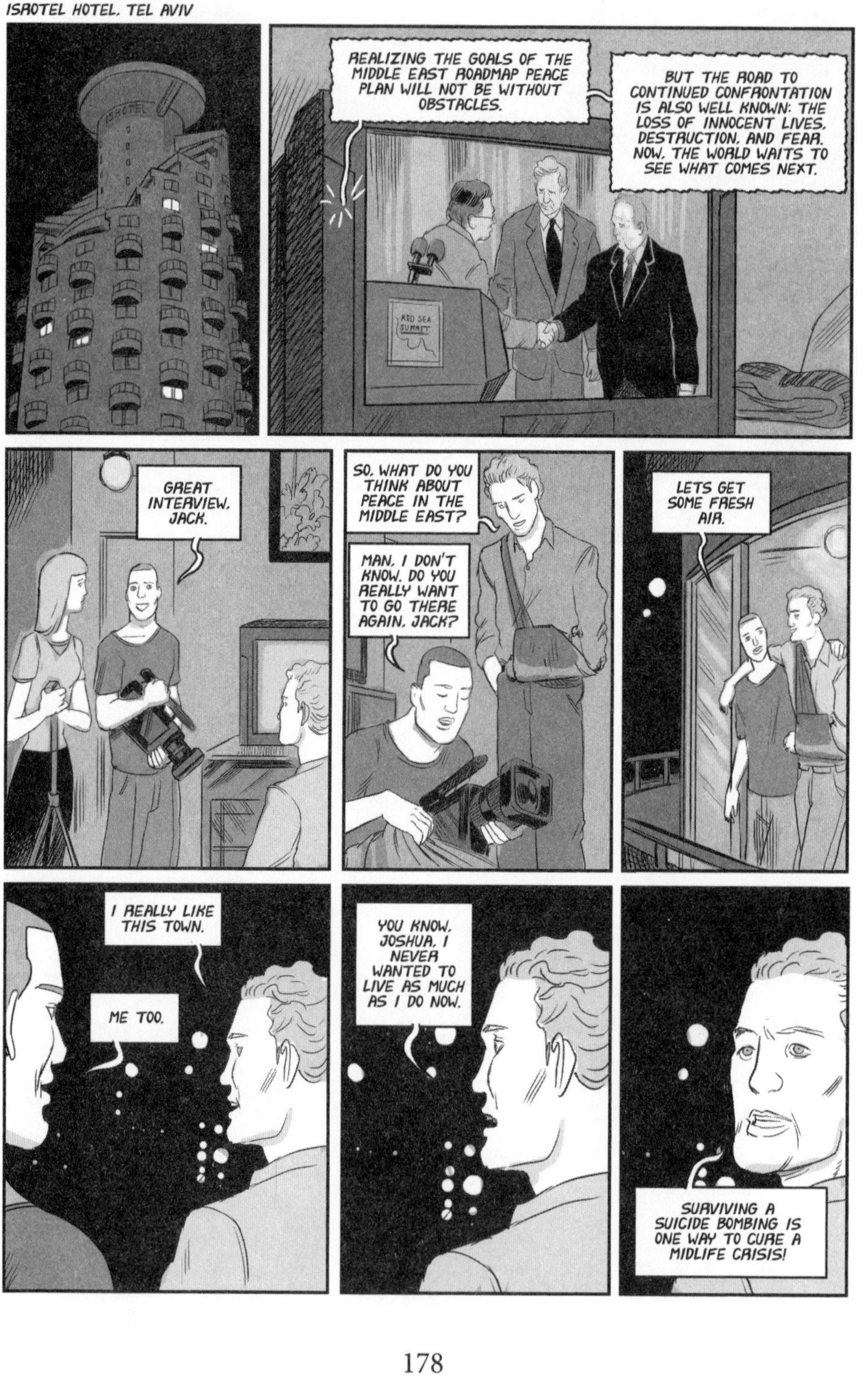
ISROTEL HOTEL, TEL AVIV
ISROTEL
REALIZING THE GOALS OF THE MIDDLE EAST ROADMAP PEACE PLAN WILL NOT BE WITHOUT OBSTACLES.
BUT THE ROAD TO CONTINUED CONFRONTATION IS ALSO WELL KNOWN: THE LOSS OF INNOCENT LIVES, DESTRUCTION, AND FEAR. NOW, THE WORLD WAITS TO SEE WHAT COMES NEXT.
RED SEA SUMMIT
GREAT INTERVIEW, JACK.
SO, WHAT DO YOU THINK ABOUT PEACE IN THE MIDDLE EAST?
MAN, I DON'T KNOW. DO YOU REALLY WANT TO GO THERE AGAIN, JACK?
LETS GET SOME FRESH AIR.
I REALLY LIKE THIS TOWN.
ME TOO.
YOU KNOW, JOSHUA, I NEVER WANTED TO LIVE AS MUCH AS I DO NOW.
SURVIVING A SUICIDE BOMBING IS ONE WAY TO CURE A MIDLIFE CRISIS!

MIKE'S PLACE, NIGHT

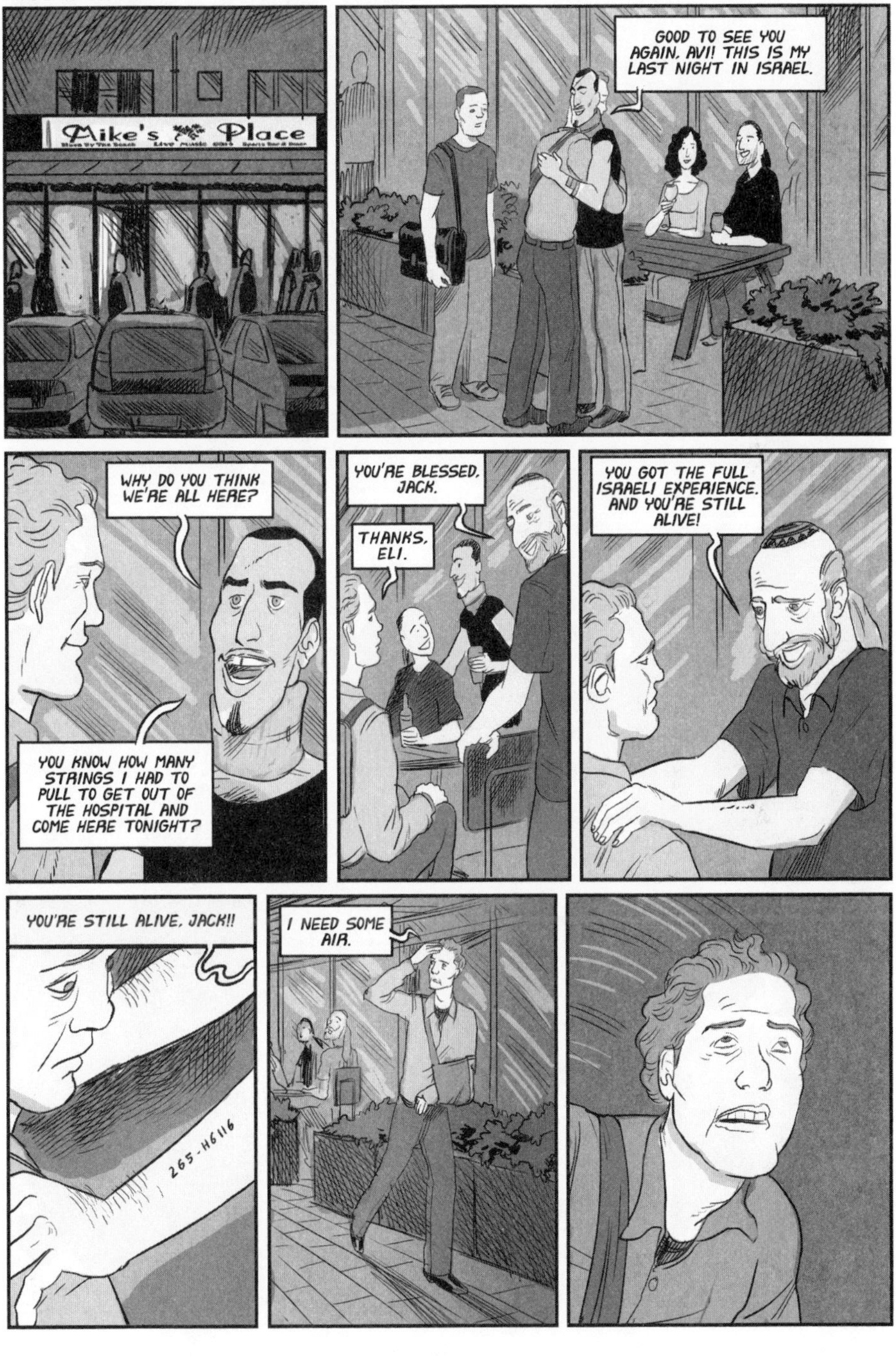
Mike's Place
GOOD TO SEE YOU AGAIN, AVI! THIS IS MY LAST NIGHT IN ISRAEL.
WHY DO YOU THINK WE'RE ALL HERE?
YOU KNOW HOW MANY STRINGS I HAD TO PULL TO GET OUT OF THE HOSPITAL AND COME HERE TONIGHT?
YOU'RE BLESSED, JACK.
THANKS, ELI.
YOU GOT THE FULL ISRAELI EXPERIENCE. AND YOU'RE STILL ALIVE!
YOU'RE STILL ALIVE, JACK!!
265-H6116
I NEED SOME AIR.

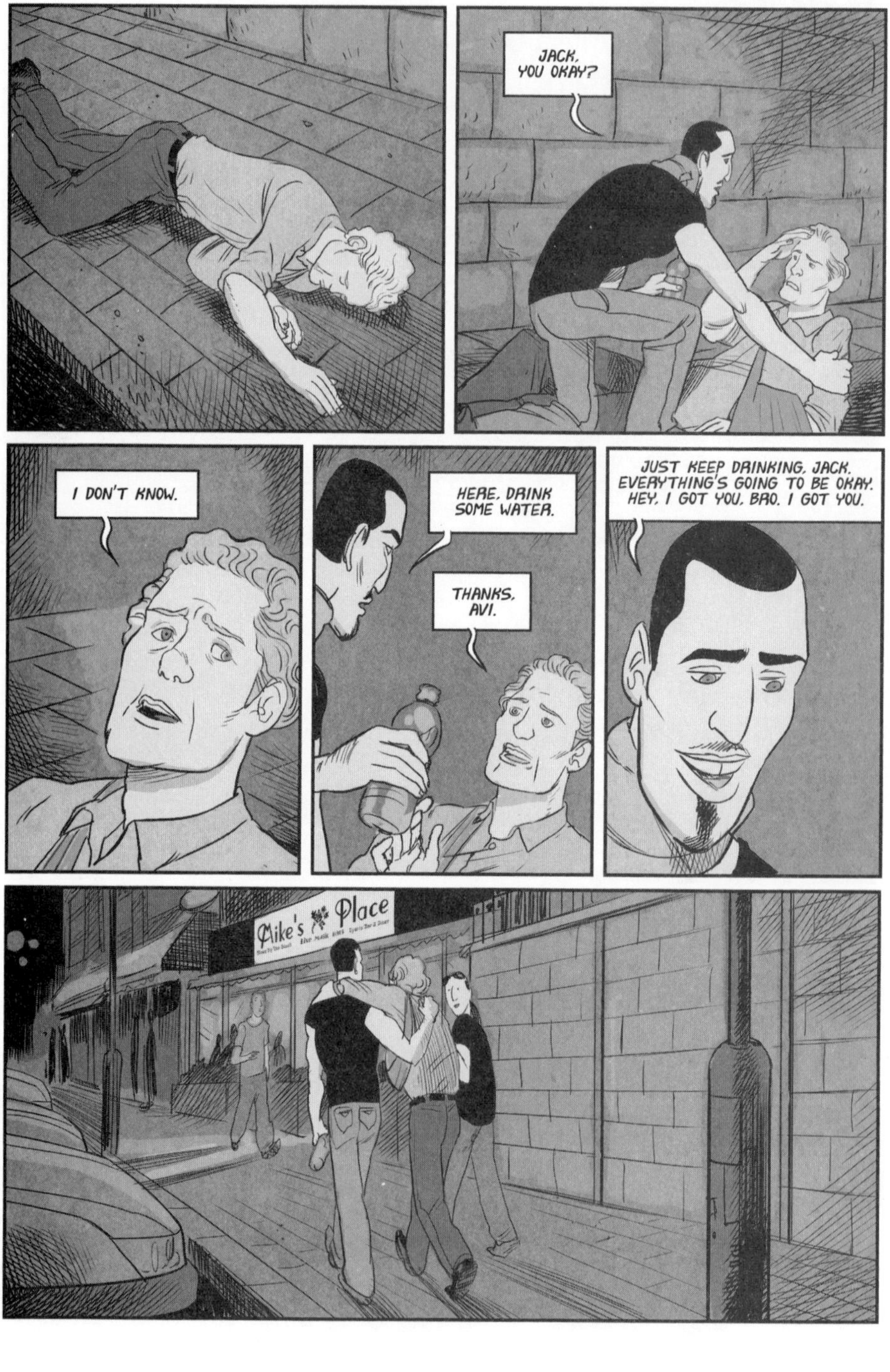
JACK, YOU OKAY?
I DON'T KNOW.
HERE, DRINK SOME WATER.
THANKS, AVI.
JUST KEEP DRINKING, JACK. EVERYTHING'S GOING TO BE OKAY. HEY, I GOT YOU, BRO. I GOT YOU.
Mike's Place

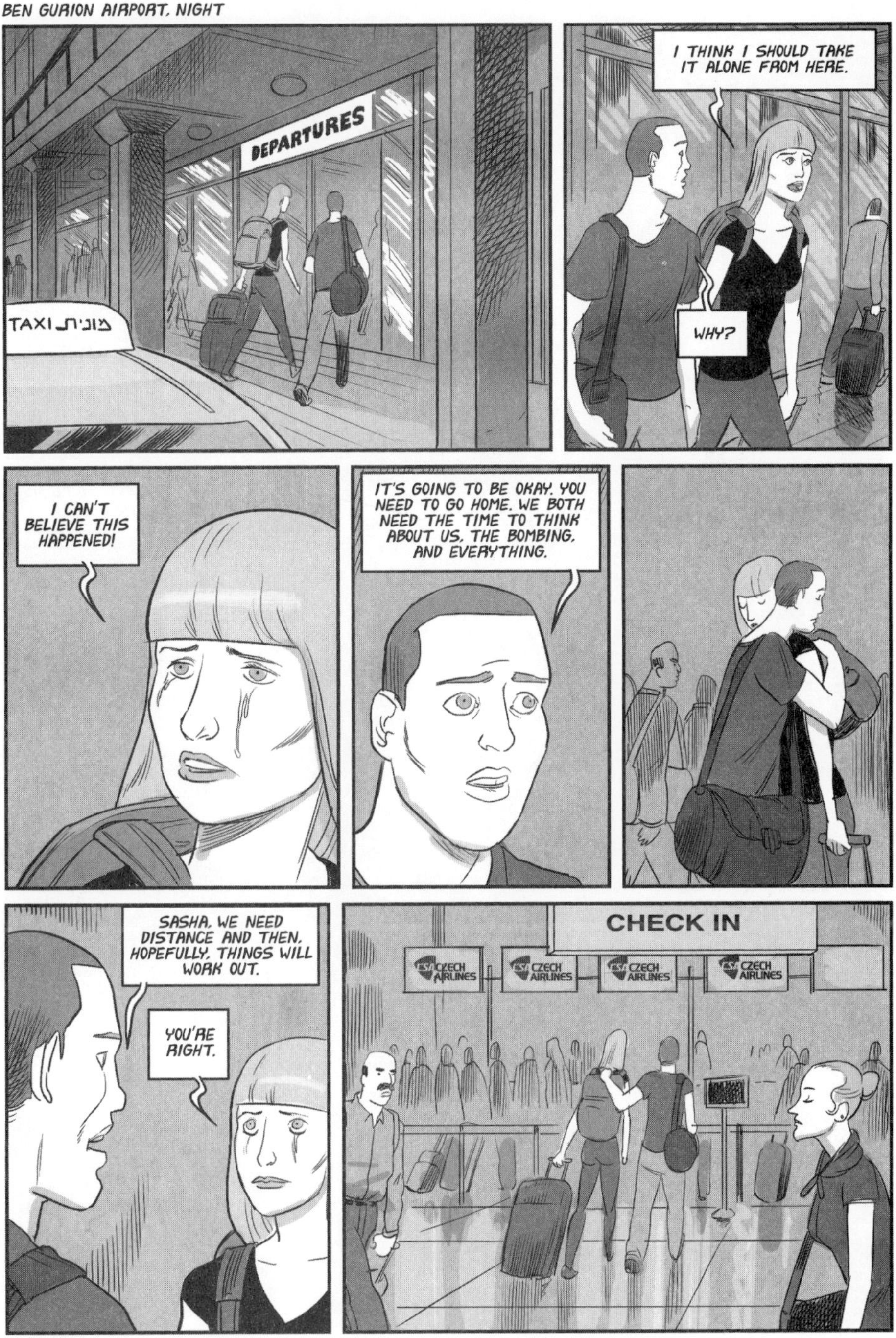
BEN GURION AIRPORT, NIGHT
DEPARTURES
TAXI מונית
I THINK I SHOULD TAKE IT ALONE FROM HERE.
WHY?
I CAN'T BELIEVE THIS HAPPENED!
IT'S GOING TO BE OKAY. YOU NEED TO GO HOME. WE BOTH NEED THE TIME TO THINK ABOUT US, THE BOMBING, AND EVERYTHING.
SASHA, WE NEED DISTANCE AND THEN, HOPEFULLY, THINGS WILL WORK OUT.
YOU'RE RIGHT.
CHECK IN
CSA CZECH AIRLINES
CSA CZECH AIRLINES
CSA CZECH AIRLINES
CSA CZECH AIRLINES

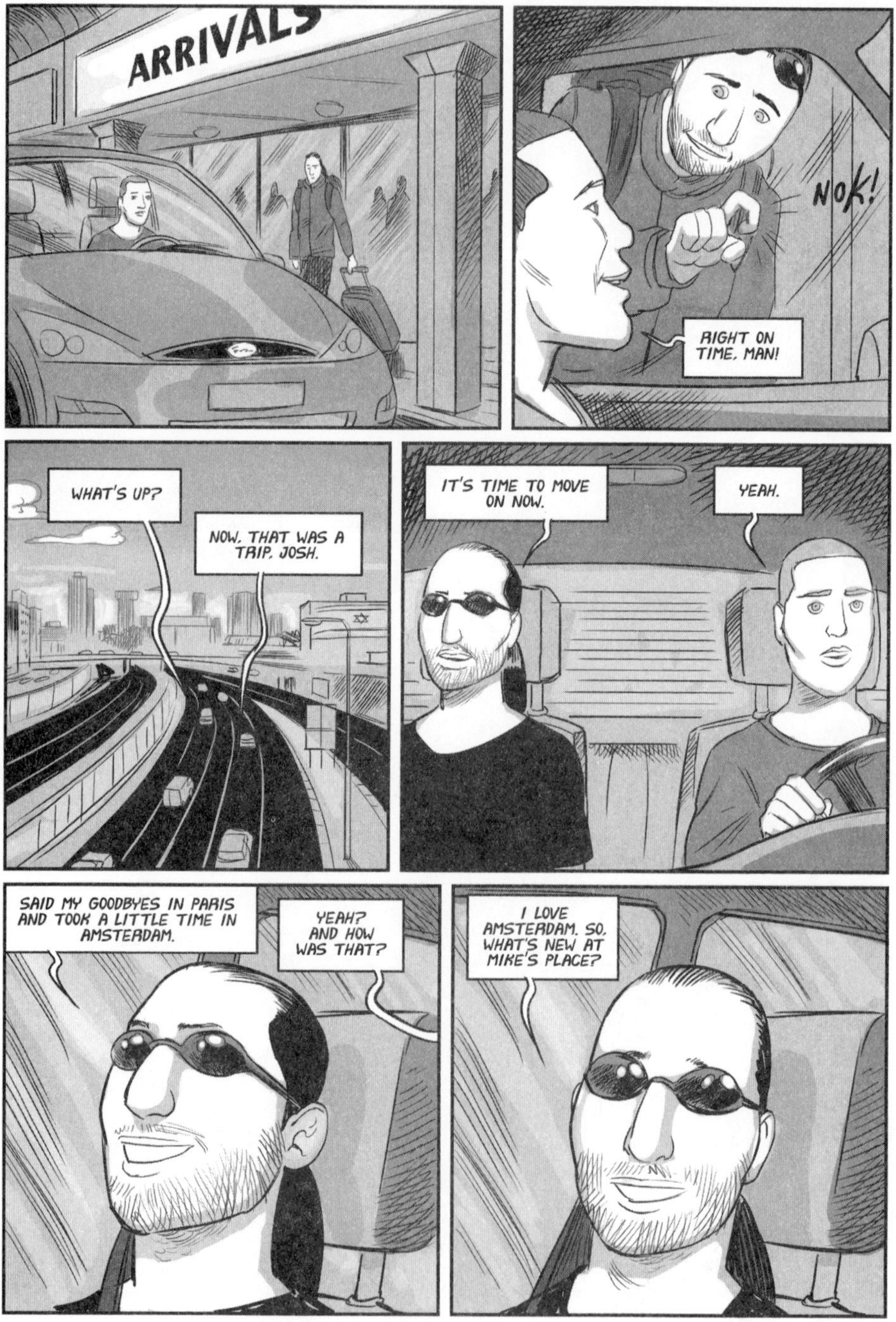
ARRIVALS
NOK!
RIGHT ON TIME, MAN!
WHAT'S UP?
NOW, THAT WAS A TRIP, JOSH.
IT'S TIME TO MOVE ON NOW.
YEAH.
SAID MY GOODBYES IN PARIS AND TOOK A LITTLE TIME IN AMSTERDAM.
YEAH? AND HOW WAS THAT?
I LOVE AMSTERDAM. SO, WHAT'S NEW AT MIKE'S PLACE?

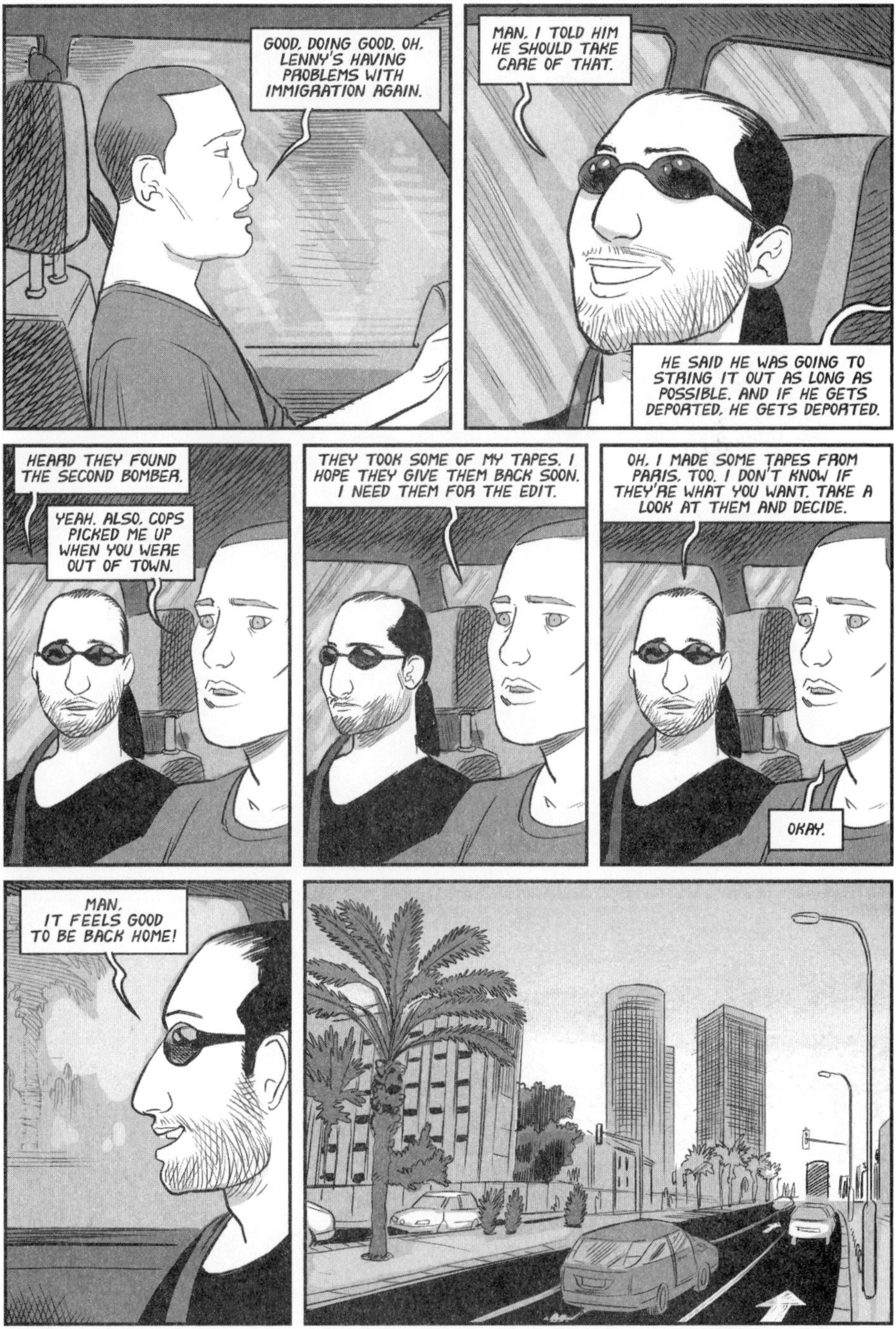
GOOD, DOING GOOD. OH, LENNY'S HAVING PROBLEMS WITH IMMIGRATION AGAIN.
MAN, I TOLD HIM HE SHOULD TAKE CARE OF THAT.
HE SAID HE WAS GOING TO STRING IT OUT AS LONG AS POSSIBLE. AND IF HE GETS DEPORTED, HE GETS DEPORTED.
HEARD THEY FOUND THE SECOND BOMBER.
YEAH. ALSO, COPS PICKED ME UP WHEN YOU WERE OUT OF TOWN.
THEY TOOK SOME OF MY TAPES. I HOPE THEY GIVE THEM BACK SOON. I NEED THEM FOR THE EDIT.
OH, I MADE SOME TAPES FROM PARIS, TOO. I DON'T KNOW IF THEY'RE WHAT YOU WANT. TAKE A LOOK AT THEM AND DECIDE.
OKAY.
MAN, IT FEELS GOOD TO BE BACK HOME!

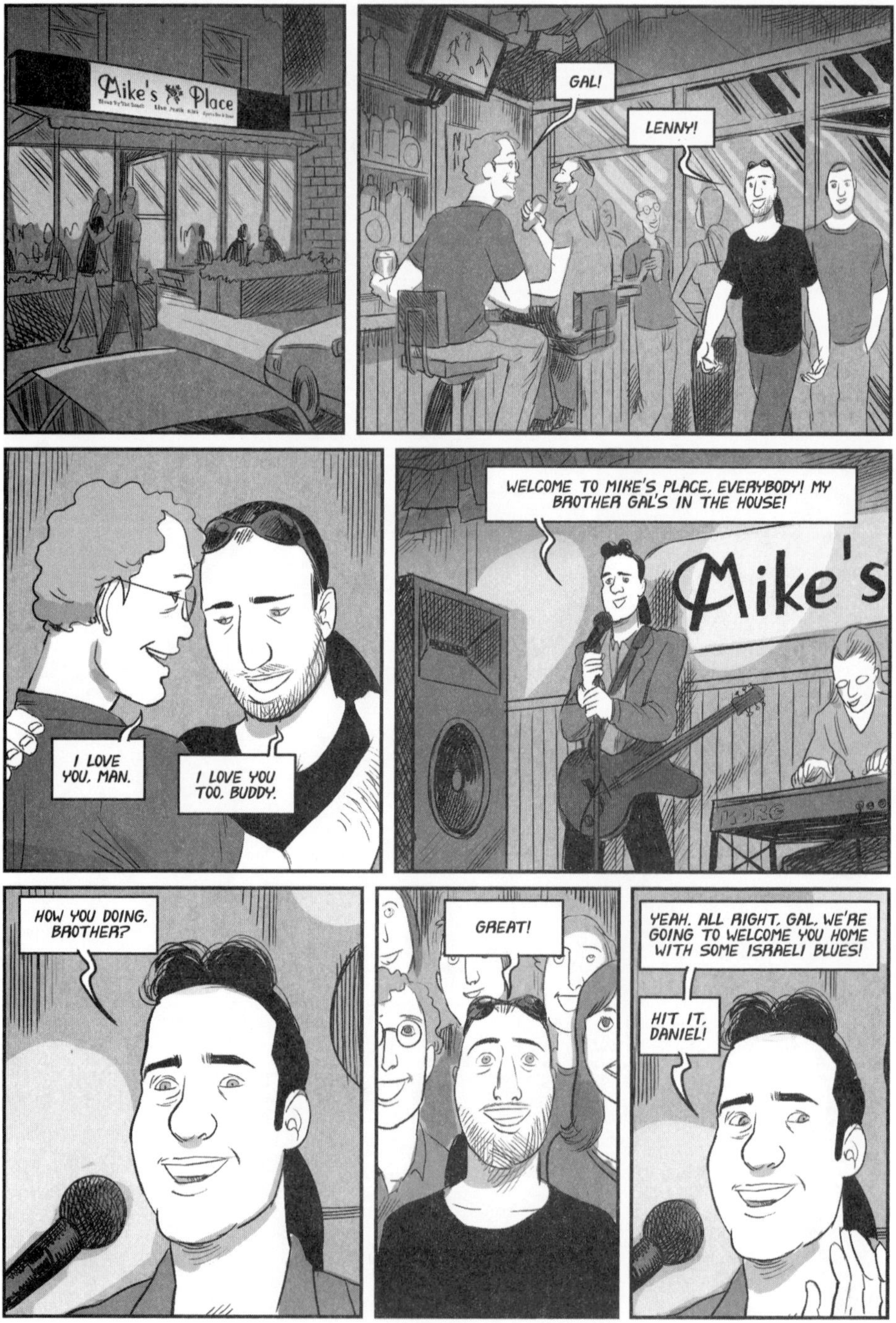

Mike's Place
GAL!
LENNY!
I LOVE YOU, MAN.
I LOVE YOU TOO, BUDDY.
WELCOME TO MIKE'S PLACE, EVERYBODY! MY BROTHER GAL'S IN THE HOUSE!
Mike's
HOW YOU DOING, BROTHER?
GREAT!
YEAH. ALL RIGHT, GAL, WE'RE GOING TO WELCOME YOU HOME WITH SOME ISRAELI BLUES!
HIT IT, DANIEL!

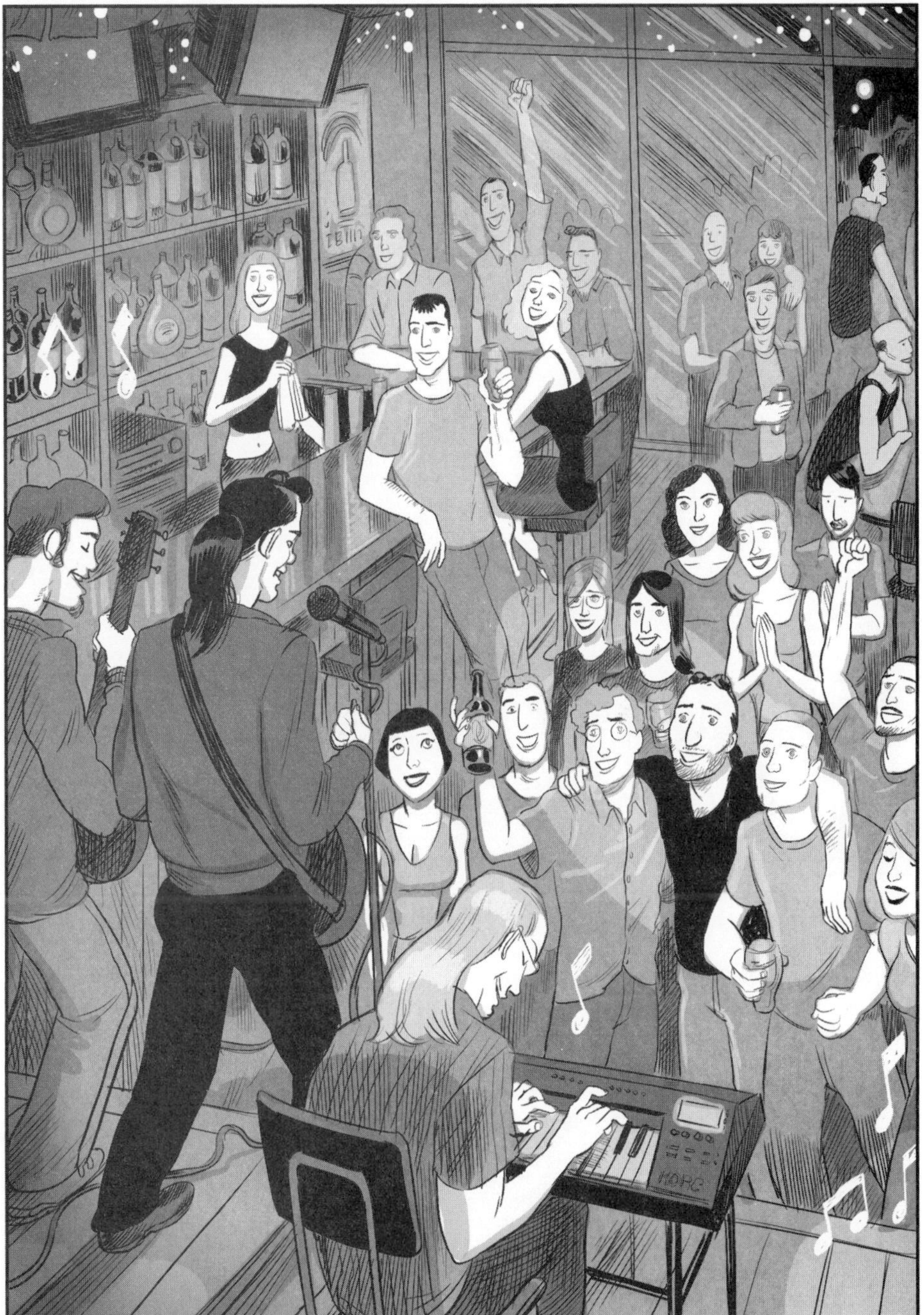
KORG

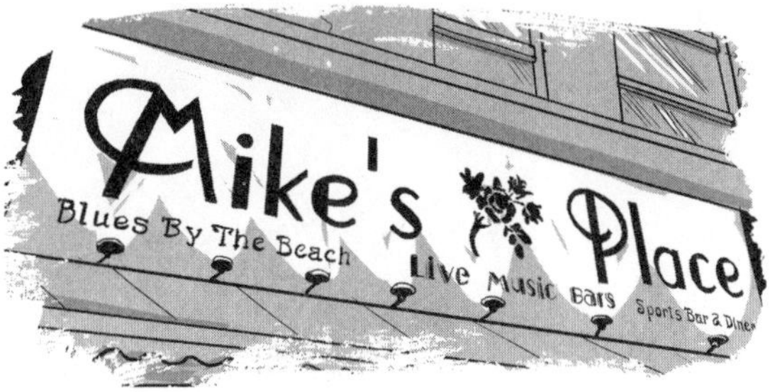
Mike's Place
Blues By The Beach
Live Music Bars
Sports Bar & Diner

EPILOGUE

We made every effort to truthfully chronicle the events around the April 30, 2003, Mike's Place terror attack. However, it was necessary to fictionalize aspects of this story for efficiency and to protect the identities of some of the characters.

To tell a genuine story while maintaining an accurate timeline required researching the official Israeli and British investigative accounts about Mohammad Sidique Khan in Israel on February 19, 2003, and Asif Hanif and Omar Khan Sharif's travels throughout April of 2003. In-depth interviews with survivors of the suicide bombing were conducted in Tel Aviv and Jerusalem in 2006 and 2008. Many of the actual scenes and outtakes from our documentary, *Blues by the Beach*, are faithfully transcribed into the plot.

After the initial explosion, Omar discarded his bomb at the scene and ran away south toward Jaffa. It has never been fully established if his explosive device had malfunctioned or if he had a change of heart when he witnessed the carnage his friend had wrought. What happened to Omar in the following days is conjecture on our part. Nevertheless, his corpse was found twelve days later floating miles north of where he was last seen by eyewitnesses.

Our long-time friend and prominent Muslim-American cleric, Imam Benjamin Bilal, helped select the scriptures from the Qur'an that are quoted at the beginning of the six chapters of this graphic novel. We wanted to show that if Asif and Omar had perhaps meditated upon and understood these sacred words things may have worked out differently for them and for the victims of the terror act they committed in the name of their religion and politics.

The Mike's Place attack was the first time in the history of the Middle East conflict that foreign nationals carried out a suicide bombing inside Israel.

One year later, in 2004, Hamas officially claimed responsibility when they released the "martyrdom video" Asif Hanif and Omar Khan Sharif made in the Gaza Strip.

On July 7, 2005, four suicide bombers attacked the London transit system. Within hours, a direct connection was made to the Mike's Place terrorists.

British suicide bombers Asif Hanif and Omar Khan Sharif pose in their martyrdom video that was filmed in the Gaza Strip.

September 1, 2005. Al-Qaeda leader Ayman al-Zawahiri claimed responsibility for the 7/7 London bombings and released the martyrdom video of Mohammad Sidique Khan. "We are at war and I am a soldier. Now you too will taste the reality of the situation."

Mohammad Sidique Khan, ringleader of the attack, was a friend of Asif Hanif and Omar Khan Sharif. All three men followed the Al Mahajiroun militant group and attended the same radicalized British mosques as convicted Al Qaeda members Richard Reid (the "shoe bomber") and captured 9/11 hijacker Zacarius Moussaoui.

Intelligence analysts suspect that Mohammad Sidique Khan helped plan the attack at Mike's Place. Khan had visited Tel Aviv on Wednesday, February 19, 2003, for only one day, just ten weeks before Asif and Omar attacked Mike's Place.

If investigators had connected all the dots back to Mike's Place, fifty-two people might not have died two years later in the 7/7 London bombings.

The Daily Telegraph

NEWSPAPER OF THE YEAR

Friday, July 8, 2005

BRITAIN'S BEST-SELLING QUALITY DAILY

www.telegraph.co.uk   FINAL

Al-Qa'eda brings terr
to the heart of Lond

Mike's Place is still open and has expanded to several locations throughout Israel. Bartender "Downtown Dave" Beck is now a co-owner of the business with Assaf Ganzman and Gal Ganzman.

In November 2005, we completed our documentary film about Mike's Place called *Blues by the Beach*. Every year on April 30, *Blues by the Beach* is screened at Mike's Place in memory of Dominique Hass, Ran Baron, and Yanay Weiss.

Shalom ❁ As-Salaam Alaikum ❁ PEACE

Jack Baxter *Joshua Faudem*

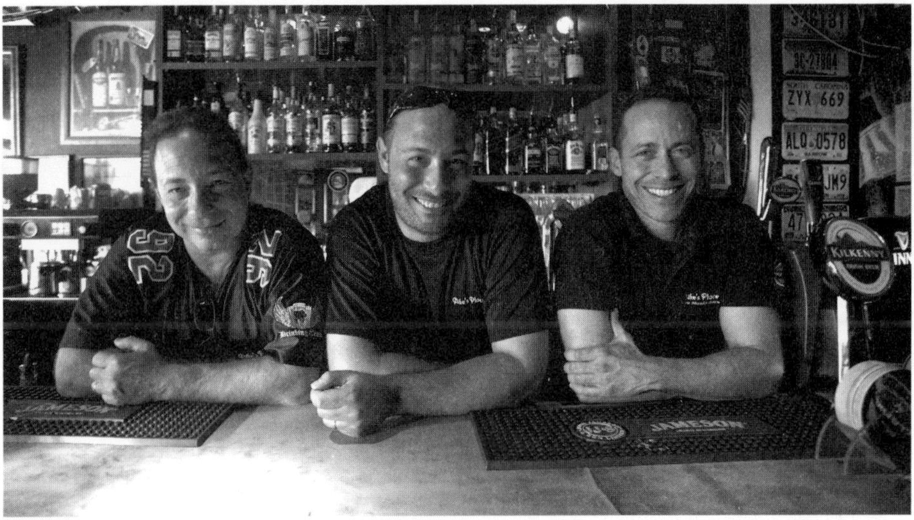
ZYX 669
ALQ 0578
KILKENNY
JAMESON

Mike's Place owners Assaf Ganzman, Gal Ganzman, and "Downtown Dave" Beck. Photo by Dror Katz.

Acknowledgments

We want to give our heartfelt thanks to family, friends, and everyone who supported us throughout the years. With a special acknowledgment to the Mike's Place family, Gal Ganzman, Assaf Ganzman, Dave Beck, Avi Tabib, David Leigh, Lenny Johnstone, Barry Gilbert, Daniel Kriman, Aaron Gluck, Lisa-Thi Beskar, Jason Jungreis, David Broza, Dr. David Bloom, Christina Kaufman, Jeremiah Kaufman, Burt and Arlene Faudem, Michelle, Jeffrey and Emily Faudem, Jeffrey, Tal, Ari and Lev Ershler, Matous Outrata, Joshua and Vlada John and the John family, Ido Aharoni, Jerry Rudes, Billy Baxter and Catherine Baxter, Barbara Psaroudis, Alexandra and Emmanuel Strauss, the Strauss Family, David Peterson, Thomas Cascione, Champagne Joy, Craig Weiss, Ian Black, Roseann Argenti, Matt Luxenberg, Sarri Singer, Judy Buchman, Dr. David Grand, Ken Ogle, Marty Stanton, Gus Simpson, Lizabeth Simpson Cooke, Harry Spillman, Helen Cunneen, Zoran Kovacevic, Inbal Lori, Phil Leclerc, Mary Sayegh, Yael Ledar, Itai and Max Leonard, Varda Seelig, Kenneth Sonny Donato, Cindy Lou Adkins, Larry Klein, David Mamet, Gilli Stern, Monika Chapman, Mena Dolobowsky, Steve Flanagan, Rene Devlin Weiss, Carol Thompson, Richard Ramos, Imam Benjamin Bilal, Koren Shadmi, and everyone at First Second Books. Forever in loving memory of Yanay Weiss and Ran Baron and Dominique Hass.

Thank you all so very much.
—Jack Baxter and Joshua Faudem

My deepest gratitude to Mary Abramson, for being there for me during my time working on this book.
—Koren Shadmi

JERUSALEM

A MISSING SON. A STOLEN ELECTION. IS THIS IRAN?
ZAHRA'S PARADISE
Amir & Khalil

STASSEN
DEOGRATIAS
A TALE OF RWANDA

The Photographer

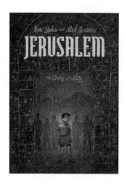

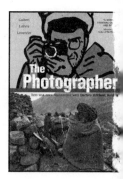